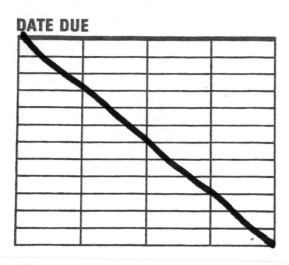

Understanding Accreditation

Contemporary Perspectives on Issues and Practices in Evaluating Educational Quality

Kenneth E. Young
Charles M. Chambers
H. R. Kells
and Associates

with the assistance of
Ruth Cargo

Understanding Accreditation

Jossey-Bass Publishers

San Francisco • Washington • London • 1983

UNDERSTANDING ACCREDITATION
Contemporary Perspectives
on Issues and Practices
in Evaluating Educational Quality
       by Kenneth E. Young, Charles M. Chambers,
       H. R. Kells, and Associates

Library of Congress Cataloging in Publication Data
Main entry under title:

Understanding accreditation.

       Bibliography: p. 459
       Includes index.
       1. Accreditation (Education)—Addresses, essays,
lectures. I. Young, Kenneth E., 1922–
LB2845.U53   1983   379.1 58   83-11260
ISBN 0-87589-570-0

Manufactured in the United States of America

The paper in this book meets the guidelines for
permanence and durability of the Committee on
Production Guidelines for Book Longevity of the
Council on Library Resources.

JACKET DESIGN BY WILLI BAUM

FIRST EDITION

Code 8317

The Jossey-Bass
Higher Education Series

Preface

When educators and others are asked whether they would be interested in learning about accreditation, the response is usually a yawn. However, if they are asked whether they want to know more about such subjects as evaluating educational quality, assuring institutional accountability, achieving and maintaining high standards, making education more responsive to students' and society's needs, and offsetting the dangers of government control of education, the interest level soars.

This book is about those topics and many others that are fundamental to the survival and improvement of postsecondary education in this country. It is intended to serve as a comprehensive, analytical guide to accreditation. (Throughout the book, the word *accreditation* is used to mean the activities carried out under that term within American postsecondary education.) Everyone who is involved in or regularly deals with postsecondary education should read this book. Its primary audience, however, is the many persons in leadership positions within colleges, universities, and other institutions of postsecondary education, people who need to familiarize themselves with accreditation—its purposes, policies, practices, and problems. As anyone reading this book will quickly discover, the major difficulty facing accreditation, and the source of many other problems, is the lamentable ignorance about accreditation that exists on most campuses. In particular, administrators and faculty members who are asked to take on key responsibilities when their institution goes through the accreditation process need to gain a better understanding of the subject.

Every publication has, or should have, its own point of view, even one involving fourteen authors. This book was predicated on several important assumptions that should be made clear at the outset:

- Accreditation is a valuable—perhaps even essential—social tool whose usefulness and effectiveness have not been fully appreciated and whose full potential has yet to be realized.
- Accreditation began as a voluntary, nongovernment process and should remain so if its inherent values are to be preserved and enhanced.
- Accreditation is a process that, at its heart, consists of guided self-evaluation and self-improvement and serves as a centerpiece to the little-understood, informal, but elaborate "system" of self-regulation in postsecondary education.
- The primary value of accreditation is to be found in the process itself, not in the formal results of the process—that is, the announced decision on whether an institution or program is accredited.
- Accreditation should be judged by its effectiveness in encouraging and assisting the institution to evaluate and improve its educational offerings. All other outcomes and uses of accreditation are secondary to this objective and should not undermine it. To be effective, accreditation must focus primarily on the institution or program, just as education must focus on the student.
- Accreditation is highly vulnerable to misuse and abuse by those who wish to turn it to other purposes. But there are enough countervailing forces—individuals, institutions, associations, as well as accrediting bodies—to offset perversions of the process or power plays. The key, however, is a broader understanding of accreditation and agreement on its basic nature, purpose, and value.

This book begins at the beginning—with the appearance
of accreditation in the early 1900s. It concludes with a forecast
of an unsettled, and unsettling, future. In between, it helps the
reader come to terms with a simple but exciting concept and
the many complexities it has engendered. Part One puts accreditation into perspective, previewing the plot and the players and
describing the essential qualities of accreditation as a voluntary,
self-regulatory enterprise. The opening chapter defines accreditation as that term is used throughout the book—as a process by
which an institution of postsecondary education evaluates its
educational activities, in whole or in part, and seeks an independent judgment to confirm that it is substantially achieving its
objectives and is generally equal in quality to comparable institutions or specialized units. Part Two explains how accreditation works from the perspective of institutions of postsecondary
education, and Part Three looks at it from the perspective of
accrediting organizations. Part Four explores accreditation's relationships with the students who are the ultimate beneficiaries
of postsecondary education, with government, and with the organization created by the postsecondary education community
to bring order and value to accreditation. Part Five discusses the
major issues confronting accreditation—issues resulting from
changes in the domain, the concepts, the practices, and the uses
of accreditation.

Several items have been appended because they are particularly helpful. Resource A is a list of accrediting bodies recognized by the Council on Postsecondary Accreditation (COPA).
Readers may want to examine the COPA documents given in
Resource B, "Provisions and Procedures for Becoming Recognized as an Accrediting Agency," Resource C, "Guidelines on
Interagency Cooperation in Accreditation," and Resource D,
"Policy Statement on the Role and Value of Accreditation." Because accreditation, like many fields, has developed its own terminology (or at least its own uses of certain terms), readers are
encouraged to refer to the Glossary in Resource E. Finally, the
Bibliography contains not only all works that are cited within
the chapters but also additional works that readers can turn to
for an even more detailed knowledge of accreditation.

Many people helped bring this book about. The Executive Committee of the Council on Postsecondary Accreditation, while I was president of that organization, endorsed this project and encouraged me to take on the responsibility of editor. Then, after I became executive director of the National University Continuing Education Association, the Executive Committee of that organization saw the value of this effort and agreed to my continuing with it.

No one anticipated that this project would stretch over a four-year period and involve so many people. Those particularly deserving of mention are, first of all, associate editors Charles M. Chambers and H. R. Kells, two of the nation's most knowledgeable students of accreditation, who helped with the organization of the book, critiqued the manuscript, and contributed three important chapters each. Second, Ruth Cargo picked up responsibilities as assistant editor in midstream and ably crafted a coherent, cohesive book out of what had been an assemblage of disparate papers. The eleven other chapter authors must be acknowledged not only for important contributions but also for their remarkable patience and adaptability during the months that elapsed while the many segments of the manuscript were melded into a coherent whole.

Others who contributed in important ways include Pamela Tate, who assisted with the book's organization and much of the early editing; Betty Lee Craig, John Enger, John Harris, James Huffman, Larraine Matusak, and Douglas Whitney, who contributed helpful draft material; Kay Andersen, George Arnstein, Sara Ayers Bagby, James Bemis, Frank G. Dickey, Gary Filerman, JB Lon Hefferlin, Michael Lambert, Richard M. Millard, Jerry W. Miller, Harold Orlans, James E. Perdue, Dorothy G. Petersen, James M. Phillips, and Mervin K. Strickler, who read the final manuscript; Earline Hefferlin, who compiled the index; Renee Marshall and Shirley Waters, who typed the material; and, of course, my wife, Mae, who suffered through these four years with me.

A decision was made early on not to commission chapters by persons actively serving as professionals in the field of accreditation (except for James F. Bemis, speaking on behalf of the regional accrediting bodies). These men and women are very busy, have stated their positions many times in many places, and are unavoidably constrained in some ways by the interests and positions of the organizations they serve. Many of them nevertheless graciously gave of their time to advise on the organization of the book, provide needed information, and read individual chapters. The chapter authors include four former staff members of accrediting bodies (two from institutional accreditation and two from specialized accreditation) and two former staff members, two former chairmen, and a former board member of COPA.

Although there were a few, perhaps inevitable, disagreements along the way—about a term here, a phrase there, or certain matters of emphasis or tone—the authors and editors found themselves in remarkable agreement on the subject. Among other things, we all concurred that accreditation is important and deserving of greater attention—particularly from decision makers in institutions of postsecondary education. We hope this book will gain their readership and their acceptance. If so, it will have served a valuable purpose.

Washington, D.C.   Kenneth E. Young
June 1983

Contents

Reviews the changes accreditation has gone through since its emergence in the early 1900s—changes in the universe it serves, its participants, its practices, and society's expectations of it. Points out that certain basic characteristics have prevailed.

Examines the various purposes accreditation serves, stressing the overriding importance of improving the quality of education. Compares the differences between institutional and specialized accrediting bodies.

The Contributors

Kenneth E. Young was founding president of the Council on Postsecondary Accreditation and now serves as executive director of the National University Continuing Education Association. He received his B.A. degree (1943) from San Francisco State College and his M.A. degree (1947) and Ph.D. degree (1953) from Stanford University. He was a Carnegie postdoctoral fellow at the Center for the Study of Higher Education, University of Michigan, and holds an honorary degree from the University of Nevada, Reno.

Young brings a broad perspective to the subject of accreditation, having served as acting dean, dean, executive vice-president, and president of various institutions of postsecondary education, as well as vice-president of the American College Testing Program. His interest in accreditation began with his doctoral dissertation—"Who Can and Should Go to What Kind of College?"—and has continued through many of the thirty articles and one other book he has written or edited during his thirty-five years in postsecondary education.

Charles M. Chambers is general counsel of the Council on Postsecondary Accreditation, where he formerly served as acting president and vice-president. He is also a professor at George

Washington University, specializing in analytic methods for management and public policy. His B.S. (1962), M.S. (1963), and Ph.D. (1964) degrees are from the University of Alabama. He spent a postdoctoral year at Harvard University and then earned a J.D. degree (1976) at the George Washington University.

H. R. Kells is professor of higher education and information studies at Rutgers University. He is former associate executive secretary of the Commission on Higher Education, Middle States Association of Colleges and Schools, and an active consultant in accreditation. He received his B.S. (1956), M.S. (1958), and Ph.D. (1960) degrees from Rutgers University.

Ruth Cargo is a freelance editor and an education consultant specializing in postsecondary education. She has edited books and other publications for the American Council on Education and the Council for the Advancement of Experiential Learning. She received her B.A. degree (1970) from Oberlin College and is working toward her M.A. degree at the University of Southern California.

Grover J. Andrews is associate vice-chancellor for extension and public service and professor of adult education, North Carolina State University. He was associate director of the Commission on Colleges, Southern Association of Colleges and Schools, and served as director of the Council on Postsecondary Accreditation's Project on Developing Criteria and Procedures for Evaluating Nontraditional Education.

Ann E. Austin is a doctoral candidate in the Center for the Study of Higher Education and assistant to the dean of the School of Education, University of Michigan. She formerly served as admissions counselor at St. Lawrence University.

Sara Ayers Bagby is professor and chairman of the Department of Home Economics, University of Montevallo. She was director of the Office of Professional Education, American Home

Economics Association, and a member of and subsequently a consultant to the Council on Postsecondary Accreditation's Task Force on Interagency Cooperation.

James F. Bemis is executive director of the Commission on Colleges, Northwest Association of Schools and Colleges. He served on the Council of the Federation of Regional Accrediting Commissions of Higher Education and was first chairman of the Assembly of Institutional Accrediting Bodies, the Council on Postsecondary Accreditation.

Louis W. Bender is professor of higher education and director of the Institute for Study in Higher Education, Florida State University. He has served on review committees for the Commission on Higher Education, Middle States Association of Colleges and Schools, and for the Commission on Colleges, Southern Association of Colleges and Schools, and as a consultant on accreditation for various colleges and universities.

Elaine El-Khawas is director of the Division of Policy Analysis and Research, American Council on Education. She previously served as director of ACE's Office on Self-Regulation Initiatives.

Lloyd H. Elliott is president of George Washington University. He served on the Board of the National Commission on Accrediting and was the first chairman of the board of the Council on Postsecondary Accreditation.

Robert Glidden is dean of the School of Music, Florida State University. He has served as executive director of the National Association of Schools of Music, chairman of the Council of Specialized Accrediting Agencies, and chairman of the board of the Council on Postsecondary Accreditation.

Fred F. Harcleroad is professor of higher education at the University of Arizona. He has been a member of the board of the Council on Postsecondary Accreditation and is chairman of the

Accrediting Commission, National Home Study Council. He previously served as president of the California State University at Hayward and as president of the American College Testing Program.

Corrine W. Larson is president of Synergic Futures, Inc. She was associate director of the Manpower Division Interstudy; director of the Manpower Division, Minnesota Department of Health; and president of the National Commission for Health Certifying Agencies. She was also appointed a member of the U.S. Commissioner of Education's Advisory Committee on Accreditation and Institutional Eligibility.

Joan S. Stark is professor of higher education, University of Michigan, where she has been dean of the School of Education. She has been director of the Center for Helping Organizations to Improve Choice in Education (CHOICE) and a member of the U.S. Commissioner of Education's Advisory Committee on Accreditation and Institutional Eligibility.

Understanding Accreditation

Contemporary Perspectives
on Issues and Practices
in Evaluating
Educational Quality

Kenneth E. Young

炸炸炸炸炸炸炸炸炸炸炸炸炸炸炸炸炸炸炸炸炸炸炸炸炸

Prologue:
The Changing Scope
of Accreditation

There is nothing more difficult to take in hand,
more perilous to conduct, or more uncertain in its
success, than to take the lead in the introduction
of a new order of things.
Niccolò Machiavelli (1513)

By most standards, accreditation is still young—only about
seventy years old—but it functions in a nation that recently
celebrated its 200th anniversary, and it is sponsored by a postsecondary education community that dates its beginnings to
the founding of Harvard in 1636. During its short existence,
accreditation has moved rather quickly from infancy through
adolescence and is just now emerging into adulthood. Only in
the past ten or fifteen years has accreditation been the subject
of any serious national attention outside postsecondary education, and that attention, unfortunately, has been limited, spo-
radic, and often misunderstood.

None of this development has occurred in a vacuum. To
understand accreditation, one must know how it started and
why it began, the ways it has changed over the years in response
to changing conditions, and its prevailing basic characteristics.

1

Only then can one sort out valid from invalid criticisms of accredition and deal effectively with the important issues surrounding this unique social enterprise. For the reader seeking a mature perspective of how and why accreditation works, this Prologue is a prerequisite. It is not a history of accreditation but rather sets the historical context of accreditation in American postsecondary education. It identifies those key events whose effects have found their way into the policies, politics, practices, and procedures of accreditation today.

Emergence of Accreditation

Accreditation had many beginnings, but it emerged as a national phenomenon on August 3-4, 1906. On those two days, in response to a proposal from George E. MacLean, president of the State University of Iowa, the National Association of State Universities convened a meeting in Williamstown, Massachusetts, of a joint committee "to present a plan . . . for establishing, preserving, and interpreting in common terms the standards of admission to college, whatever be the method or combination of the methods of admission, in order to accommodate migrating students and to secure just understanding and administration of standards" (Conference Minutes, 1906). Attending the meeting were representatives of the four existing regional associations, as well as the six-year-old College Entrance Examination Board. They met at the home of Professor A. B. Morton of Williams College and, in one productive evening and morning, agreed to—

- Recommend that the regional associations have their member colleges accept certificates from accredited schools in other regions.
- Encourage the regional associations not yet doing so to organize "a college entrance certificate board or a commission for accrediting schools."
- Propose the development of common definitions and standards.
- Establish a permanent commission "for the purpose of considering, from time to time, entrance requirements and matters of mutual interest to colleges and preparatory schools."

The ensuing National Conference Committee of the Associations of Colleges and Preparatory Schools (as it was called) assembled on June 28-29, 1907, again at Williamstown (Conference Minutes, 1907). It subsequently met annually in the New York offices of the recently created Carnegie Foundation for the Advancement of Teaching, with the president of the foundation and the United States commissioner of education in attendance (Selden, 1960). Out of these meetings, which continued for seventeen years, came (1) recommended definitions (including the so-called Carnegie Unit), (2) the modern-day admission testing program of the College Entrance Examination Board, and (3) the sanctioning and eventual nationalizing of accreditation, first at the secondary school level and then for colleges and universities, through the expansion and linking of regional accrediting associations.

During this same period, two other developments important to accreditation occurred in the Midwest—developments that led to the establishment of the two main branches of accreditation, institutional accreditation and specialized accreditation. The first development began when the North Central Association of Colleges and Secondary Schools, which started accrediting high schools in 1905, decided to accredit member colleges. Standards were drawn up in 1909, the machinery was set in motion in 1910, and the first list of accredited institutions appeared in 1913 (Pfnister, 1959). Though still in embryonic form, this activity was the first accreditation of institutions of higher education.

Meanwhile, in Chicago, the American Medical Association (AMA) established its Council on Medical Education in 1904, developed a rating system of medical schools in 1905, initiated inspections in 1906, and prepared the first classifications of institutions in 1907. Then the AMA collaborated with the Carnegie Foundation in a study of medical education that resulted in the 1910 publication of the now-famous Flexner Report (American Medical Association, 1960). Although these early efforts of the AMA (and the Association of American Medical Colleges) could not be called accreditation as that term is understood today, they did evolve into specialized accreditation and set a pattern that was to be followed by most other professional associations.

Thus, within a period of less than ten years, a radically new concept suddenly appeared on the scene, was adopted and put into operation by colleges and universities in a large area of the country, gained the attention of a major professional organization, and received the blessing and support of leaders in the higher education community, an important foundation, and a key federal agency. Why did voluntary nongovernmental accreditation come into being and achieve such rapid acceptance at just this time? To answer that question, one needs to understand the changes that were occurring in the United States during this era.

Modern America Invents Itself

During the period between the Civil War and World War I, this country was going through "a rapid and sometimes turbulent transition from the conditions of an agrarian society to those of modern urban life" (Allen, 1952, p. 7), a transition that "wrought drastic economic and intellectual changes which, in turn, profoundly affected education from its lowest to its highest levels" (Butts, 1939, p. 159). This period can be encapsulated by such terms as *industrialism, capitalism, individualism, populism,* and particularly *progressivism* ("a rather widespread and remarkably good-natured effort of the greater part of society to achieve some not very clearly specified self-reformation"—Allen, 1952, pp. 5-6).

Richard Hofstadter (1955) called this period "the Age of Reform"; Robert Wiebe (1967) described it as "the Search for Order"; and C. M. McConn (1935) labeled it "the Age of Standards." Princeton University President Woodrow Wilson captured the feeling of the period in a 1907 speech at a meeting of the Middle States Association of Colleges and Schools, when he said: "We are on the eve of a period of reconstruction. We are on the eve of a period when we are going to set up standards. We are on the eve of a period of synthesis, when, tired of this dispersion and standardless analysis, we are going to put things together into something like a connected and thought-out scheme of endeavor. It is inevitable" (Wilson, 1907, p. 89).

This mood affected every phase of American life, including higher education. Among the significant events of that time were these (Brickman and Lehrer, 1962):

- 1862—Passage of the Land-Grant Act.
- 1876—Founding of Johns Hopkins University, the first real American university.
- 1882-1910—Introduction of the elective system at Harvard University.
- 1890—Passage of the second Land-Grant College Act, providing for black institutions.
- 1895—Founding of the North Central and Southern regional associations.
- 1900—Founding of the Association of American Universities, the Association of American Law Schools, and the College Entrance Examination Board.
- 1901—Establishment of Joliet (Illinois) Junior College, the first permanent junior college.
- 1905—Creation of the Carnegie Foundation for the Advancement of Teaching.
- 1910—Publication of Abraham Flexner's report, *Medical Education in the United States and Canada.*
- 1914—Passage of the Smith-Lever Act, authorizing extension programs; founding of the Association of American Colleges.

During this same period, Harvard, Yale, Princeton, and Columbia became universities; new institutions such as the University of California, Howard University, and Stanford University were born; and such towering figures as Frederick A. Barnard, William Rainey Harper, James McCosh, Andrew Dickson White, Daniel Coit Gilman, Charles W. Eliot, James Burrill Angell, G. Stanley Hall, and Nicholas Murray Butler played leading roles.

Accreditation was therefore born during a time of ferment and hope. Accreditation not only was a product of this period but also shared the characteristics of the society that spawned it: idealistic, self-motivated, reform-minded, desiring improvement, believing in both individual initiative and voluntary collective action, and distrustful of government (though seeing government as embodying the ultimate power to right wrongs). These characteristics still infuse accreditation.

The Board of Regents of the State of New York has often been incorrectly identified as the first accrediting body in the United States (see Selden, 1960, p. 30). Historians refer to legislation enacted in 1787 that required members of the New York State Board "to visit every college in this state once a year" (Abbott, 1958, p. 23). This historical footnote, though an important benchmark, does not qualify as accreditation—even by the standards of earlier times. The process consisted of a visit, usually by a single, low-level state official and usually of one day's duration, and an acknowledgment of that visit as part of an annual written report to the state legislature. There were no established criteria, no peer review, no group judgment, and certainly no guided self-study. The New York initiative was an early precursor of accreditation. Accreditation drew from many sources and has grown and changed over time.

How Accreditation Has Changed

At its start, accreditation began with a problem of definition (What is a high school? A college? A medical school?) and the problem of articulation between high schools and colleges and between institutions of higher education. It quickly moved, however, to establishing membership requirements for an organization (for example, the North Central Association and the Association of American Medical Colleges). These early efforts understandably concerned themselves with minimum standards and defined those standards in specific, quantitative terms that were generally acceptable at the time. For example, the AMA's Council on Medical Education in 1905 adopted an "ideal standard" with the recommendation that medical schools of this country should eventually require "(1) preliminary education sufficient to enable the candidate to enter our recognized universities; (2) a five-year medical course: the first year devoted to physics, chemistry and biology; the next two years to laboratory sciences of anatomy, physiology, pathology, and pharmacology, and two years to the clinical branches, with close contact with patients in both dispensary and hospital; (3) a sixth year as an intern in the hospital" (American Medical Association, 1960, p. 7).

Within twenty years, however, accreditation—at least institutional accreditation—made a major leap forward, and the North Central Association once again led the way. In 1929 its Higher Commission appointed a Committee on Revision of Standards, which developed a research project involving fifty-seven institutions and resulting in a seven-volume report (Zook and Haggerty, 1936, and others). More important, the committee put forth a "newly developed policy which undergirds regional and professional accrediting to this day" (Geiger, 1970, pp. xiv–xv). The committee's report stated: "An institution will be judged for [accreditation] upon the basis of the total pattern it presents as an institution of higher education . . . it is recognized that wide variations will appear . . . the facilities and activities of an institution will be judged in terms of the purposes it seeks to serve" (Zook and Haggerty, 1936, p. 98). This principle —that an institution would be evaluated in terms of its own purposes and not by arbitrary standards—was adopted by the North Central Association and gradually by the other regional associations and a growing number of professional associations. It, in turn, led to the establishment of the self-study process.

This change in the approach of accreditation came at a time when the progressive education movement had taken a strong hold. "Democracy was conceived as a society in which people live freely by their own determinations and in such a way that they not only do not interfere with the free living of other people but actually aid other people to live freely for themselves" (Butts, 1939, p. 314). The belief was that "a discipline that is self-imposed and self-realized is necessary to attaining the more important end in which the person is interested" (p. 314). As one outgrowth of this movement, the Progressive Education Association set up an experiment in 1932 that led to the important Eight-Year Study (Aikin, 1942) and changes in college admission standards away from detailed specification of prerequisite courses and toward individual judgments of student quality. This new mood was also reflected in the changing emphasis in accreditation.

Other changes have been occurring in American society that have inevitably affected accreditation.

The Universe of Accreditation Is Changing. A fundamental but as yet not fully appreciated evolution has recently been taking place. The term *higher education* (by which is commonly meant degree-granting colleges and universities offering traditional academic programs and mainly serving full-time students recently graduated from high school) has been gradually giving way to use of the term *postsecondary education* (an ever-expanding variety of institutions, programs, and delivery systems in many settings and under various forms of sponsorship serving a growing diversity of learners of all ages with widely differing educational objectives). Many "traditional" colleges and universities are engaging in a growing number of educational activities not directly related to producing graduates with degrees. At the same time, a variety of "nontraditional" institutions are beginning to award credits and degrees as well as offer a great range of noncredit educational programs. Accreditation is expected to evaluate and assure the educational quality of everything from a school of welding operated by one person to a statewide system of postsecondary education, from a hospital granting both M.D. and Ph.D. degrees to a state agency offering degrees by examination, from institutions that operate campuses throughout the world to institutions that have no campuses at all. Surely, few social enterprises in history have faced such dramatic expansion and change in such a relatively short period as has accreditation.

The Participants in Accreditation Are Changing. Until World War II, the accreditation community consisted mainly of the six regional associations and a few major professional associations. Since then, a rapidly growing number of organizations have initiated accreditation activities. By 1982 the Council on Postsecondary Accreditation (COPA) had recognized fifty-one accrediting bodies and had identified more than seventy additional organizations that were operating without recognition. Many of the newer groups are well out of the mainstream of postsecondary education (for example, the Council on Noncollegiate Continuing Education, which primarily accredits for-profit purveyors of short-course learning, such as Dale Carnegie Associates and the Evelyn Wood Reading Dynamics Program). Furthermore, these more recent participants have been drawn into accreditation mainly because of its linkages to eligibility for federal funds and its credentialing value rather than for any deeply felt desire to improve educational quality.

Practices in Accreditation Are Changing. During the past seventy years, accreditation has changed—

- From a quantitative approach (expressed in specific requirements) to a qualitative approach (based on more general standards).
- From an emphasis on making institutions more alike to recognizing and encouraging institutional individuality.
- From a system heavily dependent on external review to a system based more on self-evaluation and self-regulation.
- From an initial focus on judging (and accepting or rejecting) an institution to a primary goal of encouraging and assisting an institution to improve its educational quality.

Not all accrediting bodies have yet completely implemented these principles, but the principles are generally accepted, and continuing progress toward their acceptance can be noted on many fronts. In fact, some leaders in accreditation have taken up the next goals: (1) to enable institutions to state their educational objectives in ways that lend themselves to evaluation and develop means for evaluating their achievement and (2) to foster mechanisms by which accrediting bodies can work more cooperatively and even collaboratively rather than as completely independent operations.

Society's Expectations of Accreditation Are Changing. Accreditation served important social needs from its very beginning, although its role was not generally known or understood. Accreditation has served society remarkably well by developing consensus on the meaning of a high school, a college, and professional schools; by promoting effective articulation between institutions; and by improving educational standards and practices. Over time, however, accreditation has increasingly taken on a broader social purpose. Now federal and state governments use accreditation as a consideration in determining eligibility for certain funds, in defining licensure requirements, and in other ways. To some extent, business and industry make use of accreditation in hiring and in awarding funds. Foundations and philanthropists usually make accreditation a condition for grants.

Even to this day, however, the general public has little awareness or understanding of accreditation. Most people do not take accreditation into consideration in deciding what institutions to attend or what programs to take. And they often have wildly unrealistic notions about what accreditation is, as in the following account from Persig's *Zen and the Art of Motorcycle Maintenance* (1974, pp. 141–142):

> Then one student, apparently a partisan of the governor, said angrily that the legislature would prevent the school from losing its accreditation.
> Phaedrus asked how.
> The student said they would post police to prevent it.

Basic Characteristics of Accreditation

Postsecondary education in the United States has been blessed (and occasionally cursed) with a great diversity of institutions, programs, approaches, and styles. Given so many kinds of learning enterprises under so many forms of sponsorship, to establish standardized requirements or uniform procedures and administer them through some national agency is clearly impossible. Accreditation can be properly understood, therefore, only when it is seen as a loose federation—of institutions, associations, and public representatives that also involve a variety of approaches and styles and have different forms of sponsorship. What brings them together is a commitment to the concept of accreditation as a voluntary, nongovernmental process of self-regulation focused on evaluating and improving educational quality. The basic characteristics of accreditation, then, are (1) its prevailing sense of voluntarism, (2) its strong tradition of self-regulation, (3) its reliance on evaluation techniques, and (4) its primary concern with quality.

Voluntarism. The populist/progressive age came to an end with the First World War, and the Great Depression and World War II moved this nation toward an ever-increasing involvement of government, particularly federal government, in almost all aspects of human life. Although accreditation has stubbornly held on to its roots in voluntarism, it has inevitably been affected by the growing role of government. This issue, of course, has to be addressed. Writings about accreditation, however, have been overly preoccupied with this particular problem; they have tended to exaggerate the role of government and overlook or minimize the evidence of a strong, underlying commitment to accreditation as a voluntary, nongovernmental activity. The concept of voluntarism is now enjoying a resurgence of interest in general—in the literature (see Smith and Freedman, 1972; Manser and Cass, 1976) and through the work of such organizations as the Center for a Voluntary Society, the Association of Voluntary Action Scholars, and the Independent Sector.

Self-Regulation. The term *self-regulation* is preceded in the dictionary by the word *self-regard* and followed by the word *self-reliance* (*Oxford English Dictionary*, 1971, p. 424). This trilogy of terms aptly describes the essence of this country, as perceived by de Tocqueville (1840) and epitomized by the progressive movement. Accreditation draws heavily on this tradition. Its historical roots are also found in the concept of academic freedom for faculties, which are traditionally collegial groups of independent scholars as well as educators.

The case for self-regulation in postsecondary education is also based on the following principles:

- Self-regulation is preferable to and, in the long run, more effective than any form of external regulation.
- Any system of external regulation can be effective only to the extent that it recognizes and builds on a group's willingness to engage in self-regulation.
- A substantial number of people and institutions will regulate

themselves along agreed-upon lines if they know what behavior is expected by the group and why.

- An overwhelming majority of people and institutions will
regulate themselves along agreed-upon lines if they believe
that they might be identified by their peers as not doing so.
- Only a small number of people and institutions will deliberately engage in behavior that they know will be disapproved
of by the larger group. No matter how many laws are passed
or rules written or inspectors hired, antisocial behavior by
these types cannot be inhibited or prevented.

Problems have recently developed mainly because new institutions have appeared that are not imbued with the concept
of self-regulation and because changing conditions have caused
changing practices, leaving many established institutions confused about what is acceptable behavior. Nonetheless, self-regulation in postsecondary education survives and will prevail, and
accreditation serves as the centerpiece of all self-regulation in
postsecondary education.

Evaluation. Accreditation functions as an evaluation process much more than as a regulatory process. Institutions and
programs evaluate themselves, and peers from other institutions
and programs evaluate those evaluations. The authoritative definition of *evaluation* could serve as a workable definition of *accreditation*: "Evaluation is the process of delineating, obtaining,
and providing useful information for judging decision alternatives" (Stufflebeam and others, 1971, p. xxv). *Delineating* implies defining and specifying aspects of the institution or program
to be assessed. *Obtaining* includes the collection, organization,
and analysis of information. *Providing* suggests the synthesizing
of information in a form useful for decision makers. During the
past twenty-five years, an important shift has taken place in
education evaluation—from an emphasis on process to a focus
on product (outcomes) evaluation (see Bloom and others,
1956). Now accreditation, somewhat belatedly, is reflecting
that changing emphasis.

Quality. In *Zen and the Art of Motorcycle Maintenance*
(1974), Robert Persig describes quality as a concept, not some-

thing that can be defined or measured. "Quality is just the focal point around which a lot of intellectual furniture is getting rearranged" (p. 218). Everyone seeks quality, consciously or subconsciously. If someone is talented, persistent, and lucky, that person may achieve quality at one time or another in some aspect of life. And when someone brushes up against quality, that person almost always recognizes and appreciates it—whether it is in the form of a fine symphony or an excellent motor tune-up. Persig quotes Lao Tzu from 426 B.C.: "Quality is all-pervading. And its use is inexhaustible: Fathomless! Like the Fountainhead of all things. . . . It cannot be defined" (p. 247).

What is puzzling is how often people attempt to pin quality down in ways that can be measured or itemized. This task is particularly fruitless when one is dealing with a process as multifaceted and variable as education and an institution as diffuse as a college or university. "The fact is that real authority in the university is not hierarchical, as in business or in the military; it is not even 'separate' as it is in principle in the United States Government. It is not a system of checks and balances so much as a diffusion of authority" (Pandarus, 1973, p. 572). The genius of accreditation is that it began with the impossible task of defining educational quality and in just twenty-five years evolved, by trial and error, into a process that advances educational quality.

Criticisms of Accreditation

Most criticisms of accreditation have been based on false expectations of the process or have been directed at persons and organizations who were conducting inappropriate activities in the name of accreditation. However, accreditation has properly deserved some criticism, and indeed it has received some.

One of the earliest, and most quoted, critics was Samuel P. Capen, chancellor of the University of Buffalo, who in a 1939 speech entitled "Seven Devils in Exchange for One," said: "Responsible administrators of influential institutions in various parts of the country are tired of having the educational and financial policies of their institutions dictated by a horde of irresponsible outsiders, each representing a separate selfish interest" (Capen, 1939, p. 5).

Fred O. Pinkham, first executive director of the National Commission on Accrediting, described accreditation as "an elusive, nebulous, jellyfish term that means different things to the same people" and complained that "it has been most difficult to mediate differences among people who do not agree on what it is on what they do not agree, and, I might add, on which they disagree violently, emotionally, and dogmatically" (Pinkham, 1952, p. 47).

Henry M. Wriston, a former president of the North Central Association, wrote (1960, p. 320): "The accreditation process inevitably is driven by judgments which are essentially superficial, transient in their validity, and a drain upon time, energy, and resources that ought to be put into the real obligations of the college or university. . . . Accreditation seeks not only to compare apples with grapes, but both with camels and cods."

James D. Koerner, an official with the Sloan Foundation, in 1970 delivered a paper entitled "Who Benefits from Accreditation: Special Interests or the Public?" and suggested that there were more benefits to the former than the latter (Koerner, 1970). To make certain that his point was not missed, he came back with a 1971 article, "Preserving the Status Quo: Academia's Hidden Cartel" (Koerner, 1971).

And the Carnegie Foundation for the Advancement of Teaching issued a report that was critical of both regional and specialized accreditation. It said of regional accreditation, "Among accreditors there is no agreement about the meaning of a college education, and the neglect of undergraduate education is especially disturbing" (Carnegie Foundation for the Advancement of Teaching, 1982, p. 76) and stated that "one form of self-regulation—specialized accreditation—actually threatens the integrity of the campus" (p. 78).

These are but a few examples of the criticism levied against accreditation. Why has accreditation been the target of so much criticism, much of it quite vitriolic and a great deal of it coming from within the postsecondary education community? Accreditation has never been well understood—not by the general public or, for that matter, by the institutions of post-secondary education it primarily serves. Like any dynamic process, accreditation has been evolving in subtle but important ways over the years, and the professionals and volunteers who have been actively involved in accreditation have been so busy making the process work that they have had little or no time to spend educating others about its value, limitations, and changing emphases. As a result, much of the criticism has come from misunderstandings about the proper role of accreditation.

Furthermore, accreditation by its very nature represents a "struggle over standards" (see Selden, 1960). Various interest groups within the institutions contend with one another, and external organizations try to exert their influence on institutional priorities. Inevitably, accreditation not only feels the force of these pressures but also bears the brunt of criticism from those whose interests are not served.

Accreditation is highly dependent on the unpaid services of many volunteers, who do not always perform well. They may back out of an obligation at the last minute, come unprepared for a site visit or a commission meeting, ignore accreditation standards and guidelines in favor of their own set of expectations, or behave rudely. All these things can and do happen. What is surprising, perhaps, is that they occur so rarely. Even one instance of misjudgment, however, becomes a "horror story" that is retold again and again.

Accreditation is a tool that institutions should make wise use of in their quest for educational quality. This book is designed to give institutional officials an understanding of accreditation that will help them make accreditation work for their institutions, thereby serving the entire postsecondary education community and the general public as well.

Part One

჻჻჻჻჻჻჻჻჻჻჻჻჻჻჻჻჻჻჻჻჻჻჻჻჻჻

What Accreditation Is

Accreditation began as a relatively simple idea—a voluntary effort by a small group of educational institutions to agree on standards for distinguishing a college from a secondary school. Over the past seventy years or so, however, accreditation has matured and changed into a much more sophisticated process for evaluating and improving educational quality in colleges, universities, and comparable institutions. It also has evolved into a complex arrangement of sponsors, practitioners, and users—each with its own agenda for accreditation.

Despite their many differences, accrediting bodies do share some important common agreements about the role, reach, and process of accreditation. There is a strong consensus that accreditation is essentially nongovernmental, that it exemplifies the pervasive voluntary tradition in this country, and that it serves as the centerpiece of a rather elaborate "system" of self-regulation in American postsecondary education.

Accreditation nevertheless continues to be beset by a host of misconceptions and misuses. In particular, the federal government, state agencies, professional associations, and even institutions of postsecondary education themselves often misunderstand or deliberately distort accreditation's purposes. The ultimate tests for determining appropriate uses of accreditation are serving the public interest, improving educational quality, and not compromising accreditation's basic characteristics.

1

Kenneth E. Young

ƳƳƳƳƳƳƳƳƳƳƳƳƳƳƳƳƳƳƳƳƳƳƳƳ

Accreditation: Complex Evaluative Tool

Accreditation is something like prose: A lot of people engage in it without realizing what they are doing. Michael Cardozo (1975, p. 39)

The key to understanding how postsecondary education works in the United States is to recognize that accreditation is at the center of a voluntary system of self-regulation. Accreditation is unique to this country, because in other nations establishing and maintaining educational standards is almost always the official responsibility of a government agency. A large enterprise, accreditation directly involves thousands of persons, more than 4,000 institutions of postsecondary education, and dozens of national and regional organizations. Although the concept of accreditation is fairly simple, the structures and relationships that have developed over the years have become incredibly complex and diversified. Therefore, almost every generalization that is made about accreditation can be challenged by pointing to exceptions and deviations.

That most people are confused about accreditation is not

19

surprising. More than 100 nongovernmental organizations in the United States call themselves accrediting bodies. A half-dozen other organizations not engaged in accreditation must work diligently to dispel the widespread but mistaken notion that they are engaged in accreditation. And an uncounted number of groups conduct what might be called quasi-accreditation activities, such as the listing or registration of approved programs. Of the 100 or so accrediting bodies, only 51 were recognized in 1982 by the Council on Postsecondary Accreditation (COPA).

What Is Accreditation?

Almost all previous discussions of accreditation have focused on it as an effort by external organizations and agencies to regulate institutions of postsecondary education and have failed to give attention to the strong theme of self-regulation that has consistently infused accreditation activities throughout the years.

Definitions of accreditation over time have repeatedly emphasized the role of accrediting bodies in recognizing educational institutions and programs that meet established standards:

- "The recognition accorded to an education institution in the United States by means of inclusion in a list of institutions issued by some agency or organization which sets up standards or requirements that must be complied with in order to secure approval" (Zook and Haggerty, 1936, p. 18).
- "The process whereby an organization or agency recognizes a college or university or program of study as having met certain predetermined qualifications or standards" (Selden, 1960, p. 5).
- "The voluntary process whereby an agency or association grants public recognition to a school, institute, college, university, or specialized program of study that meets certain established qualifications and educational standards, as determined through initial and periodic evaluations" (U.S. Department of Health, Education, and Welfare, 1968, p. 5).
- "[The term is] commonly used to mean that certain accepted

standards have been satisfactorily met, as judged by some group of competent experts" (Young and Chambers, 1980, p. 89).

All these definitions fall seriously short of capturing the real purpose of accreditation as it currently functions. In one sense the definitions can be said to be accurate, but they are also severely limited. They are therefore dangerously misleading.

Accreditation is a process by which an institution of post-secondary education evaluates its educational activities, in whole or in part, and seeks an independent judgment to confirm that it substantially achieves its objectives and is generally equal in quality to comparable institutions or specialized units (see the Glossary in Resource E). Essential elements in the accreditation process are (1) a clear statement by the institution of its educational intentions, (2) the conduct of a directed self-study focused on the achievement of these intentions, (3) an on-site evaluation by a selected group of peers, and (4) a decision by an independent accrediting commission that, in light of its standards, the institution or specialized unit is worthy of accreditation. Unfortunately, most discussions of accreditation emphasize the site visit and the final decision, whereas students of accreditation would argue that goal setting and the self-study are the most important parts of the process (see Chapter Seven).

The major characteristics of accreditation are the following:

1. It is predominantly a voluntary, private-sector activity and therefore cannot mandate compliance or control behavior except by persuasion and peer influence.
2. It is the premier example of self-regulation (as opposed to government regulation) in postsecondary education.
3. It focuses primarily on judging educational quality—an elusive concept—and, given the great diversity of postsecondary educational institutions in the United States, criteria tend to be general and variable.
4. It functions essentially as an evaluative process, and institutional self-study is at the heart of the process.

5. It provides outside consultation, closely tied to the institution's own research and planning.

To understand what accreditation is *not* is also important. Accreditation is not governmental, although both federal and state agencies use it—to determine eligibility for certain government programs and in relation to professional licensing. It is not mandatory, although there are strong social and political pressures and even some legal prods to encourage participation. It is not a rating system, although institutions and programs generally do get compared. It is not a mechanism for formally policing institutional behavior; accrediting bodies do not have enough staff to make regular visits to all accredited institutions to assure compliance, even if they wanted to. Rather, it depends on informal monitoring, generally through the accrediting body following up on a complaint about an institution (usually from an unhappy faculty member or student, another institution, or a state agency). It does not deal directly with credits, despite its name, although it is often used to help distinguish (sometimes erroneously) between worthy and unworthy prior educational experience. And it is not a stamp of approval on individual students or courses; it does not operate at that level of analysis, although it is often perceived that way.

Purposes of Accreditation

Like the elephant in the parable of the blind men, accreditation is often perceived, and therefore used, differently by different interest groups (see Chapter Four). Its overriding purpose, however, is to improve educational quality.

The Council on Postsecondary Accreditation (1981a) has listed six major goals of accrediting bodies:

1. To foster excellence in postsecondary education through the development of criteria and guidelines for assessing educational effectiveness.
2. To encourage improvement of institutions and programs through continuous self-study and planning.

3. To assure other organizations and agencies, the education community, and the general public that an institution or a particular program has both clearly defined and appropriate objectives, maintains conditions under which their achievement can reasonably be expected, appears in fact to be accomplishing them substantially, and can be expected to continue to do so.
4. To provide counsel and assistance to established and developing institutions and programs.
5. To encourage the diversity of American postsecondary education and allow institutions to achieve their particular objectives and goals.
6. To endeavor to protect institutions against encroachments that might jeopardize their educational effectiveness or academic freedom.

One point of confusion about the purpose of accreditation concerns the role of accrediting bodies in identifying institutions or programs that meet "minimum standards." The term *minimum standards* is often misunderstood to mean that the accrediting bodies superimpose external, objective, and quantitative standards on the institutions and programs they accredit, such as specifying student-teacher ratios or the number of volumes there should be in the library. Although some accrediting bodies do have some specific standards, accreditation as a whole is more accurately characterized as an elaborate process that involves many people making subjective judgments, individually and collectively. During the self-study, many people at the institution are engaged in evaluating the institution or program, and again during the site visit and commission review many people are involved in making judgments. Accreditation is based on subjective decisions organized within an ordered process so that gross errors and extreme judgments are detected and counterbalanced.

If *minimum standards* does not connote specific, measurable indexes, what is meant by the term? Value judgments are made to determine whether the institution or program has set and is meeting *appropriate objectives.* Appropriateness is assessed in two ways. First, are the objectives consistent with the stated mission and goals of the institution or program? (In addition, the achievement of educational objectives clearly requires some established governance and administrative processes, instructional resources, facilities, and support services.) Second, are the objectives consistent with a broad concept of postsecondary education? In this question, the accrediting body can clearly impose its view on the institution. For example, a school for thieves or a program of adult literacy education, however consistent with the stated mission and goals, would not be judged to have appropriate objectives for an institution of postsecondary education.

Finally, there are some important differences in emphasis between institutional and specialized accrediting associations (see the Glossary). *Institutional accrediting bodies* help an institution look at itself as a whole; define its objectives and evaluate its success in achieving them; assess the relative roles of the governing board, the faculty, the student body, and other interest groups; and assure a balance among these forces. The ultimate test of institutional accreditation is whether the accredited institution is acceptable to other accredited institutions (see Chapter Ten). *Specialized accrediting bodies* generally will review institutional objectives and the relationship of the program to the total institution, but they focus mainly on programs and are more likely to have fairly specific standards relating, in large part, to performance skills considered desirable, if not essential, by practitioners as well as by standards of good practice determined by consensus. As an example of the latter kind of standard, the American Physical Therapy Association (1982) states that the student-faculty ratio in laboratory experiences should in most instances be sixteen to one and that there should be no more than two students per faculty member in beginning clinical internships or four students per faculty member in advanced clinical internships. The ultimate test of specialized accreditation is whether graduates of the program are acceptable to members of the profession, credentialing bodies, and employers (see Chapter Eleven).

The Accreditation Process

In fulfilling its role, accreditation focuses on two concerns: (1) *educational quality,* defined and interpreted within the context of the institution's or program's own statement of scope and purpose as compared with similar institutions and programs, and (2) *institutional integrity,* that the institution or program is what it says it is and does what it says it does. Educational quality is evaluated and encouraged by looking at conditions that are believed to be necessary and desirable to produce educational quality (input, resources, and process) and by looking at evidence that the institution or program does indeed achieve educational quality (outcomes).

The accreditation process is designed primarily to encourage and assist the institution to evaluate itself objectively and then for the accrediting body to validate what the institution has said about itself. Basic to the accreditation process are (1) the institutional self-study, a comprehensive, internal effort to assess the effectiveness of an institution or program in light of its own publicly stated objectives, and (2) peer evaluation, expert judgment from outside the institution, usually rendered by professional educators (administrators as well as faculty members), certain specialists according to the nature of the institution or program, and sometimes others representing specific public interests. When properly done, the self-study displays the match between the institution's aspirations and its day-to-day accomplishments. From this, the visiting team can evaluate the institution and also focus sharply on areas needing improvement, in a collegial fashion that is meant to avoid the alienation that might come with official inspectors.

The accrediting associations have adopted the view that the best-qualified persons to make these value judgments are peer educators and others who are involved in or devoted to postsecondary education. Although the casual critic may scoff that this situation is ideal for conflict of interest, self-dealing, and cronyism, no one has been able to suggest other groups with sufficient insight and expertise that could do as good a job of review and assessment. In fact, volunteers who devote their time and energy unselfishly to accreditation are reluctant to condone fraudulence, spuriousness, deception, or incompetence in education. These peers, not the accrediting association staff, are the ones who make the final decisions, and they are aware that their judgments will eventually reflect on their own reputations.

Types of Accrediting Bodies

In getting to know the accrediting associations, perhaps the most useful point of reference is COPA recognition (see Resource A, "Accrediting Groups Recognized by COPA"). COPA classifies accrediting bodies as either institutional or specialized (although some organizations that accredit single-purpose specialized institutions show up as institutional accrediting bodies, and others appear as specialized accrediting bodies). *Institutional accreditation* (1) deals with the total institution, (2) is almost always the basis for institutional membership, and (3) focuses primarily on institutionwide objectives, processes, and outcomes. It encompasses both the regional accrediting bodies (comprehensive in membership, long established and well regarded, and dedicated exclusively to accreditation and closely related activities) and national accrediting bodies (specialized in membership, relatively new and therefore not as well known, and often part of organizations that perform functions other than accreditation). *Specialized accreditation* (1) generally looks at a selected part of an institution (school, division, department, program), (2) may or may not involve institutional membership (but if it does, it draws its support and participation from the appropriate specialized unit within the institution), and (3) applies criteria that relate primarily to requirements for effective professional practice.

Regional Associations. The six regional associations are the Middle States Association of Colleges and Schools, the New England Association of Schools and Colleges, the North Central Association of Colleges and Schools, the Northwest Association of Schools and Colleges, the Southern Association of Colleges and Schools, and the Western Association of Schools and Colleges. (There is no significance, other than historical, in the relative placement of *schools* and *colleges* in their titles.)

The regional associations provide the basic framework for accreditation. A college or university must in most instances achieve regional accreditation before a specialized accrediting body will review any of its parts; the regional associations are in a logical position to provide leadership for cooperation between institutional and specialized accreditation; and a significant number of states rely on the regional associations for various purposes.

The regional associations are the legal entities, but they serve as the parent bodies for several separate accrediting commissions. Only one or two commissions are concerned with postsecondary education; the other commissions deal with elementary education, secondary education, or some other aspect of accreditation. The overall association has a governing board that hires an association executive. Each commission reports to the governing board and has an executive who not only works for the commission but also has a working relationship with the association executive, as well as the executives of the other commissions. The boards and commissions are comprised of volunteers. Only the executives and their staffs, working under the direction of the board and commissions, are paid employees.

For an accrediting body to be recognized by COPA, its commission(s) must have adequate operational autonomy. Generally, this requirement is taken to mean that the postsecondary education commission, which is representative of its member institutions, develops the accreditation criteria, establishes procedures, and makes the decisions about the accreditation of institutions and that these decisions are then reported to the governing board. The board, which includes representatives from all levels of education, is expected not to overrule the commission, although it might refer actions back to the commission if they appear to be inconsistent or in conflict with association policies.

Collectively, the regional postsecondary education commissions had an accredited membership of about 2,800 institutions and had another 300 or so in candidate status in 1982.

The institutions represent all levels of postsecondary education, granting graduate degrees, baccalaureates, associate degrees, and certificates. They may be categorized as public, private non-profit, or proprietary; liberal arts, vocational, or professional; complex or single-purpose; free-standing or part of a system. In addition to traditional colleges and universities, the regional commissions have accredited institutions such as the Rand Graduate Institute for Policy Studies (sponsored by the Rand Corporation); the Arthur D. Little Management Education Institute, Inc.; the Community College of the Air Force; ICS—International Correspondence Schools; the Western State University College of Law of San Diego; and the Regents External Degree Program in New York. Each year, about 10-20 percent of the postsecondary educational institutions that are members of a regional association are reviewed for renewal of accreditation.

The regional associations vary widely in size, tradition, and character. The North Central Association, the largest regional association, with 915 institutions as of 1982, covers nineteen states. The Southern Association, in eleven states, has 722 colleges and universities and an additional 195 occupational institutions as members. The Middle States Association includes 485 institutions in five states, the District of Columbia, Puerto Rico, the American Virgin Islands, and the Canal Zone. The Western Association encompasses only two states—California and Hawaii—plus Guam and the Trust Territories, but it accredits 130 four-year institutions and 133 community and junior colleges. The New England Association accredits 194 colleges and universities and 34 vocational institutions in six states, and the Northwest Association accredits 143 institutions in seven states.

By and large, the associations' boundaries reflect certain historical, operational, and character differences. The Southern Association lost Arkansas to the North Central Association in 1923, and West Virginia followed in 1925. The possibility of a merger between the Western Association and the Northwest Association has been considered from time to time since the 1950s, and the question of boundary adjustment arose with respect to Arizona in 1980-81.

The executives of the postsecondary education commissions have worked together to coordinate practices in many areas—informally as well as formally—through, successively, the National Committee on Regional Accrediting Agencies, the Federation of Regional Accrediting Commissions of Higher Education, and the current Council on Postsecondary Accreditation. Early on, the regional associations espoused the principle of "national standards regionally applied," but they have moved slowly toward the full realization of that principle. A 1979 study found that the criteria used and their relative priorities were generally comparable among the regional associations (Phillips, 1979). However, associations still vary in important areas, such as the selection and training of the volunteers who interpret the criteria as well as the emphasis given to institutional objectives and educational outcomes, as opposed to association standards.

National Accrediting Bodies. The institutional accrediting organizations that are national rather than regional fall into two major categories: (1) associations whose members are predominantly *proprietary* schools—the Association of Independent Colleges and Schools (549 institutions), the National Association of Trade and Technical Schools (623 institutions), and the National Home Study Council (77 institutions)—and (2) associations whose members are predominantly *church-related* schools, such as the American Association of Bible Colleges (231 institutions). The Association of Theological Schools in the United States and Canada (167 institutions and programs) was classified as a specialized accrediting body but in 1981 requested reclassification as an institutional accrediting body.

The associations that accredit large numbers of proprietary schools do not restrict their membership to institutions seeking a profit. Among their members are private nonprofit institutions, religion schools, and even entities sponsored by federal agencies. These associations nevertheless reflect the interests and concerns of the majority of their members. Consequently, they tend to function to some extent as trade associations. They conduct vigorous public relations and lobbying programs as well as quite effective training activities for their members, and they view accreditation as an important tool in support of these other activities. In some of these groups, the association executive is also the key staff person serving the accrediting commission.

Accreditation has quite a different impact on proprietary schools than on public and private nonprofit colleges and universities. Of the estimated 10,000 for-profit postsecondary institutions in the United States, only about 2,000 are accredited, whereas all but about 100 of the 3,200 nonprofit, degree-granting public and independent colleges and universities have some sort of status (accreditation or candidate for accreditation) with an accrediting body. Therefore, the accredited proprietary school sees the recognition as an important distinguishing status. Only schools that are stable in years of operation, continuing sponsorship of programs, and permanence of ownership can hope to qualify for and maintain accreditation.

The two church-related accrediting bodies work cooperatively with the regional associations when institutions request both types of accreditation. The American Association of Bible Colleges accredits institutions ranging from the large, well-known Moody Bible Institute to very small schools operated as adjuncts to churches. The Association of Theological Schools accredits both free-standing theological schools and units within universities.

Specialized Accrediting Bodies. Although most specialized accrediting bodies accredit components within institutions, some accredit free-standing, specialized institutions, and some accredit programs sponsored by noncollege organizations such as hospitals and clinics. They may be categorized as four general types according to their sponsorship:

1. Accrediting bodies sponsored by organizations whose members are *units within institutions*: Examples include the American Assembly of Collegiate Schools of Business, the National Association of Schools of Art and Design, and the National Association of Schools of Music.

2. Accrediting bodies sponsored by organizations whose members are *individual practitioners*: Examples include the American Dental Association, the National League for Nursing, and the American Physical Therapy Association.

3. Accrediting bodies sponsored by organizations whose members are *both institutions and individual practitioners*: An example is the American Home Economics Association.

4. Accrediting bodies having some form of *joint sponsorship* of accreditation functions: Examples include the American Bar Association and the Association of American Law Schools, which conduct coordinated accreditations; the American Medical Association and the Association of American Medical Colleges, which jointly sponsor the Liaison Committee on Medical Education; collaborating organizations in the allied health field (including the AMA) that sponsor the Committee on Allied Health Education and Accreditation; several education groups—most notably the National Education Association and the American Association of Colleges for Teacher Education—that cosponsor the National Council for Accreditation of Teacher Education; and seven engineering societies that sponsor the Accreditation Board for Engineering and Technology.

These differences in sponsorship greatly influence the way a specialized accrediting body will see its role as well as its willingness and ability to respond to institutional concerns or the guidance of an organization such as COPA. For example, an organization of individual practitioners tends to be much more concerned about the number, quality, and status of practitioners, whereas an organization of educational units within institutions (usually represented by deans or department chairpersons) tends to focus on questions of institutional status and financial support. An accrediting body sponsored by both types is often bogged down in debates over priorities reflecting these differing perspectives. Similarly, the size and age of a professional association are significant. Accreditation is only one of many activities sponsored by professional organizations. In the large, well-established professions such as medicine and law, accreditation, though considered important, is located rather far down in the organizational hierarchy. In contrast, relatively new specializations, such as allied health and physical therapy, see accreditation as a major force for achieving recognition and acceptance. For the accrediting body supported by more than one association, such as the National Council for Accreditation of Teacher Education, accreditation is its only reason for being.

The accreditation community and the postsecondary education community must stop focusing on the exceptions and refrain from fighting old battles. Instead, they should be addressing the important issues that are facing accreditation.

Important Issues in Accreditation

Accreditation, which began with questions of definition, now—seventy years later—finds itself once again facing the same problem. The fundamental question today is "What is an institution of postsecondary education?"

This question, in turn, raises many additional questions. Can the process of accreditation, so wrapped up in academic conventions, cope with the challenges of radically new forms of learning—especially those associated with new technology? Can accreditation, grounded as it is in self-study and peer review, effectively evaluate institutions that have no full-time faculty or no faculty at all? Can accreditation, which has been so inextricably intertwined with institutional membership, continue to hold on to membership as a viable concept when members are so different from one another? Can accreditation define and maintain minimum standards for a universe of institutions and programs so diverse and ever changing?

The many stresses that this issue provokes will inevitably bring to the surface many other long-standing questions:

- Is accreditation really necessary? Does it meet an important social need? Can that need be met as well or better in some other way? Is accreditation cost-effective?
- What should be the primary purpose of accreditation—quality improvement or quality assurance? Can the same process effectively serve both purposes?
- Should accreditation be a governmental process or a nongovernmental process? Has it, in effect, become a governmental, or quasi-governmental, process? Can it serve government ends and yet remain truly nongovernmental and voluntary? Does voluntary accreditation effectively meet the needs of government?

- Can accreditation respond meaningfully to public concerns about educational quality and institutional integrity? Can accreditation effectively combine two disparate viewpoints— the institution's statement of purpose and the accreditation community's consensus about acceptable conditions and practices? Can accreditation depend on self-regulation and avoid a policing or regulating role?

- Can institutional accreditation meaningfully evaluate educational quality in institutions that are subunits of highly centralized statewide systems or in universities that are made up of virtually autonomous schools or colleges? Can institutional accreditation continue to avoid scrutinizing individual programs—especially if a program is located geographically or organically apart from the parent institution? Will institutional accreditation begin to deal with rapidly growing nontraditional programs such as summer and evening schools, conferences and institutes, independent study, and contractual offerings for business and government?

- If institutional accreditation can effectively respond to various needs, what is to be the role—if any—of specialized accreditation? If specialized accreditation addresses important concerns not dealt with by institutional accreditation, should there not logically be specialized accreditation for all educational programs? Can specialized accreditation be brought more completely into an institutional perspective and into a cooperative, collaborative mode with institutional accreditation?

- Will institutions see the value of self-study and self-regulation other than as aspects of accreditation? If so, will this strengthen or weaken accreditation?

These are some of the more important questions that will continue to be debated. This book is intended to advance such discussions by removing the many misunderstandings about accreditation and clarifying the issues. Possible approaches to answers—if not answers themselves—are suggested. If this book is successful, the reader will understand the importance of self-regulation and see accreditation as the centerpiece of that pro-

cess; appreciate why identifying educational outcomes, conducting continuing self-evaluations, and making use of peer review as valuable, low-cost consultation are all in the institution's
interest; and view the primary value of accreditation to institutions as participation in the process even more than achieving
accredited status.

Accreditation in Transition

Accreditation continues to evolve. One clear trend is that
the accreditation process will have to focus, much more than it
has, on educational outcomes. Society is moving into a time
when institutions of postsecondary education must—for their
own purposes (such as survival and institutional renewal) as well
as for socially induced reasons (such as accountability and consumer information)—engage in a continuing process of self-evaluation. This evaluative process will center on more explicit
statements of expected educational outcomes (see Chapter Seventeen). Colleges and universities will be expected to ask and answer, rather specifically, what they are about as institutions and
how they know they are achieving their objectives. Accrediting
bodies will have to ascertain that institutions are what they say
they are and do what they say they do by focusing more on
outcomes.

The future must also bring increased cooperation among
accrediting bodies. With some notable exceptions, they have
tended to function relatively independently of one another. The
result has been a growing concern among institutions of postsecondary education and others about the costs of accreditation
(especially the indirect costs to the institutions), the time demands, and what is perceived to be increasing duplication
among the accrediting bodies. However, the accrediting organizations increasingly recognize the need for working together
(see Chapter Eighteen). As they cooperate and collaborate,
they are likely to become increasingly receptive to adopting criteria and procedures that are more compatible. Common terminology would be a first step in that direction (see the Glossary).

Institutions should consciously strive to coordinate and

integrate institutional research and planning with accreditation reviews. Not only does such coordination improve the reliability of the evaluation, but it also provides the administrative framework for planning and implementing remedies for concerns raised by the accrediting body. Frequently, this capability will reassure an accrediting association about the wisdom of re-accrediting, with an interim report or two, an institution found to have deficiencies. Quite simply, the accrediting body is able to see how the institution will be able to do what needs to be done.

Each accredited institution can work as a partner with accrediting bodies in the years ahead by—

1. Dealing only with nationally recognized accrediting bodies.
2. Following guidelines for good practice in reporting their accredited status in catalogues and other published materials.
3. Centrally coordinating the institution's relations with the various accrediting bodies.
4. Providing volunteer leadership, wherever appropriate, for recognized accrediting bodies.

Because accreditation is offered through private associations, it should remain a voluntary form of self-regulation, but institutions should carefully consider how best to use what accreditation has to offer. Although an institution could doubtless abandon many of its accreditations and continue to offer quality educational programs, most institutions will almost certainly retain their current accreditations and even consider adding more. But accreditation is just too expensive to be relegated to a category of swallowing hard every so often and then rejoicing that the review process is over for a few more years. Institutions should recognize that the greatest value of accreditation is perhaps as an evaluative tool, that institutions should use the accreditation process as an unequaled opportunity for improving educational quality.

2   Fred F. Harcleroad

Accreditation: Voluntary Enterprise

> *Can there be a humane society without volunteers?*
> *Can there be a democratic society without volun-*
> *tary action? Can there be a free society without*
> *voluntarism? I think not.*
>
> Leo Perlis (1974, p. 5)

Accreditation has developed from a strong tradition of voluntary action in the United States. A useful framework for understanding accreditation—its purposes, potentials, and limitations
—can be gained through examining the voluntary sector and its
role in American society, the historical development of accreditation within this voluntary tradition, and the social and economic forces that have changed the way in which accreditation
is now viewed and used.

    Accreditation evolved as a voluntary activity in two im-

    The origins of this chapter derive from *Voluntary Organizations
in America and the Development of Educational Accreditation*, an occasional paper prepared for the Council on Postsecondary Accreditation
(Harcleroad, 1980b).

36

portant ways. First, the accreditation process is essentially one of choice. Institutional accreditation was developed by colleges and universities that decided voluntarily to regulate themselves to improve educational quality. Specialized accreditation was initiated by professional associations, but because they were often organizations of institutions, as well as groups of practitioners, the voluntary cooperation of colleges and universities was an important element.

Second, accreditation has always relied on the services of volunteers. The staffs of accrediting associations and commissions are generally quite small, often consisting of an executive and a secretary. Many people are surprised to learn that although there are probably no more than 100 persons working full-time in accreditation, thousands of volunteers participate each year in the accreditation process—in self-studies and on accrediting review teams, commissions, and association boards. Most volunteers receive no compensation for their services except remuneration for travel expenses; the rest receive token honorariums.

Accreditation is no longer a purely voluntary enterprise for some programs and most institutions—for many it is indispensable. Specialized accreditation has to some extent become linked to state government licensure of practitioners (see Chapter Fourteen) and institutional accreditation to eligibility for certain federal funds (see Chapter Thirteen), and these connections have somewhat eroded the historically voluntary character of accreditation. Nevertheless, a look at its history as a voluntary enterprise is worthwhile, to shed light on how accreditation became what it is today and to understand the changes that it is undergoing.

The Voluntary Tradition in America

How and why has the voluntary, or nonprofit, sector—or independent sector, as it has more recently been called (Gardner, 1979)—become so strong and important in American society? It preceded many current government and business forms as a method for "getting things done." In both England and the United States, "the first corporations were chartered primarily for charitable and religious purposes" (Fremont-Smith, 1972, pp. 4-5). B. A. Weisbrod, quoting W. K. Jordan, noted that voluntary (nonprofit) organizations historically preceded government provision and that in sixteenth-century England "private philanthropies [voluntary organizations] were providing funds for such wide-ranging activities as schools, hospitals, non-toll roads, firefighting apparatus, public parks, bridges, dikes and causeways, digging of drainage canals, waterworks, wharves and docks, harbor cleaning, libraries, care of prisoners in jails, and charity to the poor" (Weisbrod, 1975, pp. 185-186).

Following European social and religious traditions, colonists in this country formed voluntary associations by the thousands for every conceivable purpose, including to help widows, orphans, immigrants, debtors, and prisoners; to promote morality, temperance, thrift, and industry; to reform gamblers, drunkards, and juvenile delinquents; and to provide needed community services (United Way of America, 1977, pp. 1-10). This tradition was later reinforced by the concept of separation of powers between the judicial, legislative, and executive branches at all levels of government and between the federal and state governments. Fearing strong central government, the framers of the Constitution created the Tenth Amendment, which clearly established the states as governments with "general" powers. The federal government, however, was given only "limited" powers, those delegated to it in the Constitution. In addition, the First Amendment reserved to the people the rights to peaceably assemble, to petition the government for redress of grievances, and to have freedom of speech in these and any other activities. These citizen rights and the separation of powers helped to provide a climate in which voluntary associations could thrive.

This society's reliance on voluntary groups for responding to social needs and problems was graphically described by Alexis de Tocqueville in one of his most famous observations of the American scene in the 1830s (de Tocqueville, 1840/1946, Vol. 2, p. 106): "Americans of all ages, all conditions, and all dispositions constantly form associations. They have not only commercial and manufacturing companies, in which all take part, but associations of a thousand other kinds, religious, moral, serious, futile, general or restricted, enormous or diminutive. The Americans make associations to give entertainments, to found seminaries, to build inns, to construct churches, to diffuse books, to send missionaries to the antipodes; in this manner they found hospitals, prisons, and schools. If it is proposed to inculcate some truth or to foster some feeling by the encouragement of a great example, they form a society. Where ever at the head of some new undertaking you see the government in France, or a man of rank in England, in the United States you will be sure to find an association."

Over time, the government began to provide services that had previously been the sole province of voluntary associations, as federal, state, and local governments acquired more powers to collect varied taxes (such as corporate taxes and personal income tax) and as the social upheaval caused by urbanization, industrialization, and population growth increased dramatically. For example, many local governments have replaced volunteer firefighters with departments staffed by full-time paid employees; public schools have taken on responsibility for activities ranging from driver training to sex education; and state and federal governments have greatly expanded their roles in such areas as health, welfare, and consumer protection. However, even though the government sector and the private, for-profit sector have grown and become even more highly centralized during the last quarter century, the voluntary, nonprofit sector has also increased in size and scope and continues to provide a variety of essential services.

Today, there are no reliable statistics on the independent sector as a whole and no adequate taxonomy for classifying organizations within it. The breadth, variety, independence, and volatility of groups and organizations within this sector make classifications difficult. One of the few sources for categorizing nonprofit organizations and trusts, for example, is Section 501 of the income tax law, which enumerates some twenty separate, loosely described categories of organizations that can qualify for tax exemption. They vary from religious and cultural organizations to social welfare, health, labor, veterans', and educational associations (see Harcleroad, 1976, p. 5).

Bradley Graham, writing in the *Washington Post,* aptly

described the independent sector as "one of the least charted regions of American society" (Graham, 1979). The most complete available study of this sector was carried on by the Commission on Private Philanthropy and Public Needs (the Filer Commission) in 1973-1975. The commission's final report, *Giving in America* (1975), provides the following estimated figures and information (pp. 11-18):

> According to recent extrapolations, there may be as many as six million organizations in America's voluntary sector. . . .
> One out of every ten service workers in the United States is employed by a nonprofit organization, one out of every six professional workers. One ninth out of all property is owned by voluntary organizations . . . the voluntary sector accounts for over $100 billion in money and other resources annually.
> . . . nearly six billion womanhours and manhours of volunteer work were contributed to nonprofit organizations in 1973, the survey indicates, and the total value placed on this contributed labor is another $26 billion.
> Where does the giving go? . . . The estimated breakdown of giving in terms of ultimate recipient, in 1973, was: religion, $10.28 billion; education, $4.41 billion, health, $3.89 billion; social welfare, $2.07 billion; arts, humanities, civic and public causes, $1.67 billion; and all other, $3.19 billion.
> In 1960, private giving amounted to one ninth of expenditures by all levels of government (not counting defense spending); in 1974, giving added up to less than one fourteenth of government spending.

Thirty-one percent of Americans volunteer two or more hours a week on a regular basis, according to a recent Gallup survey commissioned by Independent Sector, an organization created in 1979 "to support and strengthen the efforts of organizations and individuals comprising the independent sector as they seek to preserve and enhance initiative and independent action" (Gardner, 1979, p. 6). When voluntary service is more

broadly defined, 52 percent of adults and an almost equal proportion of teenagers volunteer (Independent Sector, 1981, p.
15).

The Independent Sector reports, however, that although
the sector is still "alive and well," the following problems have
been developing and require immediate attention (Gardner,
1979, p. iii):

1. There has been a relative decline in giving. The report notes
    that double-digit inflation has offset the 8.9 percent aver-
    age annual growth rate in contributions and that the cost
    of running independent institutions has outpaced even the
    inflation.
2. There have been encroachments on the freedom of citizens
    to organize.
3. Changes in tax policy have had a negative impact on chari-
    table donations.
4. Independent institutions have become increasingly depen-
    dent on government funding.
5. Government has had a growing influence on the agenda of
    the independent sector.
6. The limitations of some nonprofit organizations have col-
    ored public perceptions of the sector as a whole. Some
    organizations have not been effective or accountable.
7. Public understanding of the sector is limited.
8. There is inadequate recognition of the importance of hav-
    ing alternatives and multiple sources of support for solving
    social problems.

Accreditation, one of the important activities within the
voluntary sector, is facing many of these problems. Although
accreditation began as a self-regulating activity in postsecondary
education, both state and federal governments have, since World
War II, made increasing attempts to engage in accrediting or
quasi-accrediting activities. The postsecondary education community generally supports the concept of voluntary nongovernmental accreditation, but efforts continue to use accreditation
for government-related purposes.

Accreditation as Part of the Voluntary Sector

Since education was not included among the powers delegated to the federal government in the Constitution, all educational matters, including accreditation, have been and are reserved to each of the states or to the voluntary sector. Soon after the development of the nation, in 1784, the state of New York established one of the first precursors to accreditation—the Regents of the University of the State of New York, a corporate body to "charter, endow, and control" higher education institutions as well as elementary and secondary schools, museums, and libraries in the state. The regents are required to visit these institutions regularly and maintain adequate standards (Carmichael, 1955, pp. 2-4). The regents, in turn, require regular reports, report regularly to the state legislature, and have registered all institutions under their control.

Other states, however, did not establish such an agency, and few had formal licensing systems for professional practice. As a result, professional associations were formed, such as the American Medical Association (AMA) in 1847, both to "protect" the developing professions and to combat fraud and low-quality educational programs. Following the example of the AMA, many other professional associations, from architecture to veterinary medicine, voluntarily began to review professional programs in colleges and universities, primarily to ensure that their students would be exposed to particular kinds of experiences as prerequisite for professional practice. Although this primary purpose was different from that of the regional accrediting associations being formed at about the same time, the professional associations came to use much of the same terminology and procedures as the regional accrediting bodies. They thought of themselves as voluntary accrediting bodies and, like the regional associations, used volunteers (member professionals) on evaluation teams and on the commissions or boards that received the reports and made accreditation decisions. Fairly quickly, however, specialized accreditation was frequently linked to professional certification and then to state licensure of practitioners, and it lost some of its earlier voluntary character.

Voluntary institutional accreditation actually grew out of

a concern about the unevenness of quality in high school and college education during the last quarter of the nineteenth century. When the need became clear for stronger admission standards and institutional evaluation of the rapidly expanding secondary schools and colleges in the 1870s and 1880s, the logical solution for educational institutions was to establish new, voluntary membership associations. In New England in the 1880s, leading headmasters and principals felt that "if the secondary school personnel in New England could meet and discuss problems occasionally with college leaders [mostly related to confusion in admissions practices], a better relationship between them could be achieved" (Fuess, 1960, p. 3). Charles W. Eliot of Harvard and other college presidents agreed, and the New England Association of Colleges and Secondary Schools was started for this purpose in 1885 (West, 1978, pp. 418–419). Shortly thereafter, in 1887, the Middle States Association of Colleges and Schools developed. After another decade, both the North Central Association of Colleges and Secondary Schools and the Association of Colleges and Secondary Schools of the Southern States followed in 1895, and they adopted college accreditation standards in 1910 and 1919 respectively.

Many other nonprofit voluntary groups have been active during the past century in some form of listing or accreditation activity, and various groups, including the U.S. government, have used them. From 1882 until 1963 the American Association of University Women inspected and listed institutions with standards for their graduates that were considered satisfactory to merit membership in the association. In 1905 the Carnegie Foundation for the Advancement of Teaching had to define a "college" in order to establish a pension system for college teachers (Orlans, 1975, pp. 7–8). It adopted the criteria used by the New York Regents, plus a requirement that no denominational tests be applied in choosing students, teachers, officers, or trustees. Only seventy public or private colleges qualified at that time, but the list was used for years as one basis for the federal directory listing of Higher Education and Accredited Higher Institutions issued from 1917 to 1965. Other voluntary groups that have kept lists for this same purpose at various times include the Association of American Colleges and the education boards of the Methodist, Episcopal, Presbyterian, United Brethren in Christ, and Roman Catholic churches.

From 1914 until 1948, the Association of American Universities (AAU) published its own list of "accredited" institutions, based originally on records of recently transferred students at AAU institutions (Selden, 1960, pp. 67-70). After 1928, inspection visits by the AAU as a basis for inclusion on its approved list were also used until the task of making the list became too much of a chore. The AAU voluntarily gave up the entire listing process in 1948, leaving a genuine void.

After the AAU stopped its listing, the regional and professional associations stepped up their work in accreditation. The regional associations banded together in 1949 in their own voluntary organization, the National Committee of Regional Accrediting Agencies (NCRAA), which carried on informal cooperative activities and issued its own annual list of regionally accredited institutions. At the same time, the National Commission on Accrediting (NCA) was formed as a voluntary association of university presidents who had grave concerns about the expansion of specialized accrediting associations and the cost of both membership in them and the accreditation process itself. In 1964 NCRAA was replaced by a similar voluntary organization known as the Federation of Regional Accrediting Commissions of Higher Education (FRACHE). This organization developed a number of suggested policy statements and had some success in harmonizing differences in regional standards. Later in 1972, FRACHE set up a national office next to NCA, and the two organizations worked together on various projects related to accreditation.

NCA and FRACHE dissolved in 1975, and their members became part of a new, enlarged voluntary organization, the Council on Postsecondary Accreditation (COPA) (see Chapter Fifteen).

Accreditation and the Changing Social Context

Like the rest of the voluntary sector, accreditation is directly affected by, and in turn has an impact on, the social, political, and economic conflicts in American society. Although organizations such as the Independent Sector express concerns about the increasing dependence of voluntary institutions on government funding, others are equally concerned that the corporate sector, because of its financial and political power, may exert undue influence on both the voluntary sector and the government. Further, as the Independent Sector's report stresses, because the public is not aware of the presence, magnitude, and diversity of the voluntary sector, little thought has been given to what role it should play in society in relation to the private and public sectors. Both specialized and institutional accreditation have undergone changes that are symptomatic of these broader conflicts.

Since accreditation started, relations between the federal government and the voluntary sector have changed significantly. Many diverse social and cultural needs that began as charity or social causes (such as free public schools, free libraries, hospitals, scientific research, symphony orchestras, special youth detention centers, and fire departments) are now paid for by government in whole or in part. The need for funds to support additional government services led to a search for new taxes during the first decades of the century, and when new and increasing tax funds were available, government services—social, cultural, and scientific—expanded even further. Since the mid 1930s, many former state or voluntary association programs have progressively gravitated toward federal funding and a national focus. In many cases, voluntary enterprise pointed out the needs but lacked funds to meet them satisfactorily, and federal programs developed to meet the needs. A good example is in the medical area (Commission on Private Philanthropy and Public Needs, 1975, p. 90): "In 1930, federal, state, and local governments together spent about as much as private sources in the area of medical research and health facility construction. By 1973, government was spending three and a half times as much, and this in a health field where private philanthropy has maintained one of its strongest thrusts. In medical and health spending as a whole, the change has been even greater. In 1930, the federal government was spending only 15 percent more than private philanthropy. In 1973, it was spending nearly seven times as much."

Government costs to duplicate or replace the services of voluntary organizations are often so much higher that government agencies frequently (1) pay part of the costs of voluntary organizations to keep their low-cost features operating, (2) use the results of their work without paying for it, or (3) contract with voluntary organizations for their more efficiently delivered services (Marts, 1953, pp. 182–187). The Filer Commission reported that by 1974 government itself was "contributing" (buying or contracting for services) "about $23 billion to nonprofit organizations, compared to $25 billion from private giving" (Commission on Private Philanthropy and Public Needs, 1975, p. 17). The Commission then noted (p. 17): "This trend poses a major dilemma. On the one hand, government money is needed and may even be a matter of life or death for many organizations as the amount of their private funding has advanced slowly or even declined. On the other hand, government money comes with strings attached, however invisible or unintentional they may be. The more an organization depends on government money for survival, the less 'private' it is, and the less immune to political processes and priorities." Leaving out the field of religion, which is constitutionally closed to the federal and state governments, many third-sector activities have been preempted by government efforts, primarily federal.

Although the states have been responsible for greatly expanding public postsecondary education, the federal government has also encouraged developments in postsecondary education through gifts of federal land and through its taxing and funding powers. For example, conditional gifts of land to the states were the original basis for the "land-grant" colleges formed in 1862 and 1890. Tax-exempt contributions to educational organizations such as colleges and universities have been a major source of funds for private, and some public, institutions. Government purchase of educational, social, research, and development services from educational institutions has become a significant portion of the work of many government agencies and of the budgets of many collegiate institutions.

As federal and state governments began to purchase services from educational institutions after World War II, they often depended on institutional accreditation to help determine, at an initial level, the institutions from which they could buy dependable services. Moreover, the states were persuaded that specialized accreditation would serve as a satisfactory base for screening persons taking licensing examinations. In states that contract with private institutions for degree graduates in various fields (for example, New York and Minnesota), accreditation is a basic premise of the contractual system.

Clearly, major changes have taken place during the past three decades in the relationship between the federal government and postsecondary education in general, and accreditation in particular. In 1952 the Congress, determined to correct some flagrant abuses of the original GI Bill, passed Public Law 82-250, in which Section 253 stated that "for the purposes of this act the commissioner shall publish a list of nationally recognized accrediting agencies and associations which he determines to be reliable authority as to the quality of training offered by an educational institution" (Finkin, 1978, p. 2). In analyzing this legislative action, Finkin has written that it was based on "three closely related assumptions. First, the statute assumed that 'nationally recognized accrediting agencies' existed and were of sufficient reliability that state government could permissibly piggyback its own approval of courses upon the private agency's decision-making processes. Second, reliance upon private determination of educational quality would obviate the threat of federal control of education. Third, the role of the commissioner of education in determining that such nationally recognized agencies were of sufficient reliability would be essentially ministerial" (1978, p. 2).

As Kaysen (1979, p. 41) has pointed out, the changes in federal relationships with higher education, especially since 1965, are "first and most obviously, the growth of federal regulation applicable to and applied to colleges and universities; second, shifts in the magnitude and character of federal funding for higher education." He further reported:

> In 1977, the dollar value of all kinds of federal support for colleges and universities amounted

to between an eighth and a sixth of their aggregate current fund revenues. The corresponding share for the states—the major supporters of the public institutions—was about one-third. [Federal expenditures for the support of academic science in that year were $3.8 billion. This sum was 75 percent of all expenditures for scientific research at universities and colleges and nearly 9 percent of their total current fund expenditures in that year.] Expenditures for student aid by the Office of Education, the Social Security Administration, and the Veterans Administration totaled nearly $7 billion. Most of this money goes to students, not institutions. A substantial part, but not all of it, returns to institutions as tuition, fees, room, and board. Aggregate current fund revenues from tuition, fees, room, and board in 1977 was $14 billion for all of higher education. Assuming that only 50 percent of the federal student aid returned to the institution and the remainder went to nonacademic providers of subsistence and other needs, such as books and transportation, this means that 25 percent of tuition, fees, room, and board was financed from Washington. Furthermore, nearly 40 percent of all enrolled students received some form of federally financed aid, and for some large fraction of these, aid was crucial to the decision to attend [p. 47].

The uses of accreditation by the federal government have been expanded materially, and nine uses are stated as follows (U.S. Department of Health, Education and Welfare, 1980, p. 1):

1. Certifying that an institution has met established standards.
2. Assisting prospective students in identifying acceptable institutions.
3. Assisting institutions in determining the acceptability of transfer credits.
4. Helping to identify institutions and programs for the investment of public and private funds.
5. Protecting an institution against harmful internal and external pressures.
6. Creating goals for self-improvement of weaker programs

and stimulating a general raising of standards among educational institutions.

7. Involving the faculty and staff comprehensively in institutional evaluation and planning.

8. Establishing criteria for professional certification and licensure and for upgrading courses offering such preparation.

9. Providing one of several considerations used as a basis for determining eligibility for federal assistance.

In 1979 about 400 programs in a wide variety of federal agencies delivered funds either directly to institutions of postsecondary education or indirectly through the states or their students; around 30 of these programs, or between 7 and 8 percent of them, were in the Office of Education (Young, 1979a, p. 141; 1979b, p. 213). To determine eligibility, some agencies use data from voluntary accreditation, while others establish their own lists. For example, the Bureau of Indian Affairs has "feasibility" study teams, and the Federal Aviation Agency has its own flight school approval process. In an extensive study of accreditation and the federal taxing and spending powers in postsecondary education, Trivett traced the basic difficulty to the "absence of clear authority for the federal government to spend money for education, and a subsequent inability to regulate those expenditures" (1971, p. 87). Of course, this lack of control is not confined to the field of education. The secretary of health, education and welfare reported a "ripoff" of $7 billion (much of it not from education) from the department budget of 1978 and only the hope of cutting it to a $4 billion loss with the new, tighter controls he proposed. Trivett (p. 88) went on to conclude: "It is hard to understand why accreditation is involved at all in the eligibility decision. It is an anachronistic use of a system that perhaps provided legitimacy to decisions in the past, but does not accommodate the much broader concept of postsecondary education in use today. . . . If accrediting organizations were out of the eligibility relationship, they could concentrate on identifying what they do accomplish in the way of institutional and program self-improvement, since they are nongovernment organizations with the interest of their members at heart."

The link between accreditation and federal eligibility is clearly a two-edged sword, for although it has given the institutional accrediting associations a visibility and clout they have never had before, it also has forced them into a quasi-public (some say quasi-governmental) role (see Chapter Thirteen). Interestingly, when the Carter administration proposed to separate accreditation from institutional eligibility, the regional associations opposed it.

Although both institutional and specialized accreditation are still referred to as voluntary, their increasing connections to both state and federal government uses raise several important issues about the future of voluntary nongovernmental accreditation.

1. *Is accreditation still a voluntary enterprise?* From the perspective of institutions, accreditation is not truly voluntary if they feel forced, either through political pressure or through the threat of losing eligibility for federal funds, to seek it and to abide by terms imposed by others that they would not agree to otherwise. Many nontraditional institutions in the 1970s, for example, faced this kind of pressure to participate in "voluntary" accreditation.

One response to this issue occurred when the interassociation Presidents Committee on Accreditation in 1980 declared as a major objective the separation of accreditation from state licensing of practitioners. Two of its proposals are of special interest. First, it proposed that state licensing laws refer to "accreditation by a nationally recognized accrediting agency," rather than specifying such associations by name, which bestows the powers of a state on a nongovernmental accrediting body. Second, the Presidents Committee attempted to establish that the federal government's use of accreditation was mainly linked to institutional accreditation, and then only as one element in federal eligibility, with alternatives to accreditation provided. Many specialized accrediting bodies oppose both proposals, because those organizations use accreditation primarily to enforce standards of operation that relate to entry into their respective professions. Institutional accrediting bodies do not oppose the first proposal but do oppose the second because they see the government's turning to alternatives to accreditation as diminishing their power in postsecondary education. COPA, given its diverse constituencies, may have to play a mediating role.

Although accreditation is still highly dependent on the services of volunteers, this aspect of its voluntary character is both a strength and a weakness. Accrediting bodies find it difficult to recruit and train good volunteers and to assure consistent performance. Relatively few presidents from top-ranking institutions participate actively in accreditation. Relatively few nationally recognized faculty members participate, because this kind of activity is usually not rewarded as well as scholarly and research activities. Some accrediting bodies pay small honorariums to members of review teams, and although the honorariums are not enough to constitute a payment for services rendered, the practice tends to weaken the voluntary character of accreditation.

2. *Can accreditation serve any of the purposes of state or federal government and still retain its voluntary character?* If government agencies do not recognize the limitations and appropriate role of accreditation, it cannot retain its voluntary nature and at the same time serve government purposes. For example, since states in the current economic climate can afford only a certain number of Ph.D. programs in a given discipline, some states would like accrediting bodies to identify the programs that should be retained and those that should be eliminated. Similarly, the federal government would like to use accreditation to impose on institutions certain requirements with regard to nondiscriminatory practices or tuition refund policies. If accreditation were to carry out such purposes, it would be a government enterprise, not a voluntary, self-regulating activity. Fortunately, federal officials have recently shown some evidence of wanting to use accreditation in a more restricted manner.

3. *Would accreditation survive if it were to cut its ties to state licensing and federal eligibility?* Although certain accrediting bodies would undoubtedly go out of business, accreditation

would survive. In fact, some observers argue that it would pros-
per and return to its original and primary purpose—encouraging
institutions to improve the quality of their educational programs.

4. *Should accrediting associations—and the independent
colleges and universities with which they work—join with other
independent organizations and institutions to help preserve the
vitality and strength of the voluntary sector?* The Independent
Sector's report stresses the urgent need for all voluntary organizations to do so (Gardner, 1979). To support its call to action,
the report reviews the findings of the Wolfenden Committee, a
British commission on the future of voluntary organizations in
Great Britain. In 1978 that committee concluded that England
had allowed its voluntary agency structure to deteriorate so
completely and had come to depend on its public systems so
heavily that the opportunity to have a truly voluntary sector
had been lost. Most of the voluntary organizations still in existence in England were largely dependent on government funds,
and the pattern of private support had been broken. The Independent Sector's report concludes that, when operating at its
best, the voluntary sector can expand the diversity of personal
options, represent a framework and tradition within which people can band together to pursue goals of their own choosing,
represent a seedbed for new ideas and new art forms, give people channels to experiment with activities and solutions, provide
alternatives to government action, reduce powerlessness and
help promote enpowerment, give people an opportunity for a
larger voice in how society will function, contribute to a more
enlightened electorate, monitor the responsiveness and effectiveness of government, and encourage wiser use of resources.
Reflecting a similar point of view, President Reagan in 1981 appointed a National Task Force on Private Sector Initiatives to
Stimulate Voluntarism.

To some, the basic question is perhaps whether accreditation *should* be voluntary. The pressure for government regulation has grown as the United States has become an advanced
service economy increasingly dependent on well-educated pro-

fessionals. But the accreditation process is essentially one of self-evaluation—a process that would be jeopardized if it were mandated and controlled by the government, if it were tied more directly to eligibility for government funds. Accreditation, with its several thousand constituent organizations and educational institutions, provides a form of self-regulation on which the entire society can rely, if its purposes, potentials, and limitations are understood and accepted.

3

Elaine El-Khawas

ⲒⲟⲒⲟⲒⲟⲒⲟⲒⲟⲒⲟⲒⲟⲒⲟⲒⲟⲒⲟⲒⲟⲒⲟⲒⲟⲒⲟⲒⲟⲒⲟ

Accreditation: Self-Regulation

The health of a democratic society may be measured in terms of the quality of services rendered by citizens who act "in obedience to the unenforceable."
Eduard C. Lindeman (1956, p. 217)

Everyone in postsecondary education knows something about accreditation or, at least, has some impressions and opinions about it. Campus administrators and faculty members can speak of their experiences in conducting self-studies, meeting with site-visit teams, or considering how to meet accreditation standards. Colleges and universities often have ties to several accrediting bodies, including an institutional accrediting commission and a varying number of other organizations that accredit specialized professional programs.

Not very often, however, is accreditation thought about in the abstract, as an idea about how postsecondary educational institutions meet their moral obligations for publicly attesting to the worth of their programs. Yet, the elaborate standards and procedures that are integral parts of accreditation today have their overall justification in these more lofty ideas about institu-

54

tion's responsibilities—to their students, to one another, and to the society around them.

Accreditation should be recognized as a form of educational self-regulation. Indeed, it can be understood as a central example of the procedures collectively established by colleges and universities to maintain responsible educational and administrative practice. *Accreditation* is the process by which educational institutions work together and with others to establish standards, evaluate and improve educational quality, and provide public evidence of this quality. *Self-regulation* is the broader term, encompassing a wide range of collective actions to maintain responsible practice in all areas of operation.

Many other social entities in American life, such as government agencies, hospitals, and more recently industry, also operate with self-regulatory mechanisms—including review committees, voluntary controls, and internal auditors—but postsecondary education has one of the most elaborate and delicately balanced systems of self-regulation. Interinstitutional self-regulatory mechanisms have been developed to deal with the many areas of operation in which institutions must achieve agreement among themselves on terminology, procedures, and standards. References to self-regulation usually pertain to these collective activities.

To understand how accreditation and other forms of self-regulation in postsecondary education are interrelated, an examination of the historical origins of self-regulation is useful, as well as a more detailed definition of the types and functions of self-regulation and a description of the process of self-regulation. The relationship between new self-regulatory initiatives and accreditation must also be considered, including such questions as these: To what extent do accreditation and self-regulation share similar goals and purposes? How do they differ? Should their activities be more integrated? If so, in what ways and under what circumstances?

Self-Regulation in Perspective

Institutions of postsecondary education in this country, unlike those elsewhere in the world, have practiced self-regulation from their beginnings. The first colleges were private and often church-related; they resisted government control, and religious tenets provided them with strong moral guidelines. There was no federal government for their first 150 years and a relatively weak federal government for the next 100. Colonial governments exercised little or no supervision over higher education, and state governments until fairly recently followed a similar approach, even when establishing state universities. Colleges and universities learned, by trial and error, to control themselves, and as more institutions came into being, they developed informal means for working together. These early efforts evolved into the regional organizations, beginning with the New England Association in 1885.

Accreditation, as originally conceived and practiced by these regional groups, was the first formalized system of self-regulation in postsecondary education. It initially focused on educational concerns such as defining a secondary school, defining a college, and developing agreement on certain minimum standards related to educational resources. Over time, accreditation became a more elaborate process of evaluation aimed primarily at improving educational quality. Self-evaluation was, and is, at the heart of this process. The assumption is that institutions want to improve and that they see the accrediting process, with its self-study and validating peer review, as the best means to help them become better institutions. In this sense, accreditation is a preeminent example of self-regulation.

Other self-regulatory mechanisms also came into being during the late nineteenth and early twentieth centuries. Although individual institutions cherished their own autonomy, they recognized that limited, voluntary interinstitutional agreements were useful as ways to resolve issues affecting several institutions at once. The College Entrance Examination Board was established in 1900, at a time when colleges had vastly different entrance requirements from one another (Fuess, 1950). The American Association of University Professors (AAUP), established in 1915, stands as another example of an entirely voluntary effort that gained legitimacy. Its investigation and censure procedures and its recommended policies relied on voluntary recognition and use by institutional leaders, although AAUP has recently moved into collective bargaining (Hofstadter and Metzger, 1955). Various professional associations were developed to foster generally accepted administrative norms (for example, the American Association of Collegiate Registrars and Admissions Officers) to arrive at consensus about academic programs of study. Later, in response to evidence of irregularities in college football—and amid threats of federal intervention—the National Collegiate Athletic Association was established to set and enforce certain standards among member institutions. Another example of such voluntary self-regulation is seen in the interinstitutional agreements for transfer of credit that are a distinctive aspect of American higher education.

Self-regulation has gained renewed currency in the 1970s with the view that if postsecondary education would police or regulate itself, it might avoid government regulation. This view reflected discontent about the growth in government regulation affecting postsecondary education and the fear that increasingly burdensome and intrusive regulation was becoming the trend. Beginning in 1978, the American Council on Education (ACE) and several other associations responded to these concerns by establishing a collaborative program to encourage voluntary nongovernmental action on issues subject to public concern. An important objective has been to develop a stronger capability for identifying issues that warrant new self-regulatory attention and spurring appropriate voluntary response. With coordination through ACE and the guidance of a national advisory committee, self-regulatory initiatives have recently been taken on several issues, including fair and equitable tuition refund (American Council on Education, 1979a), good practice in college admissions and recruitment (1979b), collegiate athletics policies (1979c), equitable transfer and award of credit (1980a), ways to define satisfactory academic progress of students to maintain financial aid eligibility (1981a), academic integrity and athletic eligibility (1981b), and good practice regarding employee records (1981c).

Individual and Collective Self-Regulation

Taken broadly, *self-regulation* refers to the actions of any individual or group to monitor and control its own behavior. In individual behavior, the term is applied to biofeedback and autosuggestion techniques that help people reduce physiological stress. For organizational behavior, the parallel role includes steps taken by a business firm, college, or other organization to monitor and control its actions. Fiscal and management techniques are a form of self-regulation. Better examples are found in auditing, public reporting of financial records, and customer service and complaint procedures—that is, actions and self-monitoring that are undertaken to promote the public good, especially in areas that might otherwise require external monitoring.

For postsecondary education, self-regulation refers essentially to self-monitoring voluntary actions to ensure that institutional programs and policies embody standards of good practice. It can refer not only to the policy recommendations of national associations but also to the actions of an individual institution to formulate responsible policies and assure their implementation. Student honor systems are good examples of self-regulation, as are institutional commitments to impartial appeals procedures, to faculty participation in shaping educational policy, and to the use of trustee boards for overall policy direction. Indeed, the *self* in *self-regulation* fundamentally refers to each college or university. Whatever the advice and guidance from external sources, the administrative leadership of each college and university must finally decide how to regulate the institution's affairs in a responsible manner.

Self-regulation can be directed toward almost any topic affecting the administration of a college or university, including academic matters, administrative policies, external affairs, sponsored research, and community relations. It can include preventive measures (for example, model codes of good practice) as well as policing and enforcement devices (for example, campus judicial systems or sanctions imposed by membership organizations). Although it may address a variety of issues, new or old, self-regulation is always directed toward the ability of colleges and universities to take whatever steps are necessary to maintain good practice.

Individually, colleges and universities regulate themselves

through a precarious balance of powers between governing bodies that represent the public interest, administrators who conduct the day-to-day affairs of the institution, and faculty members who play the primary role in defining and interpreting educational purposes and standards. Students, alumni, and other interest groups also often participate in this process. The activities of these various constituencies are usually coordinated through a complicated network of boards, councils, committees, and similar entities.

In the collective form of self-regulation, action is taken by a number of colleges or organizations in common. To address a particular problem, a new or existing group is authorized to set standards of proper behavior for its members and monitor adherence to those standards. Recent government pressures, especially at the federal level, have placed a burden on many groups to show that they have methods for monitoring and enforcing good administrative practice among their members. The Securities and Exchange Commission, for example, recently pressured securities dealers and large brokerages to increase their procedures for self-regulation. The Consumer Product Safety Commission reached formal agreements during the last decade with several industry groups, including chain-saw manufacturers and lawnmower manufacturers, agreements that provide industry representatives the opportunity to develop their own standards to deal with problems that have been reported to the commission. Congress and government agencies closely watched a recent voluntary initiative by hospital administrators that was aimed at cost containment.

Collective self-regulatory techniques usually begin with the development of common policies and standards; frequently a next step is the development of procedures for monitoring and evaluating member actions. Monitoring procedures include routine reporting by members of their progress toward a goal (for example, hospitals report their cost figures over several months' time); investigations conducted when complaints are filed (for example, procedures of the American Association of University Professors on matters affecting college faculty members); external reviews, usually based on peer judgments (for example, procedures of certified public accountants for verifying the accuracy of financial statements); and, rarely, punitive sanctions, which may include censure or expulsion from membership.

Especially in its collective forms, self-regulation provides society with reassurances that individual members follow prevailing norms of good practice. Thus, the medical and legal professions have long been subject to their own self-regulatory ethical bodies, and during the past decade both groups have taken steps to review and update their codes of ethics and the procedural mechanisms that support the codes.

Functions of Self-Regulation

The most important roles of collective self-regulation include identifying problems and issues, developing and distributing guidelines for good practice, monitoring appropriate responses to problems, enforcing adherence to certain procedures, and providing public assurances that sound practices exist. Other roles might be cited as well—acting as a public spokesperson and defender of members, encouraging improved practice, and educating members about new actions and requirements. The most fundamental roles are the first two, and many organizations have traditionally limited their self-regulatory activities to these roles—that is, identifying issues of public concern and developing policy recommendations for how members should address those issues. Relatively few associations have taken on the more difficult roles of monitoring and policing the behavior of their members.

In postsecondary education, accrediting bodies are the most notable examples of collective self-regulatory structures that have taken on a more comprehensive set of roles. The national and regional organizations governing intercollegiate athletics offer another example. Several other organizations have taken on policing roles in specific areas of concern; the National Association of College Admissions Counselors, for example, monitors enforcement of a rule that member colleges allow all applicants to abide by a common reply date for admissions offers.

Of the recent actions that are part of the self-regulatory initiatives, most have focused on developing policy guidelines— that is, articulating the principles that should guide institutional policy making in a given area. Often, as with the recently issued statement of refund policy, such principles are accompanied by a background statement reviewing the events that led to the development of the statement. In other instances, recent self-regulatory action has not included specific guidelines but has instead identified and described issues that college administrators should consider in providing proper oversight of programs. For example, on issues related to effective campus management of student aid, several associations jointly conducted workshops and issued publications that outlined the issues and reviewed important considerations for institutional policy.

Such broad advisory approaches—stopping short of guidelines—can often be adopted as appropriate strategies. ACE's Presidents' Committee on Athletics, for example, has sponsored informational meetings, issued advisory statements, and provided background analysis on issues of intercollegiate athletics policy. Such actions reflect a belief that the existing self-regulatory structures for governing athletics do not require additional policy guidance but would be strengthened by more active and informed participation of college and university presidents in governance and rule-setting decisions. For other issues, continuing forms of advisory assistance have been organized, as with the Academic Collective Bargaining Information Service, sponsored by several associations. Another example is the interassociation project on Higher Education and the Handicapped (HEATH), which has given colleges and universities assistance on providing access for disabled students.

Another promising approach involves preparation and distribution of self-assessment materials. Like guidelines, such materials can offer pertinent advice to colleges and universities on topics requiring their attention. They do so, however, without prescriptive guidelines and with greater attention to offering resources, options, and other detailed suggestions. This approach can be especially appropriate for issues that can be broadly applied to campus administration. An example of this approach is a legal self-audit being developed by a committee affiliated with Notre Dame's Center for Constitutional Studies. Similarly, the National Association of Student Financial Aid Administrators has prepared a guide to self-evaluation of student aid operations.

The Process of Self-Regulation

The current phase of self-regulation is new and will undoubtedly continue to evolve; new issues will come to attention, and new approaches to resolve them may be developed. However, whether the self-regulatory process results in guidelines or in other actions, whether it is directed to academic or administrative issues, the process remains the same. Self-regulation is a process that relies on the broad participation of college and university representatives in shaping whatever response is made to an issue. Recent actions have followed a careful two-step procedure. First, the associations and persons most knowledgeable on an issue take responsibility for drafting a response. Then, the draft is circulated widely for comment among other associations and persons representing the full range of institutional and professional responsibilities affected. The process seeks to ensure that self-regulatory statements offer substantive recommendations prepared by knowledgeable and experienced administrators and that the statement itself—its language, form, and specificity—has been weighed against a wide range of views and institutional circumstances.

Through such procedures, postsecondary education is gaining an improved capability for addressing new issues and problems by voluntary, self-regulating means. Education associations are now better prepared to tackle issues and take steps toward their resolution, and the process of wide participation in drafting guidelines offers a forum for discussing the issues. Through the process, campus administrators are informed about the need for and possible uses of the guidelines, and such early publicity helps encourage appropriate use of guidelines once issued.

Although the process of developing new policy standards is coordinated by a single organization, it otherwise remains largely decentralized. Many associations participate in the process, either to help draft guidelines in areas of their expertise or to comment on draft statements on other issues. Coordination helps ensure that general criteria on preparing guidelines are met and that procedures allow for wide review. This system—coordination, with decentralization of the responsibility for action on each issue—results in a flexible capability for self-regulation and requires only a modest ongoing structure. At the same time, for each of the wide variety of issues that arise, it provides expertise and a mechanism for obtaining comments from a broad spectrum of the education community.

There have been heartening signs of support for the trend toward self-regulatory action. Many elected and agency officials in the federal government are aware of and encouraged by the move toward strengthened self-regulation. Indeed, self-regulation has generated much quiet but vitally important goodwill for postsecondary education among federal officials, perhaps best symbolized by a formal statement issued by Secretary of Education Shirley Hufstedler in July 1980. Referring to the department's recognition of the self-regulatory guidelines on tuition refund, she praised the self-regulation effort and pledged the department's willingness to rely on self-regulation in the future to the fullest extent possible. Later, in May 1982, Education Secretary Terrel Bell also voiced support for academic self-regulation in a statement announcing federal acceptance of self-regulation guidelines on satisfactory progress of students. On the nation's campuses, there has also been considerable success in generating an awareness of self-regulation, an understanding of its purposes, and a willingness to make use of guidelines and other self-regulatory documents. Many college presidents have reported that guidelines have been used in reviewing and revising campus policies. Language from the refund-policy statement, for example, has been incorporated into many institutional statements on refund policy. The self-regulation statement on admissions and recruitment is frequently referred to in interpreting issues of fair admissions practice.

This new form of self-regulation led by education associations has been active now for four years, and despite difficulties, its record is a good one. Self-regulatory efforts continually confront the dilemma of seeming to some observers to move too fast and do too much, while other observers castigate self-regulation for moving too slowly and doing too little. In addition, the issues that new self-regulatory initiatives address are usually complex and defy simple-formula solutions. Fundamentally, however, the movement appears viable and is steadily gaining acceptance. Its approach is flexible; yet, it is based on important guiding principles. There is agreement that issues of public concern should receive prompt attention and that because circumstances change, institutional policies and practices need to be periodically reexamined and revised. Further, there is recognition that national policy guidelines can make a dual contribution: They provide valuable reference points for college and university administrators in reviewing existing policies, and they offer important public statements about the principles of good practice to which higher education is pledged. Finally, there is the assumption that for most issues voluntary efforts, developed by persons who have direct knowledge and experience in an area of policy or practice, will result in responses that are more workable and more effective than government directives.

Substantial problems remain to be worked out. Associations with responsibilities for particular self-regulatory policy statements will undoubtedly encounter expectations for policing their members' behavior. Some may choose not to take such steps, while others may develop a limited role, perhaps making compliance checks or responding to complaints that are filed. Still others may develop comprehensive education and compliance procedures. An increasing number of associations are choosing to develop their self-regulatory policy statements in a format that lends itself to use by institutions of postsecondary education as part of their accreditation self-study process. The National Association for Foreign Student Affairs has recently taken this approach.

Special issues face organizations that take on "policing" roles. Such organizations can easily become overzealous in pursuing good practice or improved policy; just as easily, procedural steps can gradually proliferate to the point that activism bogs down in safeguards. Balance and consistency are necessary, but difficult to achieve, in deciding how flexibly a standard can be interpreted and in determining when an existing standard needs to be changed.

Another major dilemma is how to define and establish the proper relationship between voluntary self-regulatory actions and state or federal government actions. One danger is that self-regulation, in attempting to be responsive to government concerns, will act more and more as the agent of the government and fail to exercise sufficient independent judgment about problems and what actions may be required to remedy them. Yet, some form of cooperation with state and federal government officials seems necessary. A balance must be struck and undoubtedly redefined as circumstances change.

Role of Accreditation in Self-Regulation

Accreditation plays an important role in the overall scheme of self-regulatory activity in postsecondary education, and accreditation and other forms of self-regulation have many characteristics in common. Accreditation shares many of the broad purposes of self-regulation as well as the premise that recommendations for changes in college and university practices must be responsive to differences in institutional mission, programs, and circumstances. Both self-regulation and accreditation recognize the autonomy of each college and university and seek to respect and uphold institutional rights to autonomy in decision making. They also recognize the need to balance those rights against the responsibility of postsecondary education to address public expectations about good practice. Toward that end, self-regulation and accreditation share the broad objectives of fostering institutional good practice and encouraging a commitment by each institution to the ongoing review and improvement of its programs and policies. Self-regulation and accreditation also share a recognition that their credibility and effectiveness are based on the active participation of college and university representatives, both in shaping their procedures, recommendations, and formal actions and in translating recommendations into institutional procedures and practices.

There are also important differences. Self-regulation is the broader concept and encompasses a whole array of voluntary agreements and actions by which colleges and universities work to maintain good practice and provide public assurances about their practices. Self-regulatory activities may be directed toward any area of college and university administration, educational or noneducational; in contrast, the area of purview of accreditation is primarily that of educational programs, policies, practices, and related support services. To date, new self-regulatory initiatives have focused mainly on areas of administrative practice, rather than on matters affecting educational programs. However, this pattern probably represents a response to the issues that have come up, issues that reflect larger social concerns and trends. For example, admissions practices could be expected to be the subject of public concern when enrollments are leveling off. Similarly, the recently developed policy statement on avoiding conflict of interest by members of college and university governing boards undoubtedly reflects wider social concerns about conflict of interest. Although there are gray areas in defining the boundaries between self-regulation and accreditation, nevertheless many areas calling for public accountability—for example, in public relations, development, purchasing, and fiscal management—might involve certain self-regulatory actions that ordinarily go beyond the scope of the primary purposes and expertise of accreditation.

Accreditation has a central role in self-regulation for another reason. It is distinctive in postsecondary education for its respected and carefully developed procedures, based on three fundamental precepts: (1) that the institution must publicly declare its educational purposes and should be evaluated primarily on that basis, (2) that the institution should play the major role in accreditation through the self-study process, and (3) that peer review serves as a necessary validating mechanism. Similarly, accrediting associations can stimulate other types of self-regulation by encouraging member institutions to make public their policies and procedures in important areas of operation and by calling to their attention generally agreed-to guidelines for good practice.

Accrediting bodies do not stop with the tasks of identifying and promoting standards of good practice; when necessary, they can take punitive actions such as putting an institution on probation or withdrawing accredited status. Although the latter step is rarely taken, at least among degree-granting institutions, the possibility is usually sufficient to encourage institutions to cooperate with the accrediting association. The decades-long acceptance of accreditation by colleges and universities is testimony to the importance and acceptance of self-regulation as a basic fact of life in postsecondary education.

Because most accrediting bodies have small staffs and must depend on an ever-changing group of volunteers, institutional practices, for the most part, are monitored by exception. Institutions are formally visited only every five or ten years unless they are experiencing great difficulties or going through a period of rapid change. Between visits, the accrediting bodies must depend on others to call to their attention any problems that may have developed. This arrangement works well most of the time. Institutions communicate with accrediting associations when they have difficulties, either for assistance or for "damage control." Persons within institutions, including disgruntled faculty members or students, are often the source of complaints to accrediting bodies. Other institutions will report a college or university that is believed to be engaged in questionable practices that might be damaging to the reputation of postsecondary education.

Because accreditation has shown a continuing ability to monitor and encourage good practices in educational programs, it can be expected to continue to hold a central role in self-regulation. Indeed, most other efforts at self-regulation have been limited to developing policy recommendations and have reflected a reluctance to introduce new monitoring and enforcement structures. The emphasis of other self-regulation initiatives, certainly for the present, is on issuing statements that offer advisory guidance. The underlying premise is that such statements alert administrators to the questions being raised about an issue, summarize key principles of good practice, and recommend that existing policies be reviewed, leaving institutional administrators free to exercise their own judgment about whether and how to make use of the guidelines. A "free market" principle is in place, then, whereby an advisory opinion is offered but the extent of its acceptance and use is left to the decisions of institutional officials and, ultimately, to the merits of the advice.

Whether current association activities will evolve toward greater use of monitoring and enforcement roles is an open question at present. Several organizations active in recent self-regulatory efforts have had internal discussions about ways that standards should be enforced and what sanctions might be used for members not following the standards. In business and other nonprofit sectors, many examples can be found of organizations with an initially limited self-regulatory responsibility that gradually expanded into formal monitoring functions. For the present, however, education associations have a strong commitment to an advisory role rather than a monitoring role. Association representatives and staff members share the high value placed by the educational community on each institution's ability to chart its own course. Furthermore, to the extent that education associations can rely on existing structures—especially accreditation—for overseeing the behavior of institutions, there is little motivation for them to assume a monitoring and policing role.

Future Cooperation

Are self-regulation and accreditation on different paths, one providing advisory opinion but no enforcement while the other concentrates on evaluation and enforcement? Or do they offer different, possibly competing approaches to certain issues? These are a few of the questions that arise in comparing self-regulation and accreditation as they are currently structured. They are among the questions that need to be discussed during the next few years, or the two could evolve in duplicative and inconsistent ways. The objective should be to devise appropriate articulation between self-regulation and accreditation, with a trial-and-error period, if necessary, to examine both the forms of interaction and the proper boundaries between the two. Accrediting bodies are no longer as alone as they sometimes have been in upholding the need for sound programs and practices; but new self-regulatory actions should complement, not duplicate, the ongoing work of accrediting associations.

Given that self-regulation and accreditation have broad objectives in common, a pattern of complementary activities will probably continue to develop. Indeed, to expect that accrediting bodies would carry out the full array of self-regulatory functions was never realistic. Their primary purpose has been to encourage and assist colleges and universities to evaluate and improve their educational programs, a challenging task in itself; and their nongovernmental nature, small staffs, and heavy dependence on volunteers have limited their capacity to serve as policing and enforcing bodies. What is more realistic is that the education associations will continue to identify problem areas needing improved self-regulation and will develop and promulgate guidelines for good practice. Increasingly, those guidelines should be developed in formats that lend themselves for use as part of the institutional self-study process. The accrediting bodies would then be expected to press the institutions to consider the guidelines as part of their self-study; an institution would not be required to adhere to specific guidelines, only to demonstrate in its self-study report that it had studied them, had determined how they apply to the institution's particular situation, and had made a persuasive case for departing from them if that in fact occurred.

Cooperation between accreditation and self-regulation would especially benefit institutional accrediting associations. For instance, questions that have been pressed on accrediting bodies by the federal government regarding the need for proper assurances about fair and ethical college administrative practices might more fairly be directed to education associations. In addition, self-regulatory statements should provide a valuable resource for accreditation teams that must cover many areas of campus operations in a short time; if an institution follows the recommendations of an existing self-regulatory statement, the accreditation team may be able to devote only a minimal portion of its campus visit to that topic and concentrate more on other areas of college operation. So, too, accreditation procedures could be strengthened if they were increasingly based on norms and standards emerging from the broadly participatory process that is currently used for self-regulatory guidelines. The guidelines process ensures that a policy statement has been tested to make sure it is applicable and relevant to a broad range of institutional circumstances.

A complementary structure of cooperation would undoubtedly entail some overlap between the two activities. Accrediting associations, for example, could provide "early warning" information on issues that might require policy guidelines. So, too, when new self-regulation guidelines are issued, association representatives could work closely with accrediting organizations in setting up procedures for using them.

For postsecondary education, the benefits of close cooperation between accreditation and self-regulation are substantial. Together, they offer a valuable balance between two important purposes: preserving and maintaining a vital ongoing procedure for evaluating educational institutions and programs and, at the same time, offering vehicles for renewal, a means of adapting policies and practices to changing issues and conditions. By supporting a strengthened self-regulatory approach, the postsecondary education community—institutions, accrediting bodies, and national education associations—is publicly affirming that it is willing and able to keep its house in order and accepts the challenge of remaining responsive to changing circumstances and public expectations.

4

Louis W. Bender

ƚᴁƚᴁƚᴁƚᴁƚᴁƚᴁƚᴁƚᴁƚᴁƚᴁƚᴁƚᴁƚᴁƚᴁƚᴁƚᴁ

Accreditation: Misuses and Misconceptions

*Men are disturbed not by things but by the views
which they take of them.*
Epictetus (first century A.D.)

Accreditation is often used inappropriately simply because it is
not well understood, even by the educational institutions it is
intended to serve. Twelve commonly believed myths of accreditation have been identified by Kirkwood (1973). Such myths
and other incorrect statements about the purposes and procedures of accreditation appear in articles and speeches every
year. More important, colleges and universities, government
agencies, and other organizations regularly act on the basis of
misperceptions about the role of accreditation.

Accreditation, however, suffers from more than just a
lack of understanding by users; beliefs about the role of accreditation differ among key participants in the process. Institutions
of postsecondary education and the accrediting bodies they
sponsor, particularly regional associations, have a view of accreditation that varies in significant ways from the perspective

71

of professional associations (which, in turn, have some differences among themselves).

This lack of consensus is easily understood. Because accreditation gradually evolved during a period of about seventy years in response to a variety of impulses and needs, it has changed over time in form and emphasis. Its role has been perceived somewhat differently, for example, in 1915, in 1935, in 1955, and in 1975. Moreover, because accreditation is essentially a voluntary, nongovernmental activity, it has no official definition; anyone, in effect, can define and use the term however that person would like.

The nearest to a generally accepted, current definition is the one recently accepted by the Council on Postsecondary Accreditation (COPA), which states that "accreditation is a process by which an institution of postsecondary education periodically evaluates its educational activities, in whole or in part, and seeks an independent judgment that it substantially achieves its own educational objectives and is generally equal to comparable institutions or specialized units. Essential elements of the process are: (1) a clear statement of educational objectives, (2) a directed self-study focused on these objectives, (3) an onsite evaluation by a selected group of peers, and (4) a decision by an independent commission that the institution or specialized unit is worthy of accreditation" (see the Glossary). In accepting that definition, however, COPA made clear that it was providing the definition as a guideline and was not mandating that member accrediting bodies use it. (COPA's expectations of accrediting bodies are more fully developed in its document *Provisions and Procedures for Becoming Recognized as an Accrediting Agency*. See Resource B.)

Recent Developments Affecting Accreditation

Whatever modest consensus may have occurred within the accreditation community itself, however, has recently been battered by developments that have changed not only the domain of accreditation but also public expectations about the role it should play.

Many new institutions of postsecondary education were established during the 1950s and 1960s in response to the baby boom following World War II and a growing belief that society should provide the opportunity for greater social and economic mobility through education. A number of new educational programs also appeared as a result of the knowledge explosion and the needs of a rapidly changing technological society. These developments were reinforced by the Education Amendments of 1972, which replaced the term *higher education* with *postsecondary education,* thereby encompassing not only the traditional degree-granting colleges and universities but also vocational and proprietary schools, as well as hospitals, museums, and any other social institutions that might sponsor education for adults.

That same legislation encouraged the development of state governing or coordinating boards to provide for better planning associated with the receipt and distribution of federal funds. These state bodies had appeared during the 1960s to provide for a more orderly growth of public postsecondary education, to avoid unnecessary duplication, and to ensure a diversity of opportunities for education. In some states, such as Oklahoma, a separate statewide agency was established. Other states, such as Wisconsin, created a statewide university, embracing all public institutions. In New York, the Regents of the University of the State of New York assumed both roles. Accrediting bodies had to relate to these new or changed entities.

Hand in hand with this development, state governments became increasingly concerned about accountability. The decade of the 1970s was one of accountability measures, including "sunshine" and "sunset" legislation, performance audits, management by objectives, budget-linked evaluation, and increased regulation. Although these approaches were not unique to postsecondary education, they nevertheless had a significant impact on all colleges and universities and, concomitantly, on accreditation.

A broad array of social causes emerged in the 1960s, ranging from the "Great Society" programs of the Johnson administration to student unrest and the growing demands of a variety of special-interest groups. The consumer movement of the early 1970s pressed for guarantees and protection against fraud, abuse, misleading advertising, and other questionable practices. Advocates pushed both federal and state governments for new or strengthened laws and regulations and for increased oversight. They also turned to the courts, calling for substantive and due process guarantees. And, on behalf of their special concerns, they demanded action by the accrediting associations.

Finally, the decline in traditional student enrollments that began in the 1980s—earlier in some states—has prompted changed attitudes within institutions, state governments, and the federal government. Even the psychological attitude of members of the public toward institutions of postsecondary education has sometimes been negatively influenced in a society that tends to equate success with growth in numbers. Institutions have responded in one of two ways: (1) planning for stable enrollments or retrenchment, with a consequent review of proposed and existing programs and a greater concern for qualitative outcomes, or (2) reaching out for nontraditional student clienteles, thus raising new questions concerning educational quality in courses offered off campus, through correspondence or telecommunications, by adjunct faculty members, and in collaboration with business and industry. For public institutions, because the funding policies of state legislatures have generally tied appropriations to full-time equivalent enrollments, turndowns in enrollments have caused significant funding difficulties that have been exacerbated by the budget problems in many states during the early 1980s.

These developments, and more, have combined to impose severe burdens, constraints, and demands on accrediting bodies, particularly institutional accrediting bodies. As a result, an even more difficult, yet vitally important, task is to draw clear distinctions between appropriate and inappropriate uses of accreditation.

Appropriate and Inappropriate Uses of Accreditation

Despite the many differences in perspective and practice among accrediting bodies and their clients, there have evolved over the years certain continuities and agreements. These areas of consensus can be put forth in the form of three basic principles, as follows:

- Accreditation should be used in ways that clearly serve the public interest or, at the very least, do not contravene the public interest.
- Accreditation should be used in ways that do not conflict with its primary purpose—to encourage and assist institutions of postsecondary education to evaluate and improve their educational quality.
- Accreditation should be used in ways that do not compromise its essential characteristics as a voluntary, self-regulatory, nongovernmental evaluation procedure.

These principles represent a consensus but not universal agreement. They are subject to qualification (see Chapters Ten and Eleven). Nonetheless, they form the most useful point of departure for discussing inappropriate uses of accreditation.

The groups that have most particularly attempted to use accreditation in ways that depart from generally accepted principles are (1) government bodies, both federal and state, that have seen accreditation as a potentially useful regulatory adjunct, (2) professional organizations that have viewed accreditation as a tool for association advancement, and (3) institutions of postsecondary education, or units within them, that have recognized that accreditation can be used as a lever for accomplishing certain institutional purposes.

Federal Government. When Congress enacted the Servicemen's Readjustment Assistance Act in 1952, the stage was set for both appropriate and inappropriate uses of accreditation (see Chapter Thirteen). In an effort to avoid direct involvement of the federal government in the internal operations of colleges and universities, Congress in effect created a new use of accreditation. Initially, accreditation was used as one consideration in determining institutional eligibility for certain federal funds; although accrediting bodies for some time continued to perceive themselves as private and voluntary, the federal use made them quasi-public and thus brought them into a relationship that was ambiguous and misleading (see Kaplin, 1982). Subsequently, accreditation was viewed as a potential vehicle for promoting social policies, and the primary purposes of accreditation were lost in this interpretation and application.

Because federal law called on the commissioner (now secretary) of education to publish a list of nationally recognized accrediting bodies, the proliferation of accrediting organizations was exacerbated. Institutions being denied access to federal programs first sought to be included by seeking membership in existing accrediting associations. When those attempts failed, new accrediting associations were formed, and listing by the commissioner was sought. In many cases, the new association emerged to champion the cause of the constituent members, including lobbying at national and state levels for policies that would advance the interests of the membership. Accreditation was not always the primary purpose of the organization.

Some federal agencies, including the Office of Management and Budget, have been critical of accrediting associations for not policing their members so that the status of accreditation could be used by the federal government as a general seal of approval. Such a desired use would leave little room for the concept of self-improvement and would, instead, require an expensive, ongoing monitoring mechanism including the potential for regular inspection and investigation.

Selden and Porter (1977) identified another attempted use of accreditation at the federal level whereby accrediting bodies seeking listing by the commissioner (secretary) would be required to enforce policies of the federal government when they were accrediting institutions or programs of study. The illustration given was the effort to relate admissions policies of schools of medicine to the goal of increasing the number of women in the field of medicine. Equal educational opportunity policies were also to be encompassed in the accreditation process. Although the social goals may be laudable, the means would seem neither appropriate nor effective (see Chapter Thirteen).

State Governments. Although a state has the authority to establish or disestablish institutions of postsecondary education operating within it, licensing practices are nonexistent in some states and minimal in others. An important exception is New York, where the board of regents as early as 1787 began to register and review all institutions in the state, whether public or private. No other states followed the path of New York, and when regional accreditation emerged, many states began to use it as a substitute for licensure. Thus, many state legislatures have interpreted the purpose of accreditation as being in compliance with minimum standards for operation rather than self-evaluation and self-improvement.

Moreover, in many states "sunshine" legislation attempted to make all policy-making deliberations and major administrative decision making open to the public. In this context, state legislatures and government agencies have on occasion called for accreditation reports to be made public (see Heilbron, 1976). The self-study report of the institution can thus become a self-indictment when inappropriately disclosed. A report from visiting peer evaluators can similarly be construed as evidence of weakness rather than as a collegial consultation. In some cases, problem areas identified in the accreditation process have become a justification for reducing funding.

The past decade has witnessed the growth of a rather new phenomenon: institutions offering educational programs in states other than their own. Many states have looked to institutional accreditation to cope with such interstate operations by conducting special visits to off-campus programs and establishing additional requirements for their accreditation. A further complication has arisen when institutions have established programs in accreditation regions other than their own. The regional associations have adopted a policy for dealing with this problem. Under the policy, the regional association with jurisdiction over the institution's main campus has responsibility for accrediting the out-of-state program but works cooperatively with the regional association that covers the state in which the program is located.

The degree of misunderstanding about interstate operations can be seen in the views of an executive officer of a state coordinating board who attributes the increase in state licensing of out-of-state institutions to a failure of accrediting associations to do their jobs (Ashworth, 1980). It is also evidenced by the fact that a number of states, at the urging of some accrediting bodies, have exempted accredited institutions from licensure. However, a normal assumption would be that the state agency should exercise the first level of oversight through licensure, especially given that colleges and universities must be licensed before they can seek accreditation with regional associations. The state agency would then have a logical concern that institutions comply with its minimum standards and other applicable statutes and regulations.

In some states, credit-granting practices are another topic of debate in which accreditation comes up. Two particular issues are repeatedly involved: whether credit should be granted for continuing education offerings and whether remedial courses offered by postsecondary educational institutions should be recognized as college-level course work. Some state legislatures have restricted funding for continuing education offerings because of the belief that gainfully employed adults, not public funds, should pay for their continuing education. However, institutions take the position that when continuing education offerings can be identified as credit-earning and as a required part of a degree program, they should be interpreted in the same way as the regular educational program of the institution. Accreditation is often pulled into the debate, and indeed, the question whether remedial courses should be considered college-level relates, in a way, to one of the historical purposes of institutional accreditation—to distinguish between high school and college-level work.

Professional Groups. The knowledge explosion and the development of new technologies have produced a plethora of new specializations and occupations. As each new field emerges, it organizes and then presses for recognition as a profession (see Chapter Sixteen). These new associations see accreditation as a vehicle for ensuring that specialized programs preparing practitioners meet specified education requirements. When this objective is in harmony with the institutional accrediting body's objective to help the institution evaluate and improve its educational programs, a healthy, positive result can occur. Often, however, the professional organization sees accreditation primarily as a tool to be used in the process of certifying practitioner members. This notion not only significantly shifts the focus of the accreditation process, but it also can result in an effort to use accreditation inappropriately, and ineffectively, as a means for assuring the qualifications of individual practitioners. A requirement that practitioners must come from institutions or programs having the professional organization's seal of approval in the form of accreditation not only is a misuse of accreditation but also may constitute a denial of the individual's constitutional guarantees.

With new technologies has also come a middle level of practitioners, including paraprofessionals, technologists, and technicians. These practitioners have often been thwarted in their efforts to be recognized or have been taken over by the dominant professional association in their general area, as with the American Medical Association, which has in the past played a major role in the allied health area. Many of the organizations representing middle-level practitioners view accreditation as a means for establishing the legitimacy of their occupation as well as their association. Again, such a use of accreditation could clearly be inappropriate and misleading, especially if it becomes the primary concern of the group and prompts the organization to seek federal listing simply for the imprimatur of the Department of Education. The federal list, one writer noted, "has become an exotic melange of agencies seeking the prestige that recognition implies" (Levin, 1981, p. 12).

Special-interest groups may also attempt to advance a limited cause through accreditation. For example, the American Academy of Microbiology's Committee on Postdoctoral Education Programs in 1979 successfully sought inclusion on the Office of Education list of nationally recognized accrediting bodies solely for the purpose of making its twenty-four postdoctoral candidates eligible for deferred repayment of their guaranteed student loans. Requirements for the federal loan program specified that the loans could be deferred as long as a student was in an accredited program (Committee on Accreditation and Agency Evaluation, 1979). This case demonstrates an overdependence on accreditation by both the federal legislation and the strategy of the interest group involved.

Institutions. Accreditation is frequently misused by institutions as a status symbol rather than a mechanism for quality enhancement. Recognition by both institutional and specialized accrediting bodies is published as though it were an award rather than verification that the institution is committed to ongoing self-examination and quality improvement. Some institutions have even announced accreditation as though it were an endorsement of the particular institution or program, exploiting the symbolism to attract students or gifts and grants from donors. For example, the logo of the accrediting association has been displayed prominently on advertisements and other student recruitment materials. Some institutions have even used such logos on the covers of programs distributed to audiences at athletic, performing arts, and cultural events.

College and university officials often use selective communication to mislead. On occasion, only selected parts of accreditation reports are shared with trustees, the media, or even state legislatures. This practice might be expected to involve using only the positive comments in the report and not the negative, but the reverse also occurs. For example, the visiting team may have been critical of the existing physical facilities, and the president can then imply that the institution may be in jeopardy of losing its recognition by the accrediting body unless funds are provided and a facility is built or improved. Such tactics may also be used in citing certain parts of the report to the faculty, the staff, or even students within the institution to achieve a desired purpose. As another example, a president may use discussion of the administrative organization of the institution from the accreditation report as a basis for sweeping reorganization (which may, depending on the president's motives and the actual intent of the report, be a legitimate use of the accreditation process to achieve desirable change).

The misuse of accreditation reports has resulted in accrediting bodies' adopting a policy of making a report public if the institution is misusing it. A further sanction against misuse comes from the courts, which have held in some states that the self-study report as well as the site-visit report should be treated with confidentiality in the same sense that personnel matters or land-acquisition matters would be held confidential as critical to the well-being of the organization.

Public institutions may also attempt to use accreditation as leverage for dealing with state regulatory bodies or even state legislatures. Visiting teams are often led to believe that internal problems result from inappropriate regulations developed by bureaucrats who are insensitive to the essence of academic freedom and the uniqueness of the college or university. The quest for institutional autonomy at times leads to unintended uses of accreditation.

Individuals or units within institutions often attempt to use accreditation in inappropriate ways. Instead of seeing the accreditation process as an opportunity to clarify objectives, identify strengths and weaknesses, and improve educational programs, they seize on it as a means for engaging in special pleading on behalf of increased budgetary support or improved facilities and equipment. Both the self-study and the site visit can be used to serve these ends.

The self-study is central to both institutional and program accreditation. It is the cornerstone whereby the professionals within the institution try to "look in the mirror" and see what actually is, as opposed to what their purposes and goals would indicate ought to be. Special interests can often influence the self-study so that it is used differently than intended. For example, in several cases, faculty members having an interest in a collective bargaining union have been able to gain membership on various self-study committees in such numbers or in such strategic positions that they have been able to control the direction of the self-study or the self-study report. As a result, the visiting team may not see an accurate mirrored view of the institution but rather one of vested interests. Administrative interests as well as faculty interests may be championed in the same way. In some institutions, the administration or a small faculty group has attempted to develop a self-study report that reflects its views, rather than the views of a composite of internal constituencies, with an emphasis on establishing evidence to demonstrate conclusively that stated objectives are being met.

Special interests also often use the visiting team for championing their own welfare rather than that of the institution or program. Statements and documents are selectively pointed toward accomplishing the agenda of the special interest, even at the expense of the institution or program. Visiting-team members may not be aware of the internal politics taking place and are thus inadvertently used in internal power struggles.

Misperceptions of Accreditation

Accreditation is not only misused, it is also misperceived, particularly by those most involved in the process—institutions of postsecondary education—and the public.

Institutions. Among the membership of accrediting associations are institutions that are thought to be distinguished in their own right. Prestigious institutions often accept as a given that any visiting team from an accrediting association will conclude—almost automatically—that their accreditation should be reaffirmed. Some of these institutions communicate indirectly that the accreditation cycle with its external evaluation, even if it is necessary, is merely an interruption and intrusion into their ongoing operations. Such a posture can be intimidating to some team members. Some of these institutions view accreditation as nothing more than a "threshold" process that establishes baseline standards on which other, lesser institutions should be evaluated and accredited. Of course, this approach nullifies the principles that the accreditation process is intended primarily to encourage and assist institutions to improve themselves and that no institution fully realizes its potential.

At the other end of the scale are institutions that are new, quite small, highly nontraditional, or marginal in quality. These institutions often view accreditation as threatening rather than helpful. They feel compelled to seek accreditation as a way to prove their worth within the postsecondary education community, but they are concerned that they might not "pass the test." Therefore, they concentrate their efforts on putting their best foot forward and covering up or explaining away any possible blemishes. This approach not only proves fruitless most of the time, it denies the institution the considerable value of accreditation in correcting problems and helping to identify and build on the real strengths of the institution.

If asked when accreditation takes place, most faculty members and administrators would not be able to answer, and those who did reply would probably say, "Every five or ten years." Accreditation is not seen as a continuous process of self-evaluation and self-improvement but rather as a series of widely spaced visits by representatives of an external body for which hectic preparations must be made. After reaffirmation of accreditation, many institutions cease any further self-evaluation activity until the five- or ten-year period has passed and the institution must again prepare for a visit. The fundamental purpose—institutional self-improvement and the ongoing quest for quality enhancement—is thus lost. During the intervening years some institutions, usually public, have encountered unexpected budget shifts that are critical to the ongoing health of the institution. Such institutions are often totally unprepared and are thus immediately confronted with a crisis situation that could have been avoided if continuing validation of quality enhancement had been maintained. Such a state of affairs occurs because there is no ongoing self-assessment, systematic planning process, or realistic academic program review procedure.

Another misperception that institutions have of the role of accreditation involves determining transfer credit for students seeking to change institutions or enter different programs. A view prevails that accreditation of an institution or program somehow serves to attest to course-to-course equivalencies and even to the student's abilities. These misunderstandings have been so prevalent and pervasive that the American Council on Education, the Council on Postsecondary Accreditation, and the American Association of Collegiate Registrars and Admissions Officers issued a joint statement on transfer and award of academic credit (American Council on Education, 1980a) pointing out that transfer of credit from one institution to another involves at least three considerations: (1) the educa-

tional quality of the institution from which the student trans-
fers, (2) the comparability of the nature, content, and level of
credit earned to that offered by the receiving institution, and
(3) the appropriateness and applicability of the credit earned to
the programs offered by the receiving institution, in light of the
student's educational goals. Accreditation, the statement emphasized, speaks primarily to the first of these considerations.

The Public. Accreditation is often perceived by the public
as a status symbol. Naturally, such perceptions are fostered by
the public relations policies of postsecondary educational institutions by listing accreditation in catalogues, brochures, news
releases, and other publications as though it represented an endorsement. Consequently, the public often assumes that accreditation is a general guarantee that the institution is "good" in
all respects, is responsive to most if not all public needs, is sol-
vent, and presumably always will be. Furthermore, the public
often interprets institutional accreditation as symbolizing uniform standards among similar types of institutions. The public
also views accreditation as a "quality control" mechanism rather
than a quality enhancement process and as an externally imposed control system rather than an approach that calls on each
institution to strive for self-improvement.

The public is often led to believe that accreditation forces
compliance on institutions. Although colleges and universities
are certainly expected to comply with policies, procedures, and
requirements established by the accrediting body to maintain
membership, the value and effectiveness of the entire process
nevertheless lies in the institution's own commitment to excellence and continuous self-study and evaluation. The public has
little understanding of the voluntary nature of accreditation and
the fact that compliance guarantees are not systematically built
in. Indeed, any guarantees reside in the individual institution's
seriousness of purpose and in its sincerity.

Accreditation is used in many contexts by diverse organizations, agencies, and persons. The list of uses is almost limit-
less. Furthermore, uses perceived as inappropriate by one interest may well be perceived as appropriate by a different interest.

Hence, value judgments are difficult to make because inappropriateness is often determined "in the eye of the beholder."

The uses of accreditation, whether intended or unintended, are governed by individual circumstances and by political and economic realities within the American postsecondary educational system. A variety of inappropriate uses of accreditation and misperceptions about it—ranging from those of the federal government to those of the general public—can be identified. Yet, in spite of the inappropriate uses of accreditation, its overall application and use in American postsecondary education have been constructive and purposeful. Voluntary nongovernmental accreditation has been used to foster quality education of a magnitude and scope unequaled in any other country.

Part Two

ฦฦฦฦฦฦฦฦฦฦฦฦฦฦฦฦฦฦฦฦฦฦฦฦฦ

Institutions' Role

Colleges created accreditation and are its principal underwriters, but they often view themselves as the subjects—or even the victims—of accreditation. Presidents of postsecondary educational institutions, particularly universities, especially feel beset by what they perceive as demands from "external" organizations that almost always incur new costs and that occasionally intrude on institutional prerogatives.

Colleges and universities, however, have important rights in the accreditation process—the most basic being respect for institutional autonomy. They also bear certain inevitable responsibilities if accreditation is to work as it is intended to.

Accreditation at its best calls for institutions to take the lead. The institutional self-study, if properly used, not only is the heart of the process, it can serve the institution in other fundamental ways. Enlightened educators see accreditation as a unique opportunity to reconsider educational objectives, as evidence of their accomplishment, and as suggestions for improvement. They also welcome the many possibilities for benefiting from the relatively low-cost advice offered by experienced colleagues from other institutions.

5   Lloyd H. Elliott

ᵔᵔᵔᵔᵔᵔᵔᵔᵔᵔᵔᵔᵔᵔᵔᵔᵔᵔᵔᵔᵔᵔᵔ

How to Make
Accreditation
a Constructive
Experience

> *Give me a log hut, with only a simple bench, Mark*
> *Hopkins on one end and I on the other, and you*
> *may have all the buildings, apparatus, and libraries*
> *without him.*   James A. Garfield (1871)

A SCENARIO. "Good afternoon, Mr. President. My colleagues
and I have just completed our visit to your fine campus [having lis-
tened to a number of such committees, the president cringes si-
lently at the word *fine*], and we are here to give you a brief report
on our findings." Thus begins the typical exit interview of a visiting accreditation team with the president of a college or university
being examined for possible specialized accreditation of a new
program or renewal of accreditation of an old one or being
visited again because a previous team found some deficiencies.

The chairman of the team continues, "We have been received in a most friendly and hospitable fashion, and we wish to
thank you for the many courtesies extended to us by all mem-

89

bers of the faculty, the administrative officers, and the alumni we saw, as well as your distinguished trustees. You will be pleased to know we have found many good things about your program." The use of *your* is not by accident; within a few minutes the president will learn that it is indeed *his* or *her* program —full responsibility rests in the president's lap alone. "The physical facilities are adequate. A number of faculty members seem well prepared, and we found some bright spots among the students. In summary, we have had no difficulty in concluding that your program meets minimum standards of accreditation."

There is more to come. No visiting committee will stop at that point, and the president has learned from other visiting committees that such remarks are only the introduction to the rest of the concluding conference.

"But we know, Mr. President, that you are not satisfied to have a program that merely meets *minimum* standards. In fact, we have learned something of your plans from comments, questions, and opinions expressed by your students, faculty members, and alumni. We can well appreciate that you are seeking a level of excellence for this program that will put it in the forefront with the best in the country. We just want you to know that all of us have caught from your colleagues a bit of the enthusiasm that exists on this campus for moving ahead. The further comments we have to offer, therefore, are suggestions of ways in which we think the excellence you seek can best be achieved." The president, torn between flattery and the hard realities of the budget, simply waits for the other shoe to fall. It does not take long.

"We found morale among the graduate students particularly low. I'll let Professor Jones, who gave special attention to that part of the program, comment on what he found."

Professor Jones, holding up his own institution as a prize example, makes it clear with a few oblique comments that the graduate students in this program are jammed into their study carrels, are forced to double up on laboratory equipment, are inadequately supported by either assistantships or fellowships, and look on themselves as slave labor, indentured to the faculty. To cure these ills will require a sizable expansion of both study and laboratory space, a doubling of graduate student stipends, and the addition of two more senior professors to provide minimum supervision of theses and dissertations.

The chairman of the visiting committee then turns to Professor Smith, who has given special attention during the visit to the library's holdings and library services for both faculty members and students. A rather shy and retiring man, Professor Smith speaks somewhat hesitantly but nonetheless convincingly. "The collections are inadequate, not only for the programs now offered but for the two additional specialties the faculty expects to offer next year. In fact—and I was quite shocked to find this—a number of serials are incomplete. One important journal has a twenty-year gap, from 1900 to 1920. You realize, of course, that no student or faculty member interested in the history of the field could possibly do an adequate job without that reference material. [And how could *you* be so blind as to overlook this well-known fact?] But you will be relieved, Mr. President, to know that copies of these missing volumes can be obtained from the British Museum, and your librarian has indicated to me that he is willing to go to London this spring to make arrangements for having this rather rare item purchased and delivered to your campus." Professor Smith proceeds to describe the inadequacies of library service, which also can be remedied with the addition of a few new staff positions. "However, the long-range solution must be the establishment of a departmental library . . . ." One more, thinks the president—duplicate purchases and duplicate staff, all to be provided so that faculty members and graduate students will not have to walk that one block to the main library. The rest of Smith's comments fail to register on the president, who is by this time trying to estimate what the trip to London, the purchase of the rare volumes, and their delivery will do to an already overextended budget.

Finally the conversation returns to the chairman, who delivers the blockbuster: "You have heard my colleagues' suggestions, Mr. President, and each, when put into place, will enhance the quality of your institution. However, to join the ranks of excellence, you should proceed within the next year or two to establish at least three research professorships, which would be used to attract leading scholars to your institution. In

our considered judgment, you should have such faculty positions so that you can persuade these scholars to spend a year
with your faculty and students while pursuing their own research."

The president, by this time brought home from London
by the shock treatment, meekly inquires: "Would the visiting
scholars conduct seminars or do any teaching?"

"No, no, no," the chairman interrupts, "but a book or
monograph, which would be published as a result of the visiting
scholar's year with you, would give credit in the preface to your
institution for having provided the opportunity [money] to advance the knowledge in this rapidly changing field." There are
only a few details remaining to be added. The visiting scholars
are to be paid premium salaries and provided with office and
secretarial help plus at least one research assistant each, and the
host institution will receive for all the investment either a footnote or an acknowledgment in the preface noting "the help received by the author."

The rest of the conference is ritual. The president thanks
the members of the visiting committee for their time and for
the significant contribution they have made to the host university at this historic moment. The president gives a sigh of relief
—almost. Were the president free for the rest of the afternoon,
he or she might be given to sink immediately into depression,
seek out the nearest bar, or withdraw to the handball court.
The president, however, is quickly brought back to reality. Saying goodbye to the visiting team, the president observes that the
committee from the student government has just arrived to talk
about the tuition increase announced for next year.

This scenario is imaginary but perhaps not too far-fetched.
Rarely does a visiting committee fail to suggest new or additional facilities, increased library and laboratory holdings and
equipment, more funds for student assistance, and additional
faculty positions. Rarely does a visiting committee consider the
limits of resources of either the institution or the special program being evaluated. Rarely does a visiting committee evaluating a program consider institutional fairness to other programs
on the campus, and as a result many presidents and other cen-

tral administrators regard such visiting committees as simply pressure groups whose objective is to get a bigger piece of the financial pie for a special interest.

The scenario focused on specialized accreditation. Institutional accrediting bodies, however, have also come under criticism from colleges and universities, even though they are supposedly creatures of those institutions. The complaints—aimed at the regional accrediting associations as distinguished from the other institutional accrediting bodies—are somewhat different but no less pointed than those levied against specialized accrediting bodies, as the following examples show.

• Although their criteria tend to be general and their avowed purpose is to judge an institution primarily against its own stated objectives, the regional accrediting associations often fall short of this goal in actual practice. These lapses usually relate to the quality of the team visiting the institution. A team chairman or a dominating team member who has a strong set of personal notions about what constitutes quality (usually the way that person's own institution does things) can greatly skew the review process.

• In their laudable attempt to accommodate a variety of approaches to postsecondary education, the regional accrediting associations have lost a necessary consensus about what constitutes quality education. As they move toward an emphasis on educational outcomes, they may regain this sense of agreement. They should also be aided by the efforts of the postsecondary education community to develop guidelines for good practice in a variety of areas. The regional associations, however, have been remarkably slow to respond to these developments.

• As problems of quality have related more and more to financial resources, the regional accrediting associations have not fully met their responsibility to identify such problems early on, provide expert assistance when needed, and take firm (though often unpleasant) action when it is clearly called for.

• The regional accrediting associations have failed to take the leadership that rightfully should be expected of them in seeking and making cooperative accreditation arrangements with the specialized accrediting bodies. The attitude of the regional associations has usually been "Sure, we'll cooperate with you, if you do it our way."

• Accredited institutions have every reason to expect that when they interact with other colleges and universities, accreditation has some useful meaning. Unless a president or a key administrator is on the regional accrediting commission, however, that person is usually forced to deal in the world of rumor and speculation about the status of marginal institutions. Has Institution X been put on probation? Is the problem serious or nitpicking? Did Institution Y receive a "show-cause order," and if so, what does it mean for the institution's future? Is it true that Institution Z has lost its accreditation? The accrediting associations are reluctant to announce such actions.

• One of the proud claims of the regional accrediting associations is that they stand as a buffer between institutions and outside political bodies that would inappropriately intrude into the educational affairs of the institution. On occasion, one or another of the regional associations has played an important role in protecting colleges and universities from governors or state legislators who wanted to bend the institutions to a political purpose. However, state and federal governments have grown more powerful, and the accrediting associations have been given increased stature as a means for determining eligibility for public funds. As a result, the associations appear to be losing their zeal for opposing improper interference from political officials. The accrediting associations must do more than just take a stand. They must play a leadership role in identifying and promptly addressing serious problems involving quality and integrity in postsecondary education. Prompt action will mean that ambitious politicos and bureaucrats will not have good reason to argue that the heavy hand of government is demanded because the institutions cannot police themselves.

Institutional Needs

What has been described so far is a far cry from the kind of guidance and service that a college or university has a right to expect from accreditation. Institutions of postsecondary education were primarily responsible for the creation and development of accreditation, and they provide—directly or indirectly— most if not all of the financial support for the accreditation process. Therefore, colleges and universities should understandably demand that accreditation function to assist, rather than inhibit or damage, the institution. Most college and university presidents, in fact, still view accreditation positively. However, they are increasingly critical of certain aspects of accreditation and certain accrediting bodies. Institutions have every right to expect at least four constants of the accrediting associations:

1. *Clear standards unequivocally applied.* Every institution has a right to definitive answers to the basic questions underlying accreditation: What are the standards for accreditation? Does the institution or program meet those standards? Is it accredited or not? Some specialized accrediting agencies have recently developed practices that tend to keep continuous bureaucratic chains on even the best of the programs for which they are responsible. The official letter that conveys the actions of the accrediting body after appropriate consideration of the report from the visiting committee often reads as follows:

> I am happy to report to you that the council [or commission or board] has approved the recommendation to reaccredit your program for the maximum period of [a specified number of] years. However, we are concerned about the serious limitations on space that now exist and request that we be informed in one year of the progress you have made toward solving this problem. Furthermore, you will note the council's recommendation regarding student-faculty ratios. We are also asking you to submit at the end of two years an up-to-date report on the changes you have made in both tenured and nontenured faculty positions, along with registration data for each course offering. Another concern of the visiting committee, likewise voiced by the council, was the number of non-majors who are permitted to attend upper-level required offerings, a practice that is not permitted in other approved programs. To assess the full impact of changes over the next two years, we shall need information on that subject as well.

Such demands serve to keep the director of the program or the dean of the school or college constantly beholden to the accrediting association. The institution's autonomy is eroded by such actions because both personnel and financial resources are directed not by the institution but by an exterior force—in this case, the accrediting body. Moreover, in some instances creativity and innovation are dampened as decision making in effect becomes centralized in a professional association office where staff members, often out of day-to-day touch with the profession and institutional life, greatly influence the total educational experience.

Although an institution may be expected to address problems when standards clearly relate to educational quality and can be met in specified ways, this sort of expectation must be distinguished from guildlike practices that may not improve educational quality. These practices are generally more common among specialized than among institutional accrediting bodies. Recently, however, the regional accrediting associations have been reducing the average period of accreditation and increasing requests for interim reports.

2. *Guidance for improvement.* The most important expectation that an institution has of an accreditation team is that as a result of all the information put at its disposal, it will provide bona fide counseling and guidance to strengthen the institution or program it is evaluating. The institution has a right to expect that members of a visiting committee will know about experimental efforts in other institutions and programs and also something of the results of such efforts. The committee should be able to make suggestions appropriate to the institution being visited, consistent with the uniqueness of its location, the population it serves, and other characteristics. Among the possibilities for joint exploration might be special teaching, research, or internship opportunities and special strengths or skills required of faculty members.

The spirit of collegiality, which allows new ideas to be tried, may be lost during accreditation-team visits because of the defensive posture in which the visitors sometimes place their hosts. Individual team members may not wish to precipitate a

confrontation. However, unfortunate or even unfriendly relations between the institution and the central staff of the accrediting association sometimes undermine any spirit of collegiality.
Correctly or not, institutional officials are commonly advised,
"Don't cross [the executive of the accrediting commission], or
your institution will run into all kinds of problems with its accreditation."

   3. *Protection from fraudulent and improper practices.*
Several separate but related problems come under this heading:
fraudulent institutions, fraudulent documents, and questionable
practices. Because accrediting associations are voluntary, there
are limits to the role they can play. However, they can and
should be more aggressive than has been customary in addressing these problems.

   Diploma mills and fly-by-night institutions should be controlled by adequate state licensing laws, effectively enforced.
The Education Commission of the States has developed a model
state licensing law, but some states have not adopted its essential
components or provided the necessary resources for its implementation. The regional accrediting associations require chartering or
licensing by an appropriate agency of government as a prerequisite to institutional accreditation; they should therefore insist
that steps be taken to make the licensing laws an effective instrument for separating worthy from unworthy institutions.

   Although state statutes, consumer groups, and the courts
have helped over the years to expose fraudulent practices in
postsecondary education, the task is a continuing one, never
quite completed. Institutions have the right to expect that accrediting associations will help protect them from fraudulent
diplomas, transcripts, test scores, or other vital records, especially as society becomes increasingly dependent on computers.
The accrediting associations should lead in encouraging that
guidelines for good practice be developed, and they should press
their member institutions about their practices in preserving the
integrity of documents and records.

   Because the accrediting associations have not played a
leadership role in initiating statements of good practice in many
areas of concern, other associations have had to step in to fill

the void. With the encouragement of many key national organizations in postsecondary education, the American Council on Education has established an Office on Self-Regulation Initiatives and has assisted in preparing and distributing guidelines on such subjects as tuition refund policies, admissions and recruiting, transfer of credit, and standards of progress. The accrediting bodies should encourage and assist their member institutions to consider and, if possible, adopt these guidelines (see Chapter Three).

4. *Preservation of institutional autonomy.* The tradition of institutional autonomy among colleges and universities has been so broadly embraced in the United States that little sympathy is given to those who would take away even a small measure of an institution's independence. Accrediting organizations, however, have all too often conveyed the impression of challenging an institution's autonomy in recommending, or in some cases demanding, a reallocation of the institution's resources. By so doing, an accrediting body threatens to erode the responsibility that the institution has a right, even an obligation, to preserve for itself.

An illustration may be useful. A university with accredited programs in architecture, business administration, law, and medicine may be persuaded by circumstances unique to that particular university to place, over time, a disproportionate share of resources into one of the four programs. As long as the three other programs retain sufficient support to maintain minimum standards for accreditation, the university should not be subjected to undue pressure to realign its priorities. However, virtually no visiting committee in any professional field would accept such a premise. Indeed, the bias most often found among visiting committees would be to request even more financial support for their program. The practice of specialized accrediting groups today has essentially lost sight of respect for and recognition of the autonomy of the individual college or university. Unfortunately, institutional accrediting associations, which look at the institution as a whole, are often unable to offset the pressures exerted by the specialized associations, whose teams visit more frequently and make more specific demands.

Institutional Responsibilities

If accreditation is to serve the interests and needs of institutions of postsecondary education, they must, of course, meet their responsibilities as well. Institutions have three main areas of responsibility in accreditation:

1. *Financing the accreditation function.* Accreditation is a service to the public, to students, to faculties, and, in the final analysis, to institutions themselves. Because institutions are the instruments of the educational programs that benefit all clienteles, institutions should pay the major cost of accreditation. In recent years, special problems have arisen when various jurisdictions of government have taken over accreditation, licensure, and recognition of postsecondary educational institutions and programs. The lines of responsibility between federal and state governments, between government agencies and institutions, between the public interest and institutional responsibility, and among all the various parties concerned have become so blurred as to make practically impossible the assignment of clearly identifiable roles. This confusion has allowed some colleges and universities to succumb to lethargy and slough off their primary responsibility for financing the accreditation process. In addition, as economic conditions have become more difficult, some institutions have viewed the cost of accreditation as an extra that might be cut or eliminated rather than an investment in the credibility of the entire academic enterprise. If accreditation is to remain voluntary and viable, institutions of postsecondary education must pay the costs.

2. *Managing rather than reacting.* In far too many instances, colleges and universities view accreditation as a troublesome outside force that they have to contend with periodically. Strong institutions see accreditation as a petty annoyance; weak institutions fear it as a grave threat. These attitudes—which arise with both specialized accreditation and institutional accreditation—should trouble accrediting bodies, at least those that pride themselves on serving institutions by helping them to strengthen and improve their educational offerings. More important, however, these attitudes should trouble institutions. Ac-

creditation is there to be *used* by institutions—if they would but take the initiative, singly or, if necessary, collectively.

If college and university presidents are unwilling to "take their turn" at serving on accreditation teams and commissions and to encourage some of their most able staff members to do so, then those roles may be assumed by less able people. If the volunteers in accreditatioh do not take their responsibilities seriously, then the staff members may end up running the associations themselves. If institutions do not place a high priority on defining their educational objectives and designing effective means for evaluating their achievement, then visiting team members may try to impose their own ideas. If institutions do not insist that accrediting bodies work out cooperative arrangements for data requests, self-study requirements, and campus visits, then the institutions will continue to be buffeted by widely varying demands.

3. *Making accreditation a high priority.* What is at stake here is the need for institutions to recognize that accreditation is sufficiently important to be given continuing attention as a high priority. Accreditation should be viewed as the process by which the institution defines and redefines itself as an educational institution; regularly evaluates its successes and failures; compares itself with comparable institutions and programs; identifies and keeps up with important developments; and renews its commitments to its sponsors, to the public, and to its students. What could be more important?

Mixed Responses from the Campus

At any academic gathering where deans, academic vice-presidents, chancellors, and presidents are discussing accreditation, the full range of opinion quickly emerges as each person reflects on the accreditation status of his or her institution. Two comments represent the two extremes of institutional positions about the voluntary accreditation procedures that have been built up over the decades:

1. "We're going to get our full accreditation. The visiting committee was with us two weeks ago, and we answered their

every criticism. It's just a matter now of moving the paperwork through the appropriate approval bodies."
2. "I couldn't care less" is another's response to the question whether a given professional society will continue approval of a particular program, place it on probation, or refuse to reaccredit it.

Many of the country's most prestigious institutions have taken a kind of "it can't touch us" attitude toward bona fide, well-intentioned efforts of the greater community of postsecondary education to perform the services of accreditation for colleges and universities. At the other extreme, institutions with problems, old as well as new, are continuously fearful that the highly desired status that comes from official accreditation may be lost and that the ensuing damage would be catastrophic. In many fields of endeavor, attendance at or graduation from an unaccredited program handicaps students in ways that are very difficult and expensive to overcome. Loss of accreditation is often followed by loss of student, faculty, and financial support.

Receipt of an accrediting committee's report or an official action by an accrediting body can create differences of opinion on campus. In a program where accreditation is normally granted for a definite period—for example, five years—if the institution receives less than the maximum period, different factions on campus can make different use of the committee's report. Does the shorter period of accreditation result from program deficiencies or other factors? Should the action of the accrediting body be made public if less than full accreditation is received? To call attention to deficiencies may serve to attract the support that will correct the problems in the program. However, making public those deficiencies may alert prospective students or faculty members that the program is weak, may be in danger, and should therefore be avoided. Faculty members, students, administrators, members of governing boards, and alumni all have a stake in the actions that may be taken in such a situation. Deciding which is the fairest way to proceed is often not easy, given the interests of all concerned parties. In addition, statutory requirements vary among the various states, limiting the discretion that an institution may exercise.

On some campuses, factions within a college or university may adhere to different motives when preparing self-study reports in preparation for the arrival of visiting teams. At one institution, bitterly divided over campus issues, the relatively few persons charged with responsibility for preparing the self-study report succeeded in an effort to embarrass other campus factions by reporting the worst possible picture of conditions at the institution. Fortunately, the visiting committee was sufficiently perceptive to conclude early in the visit that the institution was far stronger and of much higher quality and had many more assets than the formally prepared report indicated. As it turned out, much was gained in the long run because the work of the visiting team and the ensuing report by the accrediting body contributed significantly to the amelioration of campus animosities.

However, those who have served on accreditation teams are well aware of self-study reports that tend to represent only the strengths of the institution, cover up weaknesses, and mislead visitors. Fortunately, experienced faculty members and administrators serving as team members can quickly see through such façades.

The different ways in which accreditation is viewed and the varying values placed on it by the many publics it serves all contribute to the limitations surrounding its use. Clearly, a better understanding of the purposes, methods, procedures, and problems of accreditation by all constituencies of postsecondary education would alleviate much of the misuse that takes place.

A MORE HELPFUL SCENARIO. "The report prepared by the university for the benefit of the visitors, together with the supplementary materials, gave a very adequate picture of the institution's history, accurately described its present state of affairs, and offered an interesting preview of things to come. Those who prepared the report had no hesitancy in calling attention to matters that they felt to be problems or weaknesses. Needless to say, the absence of any attempt to cover up deficiencies made the work of the visiting committee much easier and, we believe, gave the visitors an opportunity to be more helpful in their own constructive criticisms."

The report of the visiting team, whether the oral exit interview with the president or the written report that normally comes back some weeks later, should reflect the visitors' responsibility to indicate to the administrative officers and faculties of the institution ways in which current problems might profitably be addressed. The scenario might continue as follows:

"In spite of the many steps that have recently been taken to strengthen the institution, several questions remain to be resolved. Is the institution directing its main efforts at the local community, at a regional population, or to the national clientele, or does it aspire to become one of the limited number of internationally recognized universities? Will its greatest emphasis be on graduate and professional education, or will the undergraduate programs, particularly those in the liberal arts, be the central focus of the institution? What emphasis is to be placed on research? Will new professional schools be established or new centers or institutes with special emphasis on research?

"Regardless of the answers to these questions, the institution must move quickly to remedy the glaring deficiencies in its library collections. . . .

"The visitors found that many steps have been taken to strengthen the institution since the last visit. We saw no overall weaknesses that could justify our concern. . . ."

This scenario illustrates that at least three important matters are to be addressed by a visiting team—the adequacy of the self-study report, suggestions on major unresolved problems, and a definitive response to the question whether the program (or institution) has any major problem that might affect its accreditation or reaccreditation. Evidence to support recommendations must be gleaned from interviews, reports, and other materials or from direct observation by members of the visiting team. The institution should be expected to provide the visitors with all such materials, including data from various sources. Indeed, much if not all of the data required should be anticipated by the institution. A spirit of professional collegiality between

the visitors and the hosts obviously offers the most productive
relationship for the best results.

Putting Accreditation's House in Order

Postsecondary educational institutions are faced with a
major dilemma. They must remedy the ills of voluntary accreditation or lose a significant measure of institutional autonomy.
The public interest is so great that the citizenry will not leave to
chance the potential damage to society that may come with
continued disarray in the education community. If the remedy
is not accomplished by institutions, the public will continue its
already visible turn to government for regulation.

Awareness. There may be a general understanding of such
terms as *accredited, nonaccredited, approved,* and *probation* as
they are used in relation to the thousands of training and educational programs that abound. However, the public—and even
many persons involved in education—remains vague about the
precise meaning of these terms. Clarifying them is also difficult
because the value of approval or accreditation varies among programs and institutions within different states. In some programs,
approval and accreditation are not necessary to licensure and
practice. In other fields, accreditation is looked on as the required key to open the gates to practice. With the many programs offered in different postsecondary educational institutions in the many states, for all concerned to keep informed and
abreast of changes is nearly impossible. Institutions must be relied on to make clear in publications and by other means the
accredited status of each program offered. By so doing, institutions exhibit their basic integrity. Monitoring the information
made public by each institution must become one of the fundamental responsibilities of duly organized accrediting associations and bodies.

Institutional Commitment. All too many faculty members and administrative officers in all kinds of postsecondary
educational institutions place too low a priority on matters that
have to do with accreditation. Unless persons from institutions
assume the leadership of accreditation, it is likely to continue to

suffer from neglect. All educational institutions must commit more persons and more funds to the performance of these functions if the public is to be adequately served and government intervention is to be avoided. In multipurpose institutions, the staff in the areas of academic affairs, financial matters, and general administration should include persons assigned specific and important responsibilities for accreditation. Although the president or chancellor may indeed be unable to give the time and attention to accreditation that it requires, someone who is high on the staff and has regular and immediate access to the chief executive officer should bear the responsibility. The assignment should require the person to become familiar with each of the programs for which accreditation is desirable and serve as a constant liaison with the appropriate accrediting association. In addition, each school, college, or major program should have its own cadre of informed and interested faculty members who are available to serve on accreditation teams to other institutions. Such responsibilities, if shared by many institutions, will not prove too burdensome for any one. Left unattended, voluntary accreditation will inevitably be superseded by government oversight and regulation, which may indeed require the time of many more persons and the allocation of even greater resources.

Qualitative Measures in Accreditation. One reason that accreditation has been subject to so many serious challenges over the years is the accusation that it often rests on quantitative measures and that the quality of a program seldom receives serious inspection. Defining quality is difficult, and so is devising measures that are both valid and reliable in measuring quality from one campus to another. Yet, those tasks are vital to the accrediting process. Postsecondary institutions must use some of their discretionary research funds to develop better measures of quality within all the institution's programs.

National Leadership in Accreditation. As official approval has become more important to institutions, to students, and to the public, institutions have become more vulnerable to pressures of special-interest groups. A national organization that recognizes the autonomy of institutions must have the strength to protect the individual institution from undue pressure. Such

6

H. R. Kells

༄༅༄༅༄༅༄༅༄༅༄༅༄༅༄༅༄༅༄༅༄༅༄༅

Institutional Rights
and Responsibilities

> *If an accrediting agency would assume that the institution is a good institution until the contrary is established, rather than assuming that the burden of proof lies with the institution, more might be accomplished.* John F. Nevins (1959, p. 318)

The relationship among institutions, the public, and accrediting bodies involves fundamental institutional rights and responsibilities. Institutions should not be unduly burdened by the accreditation process. In turn, they should act to ensure the integrity of the process.

Concern about the protection of institutional rights in accreditation springs from the historical development of accreditation, the autonomous nature of American postsecondary educational institutions, and recent practice in accreditation. The

Portions of this chapter were first delivered in a talk at the American Association of Higher Education meeting in March 1980 but, in light of helpful comments from many members of the accreditation community, have been revised for this book.

107

number and diversity of institutions and the pressures of competitiveness, autonomy, and entrepreneurship on them have resulted in an accreditation system that is cumbersome and duplicative. The essentially unplanned evolution of accreditation has produced a system that is at times less than sensitive to institutional needs.

For some time, accrediting bodies have recognized the potential for abridgment of institutional rights, and they are beginning to worry about instances of unreasonable practice. As early as 1966, the Federation of Regional Accrediting Commissions of Higher Education (FRACHE), one of the two forerunners of the present Council on Postsecondary Accreditation (COPA), published a code of good practice in accreditation (Federation of Regional Accrediting Commissions of Higher Education, 1966). The National Commission on Accrediting (NCA), the other forerunner of COPA, had a similar code. Although the regional commissions have since refined the FRACHE code, the basic rights guaranteed in the original code have been retained and are of fundamental importance.

The Council on Postsecondary Accreditation drew heavily on the FRACHE and NCA codes when it prepared its original "Provisions and Procedures for Becoming Recognized as an Accrediting Agency." Three of the five categories of criteria contain items taken directly from the FRACHE code. About half of the thirty-one COPA criteria were obtained from the code; virtually all those deal with procedures that protect the rights of the institution. COPA added criteria on the makeup of accrediting commissions, advance-notice requirements when accreditation standards are changed, and interagency cooperation. The COPA guidelines were more recently revised in April 1981 (see Resource B).

In the fifteen years since the original FRACHE code was adopted, many of its elements, including those eventually adopted by COPA, have become the cornerstones of good practice in accreditation today. However, two important points must be made. First, some of the elements in the COPA criteria have not been fully explored, developed, and enacted by the accrediting bodies. In short, the intention—the spirit—behind some of the criteria has often not been achieved. Second, some dimensions not included in the COPA criteria are essential if accreditation is to continue to improve as part of the voluntary, self-regulatory process of American postsecondary education.

Institutional Concerns

From an institution's perspective, accreditation often appears complex and confusing. Institution-based professionals generally know little about the purposes, policies, and procedures of accreditation. The "politics" of accreditation—whether to seek accreditation by discipline, professional level, or functional area—further complicate the issue. Rumor, myth, and anxiety tend to be fostered by the infrequency of contact with the accrediting organization, both because of the time span between accreditation-team visits and because persons from the institution rarely participate in the organization's activities on an ongoing basis. The general reluctance of educators to submit to outside scrutiny creates further problems.

Most institutions report no problems with accreditation. Clearly, some people at institutions that have had recent contact with accrediting bodies—at least the chief executive officers and the informed, relatively experienced minority—report repeatedly that accreditation, particularly the self-study, is useful and is worth the time and money (Kells and Kirkwood, 1979; Romine, 1975; Warner, 1977). At the same time, more and more institutions are speaking out against duplication of effort in accreditation and the proliferation of accrediting bodies, particularly when a single institution has multiple accreditation relationships. Some institutions are also rebelling against unreasonable procedures and the arbitrary criterion levels associated with one or more of the standards of specialized accrediting bodies. There does seem, from the institution's perspective, to be several problems that require policy direction and some corrective action.

Too Many Accrediting Bodies. There are from forty-five to sixty accrediting bodies, depending on how one counts. Because of the degree of subject matter overlap between some accrediting organizations, a given school at some universities must deal with two or three different accrediting bodies and therefore divert much time, energy, and money. This problem relates to what some institutional leaders call the right to freedom from harassment.

Not Enough Coordination. The perceived need to correct this malady varies greatly according to institution size and types of degrees granted. Only 10 percent of the regionally accredited institutions have five or more accreditation relationships, but some have more than twenty. One Northeastern university was recently visited forty times in three years. For small institutions, even two or three accreditation relationships may be a burden. More than 40 percent of institutions have two or three accreditation relationships (Kells and Parrish, 1979). A recent study clearly showed that three out of four institutions' presidents feel that there is duplication in accrediting efforts and most would welcome greater cooperation in the process (Pigge, 1979).

Relatively little progress has been made toward eliminating duplication in accreditation. COPA has been trying to develop a set of policies for accrediting bodies and has a stated concern about proliferation and duplication in accreditation (see Chapter Eighteen). However, as yet COPA has not conducted any thorough, regular review of accrediting bodies about these issues.

Some accrediting bodies have begun to send staff members to observe the activities of other accrediting bodies. COPA has sponsored conferences on interagency cooperation and has published guidelines from its Task Force on Interagency Cooperation. Some accrediting organizations have formulated bilateral cooperative agreements on self-study requirements and joint or concurrent team visits. COPA summarized many of these activities in its *Guide to Interagency Cooperation* (Council on Postsecondary Accreditation, 1981b). But progress is slow. Some accrediting-body executives are openly opposed to any interagency cooperation, while others report that their hands are tied (see Chapter Fifteen).

Accrediting-body executives interested in more cooperation can easily say that an institution that is to be evaluated soon by several accrediting organizations should stand up to them and demand cooperation, but for an institution to actually assert itself in this way is difficult. This approach works for a few strong institutions, but many institutions find that most accrediting bodies are reluctant to cooperate. The accrediting organizations usually demand individual access to the chief executive officer and individual scheduling of self-study plans and team visits. How institutions can stand up to this problem is an appropriate question, because COPA policies encourage but do not require coordination and therefore do not protect institutional rights in this matter.

Too Many Self-Studies Required. Many accrediting bodies do not yet recognize that the institution's own self-study and planning schedule should be the primary consideration. The quality of self-study and general management at institutions would improve if an articulated series of requests from accrediting bodies could reinforce and be part of the institution's own self-study and planning cycle. Where this cycle is weak or embryonic, it must be enhanced, but compounded multiple accreditation requirements only hinder it. Institutional staff members overwhelmed by reporting requirements cannot be expected to study and develop institutional programs well and prepare effective materials for each accrediting body. For example, many accrediting bodies require that the self-study report contain copies of all faculty members' résumés, often in a specified style. The cost of editing, retyping, and duplicating all the résumés is borne by the institution and its students. A cost-saving alternative would be for accrediting team members to peruse the usual set of résumés maintained at the institution. Although some accrediting bodies are working hard to reduce the load of wasteful duplication—in forms, data needs, definitions, schedules, and other specific requirements—much remains to be done.

Specific Criterion Levels Need to Be Validated. An accepted approach for determining organizational effectiveness (Campbell, 1977) is for an accrediting body to evaluate an institution as an organization on the basis of (1) the extent to which the institution seems to be achieving its clearly stated, appropriate goals and (2) the extent to which it seems to be functioning well (can survive and can continue to achieve its goals). However, most specialized accrediting bodies employ arbitrary criterion levels to express standards of good practice in the field. Because these demands (which tend to escalate and are often compounded when multiple accreditation relationships occur) can divert resources and create havoc in an institution, such criterion levels must be subject to validity studies. The ultimate test, predictive validity (for example, Will adhering to the standards create effective practicing professionals?), must be conducted during the years ahead. These studies require ascertaining attributes of good practice in a field, translating them into standards, and then testing for impact over time. Such studies are expensive but necessary. The Association of Theological Schools has completed such a study (Schuller and others, 1973, 1975, 1976), and studies have also begun in the fields of law and business.

Not Enough Assistance and Consultation. The need for accrediting bodies to explain standards, assist in self-study design, speak to the institution's professional staff, and otherwise translate cold written descriptions and standards into usable, relevant processes requires direct contact by a competent staff. The office-bound staff that sends letters and documents and tries to explain complex matters by telephone is less effective and useful. Whether staff assistance is provided on campus or at regional or national meetings, it must be effective as well as accessible.

Need for Improvement in Evaluation-Team Activities. Not all accrediting bodies engage in training activities to produce competent, well-prepared team members and chairpersons. Team members are not always carefully selected to suit institutional characteristics and needs; sometimes they bring biases based on previous experience or relationships with other institutions. Teams are sometimes not appropriate in size. For example, some specialized accrediting bodies send more people to review one program than the institutional accrediting association does, often at great cost to the institution. In general, there do not seem to be adequate guidelines for all accrediting organizations on training, team size, joint and concurrent team functioning, and conflict of interest. In addition, team reports are often not useful, timely, and objective. Frequently, an adequate oral report—covering every major issue to appear later in the written report—is not made, as it should be, before the team leaves.

Need for Hearing Procedures. Most accrediting bodies have a due process appeal mechanism for an institution to use if it disagrees with the accreditation process or the substance of an action. Many, however, do not allow all institutions the choice of appearing before the accrediting commission or council as the team chairperson presents the team report. Some have suggested that all reports should be released and all deliberations should be open, but those steps might jeopardize the accreditation process. Allowing institutions to comment directly before the accrediting commission would add another dimension to the appeal process, improve the credibility of the accreditation process, and increase institutional knowledge about accreditation, while not precluding executive sessions of the accrediting commission for further discussion and action.

Inadequate Institutional Representation in the Accreditation Process. In many instances, particularly in specialized accreditation, institutions of postsecondary education are involved minimally in the development of accreditation policies, procedures, and criteria. The accrediting bodies may print announcements in their newsletters, calling for comment, but those items are rarely seen by other than fellow professionals on the campus. Not surprisingly, therefore, the resulting accreditation processes rarely provide for meaningful institutional involvement, particularly in arranging for coordinated activities or appealing decisions on coordination (especially where there might be duplication of efforts and attendant costs to the institution). Where institutions have been provided opportunities to play a substantive role (for example, in the review of accrediting bodies by COPA or in filing grievances with COPA), they have not taken advantage of them.

A Bill of Institutional Rights in Accreditation

The accreditation community should adopt a bill of institutional rights in accreditation as an addendum to the COPA

criteria for accrediting bodies and the statement of good practice in accreditation. Such a bill of rights for institutions would
demonstrably strengthen the valuable system of mutual assistance and peer review—accreditation—as it has developed in this
country during the past century. Postsecondary educational institutions in America should be assured of the following rights
as they engage in the accreditation process.

On Proliferation and Duplication in Accreditation

  • The right to expect that the number of accrediting
bodies will not be excessive, that the accrediting bodies will not
be competitive or in conflict, and that the disciplinary coverage
in the accrediting bodies will not be duplicated.
  • The right to a well-coordinated relationship with more
than one accrediting body, including, if desired, the designation
of one accrediting body as the coordinating organization for a
given institution.
  • The right to appropriate redress for disagreements
about the frequency and type of self-study and team visits.
  • The right to have the institution's own regular self-
study, planning mechanisms, and review cycle be, under normal
circumstances, the primary focus and determinant of the nature
and frequency of accreditation activities. If the institution
chooses, accrediting bodies should not expect more than one
regular institutionwide or programwide self-study in a five-year
period. If the institution chooses to employ a joint self-study
process to serve more than one accrediting body, the accrediting
bodies should agree.
  • The right to select a schedule for regular, periodic accreditation-team visits that will be acceptable to the institution.
If the institution chooses, accrediting bodies should agree to a
joint or concurrent visit, and under normal circumstances no accrediting body should require regular visits more than once
every five years. The accrediting bodies should all adopt a similar schedule for regular visits (perhaps every five years or every
ten years), and this arrangement should be coordinated for each
institution by the institution's designated coordinating accredit-

ing body. If disagreements arise that cannot be settled by the institution and the coordinating organization, COPA or some other group should settle the matter, perhaps using trained third-party mediators.

On Effectiveness of Accreditation Activities

• The right to expect all accrediting bodies to conduct formal studies of the validity of their standards, especially any criterion levels attached to them, and to publish the results of such studies.

• The right to expect assistance, explanation of standards and procedures, and appropriate consultation with a competent and accessible accrediting-body staff and, correspondingly, that staff members will not serve as evaluators of institutions or programs. If any accrediting body cannot by itself afford to provide such services, it should work with other groups so that together they can do the job effectively.

• The right to expect that accrediting bodies will employ, with few exceptions, only formally trained evaluation-team members and chairpersons; that such visitors will be carefully selected to suit institutional characteristics and needs; that they will be competent and objective and not be biased or have a conflict of interest; and that the institution may submit a confidential evaluation of each visitor to the accrediting body.

• The right to expect oral and written evaluation-team reports that are full, relevant, timely, objective, and useful.

• The rights to appear at accrediting-commission sessions when the chairperson makes the team report and to appeal decisions.

• The right to expect COPA or some other organization to act on behalf of institutions to control the number of accrediting bodies; to work to eliminate duplication; to settle disputes between accrediting bodies and conflicts between the policies of different accrediting bodies; to protect the rights of the institution concerning schedules of visits and joint activities; and to hear appropriate appeals.

The Council on Postsecondary Accreditation has had several committees considering at least some of these matters. The COPA Committee on Recognition Criteria, which developed provisions and procedures for becoming an accrediting body (see Resource B), and the Task Force on Interagency Cooperation, which produced a set of guidelines on interagency cooperation (see Resource C), have struggled with the difficult matters of accrediting-body prerogatives and responsibilities. At the same time, the Assembly of Specialized Accrediting Bodies at its September 1980 meeting began what will perhaps be an extended and productive series of discussions on proliferation in specialized accreditation. One idea was to "cluster" similar or related accrediting bodies to permit a more effective relationship with institutions.

Institutional Responsibilities

Institutions can do much to make the system work better. Kirkwood (1978) identified five responsibilities of institutions in the accreditation process: commitment to the process, candor, coordination, the use of outcome studies, and participation. These attributes are indeed essential to the proper and effective use of the process. Institutional leaders must be committed, or the process will not function well, particularly the self-study process. Without honest self-evaluation, as well as external evaluation, the process is a sham—the concept of self-regulation fails. Institutions must exercise initiative in helping to achieve coordination of multiple accreditation relationships: If the institution does not *ask* to have a coordinated effort, it deserves what it will get from an uncoordinated multiagency effort (*caveat emptor*). The use of goal achievement, or outcome, studies is a necessity in the self-study process; they provide vital information, heretofore slighted in the process. Participation is, of course, one of many desirable elements in the process, but the real question is to what extent institutions should take the lead—to engage in the process with candor and to use the process to obtain benefits for the institution (and the system as a whole).

The following statement of institutional responsibilities

in accreditation is cast in general terms and focuses on the constituencies to whom institutions must be responsible in the accreditation process.

Statement of Institutional Responsibilities
in Accreditation

Self-regulation is a vital, distinguishing characteristic of American postsecondary education. It represents the institutions' recognition that they must take the initiative to set standards and guidelines for good practice, to work with peers to interpret them, to assess their effectiveness, and to inform others about their use. Institutions must act through self-assessment and peer action. They must be responsible for protecting quality, achieving goals, assisting other institutions to do so, and protecting the public. Institutional and specialized accreditation are part of the process of self-regulation—indeed, they are its centerpiece. They provide many ready mechanisms through which to fulfill these intentions.

Institutions and their programs must bear an important responsibility to make this system function well. Specifically, they must meet—

• *Their responsibility to the public and to their students as consumers.* Institutions must continuously examine their purposes and goals, their capacity to function well (to provide service), and their achievement of goals. Institutional leadership must remain committed to useful, candid self-analysis and to open, helpful interaction with peers through the accreditation process.

• *Their responsibility to improve their institution through accreditation.* The institution has the responsibility to protect its basic autonomy, to assess its goals and values clearly, to perform its tasks at the highest possible level of quality, and to reform and improve its practices through the accreditation process—in short, to benefit from the accreditation process. The process must not be perceived as an external exercise. It must be seen as central and useful.

• *Their responsibility to the accreditation process.* The

institution has the responsibility to be informed about the accreditation process, to participate in it and improve it, and to take the lead to seek reasonable treatment and redress. In this way, accreditation can grow and improve to meet the needs of institutions and the publics it serves.

Accreditation is at a critical stage. Institutions are under substantial pressures to streamline their functioning—to cut expenses, set priorities, and focus attention on basic activities and values. In these processes of reduction and refinement, self-regulation must not be discarded; it must be enhanced. Accreditation can be enhanced if institutions value and use the process well and if accrediting bodies protect institutional rights and continue to refine their procedures.

7

H. R. Kells

ɒɕɒɕɒɕɒɕɒɕɒɕɒɕɒɕɒɕɒɕɒɕɒɕɒɕɒɕ

Improving Institutional Performance Through Self-Study

> *I cannot begin to guess at all the causes of our cultural sadness, not even the most important ones, but I can think of one thing that is wrong with us and eats away at us: we do not know enough about ourselves.* Lewis Thomas (1978)

Until about thirty years ago, the accreditation process did not require that an institution or program conduct a self-examination, in any real sense of the term, as part of its application for accreditation or renewal of accreditation. Indeed, in institutional accreditation periodic review was not introduced until the system was between forty and fifty years old. With the end of the Second World War, interest in institutional and program study and planning increased, and some major philanthropic foundations began to require extensive curriculum reviews and

For a thorough exploration of self-study design and procedures and the relation of self-study to accreditation and institutional and programmatic needs, consult *Self-Study Processes: A Guide for Postsecondary Institutions* (Kells, 1983).

other reviews or master planning efforts as prerequisites for major grants. Since then, both institutional and specialized accreditation have gradually put more and more emphasis on self-assessment as a required, if not central, aspect of the accreditation process. In the last decade, the self-study requirement has increased in importance as demands for institutional effectiveness, accountability, and coordinated study and planning processes have accompanied the growing competition, economic constraints, and political pressures that institutions must face.

Barriers to Useful Self-Study

Mackenzie (1969), in the simplest and perhaps most useful explanation of the management of any type of organization or activity, calls for study and quality control to follow implementation of plans and then a repetition of the cycle. Nonetheless, postsecondary educational institutions and their programs do not often study themselves in a thorough, useful, and continuous way. With few exceptions, institutions do not regularly review their goals, study their processes, assess their problems, formulate solutions, and evaluate goal achievement (Kells and Kirkwood, 1978, 1979). When an institution or program does not conduct regular self-studies, accrediting bodies must ask that such studies be conducted before the accreditation-team visit. The team cannot hope to explore an institution at any depth or provide useful reactions to the institution and the accrediting body unless those responsible for conducting the programs have described, explored, and assessed them before the visit. Certainly there can be little hope of adequately judging the effectiveness of the programs and services, much less improving them, if self-assessment is not attempted first. The accrediting body will also have difficulty in determining the extent to which accreditation standards are met unless the team visit is preceded by an adequate self-study.

Saying that educational organizations ought to conduct useful self-studies is one thing; making it happen is another. There are substantial barriers to be surmounted. They stem from several sources. Some barriers are basic to the nature of American postsecondary educational institutions—complex goals, complicated and shared governance patterns, scarcity of information about goal achievement, and a general lack of data for self-study processes and their participants. Functions and entities within an institution are usually not highly interdependent. Exhibiting general disdain for evaluation, professional staff members are poorly trained for some of the things they are asked to do and tend to work better as individuals than they do in group efforts, certainly in activities seeking consensus and probing program effectiveness. Some barriers are related to institution and program leadership, particularly attitudes about the usefulness of self-study and accreditation. How the primary motivation for the effort is perceived can also be a barrier (for example, when the motivation for self-study is seen as a reaction to external forces rather than as a useful internal planning approach). The tendency of institutions to ignore human concerns in initiating and organizing such efforts can create other barriers (Kells, 1979, 1983). Finally, most self-study efforts are related to accreditation, and because program leaders are usually anxious about accreditation, the resulting self-studies are often "safe," overly descriptive, and not very useful (Kells, 1981). Much can be done to overcome these barriers.

The self-study efforts of American institutions, though far more developed than those of other nations, are mainly linked to accreditation and therefore, understandably, tend to be largely externally motivated and isolated from the ongoing management scheme at the institution. But this situation need not continue. Self-study can be useful and change-oriented. People can become excited about the processes and the possibilities for their programs and their institutions. This enthusiasm can occur in both institutional and specialized accreditation.

Institutional Accreditation. Among the purposes of institutional accreditation (Selden and Porter, 1977), two are the most important. The first is to help improve the educational quality of the institution. The second is to identify the institutions that seem to have clearly stated, appropriate goals; seem to be in large part achieving them; seem to have the human, fiscal, and physical resources to continue to do so; and meet the stated standards of the accrediting study.

Self-study must be a crucial element in an accreditation

process with these purposes, and institutional accrediting bodies are therefore in the process of increasing their efforts to improve institutions' self-study capabilities. For example, they are offering increased assistance to institutions through workshops and new handbooks. Although goal achievement is receiving more attention in self-study processes, these efforts are just beginning, and there is much to be done (Kells, 1983; Andrews and others, 1978). Too often, the processes of self-analysis are still organized for producing reports rather than evaluating and improving the institution.

Some institutional accrediting bodies are clearly further along than others in attending to these problems and are increasing their attempts to refine their standards for qualitative judgment about an institution's efforts. The absence of clearly stated criterion levels for each standard often confuses evaluation-team members (Kells, 1981). For example, a standard without a stated criterion level might read: "The institution that admits disadvantaged students must provide academic and personal support services." The addition of a process criterion level might be "must provide two counselors per x number of students." An outcome criterion level might be "must assist students so that they can reach the twelfth-grade level in reading before proceeding with college work." Some education theorists would argue, however, that the lack of stated criterion levels is consistent with the principle of institutional autonomy and the diversity of American postsecondary education.

Specialized Accreditation. To generalize about the approximately forty specialized accrediting bodies is difficult, save that they are organized nationally and usually deal with a program or a cluster of programs within an institution. However, one generalization that is probably safe to make is that although specialized accrediting bodies are interested in institutional improvement, such efforts are secondary to the primary purpose of identifying programs that meet standards of good practice in the field as established by leaders in a given profession. The standards are a mixture of categories for qualitative judgment without stipulated criterion levels and firm statements, sometimes quantitative, that are, in effect, criterion levels for a particular standard—for example, "Programs must have student-faculty ratios of eleven to one or lower in clinical areas." These standards, almost without exception, are unvalidated in that they have not yet been shown to result in better graduates or improved professional practice (predictive validity). Studies to promote more outcome-oriented standards are under way in several fields—for example, in theology, law, and business.

The self-study process in specialized accreditation also tends to be concerned mainly with meeting accrediting-body standards rather than defining problems or dysfunctions and designing strategies to improve programs. This emphasis seems to be changing, however, as accrediting bodies discover how useful the self-study process can be to programs for self-improvement. Furthermore, as accreditation standards evolve and become more predictively valid, using them in the review is bound to be a strong stimulus to program improvement.

For the most part, the professional staff members of specialized accrediting bodies do not see themselves as consultants available to assist with self-study processes. Many do function actively to help interpret accreditation standards and provide other assistance to the programs under review, but assistance with self-study design and process is relatively scarce. Much more can be done here.

Finally, institutions with several accreditation relationships feel a certain amount of duress and frustration. They face duplicative, uncoordinated, seemingly endless requests for self-studies and reports from the accrediting bodies with which they deal. Such duplication certainly hinders the development of a single, sound study-and-planning cycle (Kells, 1980a) and drains enthusiasm for improvement-oriented self-study on the part of the often inundated staff members at institutions (see Pigge, 1979). Proposals have been made to reduce the duplication (see Chapters Six and Eighteen).

Purposes of Self-Study

Self-study can serve several purposes in enhancing the life of the institution:

- *Helping institutions and programs to improve.* Institutions and programs can become more effective as a result of self-study by clarifying goals; identifying problems; studying goals achievement; reviewing programs, procedures, and resources; and identifying and introducing needed changes.
- *Providing the foundation for all planning.* Plans should be based on a clear sense of strengths and weaknesses. Honest self-analysis provides the confidence for an institution to project how to achieve newly clarified goals.
- *Leading to ongoing institutional research and self-analysis.* The capacity of the institution for change should be enhanced by self-study—should be the legacy of self-study.
- *Stimulating review of policies, practices, procedures, and records.* These reviews, though important to the institution, are usually left on the "to do" list for months or years as the press of regular business or current crises occupies attention. Self-study can also yield useful fund-raising ideas and the basic documents on which such efforts can be based.
- *Enhancing institutional openness.* Open communication, trust, listening, and group functioning—qualities needed to face and solve problems—are directly related to how people feel about themselves as part of the institutional community. If they are treated as valued, trusted members of the community and if their best efforts can be elicited to achieve organizational and personal goals, then the effectiveness of the organization will be enhanced. Those who help frame solutions to problems usually become committed to carrying out the steps required. For any institution, one of the chief payoffs of a properly designed and executed self-study is the positive identification with the institution that comes from staff members' meaningful participation in clarifying and solving problems.
- *Providing staff development.* Participation by recently hired staff members in an institutional self-study—even limited participation, such as reviewing draft reports and attending hearings at which data or new ideas are discussed—can be a useful introduction to the campus. It can be particularly valuable for new chief executive officers. Another related bene-

fit of self-study is identifying committed new leaders, who often emerge from its processes.

Self-study can also serve purposes related to accreditation, both institutional and specialized:

- *Assessing the extent to which the institution or program meets accreditation standards.* The accrediting body can thereby inform the public of institutions and programs that appear to meet the standards of good practice in the field.
- *Providing useful written materials for the accreditation team.* In the past, this purpose dominated the self-study process: The sole reason for self-study during accreditation was to produce a report for use by the team. This exercise was, and in many cases still is, wasteful, duplicative, and costly; unfortunately, it can be multiplied many times if the institution has several accreditation relationships (Kells and Parrish, 1979). Progress has recently been made in countering this practice. Many accrediting bodies have begun to emphasize self-study processes that are useful to the institution and yield, as important by-products, useful reports for the team.

Ten Desired Attributes of Self-Study Processes

The self-study process must be conducted so that its inherent rewards for the institution or a program will be realized. Problems should be assessed and solved. The following attributes are desirable in a self-study of either an institution or a program.

1. Self-study should be internally motivated rather than seen merely as a response to an outside agency.
2. The top leadership of the institution or program must be committed to self-study and must express this commitment formally, both in writing and orally.
3. The design of the self-study must be appropriate to the circumstances of the institution or the program.
4. The process should include an informed attempt to clarify goals and to assess goal achievement.

5. There should be representative, appropriate, and useful participation by members of the various segments of the education community under study.
6. The process must be well led. Effective group process, problem-clarification and problem-solving techniques, staff work, and group leadership must be used.
7. The ability of the organization to function effectively should be studied and enhanced.
8. Some improvement should occur both during and as a result of the process.
9. A readable report, potentially useful to several audiences, should result from the process.
10. A better system of ongoing institutional research, self-analysis, and self-improvement should be a major product of the process.

A recent analysis of self-study employed in the 1970s during institutional accreditation procedures (Kells and Kirkwood, 1979) indicated clearly that the first three attributes were positively related to perceived satisfaction with the self-study process. The analysis also pointed out that perceived satisfaction was not related to any particular institutional characteristics (type, size, sponsorship, degree level) or to any specified way of approaching the process (structure, cost, and participant levels). Apparently, with the right design, motivation, and leadership, any institution can have a useful self-study process.

Procedures for Self-Study

Designing an appropriate self-study process is crucial if the goals of self-study are to be achieved. Whether self-study is connected with an accreditation visit or not, it must be designed to meet the particular circumstances of the institution or program. If all institutions or programs were basically the same—in age, size, complexity, stage of development, needs, problems, goals, planning process, data system, and research programs—then all could approach self-study the same way, and all or most would achieve the goals of self-study. But, of course, they differ markedly. Thus, some institutions or programs have a need for comprehensive study, and some do not. Some must emphasize certain items on their own current agenda quite to the exclusion of other factors, because most have a list of "must fix" problems and "must do" activities. The procedures that follow are completely applicable to both institutional and specialized accreditation.

Through any type of design approach, all or most of the ten desired attributes of self-study should be achievable. In most designs, the basic procedure is intended to obtain answers to the following groups of questions:

- What are the institution's or program's intentions or goals? Are they clear, appropriate, and useful? Are they understood? Is there a consensus on them?
- Are the resources (human, fiscal, and physical) available to carry out the programs and services? Will they continue to be available?
- Are the goals being achieved? How can systematically gathered evidence about the extent of achievement be used to improve the institutions or programs?

When a self-study is related to an accreditation visit, the procedure should also seek to answer another set of questions:

- Are the standards of the accrediting body being met? If there are specific criterion levels for some of the standards, are they appropriate for the program(s) concerned? If not, why? What is appropriate? Why?

Steps in the Self-Study Process. Five steps are usually taken to help answer these questions. They must be present in any self-study process if the purposes and goals (the ten desired attributes) are to be realized by a given institution or program. These steps have been established through analysis of successful self-study processes (Kells and Kirkwood, 1979), and they continue to be confirmed as essential to the process by graduates of self-study workshops. The five steps are as follows:

Step One: Prepare for and Design the Study Process.

- Establish leadership and internal motivation.
- Draw up a specific list of local needs or issues.
- Identify local circumstances to take into account in designing the study.

Step Two: Organize the Study Process.

- Define tasks and roles.
- Establish a means for guiding the study—a steering structure.
- Select, orient, and train people.
- Obtain resources.
- Establish work groups.
- Define the sequence of events.
- Establish coordination and communication mechanisms.

Step Three: Pay Attention to the Mechanics
of the Study Process.

- Work with stated intentions (goals)—clarify them and study them for consensus, completeness, and priority.
- Examine input, environment, program, and process.
- Review accreditation standards—use useful, valid criterion levels applicable to the institution or program.
- Use instruments to assist with gathering facts and opinions.
- Undertake goal achievement (outcomes) studies.
- Discuss results and prepare a useful report.
- Use the results—implement changes.

Step Four: Use Peers.

- Use consultants.
- Use the team visit.
- Work well with outside organizations.

Step Five: Establish Cycles of Study and Planning.

- Use self-study as a basis for planning.
- Increase ongoing institutional research.

Nature of the Work. Most institutions use both work groups and assignments to individuals to accomplish the study task. The overall effort is usually managed by a steering committee or coordinating group. To achieve the goals for self-study, certain activities must be conducted. Records must be reviewed, and data must be assembled from within the institution. Facts and opinions must be gathered from many persons. In the process, questions must be posed, and answers to questions and solutions to problems must be sought. New ideas must be generated. Final documents must be produced, following the drafting of materials, discussions, written reaction, and final editing. When the documents are in final form, the results must be discussed and implemented.

The exact configuration of work groups and other assignments will vary depending on the study design. A comprehensive self-study process usually employs a series of work groups in some sequence that will work well for the institution in question. These groups are usually charged with considering the status, strengths, weaknesses, problems, and proposed new solutions in areas such as these:

- Goals (or mission, goals, and objectives)
- The student body
- The faculty (or faculty and instruction)
- The program (possibly taking undergraduate and graduate programs separately)
- Student services
- Educational services (possibly a separate group for the library or learning center)
- Administrative services (including physical plant)
- Organization and governance
- Finance
- Research (if research is a function of the institution)
- Public services (or continuing education or community services)
- Goal achievement (outcomes)

A less comprehensive study may touch on only some of these areas. Such a study may also employ work groups to explore special topics in depth and over varying periods of time according to the design developed for the study. Of special concern, for example, and therefore receiving special attention, may be such topics as governance, financial planning, or the relation between liberal and career studies.

Preparing a Useful Report. Only part of the impact of a self-study is expressed through the final report. Some improvements should have occurred before the report is written. But the report conveys most of the messages and all of the remaining commitments to study, to act, and to change. Obviously, it ought to be well done.

The report should be clearly written and well organized. Readability is very important and may make all the difference for some readers. Some people discard or strongly discount a poorly written report. The report should be concise. Bulky reports are often necessary for large institutions, but a self-study report longer than 200 pages is too fatiguing for the reader. A good size is about 100 pages or fewer—back-to-back and single-spaced. The report should be a frank and balanced view of the institution or program. Both strengths and areas for improvement (and the strategies and commitments to change) should be included. The report should be useful for several audiences—a point often forgotten. When a report describing an institution and its strengths and opportunities is well written, it can conceivably be used with the board of trustees, potential donors, state agencies, staff members, student leaders, and one or more accrediting bodies. Finally, if the report is to be used for accreditation purposes, it should include systematic references showing how the standards of the accrediting body are met and how the definition of an accredited institution is met. For topically oriented reports, an indexing scheme is useful in this regard.

Improving Self-Study Processes

Increasingly, the leaders of American postsecondary education—including the officials of its accrediting bodies—are coming to the conclusion that self-regulation is important to the autonomy and viability of institutions and programs. Self-regulation requires two levels of effective action. The first is strong internal management—planning, organizing, staffing, directing (which includes motivating and leading), and control (consisting of study as well as action). Strong internal management permits the institution to stay in control of its destiny and prevents government agencies from stepping in, thus protecting the public trust in the institution. The second level of action required by self-regulation is collective nongovernmental activity by institutions. Collective action by peer institutions serves to strengthen internal activity by a single institution toward achieving the same goals.

Self-study that is properly integrated into an ongoing, useful cycle of study and planning at the institution can effectively improve internal management. The process of self-study itself can be improved if the following steps are taken:

1. Institutional leaders and program directors can improve self-studies by giving them high priority and demanding that the investment in the process yield benefits for the institution or program. Just getting or staying on the accredited list is usually expensive and energy-diverting unless the programs being studied produce other direct benefits as well.

2. Self-study efforts must be designed to yield desired results, taking into account institutional circumstances and studies being conducted for other accrediting bodies. Design affects organization, cost, attitudes, timing, and results.

3. More attention must be given to making work groups function better. Group skills, group leadership, problem identification, and problem solving must be improved if self-study, planning, and similar processes are to be more effective.

4. Self-study processes can yield—and should be expected to yield—a much stronger capacity for ongoing institutional research.

5. Self-studies should be conducted more frequently, be less comprehensive, and have a sharper focus. They would then be more acceptable to participants and more useful to institutions.

6. Self-studies and ongoing planning processes should be more

integrated, more interdependent, and more continuous. The self-study process should not be terminated until the first stages of the subsequent planning process are begun. External requests can be more readily satisfied by a solid cycle of study and planning.

Institutions must move to improve self-study processes if they hope to decrease external influences and retain control of their destiny. The heart of the accreditation process—self-study—should become the heart of the institution's efforts to plan, manage, and improve its programs and services.

Part Three

჻჻჻჻჻჻჻჻჻჻჻჻჻჻჻჻჻჻჻჻჻჻჻჻჻

Accrediting Bodies

Voluntary, nongovernmental accrediting bodies are not completely private entities. Over time, in fact, they have become quasi-public organizations and as such must serve a broader social purpose beyond just meeting members' needs. How can "social need" be judged, and who should make that determination? These are central questions that continue to be debated.

The debate is complicated by the fact that accrediting bodies actually carry out many related activities; they sponsor or conduct research, develop policies, issue publications, operate training programs, and influence the directions of postsecondary education in a number of ways. Their most central role, however, is to organize and conduct an effective accreditation program; and this responsibility involves a sequence of actions and a host of participants—most importantly, the key people in the institution undergoing accreditation.

Although accrediting bodies have many common characteristics, they also differ widely in scope, sponsorship, and structure. The most significant difference relates to their focus,

133

the two major forms of accreditation being institutional and specialized (or program). The regional organizations are the best known of the institutional accrediting bodies; and even they vary in history, size, organization, and personality. The specialized accrediting bodies, however, are even more disparate. Decision makers in colleges and universities, outside a given specialization, rarely are familiar with these groups and the important roles they play.

8

Charles M. Chambers

‍‍‍‍‍‍‍‍‍‍‍‍‍‍‍‍‍‍‍‍‍‍‍‍‍‍‍‍‍‍‍‍‍

Characteristics of an Accrediting Body

> *This fear of the untypical, this quest for security within the walls of secular uniformity—these are traits of our national character we would do well to beware of and to examine their origins.*
> George F. Kennan (1953)

Seventy years ago there were no accrediting bodies. Today there are more than fifty that are nationally recognized as members of the Council on Postsecondary Accreditation (COPA). Approximately three times that number of associations are currently developing some type of credentialing process to apply to some aspect of postsecondary education. At least two dozen of these groups have initiated formal accreditation activities over the last few years. Although not every discipline or specialty has an accrediting body, some are covered by two or more competing groups. With so many accrediting bodies already, whether to create any new ones is a substantial, complex, and difficult question.

Accrediting bodies, both old and new, in general tend to

justify their work in terms of assuring educational quality and protecting the public. Further, new accrediting groups often point to emerging bodies of knowledge and argue that a need for accreditation, which did not exist before, does now—particularly to avoid confusion among students and the public about which programs are quality programs. Although the college or university is the major supporter and the primary user of accreditation, as well as the source of most volunteers, outside groups—particularly accrediting bodies—exert a profound influence on postsecondary educational institutions. And although the vast majority of small colleges rarely have more than three accreditations, several hundred institutions—such as state university systems and large community college districts—must undergo numerous evaluations from outside groups on what seems an almost perpetual cycle.

Accreditation is often described as a voluntary process. The obvious inference is that if institutions were not getting what they wanted, they could easily drop any superfluous accreditations. In reality, large institutions are complex organizations, and the reasons, pro and con, that influence a decision to invite an accrediting body to the campus are frequently intertwined with many other aspects of institutional and professional life. Careful analysis is required to determine whether the decision is sound.

In addition, given the growth of accrediting groups in the wake of the post–World War II boom in veterans' education, the postsecondary education community has been scrutinizing quite carefully all proposals for new accrediting bodies. There is never any question that what is good can be made still better, but the growing effort to further fragment and subdivide disciplines and, usually, to create attendant accrediting bodies appears to many college officials to have reached the point of diminishing return. Their view is increasingly that the American postsecondary education enterprise must give careful consideration to the costs and benefits involved in taking such steps. Indeed, given the difficulty in assessing the benefits of accreditation, whether the accrediting body is helping the institution or vice versa is in many cases not clear.

These decisions—whether to support the creation of a new accrediting body and invite yet another accrediting body on campus—can be better made when the environment in which accreditation operates is better understood. What are the legal responsibilities of an accrediting body? How can social need be determined? How can quality in accreditation be assured? What governance processes, formal and informal, can be established to help balance the interests of the accreditors against the interests of the postsecondary education community and the public? Accrediting bodies, too, must thoroughly understand these issues to be effective and responsive to the needs of their constituencies.

Legal Nature of Accreditation

The interest of government in public safety and well-being has led to pervasive legal regulation. We obtain licenses to drive and to marry; we register cars and boats; the titles to our real estate are carefully searched, and deeds are properly recorded in local land records; our foods and medicines are inspected; our water is chlorinated; and our home mortgages are approved by the government. Teachers, nurses, engineers, and lawyers are certified, registered, licensed, or otherwise authorized to practice by various government agencies. Therefore, a not unreasonable assumption is that accrediting bodies, which have a quasi-regulatory effect on colleges and universities, are part of, or receive their authorization and jurisdiction from, some related government department or agency. The assumption is, of course, false.

Although statutes in several states authorize their education departments to "accredit" colleges and universities within their boundaries, the more widely accepted use of the term in education is for the process of self-study and peer review carried out by nongovernmental, private associations. Exercising their First Amendment rights of free assembly and speech, these groups establish their own scope of activities, define their own membership, and adopt their own standards, policies, and procedures. There are no laws or regulations that must be met or

government approval that must be obtained before an organization can function as an accrediting body. Usually, the only for-
mality is to obtain a charter to operate as a nonprofit corporation
or association from the state in which the parent organization is
located. At the same time, no accrediting body has any legal
authority to make any institution do anything. Put simply, anyone can become an accrediting body in any state. No permission
must be obtained nor any jurisdiction granted from any government department.

If an accrediting body has no legal power to control institutions, then how does it maintain its prominent position of influence in education? In the ideal situation, an accrediting body
establishes and maintains its reputation through a tradition of
competent activities and reliable decisions for the many users of
its services. This ideal view must be tempered by the realities of
postsecondary education administration. First, colleges and universities are complex organizations with power dispersed and
authority shared at all levels. Some accrediting bodies function
as advocates for their special interests within the institution,
and they can maintain their role because their clientele desires
accreditation. Second, other accrediting bodies have their accreditation linked to licensure or career mobility for graduates,
and most institutions have little choice but to invite them to
campus. Many accrediting bodies actively pursue close working
ties with government agencies to gain influence. For example,
accrediting bodies may be listed by the federal government to
establish part of the eligibility of their member institutions and
programs for certain federal funds. Or state licensing bodies
may use accreditation as a qualification for graduates to be considered for, or to receive, licenses to practice certain crafts or
trades.

An unfortunate consequence of the fact that accrediting
bodies are nongovernmental is that purveyors of fraudulent education are able to contrive their own accrediting groups to "accredit" their own "diploma mills." Over the past twenty years,
there have been a number of such organizations, and at least
two were in existence in 1982. Such accrediting bodies are, of
course, illegal in that they operate to defraud the public and

therefore violate any corporate charter issued to them by the
state. However, such violations do not deter the operators of
sham schools. Because there are no laws controlling the use of
the term *accreditation,* and accrediting bodies are not regulated
by government agencies, how can one determine whether a particular accrediting body is reputable? The education community
has evolved a voluntary system of oversight and self-regulation
for governing the accreditation process, and some accrediting
bodies are identified as nationally recognized, which in some
measure serves to separate the legitimate groups from the bogus
ones.

The Cost/Benefit Balance: Establishing Social Need

Within the postsecondary education community, there is
a wide range of views about the value of accreditation. At one
extreme are those who take the position that one can never
have too much of a good thing. Because a central purpose of accreditation is to identify where educational quality can be
found, students, in particular, will presumably be best served by
having a separate accrediting body for each specialty. The benefits are considered so overwhelming that they discount or offset
any concerns about the financial or other costs. At the other extreme are those who feel that the appropriate control site of
educational quality is the collegial governance of academic affairs by duly established faculties. Excellence in research and
scholarship is maintained through peer review within each discipline, and any supervision or control by an external group, such
as an accrediting body, can only diminish the vitality and vigor
of the educational enterprise. In this view, the standards, criteria, and guidelines of the accrediting body, regardless of how
skillfully and sensitively they are applied, inevitably tend to
stifle freedom of inquiry and lead to standardization and rigid-
ity, if not outrght dogmatic conformity. Any cost is too much
to pay, no matter what benefits might be obtained. Clearly, the
desirable situation lies somewhere between these two extremes.
Finding the balance to be struck when a new type of accreditation is proposed is indeed no small task. Yet, it must be mas-

tered if institutions are to honor their responsibilities while preserving their rights.

The cost/benefit concept can sometimes be applied in a
mathematical, dollars-and-cents fashion. The expenses incurred
to achieve a desired goal can be calculated, and if the benefits
are indeed worth more than the costs, then the proposal is approved. In an area as subjective as quality in education, the
terms *costs* and *benefits* must be interpreted broadly. Costs encompass the whole range of onerous burdens and potential compromises associated with a new accreditation process. Similarly,
benefits include all salutary consequences among many varied
constituents.

Of course, one person's costs may be another person's
benefits. For example, the ability to control entry into a profession through rigid accreditation standards might be considered
an important benefit in some quarters and an unacceptable cost
in others. In any event, the cost/benefit approach clearly provides a framework so that a decision-making process, broadly
representative and reasonably objective, can strike a balance between competing viewpoints. If after comprehensive, representative, and responsible review, the benefits of a proposed accreditation are found to exceed the costs, then a social need is
said to exist for that accreditation.

Each proposal for a new accrediting body or accreditation process or program must be examined on its own merits,
with reference to the community of interests ultimately affected. Therefore, whether social need exists cannot generally
be predicted, except in institutional accreditation, where society has fairly well established that the overall value exceeds (by
some measure) the costs involved. Further, there are established
accrediting bodies for virtually every type of postsecondary
educational institution. In specialized or programmatic accreditation, each proposal must be examined separately. Only a few
general observations can be made about establishing social need
for a new accrediting body.

Scope of an Accrediting Body. The starting point in assessing social need is a detailed statement of exactly what is to
be accredited. The scope of an accrediting body is generally

specified by demarcations such as geographical location, degree level, or discipline or field. For specialized accreditation, the nature of the profession needs to be specified, including any entry-level requirements, certification or licensing processes, and the relationships that exist with other disciplines and professions. Surprisingly, many new accrediting bodies pay little attention to this aspect and are able to give only a vague general description of what they seek to accredit.

By reasonably well-established national policy, accreditation in professional areas is limited to the educational programs that prepare students to begin working in that profession —known as first professional programs or entry-level programs. With a new accreditation process, the argument is frequently made that one of its intended benefits is to bring order and direction to a discipline. Although bringing focus to an emerging discipline is a worthy goal, introducing formal accreditation prematurely is generally recognized as hindering rather than helping. The reason for this apparent anomaly is that accreditation is, at its core, the professional judgments of a group of peers, and to be true peers, the group must share a mutual dedication to a well-defined area of study. Put simply: no peers, no accreditation. Establishing an accreditation process will do nothing to bring about a strong peer community if one does not exist. In fact, precisely the opposite can happen. For example, each of the three major theories of psychotherapy has its own group of dedicated practitioners, and each is seeking to establish its own accrediting body. However, until programs preparing psychotherapists become cohesive, an accrediting body representing any one theory would inevitably limit the influence of the other two, thereby perhaps eroding the overall peer community of therapists. Thus, accreditation is built on programs and not the other way around, and a well-defined scope related to a well-established area must be delineated clearly at the outset.

Clientele. Once there is a clear idea of what is to be accredited, the next step is to identify the particular institutions or programs that will be eligible to apply for accreditation if the accrediting body is established. Although there are no numerical quotas that an accrediting body must meet, information about the number of eligible institutions or programs is useful in determining how well established the area is within postsecondary education. In some highly specialized health professions, such as podiatry, the clientele could be as few as a half-dozen institutions, whereas in broad areas, such as teacher education, engineering, or business administration, several hundred would be normal.

Community of Interest. Accreditation, like most social activities, does not operate in a vacuum. Any accrediting body, existing or proposed, affects, to differing degrees, a host of related persons and organizations. Collectively, these outside groups, which have a strong influence on the cost/benefit balance, are generally referred to as the community of interest for the accrediting body. There is no formal definition for this community of interest, and its exact composition varies significantly from one area to another. Certain constituencies, however, are found in any such community, and in justifying the social need for new accreditation, there should be convincing evidence that each essential constituent strongly supports this need.

Essential constituencies in the community of interest include not only the institutions offering the education but also other professional societies and education associations in the same or related areas, employers of students graduating with accredited credentials, the students themselves, and the general public. The degree of concern that each of these groups has about the accreditation depends on the circumstances, but eight constituencies that have been identified as being the most integral parts of the community of interest can be listed in the following rough order of priority:

1. Chief executive officers of institutions to be accredited.
2. Deans, directors, and faculty members of specialized programs to be accredited.
3. Affiliated groups of students.
4. Professional societies and individual practitioners in the field to be accredited.
5. Employers of graduates of accredited programs.
6. Groups representing related disciplines and professions.

7. Other organizations carrying out accreditation in the same or closely related areas.
8. Agencies responsible for certification and licensing of practitioners, state education planning and coordinating boards, and similar bodies.

Given the diverse types of education available throughout the country, even such an extensive list might not include interested parties whose views should be considered in a particular case in judging the overall social need. Accordingly, to be sure that no important viewpoint is overlooked, an open call for comment from any interested member of the public must generally be published. New accrediting bodies sometimes argue that this approach should be the only way comment is obtained. Their feeling is that postsecondary educational institutions and related professional societies should not be surveyed directly. Rather, if they decline to respond to a public call for comment, then they presumably have no objections to the new accrediting body. At the same time, such a group would doubtless campaign vigorously among its own supporters to be sure there was a healthy, positive response. Obviously, the fallacy in this approach is that no legitimate social need can be established unless the opinions of the primary constituents are directly solicited. No formal ballot is taken to show that a majority of the community of interest supports the new accrediting body. Rather, a considered judgment must be made, based on all the responses, that there is (or is not) a convincing consensus within the community of interest that social need does exist for some additional form of formal quality assessment.

Appropriateness of Accreditation. Is accreditation the appropriate process for evaluating and assuring educational quality? There are a host of evaluative methods that can be applied to education, and accreditation is one of the most complex and costly of the lot. The need for quality assessment might be fulfilled by an alternative such as state registration, certification, program approval, and validation. If an alternative is less onerous and still serves the intended goals and social needs, then accreditation should not be considered. The relative complexity of accreditation stems from the fact that it rarely seeks to impose prescriptive standards or quantitative criteria of measurement in evaluating education. Rather, it attempts to assess the soundness of the goals established by the institution or program and how well they are being achieved, while permitting a large amount of flexibility, diversity, and innovation. To obtain sound results, an elaborate and expensive process of comprehensive self-study by the institution is required, as well as a carefully structured external peer review in which judicious standards and criteria are applied.

Appropriateness of the Organization. Must the accrediting body proposing the accreditation process be the one to conduct it? This question is frequently an uncomfortable one for a new accrediting body. Because it first brought forth the idea of the new accreditation and doubtless has devoted much time and effort to developing the process, it understandably feels that it has some sort of "patent" that makes it the only organization that should offer the process. However, social need is built on a much broader perspective, and the best cost/benefit balance must be sought among all the participating groups and not just from a single organization, the one that happened to step forward first.

Relationship to Other Accrediting Bodies. The final element in establishing social need is to determine how the actual service can be provided most effectively and efficiently. If there is an existing accrediting body in a closely related area, then whether the need can be met through that body, either alone or in collaboration with the proposed new accreditation body, must be explored carefully. Creating a new umbrella organization to cover any existing related ones and the proposed new accrediting process may even be beneficial. In addition to possible financial savings, this approach can avoid undesirable duplication among closely related accrediting bodies—a situation that can pose an extra burden for educational institutions, result in inconsistent and contradictory accreditation decisions, and cause confusion among students, employers, institutions, and the general public about the quality of the programs being offered.

Social need is complex, but it cannot and must not be ignored. Accreditation entails a heavy burden of added expense to the educational process. It also carries inherent risks of standardization and narrowness in curricula, as well as the disintegration of professional preparation in those parts that do not have accreditation and possibly the larger curricular area. Consequently, the need for a new accreditation process should not be established simply because a group of well-intentioned educators considers it desirable but rather because there is a widely accepted and generally endorsed need for the accreditation and strong benefits to be obtained by institutions and their students.

Quality in Accreditation

Like educational institutions, accrediting bodies are organizations of people, policies, and procedures, each of which directly influences how effective the accreditation process is. Because accreditation is concerned with quality in education, and because an accrediting body's decisions will be given much deference and relied on by many persons both within and outside education, society should expect—even demand—that any accrediting body will offer only the most reliable services of the highest quality. Done well, accreditation is an expensive process, but if the social need exists, then the benefits almost always outweigh the costs. Several significant factors enter into the judgment concerning the quality of a proposed accreditation process. None of them alone guarantees quality, but taken as a whole, they strengthen an accrediting body.

Autonomy. The accrediting body must have some degree of autonomy and operational independence in making accreditation decisions. Such autonomy ensures that the accrediting organization is not unduly subjected to political pressures and other forms of influence from a parent association that may have too narrow a perspective, such as a professional association of practitioners or a state licensing body. No one organizational structure guarantees or prevents such operational independence. Rather, the nature of each accrediting body and its relationships to closely affiliated groups, especially those that provide funding, must be examined on a case-by-case basis. At the minimum, an accrediting body must be nongovernmental, because accreditation is a process of self-study and peer review. The self-study is intended to be an inherent part of the ongoing self-regulation of a duly constituted faculty and staff rather than an administrative process to produce a report imposed by an external agency. In addition, the word *peer* in *peer review* is closely entwined with the concept of academic freedom. A group of officials from a government agency, however well intentioned or well qualified, could not be considered peers because their loyalties would necessarily be to the government, not to the education community.

Due Process. Another important area that reflects the quality of an accrediting body is its attention to due process for institutions and programs. In the legal arena due process can be quite involved, relating to such detailed matters as the right to a free transcript of a trial. In accreditation due process pertains to basic elements of fairness and equity between the two parties. For example, a good accrediting body is expected to describe fully in official publications its scope, evaluative criteria, and procedures. It is also expected to process applications for accreditation fairly and to provide for appeals of accreditation actions and decisions. Further, it is expected to evaluate an institution or program only at the invitation of the chief executive officer and to maintain clear definitions of each accreditation status as well as written procedures for granting, denying, reaffirming, modifying, suspending, revoking, or reinstating accreditation.

A good accrediting body is expected to give appropriate consultation and guidance to institutions and programs about its accreditation process and to provide opportunities during the campus visit for discussion between team members and faculty members, staff members, administrators, students, and other interested parties. Further, ample due process permits the chief executive officer of the institution to have both the opportunity and the time to comment on the report of the visiting team before accreditation actions are considered. An accrediting body is also expected to provide written notification of decisions, giving reasons for the actions. Good practice in accreditation requires that the institution receive an evaluation report, which it is free to distribute, but that the accrediting body will, insofar as possible, maintain the confidentiality of aspects of the accreditation process that, if disclosed, would jeopardize the purposes of accreditation and weaken the process. During the preliminary review phase, a degree of confidentiality is necessary so that mutual reputations are not called into doubt before an objective judgment is made and political maneuvering and public grandstanding do not erode the ability of the accrediting body to make a sound review. Finally, an accrediting body committed to due process will permit the withdrawal of a request for accreditation at any time and will not change the current accredited status of an institution or program until all appeals have been exhausted.

Accountability. A feature that is a hallmark of excellence in accreditation is an accrediting body's accountability to the public. In recent years, the attention given by an accrediting body to the public interest has become an increasingly important element in litigation. Because many public groups are using accreditation decisions more and more, courts are requiring greater public responsibility by accrediting bodies (Kaplin, 1982). Regardless of judicial pressures, a reputable accrediting body that takes pride in having its accreditation decisions relied on and deferred to by business, government, and education should willingly adopt policies protecting the public interest. One important policy involves public representation in the affairs of the accrediting body. Another is public disclosure of significant information about its accreditation activities.

Of particular importance is effective public representation in an accrediting body's evaluation, policy-development, and decision-making processes. At the very least there should be public representatives on the accrediting commission. Some accrediting bodies also use them on visiting teams. Although the question of who can best represent the public is difficult to answer, the purpose of public representation is to avoid self-serving activities by a group of people who share a strong allegiance to a particular area. Despite honest intentions, experience has shown that such groups tend to favor vested interests over the public good. Further, because accreditation of postsecondary educational institutions is technically complex, public representatives should ideally be generally knowledgeable about education and, to a lesser degree, accreditation. They should also have no professional affiliation with the institutions or programs being accredited or the related career fields.

Increasingly, public accountability for accrediting bodies also involves public disclosure. A responsible accrediting body makes all official documents describing its activities and procedures publicly available. At least once a year it also publishes a current listing of all institutions or programs accredited. It makes public all final accreditation actions taken; if, after all appeals and other opportunities for mediation are concluded, an accrediting body does not disclose a negative decision, then its public credibility is greatly compromised. Although there should be confidentiality during the evaluation phase, the need no longer exists when a final decision is reached. To fail to disclose a final decision would only reinforce the impression that accreditation is little more than a private club devoted solely to the vested interests of its members, not to the interest of the public at large. The exact details of the accreditation review, such as those found in the team report, may remain confidential between the accrediting body and the institution. Should the institution release distorted and misleading information about its accreditation, however, the accrediting body has a responsibility to correct the public record by releasing part or all of the official report. Finally, the responsible accrediting body makes publicly available the academic and professional qualifications of persons serving in policy, decision-making, and administrative capacities.

Other Characteristics. Quality in accreditation is, of course, frequently related to the separate steps in the process. For example, each accrediting body should—

- Have fiscal integrity in its budgetary support.
- Have a staff well qualified to maintain effective evaluation procedures.

- Appoint to visiting teams only persons who are competent by virtue of experience, training, and orientation to develop and articulate objective opinions and decisions that are free of self-interest and professional bias.
- Design data-gathering instruments that stimulate self-evaluation and improvement, but which require only data directly related to the accreditation process and make maximum use of information already available in the institution.
- Review its evaluation criteria and procedures periodically and modify them when necessary, but only after providing advance notice and opportunity for comment by affected persons, institutions, and organizations.
- Recognize the right of institutions or programs to be evaluated in light of their own stated purposes, as long as those purposes are consistent with purposes generally recognized by the postsecondary education community and are appropriate to the scope of the accrediting body.
- Develop and interpret its evaluation standards and criteria to not merely allow but also encourage institutional freedom and autonomy and ensure that they are clearly relevant to evaluating the quality of institutions or programs.
- Evaluate an institution or a program in relation to the operational goals of the total institution, to the expected educational outcomes of the program or programs, and to the carefully developed criteria or standards of the accrediting body.

Just as quality in education is subjective, so too is quality in accreditation. Many new accrediting bodies approach their task by reproducing, with appropriate editorial changes, the handbooks, criteria, standards, and other written materials of an established accrediting body. They then feel secure that they are doing as good a job as anyone else. Unfortunately, this approach overlooks the fact that good accreditation is predominantly substantive rather than procedural. An emphasis on format and process can give a false impression of quality. The history of accreditation has shown that an accrediting body must devote years of continued attention to the substantive aspects of accreditation before it is recognized as a true equal among its peers.

For specialized accreditation to work, the subject area of the programs to be accredited must reflect a recognized body of knowledge organized around an established faculty devoted to the field. Proposals to accredit spin-off programs, which may be only variations on the theme of a more established discipline, must be viewed cautiously to be sure that the peer-based evaluation inherent in accreditation can actually be accomplished. With a newly emerging subspecialty, a need for evaluation (for licensing, for example) should not, in and of itself, call for accreditation unless and until the subject matter base on which accreditation exists has been developed.

Governance of Accreditation

Any accrediting body is unlikely to be so motivated by altruism and public service that it would take on and pursue to an absolute conclusion all the matters presented in the preceding sections of this chapter. Yet, the fact that an ideal may be Olympian in its challenge is no reason not to work toward it. Some accrediting bodies are serving these ideals, postsecondary education, and the public well indeed. These goals are not as elusive as a new accrediting body might want to pretend. The question is, therefore, what practical incentive is there for any accrediting body to serve legitimate social needs in the highest-quality fashion?

Accreditation is the postsecondary education community's main form of self-regulation. The *governance* of accreditation is itself an important element of self-regulation. In a country where *caveat emptor* ranks only slightly behind motherhood and the flag, institutions might conceivably turn down accreditation services from the shabbier accrediting bodies. Unfortunately, accreditation does not operate in a freely competitive market; consumer forces alone cannot improve its quality (see Chapter Twelve). In fact, some institutions might prefer a less demanding, marginally effective accrediting body, and Gresham's law would operate, so that the truly sterling accrediting bodies would be driven out by the inferior ones. The problem of governance is further complicated by the inordinate leverage that accrediting bodies, as centralized, coordinating organizations, have over individual institutions. The cyclical evaluation by an accrediting body is not often a time of great institutional courage. Few institutions want to risk censure before their peers. Even if all the institutions held an accrediting body in disregard, probably not a single one would break ranks, for fear that it would lose accreditation and be judged inferior to the others. The potential therefore exists for the entire accreditation process to deteriorate to little more than a cunning charade by an institution to keep its accreditation while it ignores the goals and spirit of accreditation.

Clearly, the hope that all the best aspects of accreditation will come together spontaneously—simply because all the constituents have a fair and balanced view of their roles and responsibilities—is unreasonable. The internal tensions are just too strong. As long as thirty years ago, the postsecondary education community realized that it needed to bring about direct national supervision and coordination of accreditation, so that institutions would be well served and the public interest protected. This form of self-regulation, sometimes called "accrediting the accreditors," was conducted for specialized accrediting bodies by the National Commission on Accrediting (NCA) from 1948 until 1975. It then merged with the Federation of Regional Accrediting Commissions of Higher Education (FRACHE) to form the Council on Postsecondary Accreditation (COPA). With offices in Washington, COPA reviews its member accrediting bodies at least once every five years. COPA is supported by the postsecondary education community as the chosen instrument in accreditation and is the only nongovernmental organization through which an accrediting body can formally achieve national recognition.

In its work with accrediting bodies, COPA functions in two distinct roles. First, COPA conducts an exploratory process to enable both it and interested groups to determine whether there is social need for accreditation in a new area and, if so, which body or bodies can be expected to deliver the services that meet the standards for national recognition. In essence, COPA has organized a cost/benefit analysis in what it terms the preapplicant process. Second, COPA conducts a formal process of review through which accrediting bodies are officially recognized. COPA has developed specific provisions and procedures that assess how well an accrediting body is meeting standards of good practice (see Resource B). The purpose of recognition is to enable institutions to identify competent, reputable, and experienced accrediting bodies that follow national standards of good practice and professional responsibility.

Although the process is supposed to be voluntary, and each postsecondary institution is theoretically free to engage in as many accreditation relationships as it considers appropriate, formal recognition of accrediting bodies by a national coordinating council provides third-party assurance that an accrediting body is reputable and its services generally acceptable. Further, because recognition is based on compliance with COPA's published provisions, an institution that feels it has not been treated fairly by a recognized accrediting body can request COPA to review that body's continued compliance with the provisions. Institutions are encouraged, but not required, to deal only with COPA-recognized accrediting bodies and are urged to exercise great caution in inviting nonrecognized accrediting groups to their campuses. Not only might they find the experience less than satisfactory, but affiliation with a nonrecognized accrediting body gives it perhaps undue stature with other institutions.

An accrediting body that fulfills a well-documented social need and meets standards of good practice can achieve recognition in the postsecondary education community through COPA; it will then have established its credentials as a reliable and reputable accrediting body. Without COPA endorsement, an accrediting body cannot truly be considered to have become nationally recognized. COPA addresses the accreditation concerns not only of institutions and their leaders but also of accrediting bodies and the public, who are represented in COPA's policymaking and recognition activities. Becoming a recognized accrediting body is an arduous task, but perhaps nowhere other than in accreditation is the adage more applicable: "If something is worth doing, it is worth doing well." By supporting COPA, institutions support quality in accreditation and, therefore, quality in education.

9

H. R. Kells

ᖰᎾ

Roles of
Accrediting Bodies

> *The administrators of all institutions of higher edu-*
> *cation . . . and all so-called professionals should*
> *definitely have a close and accurate understanding*
> *of accreditation in all its ramifications, general and*
> *special. The accrediting process cannot live and*
> *prosper without their appreciation and sympathic*
> *support.*   Roy J. Deferrari (1959, p. iv)

The nature of power and decision making in accrediting bodies and the policies and procedures they use are only vaguely
understood by most people in postsecondary education. Historians of education and students of American academic governance are beginning to view accreditation as a unique enterprise worthy of study, and representatives from an increasing
number of other nations have been seeking information about
this interesting voluntary activity and the groups that conduct
it. On the campus, however, knowledge about accreditation is
scant and probably varies with position in the institutional hierarchy and with the nature of the accrediting body, the activities
of its staff, and how much time has elapsed since the last major
review of accredited status.

The mythology about accrediting bodies—that the "agency" says this and forbids that, always does this and expects that —is pervasive and often untrue. These myths are not surprising, however, because the average length of tenure in postsecondary education leadership positions is probably now no longer than the average length of time between the review cycles in accreditation, and the leaders in the institution or the program are the major points of contact for the accrediting bodies. Although the process seems to be more open now, involving more people in more junior positions, general knowledge about accrediting bodies and their specific role in the process is meager. Understanding the nature of accrediting bodies as they continue to evolve is important in illuminating the expectations—both reasonable and unreasonable—that people have of them.

Accreditation is one expression of a unique American voluntarism, a form that has developed over the last century and is still maturing—still defining its terms, its boundaries, its forms, and even its purposes (see Chapter Two). Accrediting bodies are (or are part of) nonprofit corporations that are chartered in one of the states but operate nationally or regionally. Each accrediting body usually pursues general educational purposes and, as expressed in its bylaws, the specific purposes of (1) identifying institutions or programs that seem to be achieving their goals and are judged to meet the standards of the accrediting body and (2) helping institutions and programs improve. The general purposes, organizational structure, staffing patterns, and nature of the accreditation process of all recognized accrediting bodies have certain similarities: They are required to meet the criteria for recognition by COPA, the Council on Postsecondary Accreditation (see Resource B), and they have an official accrediting commission, a staff, standards, procedures, an office, and a base of financial support through dues or fees.

Although the recognized accrediting bodies share certain characteristics to a greater or lesser extent, they are quite diverse in their form and their processes, as well as their budgets (see Chapter One). The latter range from a few thousand dollars a year to several hundred thousand. Accrediting bodies vary in the nature of sponsorship from those sponsored by vast numbers of entire institutions organized through a regional association (such as the North Central Commission on Institutions of Higher Education, one of several operating units of the North Central Association of Colleges and Schools) to those sponsored by a handful of schools or programs in a single discipline operating through a committee or board that functions for the professional association or society in that discipline (Council on Postsecondary Accreditation, 1978a; Petersen, 1980). Some accrediting bodies actively cooperate with one another to establish common terms, data and self-study requirements, time schedules, and the potential for joint or concurrent evaluation-team visits. Other accrediting bodies may be working in total isolation.

Accrediting bodies range in size from memberships of about a dozen programs or schools to as many as 1,000 institutions or 3,000 programs. The staff may consist of a single person or a large group of professionals. The role of the staff varies substantially from office-bound to field-based, from relatively passive servants of the accrediting group to active, nationally visible leaders who guide the development of policy, and from consultants to member institutions to active participants in the evaluation process.

The nature of the self-study process expected by accrediting bodies ranges from the filling out of forms by an officer of the institution (not a study process in any sense) to a useful, thorough, well-designed, participatory process. The accrediting body's criteria may or may not have evolved through serious study of the desired outcomes of programs and may or may not have been subjected to any type of validation over time (American Assembly of Collegiate Schools of Business, 1980). The accreditation decision may be made by a small committee in a larger organization, or it may be an action of the entire sponsoring membership of the association or society (Council on Postsecondary Accreditation, 1978a).

One dimension of what accrediting bodies are strikes at the very heart of the American postsecondary educational system (or "nonsystem," as our European friends and forebears have often exclaimed), and it is something that educators neglect at their peril. Accrediting bodies are the institutions and programs that compose their membership, or they should be. If institutional leaders are not familiar with the members of the institutional accrediting commission, its staff, and the criteria it professes, accrediting bodies are weaker and less responsive as a consequence. If an accreditation review is something to be "dealt with," handled rapidly, and forgotten—rather than a rare and useful opportunity to promote self-knowledge, improvement, and useful interaction with peers—then the postsecondary education community is less strong and less accountable, and self-regulation is less than effective. If chief academic officers do not become acquainted with the specialized accrediting bodies that accredit their programs, they will be making decisions about these programs without vital information. If department heads or program directors do not participate actively in the improvement of specialized accreditation procedures, the ongoing validation of criteria, and the organized, effective life of the discipline and its self-regulation, the system is weaker. *We,* not *they,* should be at the center of educators' consciousness about standards and improvement, both in specialized fields and throughout institutions.

The first message, then, about the role of accrediting bodies, and what institutions and programs can expect when working with them, has to do with knowledge and participation. The institution or program that wants to get the most out of interacting with an accrediting body must first know it—its organizational affiliation, financial base, accrediting-commission members, staff members, services provided, policies, criteria, procedures to be followed, and how policies and procedures are formulated and reviewed. If the accrediting body's publications do not provide the information, institutions must ask for it. For leaders in a system of postsecondary education that is characterized by self-regulation, not to know, understand, and participate in the major processes of self-regulation can only lead to unfortunate circumstances for the system and its institutions.

If institutions are to gain the most useful experience and play a responsible role in governing and improving the accreditation process, they must understand the five major roles of the responsible accrediting body. Not only are these roles manifest in the activities of accrediting bodies, but they also point to what institutions should expect from accrediting bodies.

Role Number One:
To Become Recognized by COPA

Recognition by the Council on Postsecondary Accreditation serves to assure the public that the accrediting body has sufficient status in the field, resources, and experience to effectively fulfill its responsibilities. Such recognition also serves to identify appropriate accrediting bodies and thereby to limit confusion, duplication of effort, and the dispersion of valuable time and talent by institutions, programs, and accrediting bodies. Institutions are probably wise to work only with recognized accrediting bodies. For fields or professional areas without a recognized accrediting body, the institution should greet any suggestion that it seek accreditation from an unrecognized accrediting body with carefully posed questions about sponsorship; resources; reasons that the organization is not recognized by COPA; staff assistance available from the agency; how, when, and by whom the standards were formulated; costs; and due process.

Role Number Two:
To Involve Institutional Leaders and the Public in the
Governance and Administration of the Accreditation
Process, Including the Formulation of Standards

Some of the most knowledgeable persons in the field should be included as leaders. As elected (or appointed) members of the accrediting board or in other capacities (evaluation-team chairpersons or team members, consultants, and advisers), they should assist the staff of the accrediting body.

Through involvement of institutional leaders, the accrediting body should maintain policies and procedures at the highest professional level. Accreditation standards should be reviewed regularly and studied over time for their validity. Such studies can culminate in evidence of predictive validity for some of the standards—evidence that shows that application of the standards will result in competent professional practice by graduates or in other intended outcomes of the programs being accredited. Although many accrediting bodies circulate their standards widely for review during the formulation process, relatively little effort has been expended by accrediting bodies toward more sophisticated analyses. Several accrediting bodies are conducting opinion surveys of their constituencies concerning the validity of their standards. A few, such as the Association of Theological Schools, have launched extensive predictive validity studies. Others, such as the American Assembly of Collegiate Schools of Business, are making a concerted effort to base standards on intended program outcomes.

The institution or program interacting with an accrediting body should certainly ascertain whether the leaders in its peer group are involved with the accrediting body; whether the policies, procedures, and standards have been widely scrutinized and are examples of the best professional practice; whether the standards have been or are regularly reviewed and studied; and whether there is a role for its best people in these processes. Positive, professional responses from accrediting bodies to such inquiries may reasonably be expected; yet, accrediting bodies are only recently becoming more active in this area, and much remains to be done.

The public is now represented in the accreditation process through membership on the accrediting commissions or advisory boards. During the past ten years, accrediting bodies have recognized their quasi-public role—which came about through the federal government's use of accreditation in questions of eligibility for certain funds—by placing members of the public on these boards (see Selden and Porter, 1977; Kaplin, 1982). In addition, the consumer movement has resulted in increased awareness of certain public-interest issues in accreditation standards. A recent example is the increased awareness of the COPA requirement that accrediting bodies publish all final accreditation actions for institutions or programs. Institutions can therefore expect accrediting bodies to show greater concern about the public interest in general.

Role Number Three:
To Secure Resources and a Staff Qualified to Conduct
an Effective Accreditation Program

Institutions and programs should expect to receive clearly written, complete, and useful publications; to be served by a procedure that can be conducted in a timely manner; to have effective access to an accrediting body's staff members by telephone, correspondence, and training sessions or field visits; and to interact with well-trained staff members who have experience, stature in their field, and an understanding of the theoretical and practical aspects of evaluation and organizational development.

Many accrediting bodies serve national constituencies or large regions of the country. An underfunded group therefore cannot provide staff services on other than an office-bound, "come to us" basis. Its ability to respond to inquiries in a timely and effective way, or with its general program of review, will necessarily be limited. Staff members without stature in their field or region cannot command the necessary respect of campus leaders and will have difficulty gaining the necessary level of participation by busy leaders or "flagship" institutions or programs. When staff members lack understanding of evaluation and improvement strategies, the result can be faulty or severely limited standards, guild-oriented programs, and an accreditation process that is not useful to the institution. The role and competence of accrediting-body staff members and staff development for them have, unfortunately, received almost no attention in formal studies.

Role Number Four:
To Organize and Conduct an Effective
Accreditation Program

The recipient of accreditation services should expect, of course, to periodically experience a basic sequence of three steps: (1) an opportunity for useful self-analysis in light of accreditation standards and stated organizational or program goals;

(2) a visit by qualified and appropriate peers who examine the institution or program in light of its self-examination to verify satisfactory compliance with accreditation standards and goal achievement and, if possible, to assist the institution to develop; and (3) an accrediting action by the body empowered to act that takes into account the self-study report, the visitors' report, and any institutional response. Each step entails an additional sequence of activities that institutions and programs should understand.

Self-Study. Institutions and programs seeking accreditation should expect the accrediting body to include self-study as part of its operating procedures. The focus should be on self-study as a useful process, as opposed to the mere requirement to fill out some forms or produce a report. The institution or program should be provided with handbooks and any necessary staff advice or assistance, preferably through well-run training sessions or on-campus contact. If the accrediting body does not sponsor self-study workshops, and most do not, it should assist institutional representatives in enrolling in workshops conducted by other accrediting groups. In general, staff assistance with self-study processes by accrediting bodies is superficial. Institutions with multiple accreditation relationships should strive to create a sequence of self-study that will, with a minimum of duplication, meet the needs of the institution and each of the accrediting bodies with which it deals.

Evaluation-Team Visits. This aspect of the accreditation process can be and often is quite effective, but it varies greatly from one accrediting body to another. Many leaders in accreditation think it needs much more emphasis.

At the minimum, institutions and programs receiving an accreditation review should expect that the accrediting body will select a group of visitors with ample and appropriate subject matter expertise who have been trained in some way to conduct an effective evaluation visit. The purpose of the visit should be to examine the institution or program in light of the standards of the accrediting body, and the evaluation team should begin its work by reviewing the self-study report. The teams, particularly those from institutional accrediting bodies,

should also focus on the extent to which the goals of the organization seem to be achieved and whether major programs and
services are effective. The visiting group should be expected to
interact thoroughly with the professional staff and students,
perhaps with alumni and community representatives, with members of the executive staff, and, in institutional reviews, with
the board of trustees. The team should strive to reach consensus on the elements of its report, present an oral summary before leaving the campus, and submit the written report shortly
after the visit.

There are many subtleties and variations in the purposes
of evaluation-team visits (many, for instance, are also intended
to assist the institution by providing advice) and the role of
accrediting-body staff members (some accrediting bodies send
a staff member with the team or even include one as an official
team member; many do not). There are also great variations in
team size and in attention given to matching the team with the
institution or program being evaluated. Some accrediting bodies
try to construct the team in a way that will match the nature of
issues addressed in the self-study. Most have their staff formulate a draft team roster and present it to the institution for comment or to eliminate possible conflict of interest. One accrediting body even permits the team chairperson to select the
members. Most accrediting bodies strive for complete objectiv-
ity in the evaluation team, in part by selecting team members
from other geographical areas to eliminate obvious program
competitors or detailed familiarity with the institution being
visited. Unfortunately, other accrediting bodies select team
members from relatively nearby institutions, a practice that can
produce a certain provincialism and even conflict of interest.

Of course, there is great variation in practice and—if intentions can be inferred from practice—in the apparent goals
for evaluation visits among the various accrediting bodies. Some
have been models of accountability, useful interaction, and professionalism. Most have functioned reasonably well. Some, however, have been bland, tedious, largely wasted exercises employing useless classroom visits to observe instruction and seeking
detailed verification of often unimportant facts presented in the
self-study documents. The most flagrant recent example was a

four-day visit by a specialized accreditation team that spent most of its time in such useless classroom visits and gave no oral summary report to the institution. The team chairperson permitted no discussion of the team's reactions to major issues in any group session or open meeting. During the visit, the team was preoccupied with details. It asked where the "seventh restroom listed in the facilities list" was—it could find only six. The team consisted of five professionals who had come a great distance at considerable expense to visit an institution that was in the middle of serious curriculum review and general reorganization. The institution was seeking, and could have benefited from, serious dialogue with the visiting team; it was afforded no opportunity for such interaction. Fortunately, this team's failure to fulfill the substantial potential of the evaluation-team part of the accreditation process is not the typical experience. Yet, it provides powerful evidence of the need to support a vigorous, cooperative interagency program of training for evaluation-team visitors.

Baysore (1971) examined the extent to which accrediting bodies trained team members, what they were taught, and how. The results were disappointing. Informal processes prevailed, and few structured, "hands on" workshops or simulation experiences were used. Although COPA reported in 1978 that almost all accrediting bodies conducted a periodic training workshop or seminar, recent studies indicate that much remains to be done to develop useful training materials and experiences. Training of evaluators should be based on theory as well as on hints about practice, moving well beyond the passive tools of lecture and visual aids. The training should be a dynamic process involving the evaluators in learning-by-doing through systematically guided practice. Some accrediting bodies are beginning to address the issue of training, and the comments and participation by member institutions and programs should stimulate further developments.

Institutions should fully explore the specific procedures and rationales for evaluation-team visits of the accrediting body with which they are working. The full potential of the visit can be achieved only if the institution actively helps the accrediting body set the tone for the visit. The institution should establish expectations for the visit that help to ensure a truly professional, useful, and objective interaction, meeting the needs of both the accrediting body and the institution.

Action by the Accrediting Commission or Board. Institutions and programs should have five general expectations of actions by accrediting commissions and boards. First, they should expect that the accrediting action will be based on a review of both the institution's self-study report and the report of the evaluation team. Some accrediting bodies also include a written response from the institution to the team's report as part of the material considered by the body taking the accrediting action. Second, the action taken should be that of the accrediting body, not its staff. The staff members of an accrediting body often serve as advisers and consultants to the program or institution being examined. Sometimes they serve as evaluation-team members, a questionable practice. Fairness requires that an independent, objective review of the evidence, one that is not based largely on staff recommendations or analysis, be the basis of accreditation decisions. An independent action that represents the field or the institutional members and acts for the public at large should be made. Third, the accrediting body should have diverse membership—professionals from the field, laypersons, and faculty members. This pattern is now the general one with few exceptions. Fourth, the accrediting action should state why accreditation was not granted or why a particular status was awarded in terms of stated standards or other previously defined requirements. In other words, the accrediting body's definition of an accredited institution should have been previously spelled out. Finally, institutions and programs should expect actions that observe due process within a reasonable timetable. An institution or program should expect to have access to an established appeals procedure if it feels that the accrediting body did not proceed according to its stated procedures or did not observe other aspects of due process.

Institutions and programs should be aware that accrediting actions are made as professional judgments. Except in those instances in which accreditation standards include measurable criterion levels (such as required numbers of items, staff levels, or numbers of pieces of equipment), accreditation standards are qualitative and require judgment by an evaluation team followed by judgment by the accrediting body. Unless due process has not been observed, or in the rare case in which conflict of interest or other complications can be proved, the courts are reluctant to impose their judgment over that of a recognized professional or institutional accrediting body.

Ongoing Assistance and Protection. Accrediting bodies usually perform services that extend beyond the accreditation process itself. Depending on their size, resources, and purposes, accrediting bodies—largely through the actions of their staff members—may strive to assist member institutions or programs and the discipline or field at large by sponsoring professional meetings, publications, consultation services, and training activities. They also attempt to protect the membership from unreasonable political or other pressures—both external and internal—that might diminish quality or good practice in the field. Most accrediting bodies subscribe to policies that promote freedom of inquiry and seek reasonable autonomy for the institution or program so that goals can be achieved and standards of quality upheld. The ability of the accrediting council or commission to conduct such activities may sometimes be hindered by the policies or structures of a parent association or organization. For instance, certain regional accrediting commissions have recently been curtailed by overall association policies or procedures determined by board members representing other interests, such as elementary or secondary schools. Such interference could and occasionally does threaten the very foundations of voluntary self-regulation in postsecondary education and requires thorough examination.

Increasingly, accrediting bodies are being asked to be sensitive to the academic and administrative impact on campus of their policies and procedures, particularly when an institution is working with more than one accrediting body. Institutions should expect that the accrediting body will try to accommodate the institution's primary cycle of study and planning as accreditation review cycles are established and that accrediting bodies will cooperate with one another in establishing requirements at an institution they each accredit. Most institutions must respond to state and institutional planning cycles as well as institutional accreditation schedules that typically consist of a ten-year evaluation with intervening five-year progress review reports. All accrediting bodies should attempt to accommodate these cycles and not force unnecessary additional major study efforts. However, institutions must seek such accommodation if they choose to do other than respond to arbitrary requirements.

Role Number Five:
To Foster Self-Regulation and Accreditation

This category concerns purposes that extend beyond the actual accreditation function. Accrediting bodies expend much time and effort explaining their roles to a host of audiences—a time-consuming and costly business because their roles and functions are little known and often misunderstood. They also take the lead in fostering the concept of self-regulation. In doing so, they must maintain relationships with other accrediting groups, with many associations and government bodies, and with special groups that spring up to question their procedures. Maintaining themselves as healthy organizations also takes time and energy. Bylaws, governance, policies, dues structures, and professional development all demand attention and get it in increasingly professional ways as these organizations mature.

Both the institution or program and the accrediting body have several expectations about the role of the accrediting body in the accreditation process. The recipient of accrediting-body services and actions—the college, university, or specialized program or institution—must become aware of general accreditation practices. It must also gain knowledge about the specific procedures and persons in the accrediting body it seeks to engage. Furthermore, it must participate fully in the accreditation process and in the general life of the accrediting body. Although accreditation is diverse and has perhaps proliferated to too great a degree, it is a vital and constantly improving element in the governance and regulation of American postsecondary education. To use it well, institutions must gain a better understanding of its potential and practices.

10

James F. Bemis

)O)O)O)O)O)O)O)O)O)O)O)O)O)O)O)O)O)O)O)O)O)O)O

Regional Accreditation

We needed not only to define the characteristics of a college but also to define the characteristics of an acceptable college.
Norman Burns (1959, p. 252)

Institutional accreditation as it exists today is relatively recent and was not conceived by the founders of the six regional associations: the New England Association of Schools and Colleges, founded in 1885; the Middle States Association of Colleges and Schools, in 1887; the North Central Association of Colleges and Schools, in 1895; the Southern Association of Colleges and Schools, also in 1895; the Northwest Association of Schools and Colleges, in 1917; and the Western Association of Schools and Colleges, in 1962. During their formative years, the work of the associations centered on establishing closer relations between colleges and secondary schools and preparing high school students for higher education; accreditation was not a formal pursuit of the associations.

The North Central Association led the way by adopting

standards for accrediting colleges in 1909. In 1913 it published the first list of accredited colleges. The Commission for Accreditation of Institutions of Higher Education was authorized by the Southern Association in 1917 but did not become operational until 1920. The Middle States Association established a Commission on Institutions of Higher Education in 1919. A single commission on accreditation served the Northwest Association until 1923, when two parallel commissions—one for secondary schools and one for higher education institutions—were organized. The New England Association did not function as an accrediting body for colleges and universities until 1952, sixty-five years after its founding. The two postsecondary education commissions of the Western Association were established in 1962, although the old Western College Association had been accrediting since 1948.

Although institutional accreditation by the regional associations has become more important over the years, it is not well understood or appreciated by students and the public—or by professional educators, for that matter. Inappropriate demands are sometimes made of the accrediting commissions, expectations that cannot be met. The regional accrediting bodies are voluntary associations of institutions engaged in the self-regulatory process of assessing and improving educational quality. They serve to assure the public that an institution's purposes are appropriate and soundly conceived, that its educational programs have been intelligently devised, that its purposes are being accomplished, and that the institution should continue to merit confidence because of its organization and resources.

To comprehend institutional accreditation, one must examine its procedures—the standards and criteria that are applied, the self-study process, the system of peer review, requirements for disclosure, and appeals mechanisms. The formal structures of institutional accreditation must also be understood—the division of the country into six regions, the accrediting commissions within the regional associations, the interrelationship of the associations, and the relationship of the associations with federal and state government.

Procedures of Institutional Accreditation

For the most part, the regional accrediting associations have only broad standards and criteria for evaluating institutional effectiveness. The emphasis is more on the two main stages of the evaluation process: self-study and peer review. In the assessment of institutional quality through self-study and peer review, careful attention is given to institutional integrity, meaning that an institution delivers the kind of education that it promises. Requirements for disclosure are usually aimed at providing the public with essential information while protecting the confidentiality of the details of the evaluation findings. All six regional associations have appeals mechanisms for institutions that are not happy with the accreditation process or its outcome.

Standards. The successful application of standards for the improvement of secondary schools in the early 1900s eventually carried over to institutions of higher learning. At first the standards were quite specific and arbitrary and did not provide much leeway for institutional differences, but by 1921 the American Council on Education had formulated standards for four-year institutions, junior colleges, and teacher training schools that had a significant influence on some of the regional associations. Although the formats of the standards were similar, there were differences in content for the three types of institutions. There were seven standards, mainly objective, that apparently met the needs of the times. They dealt with structure rather than function and were considered to cover minimum essentials.

Criticisms of the objective standards—that they were too mechanical and required superficial information of a college—increased during the early 1930s. In 1936 the North Central Association led the way again by developing a qualitative approach that evaluated an institution of higher learning mainly on the basis of the purposes it sought to serve. Other institutional accrediting bodies followed suit and initiated the qualitative approach to evaluation. Despite significant changes in policies and practices since 1936, the principle of evaluating each institution primarily in relation to its own particular purposes still holds.

The minimal qualitative standards, though modified and improved over the years, subsequently came under attack. General criteria statements, sometimes called standards or principles, directed attention to the various features to be reviewed in several areas but did not establish any clear-cut minimum requirements. Institutions tended to submit self-descriptions rather than self-studies. Reports were usually unduly long, with a minimum of analysis and appraisal.

Thorough revisions of the qualitative standards have been made since the early sixties, and ongoing revisions designed to stimulate institutional improvement continue. New criteria have been developed for such areas as off-campus educational activities, computing services, nontraditional degrees, and experiential learning. Nevertheless, the criteria continue to place strong emphasis on institutional structure and process, which are thought essential to quality outcomes. Critics, however, charge that the criteria for institutional accreditation do not provide reasonable assurance of educational quality, that there is little or no demonstrable relation between the criteria and educational outcomes or results.

The long-held principle of evaluating an institution against its own educational purposes has also come under closer scrutiny. Although the accrediting bodies insist that an institution seeking recognition have clearly defined educational purposes that are appropriate to postsecondary education, the range has become increasingly broad. The great diversity among institutions that the regional associations have supported has recently been of increasing concern. Critics charge that the requirements an institution must fulfill to apply for consideration are too general and, further, that the qualitative standards for accreditation are so flexible that the regional associations are no longer distinctive. Examples to support the critics' position are institutions that minimize structure and process to provide more direct and less costly educational services, free-standing specialized institutions in a widening variety of fields, and educational enterprises of business corporations. The "education zoo," as some critics have described the membership of the regional accrediting associations, has placed accreditation in a dilemma. On the one hand, the regional associations have a commitment to support the diversity of postsecondary education that has served the United States so well; on the other hand, they have a commitment to maintain among their membership a collegiality that has recently been strained.

Self-Study. Basic to the institutional accreditation process is the self-study. Here, the faculty, administration, and governing board declare what they want the institution to be and make their own appraisal of its present accomplishments and future potential. The aim of the self-study is to understand, evaluate, and improve rather than merely defend what already exists. The on-site evaluation by peers that usually follows gives added impetus to the self-study, and the views of the visiting team sharpen the impact.

The self-study is the part of the evaluation process that has primary importance for the institution. Its benefits are proportional to the incisiveness of the inquiry. A well-conducted self-study usually results in a renewed common effort within the institution to consolidate and improve the whole. Surveys by the regional associations indicate that institutions are well satisfied with the self-study process as currently organized and conducted.

The criticisms of the qualitative standards also apply to institutional self-studies. Because the criteria for institutional accreditation emphasize structure and process and tend to minimize educational outcomes or results, self-studies follow the same pattern. In general, institutional self-studies do not adequately assess student achievement against the programs and services offered to accomplish the educational purposes. More than ever before, state agencies and various constituencies expect an institution to show clearly that the achievements of students who complete programs are commensurate with the certificates, diplomas, degrees, or other recognition awarded. The institutional accrediting bodies have given more attention to the measurement of outcomes through institutional self-study during recent years, with varying degrees of success.

Peer Review. After the completion of an institutional self-study, peer review is the second stage of the long-range evaluation process, and the regional accrediting associations are somewhat similar in their approach. Because peer review is the hallmark of nongovernmental accreditation, the teams are made up mostly of full-time faculty members and staff members from accredited institutions. The function of the evaluation team is to make an independent analysis of the effectiveness of an institution's procedures, the quality of its performance, and the adequacy of resources for maintaining and improving its performance. In general, the evaluation team looks for coherence between what the institution says and what it does. It checks for agreement between institutional documents and actual performance. The team determines whether the institution's purposes are appropriate and whether they provide reasonable ends for which the means of achievement can be assessed.

The evaluation committee functions as a unit. Its members have particular assignments that are often pursued independently, but each evaluator has an equal responsibility to the committee as a whole. Close cooperation and frequent conferences among the members are essential. Information is shared in detail and cross-checked to provide reasonable assurance that the institution is evaluated critically and constructively. Fairness and accuracy are of utmost importance. Yet, the evaluator approaches the evaluation as a colleague, not as an inspector. Because the criteria are qualitative, there are no formulas to use, rating scales to apply, or formal patterns to impose. As a colleague, the evaluator helps to identify the institution's significant strengths and to suggest ways of addressing its most critical problems.

Whether the evaluators are thought of as generalists or specialists varies among the regional accrediting associations. Because regional associations accredit total institutions, not components or programs, some of them assign evaluators primarily by broad areas within the institution, such as the educational program or the instructional staff. Others believe that more specialists in programs and service areas are required because institutional accreditation indicates that each constituent part or related unit has been evaluated and found to be achieving its own particular purposes satisfactorily, though not necessarily all at the same level of quality. Although to assign an evaluator for each program offered is usually not possible, related programs are organized into clusters for evaluation by a team member. A regional association that relies primarily on generalists, such as the North Central Association, typically has an evaluation team of four or five, whereas an association that uses a combination of generalists and specialists, such as the Northwest Association, usually has a team of more than eight. The Southern Association uses relatively large teams and relies on specialists as well as generalists. To evaluate library resources as part of an institutional review, the college commission of the Southern Association assigns a professional librarian to virtually every team; the North Central Association does not usually assign librarians. Others make a practice of using librarians primarily when evaluating large, complex institutions.

The regional associations have devoted increasing time and attention to the selection, training, and evaluation of team members, particularly during the past ten years. All the regional postsecondary education accrediting commissions conduct orientation and training sessions for inexperienced evaluators. Much of the impetus came through two statements in October 1972 issued by the Federation of Regional Accrediting Commissions of Higher Education (FRACHE), one on the selection and training of evaluators and the other on constructing, placing, and evaluating the evaluation team.

Size and makeup of evaluation teams differ among the regional accrediting associations. Although evaluators for most of the regional associations serve without compensation except for expenses, evaluators for the Middle States Association, the North Central Association, and the college commission of the Southern Association receive honorariums, and team chairpersons receive an additional amount. Evaluation visits are usually three days in all the regions. The size of the evaluator pools varies considerably. For example, the North Central Association's consultant/evaluator corps for postsecondary institutions is about 600, approximately the same as that of the commission for senior colleges of the Western Association. The Middle

States Association has more than 2,000 evaluators, and the college commission of the Southern Association has nearly 3,000.

The final written report of the evaluation committee is a major part of the accreditation process. Reports vary in length among the regions. Generally, smaller teams composed primarily of generalists produce shorter, more succinct reports, and larger teams with a combination of generalists and specialists prepare more detailed reports. Neither is necessarily better than the other. A well-written report analyzes, interprets, gives perspective, provides a detached point of view, and weighs the quality of the institution's achievement. It is fair and accurate. Assumptions and unsupported generalizations are not made. It provides a balanced analysis, recognizing accomplishments as well as problems. The well-written report concentrates on matters of continuing significance, avoiding the temporary and trivial. Finally, it is compressed and succinct for readability and comprehension. In October 1972 FRACHE also approved a statement on the nature of the evaluation report.

In all the regions the chairperson of the evaluation team is responsible for the content of the team's final report, but in some regions the chairperson's responsibility is greater. Some chairpersons write substantially the entire report from team members' written notes and oral reports. Reports prepared through this procedure, though shorter and sometimes more general, usually have the characteristics of a well-written report. When the committee report is more a shared responsibility, the chairperson assigns team members responsibility for drafting certain sections. The chairperson writes the introduction and conclusion and possibly a section on administration but only edits the other sections of the report. This type of report is sometimes more helpful to the institution because of the amount of detail. However, there is also the risk that such a report will lack continuity and read poorly because of different writing styles and content, and there are more chances for errors and inconsistencies.

The criticisms of institutional self-studies also generally apply to evaluation-committee reports. Because self-studies deal heavily with structure and process, evaluation-team reports tend to do the same. When data required for goal achievement studies have not been assembled by the institution, a team cannot readily make an assessment of outcomes. The reports often cite the criteria of the respective commissions for which they are written. Because the criteria are qualitative and describe conditions and principles that characterize educational effectiveness, the citations do not deal directly with goal achievement. Team reports in general give much more attention to institutional improvement than to quality assurance.

Disclosure and Appeals. Except for membership directories that provide basic institutional information, regional accrediting associations differ in their treatment of adverse decisions. The Western Association and the Northwest Association both publish negative accrediting decisions; however, the Western Association publishes the names of institutions under showcause orders as to why their membership should not be terminated, whereas the Northwest Association considers show-cause orders confidential. The New England Association, the North Central Association, the Southern Association, and the Western Association have a probationary status; the Middle States Association and the Northwest Association do not. The college commission of the Southern Association has both a private and a public probation. The occupational commission of the Southern Association has a single probationary status but also has a warned status.

Confidentiality is an important consideration. A client/ practitioner relationship exists between the institution and the accrediting body. If the institution is to address delicate and sensitive problems in its self-study, the institution expects the information to be used discreetly. The evaluation team also expects the information in its report to be used discreetly. There was no significant problem with this relationship before the link between accreditation and eligibility for federal funds and before increased oversight of postsecondary education by the states. Although institutional accrediting bodies recognize their public service function and are usually considered quasi-public agencies, an important element in nongovernmental accreditation would be lost if accrediting bodies were required to make all institutional and evaluation committee reports public. Nevertheless, the regional accrediting associations do not prevent institutions from making self-studies and evaluation committee reports public should they care to do so. In the case of publicly supported institutions, reports are usually made available to the public, though not widely publicized in their entirety. Independent colleges tend to be more circumspect in their publication of sensitive information.

Although the regional accrediting associations need to maintain an appropriate confidential relationship with postsecondary educational institutions, they also require institutions to publish and openly distribute accurate, detailed information about themselves. A basic eligibility requirement of all the regional associations in considering institutions for recognition is a catalogue and other official publications available to students and the public that set forth institutional purposes and objectives, entrance requirements and procedures, rules and regulations for conduct, programs and courses, degree completion requirements, costs, refund policy and procedures, and other information about attending the institution or withdrawing from it.

All the regional associations have published their own policies and procedures on appeals of accrediting decisions. Because the number of appeals and the amount of experience in dealing with them are limited, the regional associations continue to be concerned about their appeal procedures. The procedures of the New England Association and the North Central Association have recently undergone extensive revisions. In 1980 the regional associations, through the COPA Assembly of Institutional Accrediting Bodies, began work on a common appeals procedure in cooperation with the National Center for Mediation in Higher Education. Two drafts were prepared and considered. Great effort was made to avoid, through the suggested procedure, adversarial situations that could lead to expensive and counterproductive litigation. Because of differences in organization among the regional associations and the complications involved in putting the procedures developed by the National Center for Mediation into effect, the COPA Assembly in

1981 decided not to recommend the procedures for consideration. The assembly did, however, approve the use of the mediation procedure in principle. Contact with the center is expected to continue.

Structures of Institutional Accreditation

The formal structures of institutional accreditation—the regional divisions, the accrediting commissions and their staffs, the interrelationship among the associations, and the relationship with government—are often the result of historical tradition rather than planned development. Recent efforts to make these structures more rationally designed have, for the most part, met with almost no success. The greatest area of success has been in the formation of a national coordinating body for accreditation that provides a forum and a mechanism for approaching the other issues.

Definition of Regions. The regional associations did not develop cooperatively with any plan in mind for a rational organization to serve institutional accreditation. Regions grew and were defined at random without much attention to size or regional continuity. As a consequence, the current boundaries of the six regions make little sense. The North Central Association serves nineteen states, stretches from West Virginia to Arizona, and serves about 950 postsecondary educational institutions. The Western Association, organized as an accrediting region in 1962, includes only two states, California and Hawaii, plus American Samoa and Guam. The Northwest Association serves a region of seven large states, most of which are sparsely populated, but includes about three-fifths as many postsecondary institutions as the Western Association and only one-sixth as many as the North Central Association.

During the past decade, considerable time and effort have been devoted to regional realignment, but with no success. In 1974 the Danforth Foundation funded a project that initially involved representatives of the North Central, Northwest, and Western associations. The thought was that accreditation and the institutions in those regions would be better served by organizing a region that included the states of the Northwest Association and the Western Association, plus the four Western states—Arizona, Colorado, New Mexico, and Wyoming—of the North Central Association. After the first meeting, the North Central Association showed no interest in the reorganization. The Northwest Association and the Western Association continued their efforts during meetings held between July 1974 and June 1976. The final proposal, which had the support of the commissions and trustees of the two associations, was for a confederation of the two bodies rather than a merger. Despite the modesty of this proposal, it failed to receive the required two-thirds favorable vote by the institutional delegates of the Northwest Association at annual meetings in 1977, 1979, and 1980. Although a large majority of postsecondary institution delegates favored the proposal, there was strong opposition from secondary school representatives, particularly from Montana, Idaho, and Utah.

In 1978 the public universities in Arizona, governed by a single board of regents, expressed a strong interest, through a resolution, in becoming part of a united accreditation region currently served by the Northwest Association and the Western Association. Because of the problems encountered by the two associations in trying to achieve a modest confederation, the Arizona board of regents pursued the matter for an alignment with the Western Association. As in the Northwest Association, secondary school representatives in Arizona were not interested. Consideration by the Arizona regents has discontinued. Thus, no matter what reasons are presented for a realignment of regional boundaries, it is difficult to achieve.

Internal Organization. There are nine postsecondary education accrediting commissions in the six regional associations. Three of the associations—Middle States, North Central, and Northwest—have a single accrediting commission for postsecondary institutions. The Western Association has two accrediting commissions, one for senior colleges and universities and a second for postsecondary institutions that offer less than a baccalaureate degree. The New England Association organized a commission for higher education institutions in 1952, and in 1970 it established a commission for vocational, technical, and career institutions at the secondary and postsecondary levels. The Southern Association's Commission on Colleges is for institutions that grant associate degrees and higher degrees; its Commission on Occupational Education Institutions for postsecondary non-degree-granting schools was created in 1968.

The reasons that the associations organized different commissions to serve postsecondary institutions vary. When the Western Association was organized in 1962, organizing two postsecondary education commissions was natural because the Western College Association had served an accrediting function for senior colleges and universities since 1948 and there was a strong professional organization of California community colleges. In the Southern region, unlike the others, the large number of non-degree-granting postsecondary occupational schools led to the organization of a separate accrediting commission for such schools. In the other three regions, single commissions have served the diversity of postsecondary educational institutions reasonably well. Some consideration has been given to reorganizing the commissions from time to time, but there appears to be little support for any basic reorganization.

The regional postsecondary education accrediting commissions vary significantly in their organization and operation, owing in part to differences in size. They have undergone considerable change over the years to handle the increased work load that has resulted largely from the greater number of postsecondary institutions to serve. As an illustration of the differences, the postsecondary education commission of the North Central Association consists of about sixty-five persons. Meetings had traditionally been held at the time of the association's annual meeting, but because the meetings of the commission had become *pro forma* sessions, in 1977 the authority of the commission was transferred to the fifteen-member executive board, which meets four times a year. In the Northwest Association, a twenty-five-member postsecondary education commission meets twice a year in regular session. The commission has been able to consider and act on each application, either through the commission meeting as a whole or by organizing two sections of the commission when the review schedule is heavy.

During much of their history, the administrative affairs of

the regional postsecondary education accrediting commissions were handled by part-time staff members and volunteers. Currently, the nine postsecondary education commissions in the six regions have about twenty-seven professionals to serve more than 3,100 postsecondary educational institutions, a ratio of about 1:115. Again, there are significant regional differences. The college commission of the Southern Association has a staff of nine to serve about 750 members and candidates, whereas the postsecondary education commission of the North Central Association has only five professionals for the approximately 950 institutions in its nineteen-state region. The staff load of institutions in the North Central Association is thus more than double that in the Southern Association.

Staff size determines, in large measure, how a commission operates to accomplish its mission. The staff members of the college commission of the Southern Association are field-oriented. A commission staff member accompanies each accreditation team during the on-site evaluation. Field work of the staff of the North Central Association is more limited. A staff member is not usually present during a site visit. In regions with a smaller ratio of staff members to institutions, more services can be performed by professionals that otherwise need to be delegated to volunteers. Although all the regional associations recognize the importance of volunteers and rely heavily on volunteer services, a regional accrediting commission must also have a competent staff of a reasonable size to provide continuity and consistency to its operation. A balance needs to be struck that continues to emphasize the volunteer but also provides adequate staff support for the volunteers to operate effectively and efficiently.

Relationships Among Associations. Before 1951 there was limited contact among the regional accrediting associations. There were about half as many accredited postsecondary educational institutions in 1951 as in 1981; most accredited institutions in 1951 had not been visited since their initial accreditation; and the staff work of the commissions was accomplished mainly by part-time staff members and volunteer help. Then, in 1951, the National Committee of Regional Accrediting Agencies (NCRAA) was formally organized. The committee, composed of the executive secretaries (directors) and chairs of the regional commissions of postsecondary education, usually met once or twice a year to exchange ideas and information about accreditation and discuss problems of common concern.

By the early 1960s, the NCRAA, having served a useful purpose, was clearly no longer enough. Increasingly, the concerns of postsecondary education needed to be dealt with at a national level. Large private foundations were exerting strong influence on American postsecondary education, and the federal government, through various agencies and acts, was assuming a greatly expanded role in postsecondary education. The regional associations needed a mechanism to enable them to jointly address issues of national scope. Accordingly, the postsecondary education commissions of the six regional associations organized the Federation of Regional Accrediting Commissions of Higher Education, and in March 1964 the Articles of Agreement of FRACHE were approved.

The history of FRACHE may be divided into two periods —1964-1972 and 1972-1975. During the earlier period, Norman Burns, executive director of the postsecondary education commission of the North Central Association, also served as the part-time director of FRACHE. A council of eighteen members, consisting of the executive directors and two commissioners from each of the six regions, met semiannually. The executive directors of the commissions also held separate meetings to do staff work for the council. The FRACHE Council served as a valuable forum for sharing institutional accreditation concerns. Some progress was made in creating a more common approach to institutional accreditation. Eighteen policy statements were adopted and published.

In 1969 the FRACHE Council authorized an independent study of the organization and its constituent members. The study, under the direction of Claude E. Puffer, professor of economics and vice-president for business affairs at the State University of New York at Buffalo, was completed in the fall of 1970. The report of the study, known as the Puffer Report, commended FRACHE for what had been done but noted that it could do little more because of its limited authority, limited functions, and limited national visibility. A thoroughly revised FRACHE organization was recommended that would have paramount authority over the regional accrediting associations for postsecondary education (Puffer, 1970).

By fall 1971, in response to the Puffer Report, bylaws for a reorganized FRACHE were approved that empowered FRACHE to establish and coordinate national principles and policies for the regional accrediting commissions. The FRACHE Council was enlarged to include six public representatives and the director of the National Commission on Accrediting (NCA), an organization created in 1949 to control the proliferation of specialized and professional program accreditation. Another decision was to establish an office in Washington, D.C., with a full-time director and staff.

Within a year after the reorganization of FRACHE, serious attention was given to a merger with the National Commission on Accrediting. Because of the serious problems caused by the increasing number of demands made on many colleges and universities by specialized accrediting bodies, seven Washington-based education organizations sponsored NCA. The specialized accrediting bodies were required to submit extensive documentation and be reviewed by NCA before they could be recognized, but they were not represented on the commission. In 1973 the Council of Specialized Accrediting Agencies (CSAA) was organized to represent their interests. Following the organization of CSAA, meetings of executive officers of key education organizations in Washington, representatives of specialized accrediting bodies, the executive directors of the regional accrediting commissions, and other interested parties were held to consider the issues of governance in accreditation and future relationships among institutional and specialized accrediting bodies. The outcome was the organization of the Council on Postsecondary Accreditation (COPA) in January 1975.

The consensus among the executives and commissions of the regional accrediting associations has been that the regional associations have not been as well served by COPA as they were by FRACHE. However, cooperation among the regional associations to develop common policies and practices for regional application has not progressed a great deal since the creation of COPA. A number of FRACHE policy statements still apply, but some of the regional associations have acted unilaterally in revising policy statements and adopting new ones. Fortunately, a return to the cooperative approach has begun under the COPA Assembly of Institutional Accrediting Bodies.

Relationships with Government. The regional accrediting associations have provided a tremendous service to federal and state governments that could not have been provided as effectively or efficiently by any other group. Some people misunderstand the limitations of nongovernmental accreditation; they expect a day-by-day regulatory function that cannot be accommodated by the regional associations. In the oversight of postsecondary education, the roles of the federal government, state government, and the private accrediting bodies—known collectively as the triad in accreditation—need to be better understood and articulated. The problem of cooperative relationships between state government and regional accrediting associations is particularly difficult because each state is different. Not only are the regulatory statutes significantly different, but the state offices and agencies for administering the regulations vary greatly. The problem is compounded by the turnover and reassignment of personnel.

The Tenth Amendment to the Constitution established that the federal government does not have specific powers regarding education and that educational affairs are reserved to the states and the people. However, the federal government has provided financial support to postsecondary educational institutions and their students through a wide variety of programs. With that support has come a federal interest in determining the soundness of institutions and programs. Since nongovernmental accreditation is an effective procedure for determining educational quality, a relationship has been established between accreditation and the process for determining eligibility of institutions to apply for federal support (see Chapter Thirteen).

A possible reason that the regional associations have not received the recognition they deserve for assisting the federal government in determining institutional eligibility for certain programs is that accrediting commissions operate with a very low profile. Unacceptable applications have usually not been announced. Public notice has not been made of institutions that begin the process but withdraw. Nevertheless, during the past eighteen years, the nine commissions in the six regions have organized and conducted well over a thousand initial and follow-up visits to nonaccredited postsecondary educational institutions. Although the regional associations' purpose in conducting these visits was not to serve a function for the federal government, the eligibility link between the nongovernmental accrediting associations and federal funding programs has worked remarkably well.

Determining institutional eligibility could not have been performed as efficiently or effectively by relying on the fifty states. Although the states have the basic responsibility of chartering or incorporating educational institutions and authorizing them to operate, they vary enormously in the extent to which they monitor institutions within their borders. In a few states a charter for a college can still be obtained from the secretary of state by a person completing a simple document with no significant questions asked and paying a modest filing fee. Those states have literally no requirements for institutions offering degrees.

The work of regional accreditation is therefore of special importance. The regional accrediting commissions, through FRACHE, cooperated with the Education Commission of the States (ECS) in 1972 when a task force was organized on how the states should deal with unethical and fraudulent practices in postsecondary education. In June 1973 the ECS task force published a widely distributed report, *Model State Legislation for Approval of Postsecondary Educational Institutions and Authorization to Grant Degrees* (Education Commission of the States, 1973). Parts of the model were used by many states, and other states were encouraged to revise their regulations. Nevertheless, despite the remarkable progress that the states have made during the past decade in enacting more effective legislation to regulate postsecondary education, state governance remains uneven. The requirements in some states are in such general terms as to be unenforceable. Others have established no administrative mechanisms for monitoring institutions. There are unresolved issues of conflict of interest and state jurisdiction, particularly as applied to independent (private) postsecondary education. The situation is complex, and no two states are the same. There is virtually no chance for a uniform approach among the states for incorporation, registration (licensure), and the authority to grant degrees.

Although the regional accrediting associations have strongly supported the necessary state regulatory functions in authorizing institutions to operate and to grant degrees, much better working relationships need to be developed between the two. By using regional associations as a check, states have a chance to insulate regulatory decisions from local politics. Lack of understanding of the value, nature, and function of nongovernmental accreditation has contributed significantly to the problem. Important state agencies too often have misconceptions of the meaning of accreditation and how it operates. Expectations generally go beyond the role of accreditation in attesting to and encouraging the improvement of institutional quality and integrity.

Few problems of the regional accrediting associations need more immediate attention than the one concerning state relationships. This important problem must be faced by the states as well. It is particularly difficult because the organization and operation of state oversight over postsecondary educational institutions differ significantly. An appropriate working agreement for one state might be inappropriate for another. Agreements need to be reviewed and updated periodically. Unfortunately, the small professional staffs of the regional associations are kept busy with the day-to-day activities of the commissions and postsecondary institutions seeking initial accreditation or reaffirmation of accreditation. Nevertheless, good working relationships with appropriate state agencies and officials need to be nurtured and developed by the regional associations.

Nongovernmental accreditation of postsecondary educational institutions must be kept in proper perspective. On balance, this unique American system is a dynamic self-regulatory mechanism of postsecondary education that has admirably served its mission of assessing and enhancing institutional quality and integrity. Significant improvements have been made over the years, and many more are under consideration. Understanding and support are needed not only by institutions but also by their publics. The unacceptable alternative is direct quality assurance by state and federal agencies or bureaus, an alternative that would destroy the independence of postsecondary educational institutions and—in a supreme constitutional compromise—make them merely another extension of government.

11

༼༽༼༽༼༽༼༽༼༽༼༽༼༽༼༽༼༽༼༽༼༽༼༽

Specialized
Accreditation

*Even though it must remain a purely advisory body
and have no legal status, the Council on Medical
Education of the AMA will undoubtedly exercise a
strong, indirect control over medical schools by its
schemes of reports and inspections and by scatter-
ing broadcast the results of their inspections.*
Dr. Henry B. Ward (1908)

Specialized accreditation was born out of the concern of a
profession about the quality of educational programs that
were preparing its practitioners. By the end of the nineteenth
century, the status of medical education in the United States
was deplorable, and a number of steps were taken to rectify
the situation. The first efforts to develop a means for determining and improving educational standards in professional education came from the institutions themselves. Between 1876 and
1889, the short-lived American Medical College Association attempted to create a register of medical schools meeting certain
agreed standards. Then the Association of American Medical
Colleges (AAMC) was established in 1890, requiring a three-year

medical course as one condition of membership. Additional requirements were approved in 1894 and again in 1900, and the secretary-treasurer in 1903 was authorized to visit each member college and make a detailed study and report (Smiley, 1957, pp. 512–518).

Shortly thereafter, the American Medical Association (AMA), the major organization of individual practitioners, became more actively concerned about educational standards. One of the first acts of the organizational meeting of the AMA in 1847 had been the appointment of a committee on medical education. During the next fifty-seven years, the committee advocated higher standards in medical education but took no formal action until after the reorganization of the AMA in 1902. Then, in the next several years, the Council on Medical Education was made a permanent body, an "ideal standard" for medical education was developed, and tables were published listing medical schools in four classes based on the percentage of state licensure examination failures. A rating system with ten categories of qualification was developed, and inspections were begun in 1906 (American Medical Association, 1960, pp. 1–9).

In the meantime, the states had also been active. By 1900 twenty-six states had instituted licensure requirements for medical school graduates (Wiggins and Shepherd, 1959). The National Confederation of State Medical Examining and Licensing Boards adopted the AAMC's standard curriculum in 1905 (American Medical Association, 1905) and its minimum medical school equipment list in 1907 (American Medical Association, 1908).

Although the AMA became actively involved after the AAMC, it quickly seized the initiative, joining forces with the Carnegie Foundation of New York, which was planning "to investigate all the professions: law, medicine, and theology" (American Medical Association, 1960, p. 10). Discussions between the two groups led to an agreement that although Carnegie "would be guided very largely by the [AMA] council's investigation, to avoid the usual claims of partiality no more mention should be made in the report to the council than any other source of information. The report would therefore be, and have the weight of, an independent report of a disinterested body" (American Medical Association, 1960, p. 10). N. P. Colwell of the AMA Council and Abraham Flexner of Carnegie conducted a study, which became known as the Flexner Report (Flexner, 1910). AAMC was kept informed of the study, and its members generally cooperated in the visits.

The Flexner Report severely criticized medical education in this country and advocated (1) the incorporation of medical schools as organic departments of universities, (2) the elimination of proprietary schools, (3) the requirement of basic scientific courses taught by full-time faculty members, and (4) the use of teaching hospitals for clinical experience. The report had a considerable impact; 160 medical schools in 1905 were reduced to 85 by 1920 (American Medical Association, 1960, p. 11). The motivation of the medical profession may have been not only to eliminate marginal and substandard schools but also to reduce the excessive number of physicians being trained (Selden, 1960, p. 45).

Similarly, the Association of American Law Schools (AALS) began in 1900, adopting standards for membership that dealt with the quality of legal education (including a three-year course requirement after 1905) and subsequently introducing a system of school visits. The American Bar Association (ABA), which had played a role in launching AALS, did not start its own inspection activities until 1921, when it began to publish an annual list of law schools "in compliance with a set of minimum standards" (Cardozo, 1975).

These early efforts to address the problems of educational quality in the professions of medicine and law are useful to understand for several reasons. First, they set a pattern that was followed in most other professions. Second, most of these early efforts could not be called accreditation as that term is now understood; for example, the institutional self-study was not introduced by AMA/AAMC until 1977. Third, professional associations of practitioners, associations of professional schools, and state agencies acted—separately and on occasion cooperatively—in dealing with the same set of problems. Fourth, institutions, through membership requirements and other self-regulatory efforts, played a little-recognized leadership role, although the professional association often later became the dominating partner. Finally, in the professions of medicine and law were the first instances of conflict over standards and practices between a profession and the institutions that prepare its practitioners, a tension that has existed to some degree ever since.

By the end of the 1920s, dentistry, landscape architecture, library science, music, nursing, optometry, teacher education, and collegiate business education had established visiting and listing activities (Selden and Porter, 1977, p. 2). In at least one of these cases—music—self-regulation and peer review procedures were developed by a group of institutions largely to control unethical practices in the recruiting of students and faculty members. In another case—business—an association of institutions had been formed earlier (1916), and then program guidelines that later became accreditation standards were developed. Eight additional fields joined the specialized accreditation ranks during the 1930s, and by 1952 the National Commission on Accrediting recognized twenty-two specialized accrediting bodies. That number had grown to twenty-eight by 1965. The 1980–82 *Guide to Recognized Accrediting Agencies* published by the Council on Postsecondary Accreditation (COPA) included forty-seven accrediting bodies that are considered specialized or programmatic, but only thirty-nine of those were recognized by COPA for their accreditation activities (Petersen, 1980).

Types of Specialized Accrediting Bodies

Specialized accreditation is also called programmatic accreditation and professional accreditation. It applies mainly to the approval of programs, curricula, disciplines, or units within institutions of postsecondary education. In some instances—art, chiropractic, music, osteopathy, and theology, for example—specialized accrediting bodies accredit single-purpose, freestanding schools as part or all of their responsibility. The specialized accrediting bodies are all national in scope, but they vary greatly in size. Some, such as the Committee on Allied

Health Education and Accreditation, the American Dental Association, the Accreditation Board for Engineering and Technology, the National Association of Schools of Music, the National League for Nursing, and the National Council for Accreditation of Teacher Education, are large, each accrediting more than 500 programs. Others, such as those in the fields of construction education, optometry, osteopathy, veterinary medicine, chiropractic education, and industrial technology, accredit fewer than twenty-five programs each. Most specialized accrediting bodies accredit "first professional degree" programs, at whatever level that may apply in a particular institution. Some (such as construction education, dietetics, home economics, and industrial technology) restrict their activities to the baccalaureate level, and a few (health services administration, public health, rehabilitation counseling education, speech pathology and audiology, and theology) accredit only graduate programs. One, the American Psychological Association, considers only doctoral programs, as indeed is true of a few others in the "first professional degree" category. Art, business, journalism, interior design, music, nursing, social work, and teacher education are recognized by the Council on Postsecondary Accreditation for both undergraduate and graduate program accreditation.

Perhaps the most important categorization of specialized accrediting bodies is determined by the nature and makeup of the sponsoring organization. Some accrediting bodies are associations of institutions, associations that were formed specifically for the purpose of accreditation or for which accreditation has become one of their primary reasons for being, even if they were not originated for that purpose. The National Association of Schools of Art, the American Assembly of Collegiate Schools of Business, the Association of American Law Schools (which shares accreditation responsibility in the field of law with the American Bar Association), the Association of American Medical Colleges (which shares responsibility with the American Medical Association), the National Association of Schools of Music, and the Association of Theological Schools in the United States and Canada are, as indicated by their titles, in this category. Because these accrediting bodies are associations of institutions, they, more than some of the other specialized accrediting bodies, tend to share with the regional accrediting associations a common philosophy and attitude about the function of accreditation.

Most specialized accrediting bodies, however, are arms of associations of individual members from a profession or councils formed by several individual-membership groups representing a profession. For example, professional associations such as the American Bar Association, the American Dental Association, the American Library Association, and the National League for Nursing, to name but a few, have committees or commissions designated by their membership to carry out the accreditation function for their profession. Other accrediting bodies, such as the Accreditation Board for Engineering and Technology, the American Board of Funeral Service Education, the American Council on Education for Journalism, and the Council on Rehabilitation Education, were formed and are supported jointly by several professional societies in their respective fields. For example, the Accreditation Board for Engineering and Technology is supported by eighteen different groups of professional engineers. And finally, several specialized accrediting bodies are jointly supported by individual-membership groups and associations of schools in their professions. The American Council on Education for Journalism, the National Architectural Accrediting Board, Accrediting Commission on Education for Health Services Administration, and the National Council for Accreditation of Teacher Education (NCATE) all belong to this category. NCATE, for example, has ten constituent member organizations, the two major ones being the National Education Association and the American Association of Colleges for Teacher Education and the others being individual-membership groups from the education profession.

The Committee on Allied Health Education and Accreditation (CAHEA) is an interesting case that is virtually a category in itself. CAHEA was formed in 1976 as a result of the need for coordination and cooperation in the accreditation of health-related educational programs, taking over a function previously performed by the American Medical Association. As of 1980,

"CAHEA collaborates with twenty-one review committees, representing forty-five collaborating allied health organizations, in the accreditation of programs in twenty-six areas of allied health" (Petersen, 1980, p. 131). In all, CAHEA accredits more than 2,900 programs in allied health.

How much difference exists in attitudes or in actual accreditation practices among these categories of accrediting bodies is difficult to generalize about or to document. There may be as much difference within categories as between them. However, one difference between categories that might be expected is that the persons involved in decision making from associations of institutions are likely to be predominantly educators—that is, peers from institutions—whereas persons executing the process for accrediting bodies that are supported by individual-membership organizations from the profession are more likely to be peers from the profession itself. In other words, one review is likely to be oriented more toward the interests of the institution and the other toward the interests of the profession. Certainly, one of the chief causes of tension between institutional leaders and specialized accreditation is the question of who is being served by the accreditation process, the institution or the profession. In the best of worlds, of course, a balance would be struck. Appropriate professional standards must be upheld, not only in the interest of the professions but for the good of society, and specialized accreditation regards that mission as its function. However, the accreditors must understand the problems of resources and curriculum balance within institutions.

Procedures of Specialized Accreditation

The basic pattern of procedures by which specialized accreditation is carried out is common to nearly every specialized accrediting body. (For details about these procedures, and for other detailed information about accrediting bodies, see Petersen, 1980.) Standards or criteria for accreditation are established by the sponsoring organization(s); the program aspiring to accredited status conducts a self-study according to those criteria and other rules of eligibility; an on-site visit is conducted by a group of peers; and an accrediting decision is made by an accrediting commission or committee from the sponsoring organization. Only one recognized specialized accrediting body varies significantly from this basic pattern, the Council on Rehabilitation Education, which requires no on-site visit but rather collects detailed data and analyzes them by computer.

Although institutional accrediting bodies commonly give important consideration to an institution's performance according to its own stated objectives, most specialized accrediting bodies are much more interested in a program's compliance with a set of national standards that have been established within the field. In years past, perhaps as recently as a decade ago in some accrediting bodies, a committee of leaders from the profession or from the institutions would have, not uncommonly, been involved in developing such standards with relatively little input from the field as a whole. Today, the usual practice by far is for statements of proposed standards or criteria to be drafted, circulated widely, subjected to hearings at regional or national meetings, and then voted on by an assembly of the sponsoring organization(s). Although the degree of specificity varies widely from one accrediting body to another, the standards for specialized accreditation usually include statements on (1) the organization, administration, and governance of the program, (2) faculty qualifications, teaching loads, and student-faculty ratios, (3) admission and retention of students, (4) curriculum content and balance, (5) the library, (6) facilities and equipment, and (7) financial resources (see Petersen, 1979, pp. 74-99, 115-141).

Specialized accrediting bodies typically require compliance with other rules of eligibility in addition to the standards in these seven areas. For example, twenty-seven of the recognized specialized accrediting bodies require accreditation by the appropriate institutional or regional accrediting association, particularly if the program exists in a college or university setting. Fourteen of the specialized accrediting bodies specify that at least one class of students shall have been graduated from the program under consideration.

The self-study is generally considered one of the most important aspects of the accreditation process. Such an assessment is required by every specialized accrediting body, and in most cases the self-study guidelines provided by the accrediting bodies are quite specific. Many specialized accrediting bodies encourage participation by as many faculty members as possible, believing that the value of the accreditation process is enhanced by faculty involvement in program evaluation according to national standards. This faculty involvement is one of the advantages of specialized accreditation to an institution, because even in large programs most or all faculty members can be engaged in the self-study if the department or college encourages such participation. From the opposite point of view, one of the commonly heard complaints about specialized accreditation is that self-study requirements are excessive, calling for information and, particularly, quantitative data that are superfluous to the task at hand. Self-study reports are often voluminous, and the cost of typing and duplication alone can be large. The accrediting bodies contend that the information required is essential for a valid program review and that the costs are minimal in relation to the benefits to the institution if the self-study is conducted conscientiously and if it involves a majority of the faculty members in the unit.

The greatest variability in the cost of specialized accreditation is the cost of the on-site visit. The size of the visiting teams varies from two to nine or more, but in some cases the cost of the on-site visit is borne by the accrediting body rather than by the institution. The average visiting committee from the American Dental Association (ADA) to dental schools usually numbers fifteen; but ADA's teams, like those from other individual-membership professional organizations (such as the American Osteopathic Association, the American Podiatry Association, and the American Veterinary Medical Association), are supported by the professional organization. To generalize about the cost of on-site visits for specialized accreditation is nearly impossible. Some accrediting bodies charge a flat fee for the visit, regardless of the number of visitors required by the size of the program or their expenses. Others charge the actual expenses of the visiting team only, having built the other costs of review into an annual dues structure. Some charge a fee for the review (ranging from a few hundred dollars to several thousand) in addition to the expenses of the visitors. Still others levy a flat charge per visitor (ranging from $125 to $1,100), the variable being the size of the team. The only generalization possible is to estimate, on the basis of the most recent information available (Petersen, 1980), that the average direct cost of on-site visits for specialized accrediting bodies is in the range of $1,500 to $2,000. Although on-site visiting teams are assigned by the accrediting body in all cases, some accrediting bodies allow the institution to select from a list of nominees, and some provide the institution opportunity to veto individual visitors if they are believed to be inappropriate choices for some reason.

In most specialized accrediting bodies, the committees, commissions, or boards of review that make accrediting decisions are appointed, although among associations of institutions the commissioners or committee members are commonly elected by the entire delegate assembly. Most accrediting commissions include two or three public members, and they are usually appointed regardless of the selection process for other commission members. In some accrediting bodies the public members have full voting rights; in others they serve in an advisory or consultant capacity. Some specialized accrediting bodies, such as the American Veterinary Medical Association (AVMA), are very specific about the makeup of their accrediting commissions—AVMA specifies for its twelve-member Council on Education one or two members from each of ten specializations or levels of study within the field. Specialized accrediting bodies that are sponsored by multiple organizations designate a certain number of seats on their accrediting commissions for each of the participating groups, allowing those groups to elect or appoint their representatives. The size of the accrediting committees or commissions in specialized accreditation varies from seven to twenty-seven, the average being thirteen.

The terminology used to define the categories or levels of specialized accreditation is not all standardized, which presents few problems within any one field but is confusing to those who need or desire an overall understanding. Most specialized accrediting bodies recognize at least two levels of accreditation, one for preaccreditation and one for accredited status. The term *provisional* is not used consistently from one specialized accrediting body to another, however, and therein lies one basis for confusion. Some accrediting bodies use *provisional accreditation* to indicate initial accreditation or preaccredited status for developing programs that are not yet fully operational, a second review being required before full accreditation is granted. Other accrediting bodies use the term *provisional* to indicate that serious deficiencies in the program are in evidence. A discussion of these differences may be found in Petersen's *Accrediting Standards and Guidelines* (1979, pp. 70-72, 107-109). The specific terminology used by each recognized accrediting body is included in COPA's 1980-82 *Guide to Recognized Accrediting Agencies* (Petersen, 1980).

There is also wide variation among the specialized accrediting bodies in the length of the term for which accreditation is granted. Two accrediting bodies grant accredited status for as brief a term as one year, whereas at least six others have a standard maximum term of ten years. The average length of term is six years, and the most common is five. Most accrediting bodies require annual reports, some used strictly for statistical purposes such as summary reports, others used to note significant changes in a program's operation. Further, most accrediting bodies have procedures for follow-up reports about particular deficiencies found at the time of review, and some reserve the right to call for a full review before the end of the term if there is evidence of a significant decline in program quality.

As in most other matters, the specialized accrediting bodies vary in the scope of their accreditation. Some accrediting bodies, such as those for home economics and music, accredit "all or none" of a department's or school's programs. The advantage of this policy for the accrediting body is that a school is usually willing either to upgrade or to eliminate a particular program that is found deficient so that it can maintain its accredited status. Other accrediting bodies—such as those for engineering, teacher education, and journalism—accredit individual programs, allowing institutions to choose those programs for which they will seek accredited status. NCATE, for example, accredits 2,867 programs in 561 institutions (Petersen, 1980, pp. 212-213).

Issues

Some leaders in postsecondary education, particularly certain university presidents, argue that specialized accreditation serves no useful purpose; that institutional accreditation can and should meet the need for evaluating and attesting to the quality of an institution's total offerings (and indeed is presumed to do so); that specialized accreditation does not exist in many fields of study and therefore is obviously not essential; that specialized accreditation as it currently operates does not address the fundamental question of the competency of the individual who completes a professional program; and that the professional associations should concentrate on improving the licensing, certification, and continuing education of practitioners. However, not only spokespersons for specialized accreditation but others who have studied accreditation would contend that institutional accreditation, if left to its own devices, might become provincial and self-serving and that the stimulus of external standards and evaluation is highly desirable, if not necessary.

In 1981, COPA issued a statement on quality assurance in professional accreditation that stated, "Specialized accreditation exists primarily for the purpose of providing some assurance to the public of the quality of education professionals receive, a responsibility for which members of an organized or licensed profession have traditionally been held accountable" (Council on Postsecondary Accreditation, Assembly of Specialized Accrediting Bodies, 1981c, p. 1). The statement lists the value of specialized accreditation to the public, to students, to educational institutions, to the professions, and to institutional accrediting bodies. The basic assumption is that specialized accreditation serves to assure educational quality.

What constitutes educational quality, and who is best

able to determine it? These are the questions that have caused the greatest contention between the institutions and the professions and, on occasion, between competing professional groups. In recent years, a consensus has been reached that all accreditation, institutional and specialized, should begin to focus primarily on educational outcomes (see Chapter Seventeen). However, practice has been slow to catch up with theory. Several specialized accrediting organizations—the Association of Theological Schools, the National League for Nursing, and the American Assembly of Collegiate Schools of Business, for example—have initiated long-term research projects intended to achieve agreement on the competencies or proficiencies expected of a practitioner; and the Kellogg Foundation has funded a pilot project under which Pennsylvania State University has been working with selected professions to identify proficiencies and design educational experiences to achieve them (Continuing Professional Education Development Project, 1981).

Institutions still complain regularly, however, that many visiting teams interpret accreditation criteria quite rigidly and tend to focus on specifics such as budgets, teaching loads, facilities, and organizational questions. There have also been some disquieting signs that, faced with enrollment declines and financial cutbacks, some professional groups are talking about strengthening specific requirements such as the number of full-time faculty members and student-faculty ratios. Working through an interassociation Presidents Committee on Accreditation, the American Council on Education in 1980–81 took the lead in encouraging COPA to arrange meetings between concerned presidents and representatives of the professional associations that were causing the greatest concern. Out of these discussions has come a better understanding by the presidents that some of the problems they are experiencing may actually have been the result of actions within their own institutions. There were also acknowledgments by the accrediting bodies that certain of their practices needed to be reviewed or modified.

The move toward specifying educational outcomes should eventually provide a common point of reference for evaluating educational programs and improving professional credentialing.

In addition, periodic meetings between institutional and professional association representatives should increase their mutual understanding and agreement. However, a certain—perhaps necessary—element of tension will probably continue.

Professional associations, particularly those made up of individual practitioners, view accreditation from a much different perspective than do institutions of postsecondary education. The professional association sees its main objective as protecting and improving the status of the profession and its practitioners. Accreditation is viewed as one of several tools to be used to achieve that goal, and it is usually regarded as a supportive rather than a primary tool. State licensing is sought by many professional groups; others develop their own system of certification. Accreditation of professional programs is usually pursued as an adjunct activity, at least by many of the senior professions, which often commit relatively minor resources to this function. The American Bar Association, for example, in 1981 had an accreditation staff consisting of a "consultant" (an associate dean at a law school devoting most of his time to accreditation activities) and a secretary. The smaller and newer fields of specialization, however, view accreditation as important to securing their future acceptance and therefore devote correspondingly more resources to this activity. New professional and occupational organizations not yet involved in accreditation have also been prompted to consider establishing their own accreditation mechanisms.

Indeed, the presence of a structure for accrediting educational programs seems to enhance the status of a profession or discipline, at least in the minds of some. If accreditation performs a valued service for such professions as engineering, law, or medicine, it is attractive to any professional group that has or desires its own identity. Emerging specializations, some from within larger professional groups, tend to view accreditation of the programs that prepare their practitioners as a means toward achieving credibility and perhaps as a mechanism by which to gain leverage for resources within the institution, where they are still viewed as newcomers. Not surprisingly, the Council on Postsecondary Accreditation has had inquiries from many groups that want information about establishing accreditation procedures. COPA has responded to inquiries from seventy-two such groups in recent years—a number that is particularly staggering given that COPA's 1980–82 *Guide to Recognized Accrediting Agencies* listed a total of only sixty-one accrediting bodies, forty-eight of which are considered specialized, and of those forty-eight, COPA recognized thirty-nine for their accreditation activities (Petersen, 1980). In other words, the number of groups inquiring about recognition in recent years is nearly double the number of existing specialized accrediting bodies recognized by COPA. The concern about proliferation, therefore, is not only real but justified.

Indeed, the most commonly heard complaint from institutional leaders about accreditation is the proliferation of accrediting bodies. Some college and university presidents, particularly some of those from large universities with several professional schools and programs, have been greatly concerned about the proliferation issue. Accordingly, the proliferation of accrediting bodies has occupied a prominent place, normally top priority, in every long-term agenda of the Council on Postsecondary Accreditation since COPA's inception in 1975, and it was certainly a constant and major concern of the National Commission on Accrediting (NCA), one of COPA's forerunners, as well.

NCA recognized thirty-six specialized or programmatic accrediting bodies when it merged with the Federation of Regional Accrediting Commissions of Higher Education to form COPA in 1975. From 1975 to 1980, COPA awarded recognition to only three additional specialized accrediting bodies, bringing the total to thirty-nine in 1980. COPA published a statement on proliferation in 1978 that defines some of the problems (Council on Postsecondary Accreditation, 1978b). The document also suggests some alternatives to accreditation for aspiring groups and recommends actions to the COPA staff and elected leadership for the control of proliferation in the future.

Interestingly, the COPA statement on proliferation, written by the Task Force on Proliferation and Specialization, avoided the issue of social need for accreditation that was so long a stated criterion for recognition by NCA. COPA also skirted the issue of social need in its *Provisions and Procedures for Becoming Recognized as an Accrediting Agency for Post-secondary Educational Institutions or Programs* (Council on Postsecondary Accreditation, 1975). Instead, it emphasized a requirement that an accrediting body demonstrate that it had achieved wide acceptance among institutions and other appropriate groups (see Chapter Fifteen).

Social need is difficult to define, at least in terms that are acceptable to the entire postsecondary education community. There is little argument about a social need for quality assurance in the education of practitioners in health-related fields, and probably the same is true for a profession such as engineering. But how does one judge the social need for accreditation in a field such as journalism or library science or theology? Poorly educated medical doctors or dentists or engineers represent a threat to our well-being, to be sure, but poorly educated journalists or librarians or theologians also represent a certain kind of threat to society. Furthermore, in this age of consumerism, an argument can be made that the public has the right to some kind of determination of quality, or at least of minimum standards, for any specialized educational program. The answer to proliferation in accreditation will most likely have to come from criteria that can be more readily determined than social need.

Some of the concern about the proliferation of specialized accreditation among institutional leaders is undoubtedly prompted by their own personal experiences with specialized accrediting bodies. Some institutional leaders have few complaints because they have a manageable number of accredited specialized programs on their campuses, have not been besieged by excessive demands for new facilities or equipment or higher salaries, and have benefited from the insights provided by outside evaluators from the professions or other educational institutions. Others have experienced excessive demands, have hosted ten or more visiting teams within one academic year, and have felt that the outside evaluators were more concerned with the vested interests of their profession than with educational quality.

Generally, however, presidents' attitudes about specialized accreditation are more positive than negative. A nationwide study of opinions about accreditation and interagency cooperation conducted for COPA in 1979 revealed that 75 percent of institutional presidents or chief academic officers believed both institutional and specialized accreditation to be important and necessary (Pigge, 1979, p. 35), although 40 percent of the same group expressed the opinion that specialized accrediting bodies are too demanding (p. 36). Of the heads or representatives of accredited academic programs or units within the same institutions who responded to the same items in the Pigge study, 86 percent believed both institutional and specialized accreditation to be important and necessary (Pigge, 1979, p. 35), and only 20 percent believed specialized accrediting bodies are too demanding (p. 36).

Two points need to be made about the concern, and sometimes frustration, of institutional presidents about specialized accreditation. First, some of specialized accreditation is completely voluntary. The system of voluntary accreditation in the United States—referring, of course, to a system of nongovernmental self-regulation and peer review—is a source of pride. The immediate response of the specialized accreditation community to charges of excessive demands, excessive costs, or stifling of innovation and experimentation in education is that accreditation is voluntary and institutions that do not want to "pay the price" for the accreditation of a particular program should not seek it. Yet accreditation is not really voluntary, when, for example, federal funding of a particular program is contingent on its accreditation, as is sometimes true in health-related fields. The institution's alternative is not to forgo accreditation but perhaps to excise the program. Further, in at least ten professions (primarily law, engineering, and health-related professions), graduation from an accredited program is the accepted route toward licensure in many states. Even though alternative access to licensure or certification is available in some professions or in some states, the tie of licensure to accreditation tends to reduce the voluntary nature of accreditation in those fields (Grimm, 1972, pp. 14-15). For example, when an institution is presented with a demanding bill of particulars for continuation of accreditation in a field in which licensure is at stake for students already enrolled in the program, it has little choice but to meet the demands of the accrediting body. To forgo accreditation would in one sense be a breach of contract with students who enrolled with the understanding that a degree from the institution would qualify them to sit for the licensure examination. Even if the requirements placed on the institution by the accrediting body are totally justified, the institution's situation of "no choice" is understandably frustrating to a president when financial resources are already strained to the limit.

Second, in cases in which the requirements of licensure for a profession are not at issue—in which specialized accreditation is indeed voluntary—the pressures for accreditation that institutional leaders feel are often from within their own institutions, not from accrediting bodies. Of the forty-eight specialized accrediting bodies included in the 1980–82 COPA *Guide to Recognized Accrediting Agencies,* at least twenty-two indicate no tie to either licensure or certification for the profession (Petersen, 1980). In other words, although loss of accreditation in those fields (such as business, journalism, music, and psychology) may result in a loss of institutional pride and stature and probably in the ability to attract good students, it would not affect licensure or certification of practitioners, either because there is none in the field or because it is not tied to accreditation. The desire for accreditation in those fields derives from faculty members' pride in their program as well as the desire to have their program recognized in their profession as a program of quality. Of course, the institution has the option of denying a department's request to seek accreditation or of resigning from accredited status if the costs and demands seem excessive. Accrediting bodies do not review a program unless they are invited to do so by the institution, usually with the approval of the president or chief academic officer. In some cases, accrediting bodies may simply be a convenient target for general resentment.

The costs of accreditation are often cited as a major concern of institutions, but they are probably perceived as a serious problem only when large, complex institutions add up their total accreditation bill. In Pigge's study of opinions about accreditation and interagency cooperation, only 22 percent of the 483 presidents or chief academic officers who responded, and 16 percent of the 1,167 program heads, agreed with the statement that "accreditation is too costly for what it accomplishes" (Pigge, 1979, p. 33). In the same study, 65 percent of the presidents and 50 percent of the program heads agreed with statements about fees and site-visit expenses presenting burdens, but a greater percentage of each—80 percent of the presidents and 69 percent of the program heads—felt that the preparation of reports is a burden on institutions (pp. 42-43). In other words, educators consider the costs of accreditation a burden, but not as much of a burden as the time required to tend to accreditation matters and not a serious concern relative to what accreditation accomplishes.

Many issues concerning the standards and guidelines of specialized accrediting bodies were brought out in Petersen's study for COPA (Petersen, 1978, 1979). The study examined the evaluation standards and guidelines of COPA-recognized accrediting bodies and sought to answer such questions as these:

- Are accreditation standards predominantly quantitative rather than qualitative in their requirements?
- Do accreditation standards inhibit educational innovation and experimentation?
- Do accrediting bodies fail to keep their standards abreast of current developments?
- Are accrediting bodies more interested in form than in substance?

Petersen's summary statement referred to all accrediting bodies, institutional as well as specialized, but she concluded in response to these questions that "with some exceptions, accrediting standards and guidelines are more qualitative than quantitative, more general than specific, more flexible than rigid, and more up-to-date than outdated" (1978, p. 313).

Petersen's study found that, in general, there is no basis to the sometimes-heard criticism that accreditation restricts institutional autonomy, at least in the broad, general statements on institutional governance that dominate most of the standards (Petersen, 1979, p. 155). Petersen did find requirements in some specialized accreditation standards that raise questions of infringement on institutional autonomy, however, particularly requirements on number of faculty members, faculty-student ratios, or faculty teaching loads. She also found that, in general, the standards and guidelines of specialized accrediting bodies are more prescriptive than those of the regional associations. This finding is not surprising, because the specialized accrediting bodies deal with the disciplines in more specific terms than would be appropriate or practical for institutional accreditation.

Future of Specialized Accreditation

The outlook for the immediate future in postsecondary education suggests that specialized accreditation may play an increasingly important role, and perhaps an increasingly controversial one, during the next two decades. Combinations of conflicting factors, such as declining enrollments and higher costs, will make maintaining and improving educational quality increasingly difficult. As a result, assurances of program quality will be more and more important to prospective students and to the public in general. The pressures on accreditation to deliver valid assurances of quality will surely grow, but at the same time institutions will be ever more watchful of the costs and time required by the accreditation process. In addition, institutions or programs that suffer a decline in quality to the degree that they are threatened by removal of accreditation will be likely to make their cries of infringement on institutional autonomy and other recurring criticisms ring louder and louder. Tensions between institutions and specialized accreditation will probably increase, but the accreditation process will also probably be more important than ever.

Specialized accrediting bodies must be credited for their efforts to improve their operations. Several of them have recently made major efforts to study and validate their standards. The Association of Theological Schools in the United States and Canada has been engaged in such a study, and the American Assembly of Collegiate Schools of Business has recently received a major grant to embark on one. Because the requirements that society places on its professions are changing at an ever-increasing pace, many specialized accrediting bodies must conduct continuous reviews to update their standards. Others engage in periodic major revisions. The National Association of Schools of Music, for example, has recently revised and updated all graduate degree standards after a two-year study and hearing process.

The specialized accrediting bodies have been somewhat slower to revise procedures than standards. The number of on-site visitors, the type and amount of information requested in the self-study, and the procedures by which decisions are made have not been subjected to the same internal scrutiny as have standards and guidelines. The future will probably see an increased emphasis on efficiency in accreditation operations, particularly when institutions insist on it. As one example, the computer age should enable accrediting bodies to make better use of the information they collect in annual reports and therefore alleviate some of the requirements for quantitative information in self-study reports. In addition, better interagency cooperation could reduce the amount of time that institutions devote to specialized accreditation, although whether cost savings would actually be realized remains to be proved. Certainly, better cooperation between regional and specialized accrediting bodies would be to the benefit of institutions. The future may also see some clustering of accrediting bodies in related disciplines under umbrella organizations, such as the Committee on Allied Health Education and Accreditation. The extent to which such clustering is practicable with existing, autonomous accrediting bodies is questionable, but it could alleviate the pressures of proliferation while providing recognized accreditation for emerging professions.

Despite the criticisms that will always be made, specialized accreditation has served postsecondary education, the pro-

Part Four

༄༅༄༅༄༅༄༅༄༅༄༅༄༅༄༅༄༅༄༅༄༅༄༅

Beneficiaries, Users, and Special Interests

Who benefits from accreditation—institutions that are accredited, special interest groups involved in accreditation, various users of the results of accreditation, the general public? Students are, or are supposed to be, the focus of education; but accreditation has not always kept their interests at the forefront. Only infrequently have students been directly involved in the accreditation process; and as a general rule they are not aware of, let alone informed about, accreditation. In recent years, however, increasing efforts have been made to involve students in accreditation, to use accreditation to protect students from flagrant consumer abuses, and to orient accreditation more toward student outcomes.

Probably the most dominating user of accreditation in recent years has been the federal government, as it turned to accreditation as one consideration in determining institutional eligibility for certain federal funds. This growing involvement with the government and with dollar rewards has brought into question the voluntary, nongovernmental nature of accreditation. It also has altered some aspects of the process, as well as perceptions of the process.

State governments also use accreditation, but their impact has been less dramatic. The states have interacted more with accreditation through their chartering of institutions, licensing of practitioners, and consumer protection activities. But increasing state initiatives of a quasi-accrediting nature have raised questions concerning roles and relationships.

Early efforts to create a national organization to deal with the many issues inherent in accreditation have led to the formation of the Council on Postsecondary Accreditation. COPA has a broad mandate, a diversified membership, and limited powers and resources. It remains postsecondary education's only hope for assuring the integrity and viability of nongovernmental accreditation.

12

Joan S. Stark
Ann E. Austin

 жжжжжжжжжжжжжжжжжжжжжжжж

Students
and Accreditation

*In an American college of the eighteenth and nine-
teenth century any proposal that the students
should be asked to state in public what they
thought of their teachers and teaching, would not
merely have been considered horrible. It would
have been horripilant. Chills and fevers of outraged
authority would have shaken the whole faculty
from the president down to the youngest assistant
instructor.*

Boston Transcript *Editorial (1926)*

A recent report from a liberal arts college states: "Today, most
American educators would probably agree that the learner—
not the teacher—is at the center of the educational universe"
(Alverno College Faculty, 1979, p. 1). Indeed, most statements
of purpose published by widely differing postsecondary educational institutions—from state universities to community colleges to proprietary trade schools—similarly imply that an educational experience of high quality provides direct benefits to
students, in both their personal and intellectual development as

211

well as in later employment possibilities. Nevertheless, accrediting associations, which have historically functioned as the guardians of educational quality, have less often emphasized direct benefits to institutions and professionals while focusing only indirectly on benefits to students. Although students do not yet appear to be of central importance in the accreditation process, new developments will probably make accreditors increasingly responsive to an emphasis on learners' experiences.

Students as Beneficiaries of Accreditation

The process of voluntary accreditation has three potential beneficiaries: postsecondary educational institutions (including various disciplinary and professional units within institutions), students, and society. Ideally, the accreditation system should serve all these beneficiaries equally well, because service to one group implies advantages for the others: The institution is encouraged to evaluate and improve its educational offerings, the student is assisted in choosing a school that demonstrably accomplishes desired objectives, and society's investment in both institutions and students is protected and enhanced. In reality, the history of voluntary accreditation shows that the three beneficiaries have profited to different degrees at different times. Because the social context is continually evolving, emphases will necessarily change in the future. Traditional accreditation procedures may be supplanted by new modes of quality determination more appropriate to an extremely diverse student population and to a society seeking more rigorous levels of accountability.

When regional accrediting associations originated, in the early twentieth century, institutions of higher learning were the intended beneficiaries as the associations tried to determine that students presenting certain credentials were qualified for study beyond high school. Somewhat later, these associations provided protection for their institutional members against competition from schools that were considered less adequate in their educational offerings and were not accredited. Eventually, these activities evolved into a concern for upholding minimal educational standards among member institutions (Selden and Porter, 1977, pp. 2-3). Although students and society certainly benefited as more consistent standards were gradually established, institutional gains were somewhat more easily identified. Colleges that conducted peer reviews began to achieve status, thereby attracting the best-prepared students.

Possibly because of this tradition, specific references to the benefits of accreditation to students—either in materials published by particular accrediting bodies or in the general literature on accreditation—are hard to find. In a 1979 document on accreditation standards by the Association of Independent Colleges and Schools (AICS) Accrediting Commission (1979, p. 9), accreditation was found to be useful to three constituencies: (1) agencies and authorities concerned with education that desire to identify institutions that meet particular standards, (2) employers who wish to gauge the strength and reliability of an instructional program or institution, and (3) the institution that is striving to maintain quality in its program. In its revised 1980 document, the AICS Accrediting Commission cited the accreditation process as being useful to both institutions and students by encouraging quality programs (1980, p. 12). In a review of accreditation standards and guidelines, Petersen (1979) indicates that regional associations give little attention to student issues beyond specifying a review of student services. Institutional associations devote some attention (but little) to ethical practice in student relations and specifying student outcomes. The greatest emphasis on students as beneficiaries of accreditation is found among specialized accrediting associations. These groups, particularly in the health care fields, are concerned about providing for students' individual differences and about guarding against exploitation of student trainees. In general, however, accreditors' statements on students are vague and varied, with greatest emphasis on the admissions process.

Similarly, in analyzing the goals of accreditation, experienced members of the accreditation community have distinguished among the several uses of accreditation: (1) internal uses, (2) external uses, (3) professional uses, and (4) social uses (Selden and Porter, 1977, p. 4). Students are mentioned only briefly, as one group of external users of accreditation. The implied value of accreditation is to the institution. The link between evaluation and improvement of educational quality, on the one hand, and student needs or benefits, on the other, is not directly discussed.

Some critics would hold that this omission occurs because such a link cannot be demonstrated. Numerous researchers (Jacob, 1957; Lehman, 1963; Chickering, McDowell, and Compagna, 1969; and others) have found minimal or nonexistent relationships between the college characteristics usually considered by accreditors and certain aspects of student change and development. Although one cannot assume the absence of a relationship between the criteria generally used by accrediting associations and the quality of an institution, research does not "substantiate the claim that certain accrediting association criteria assure institutional quality" (Troutt, 1979, p. 208). Accreditation has been compared to health-department approval of a restaurant: "It reassures a patron that he or she is unlikely to fall ill as a direct result of eating in the establishment, but there is no assurance of a tasty meal or even a nutritious one" (Atkin, 1978, p. 3). Regardless of what future research may show, supporters of accreditation can justifiably claim that the process yields substantial indirect benefits for students. Now, however, they are being urged to make clearer the direct benefits. There seems little question that recent changes in postsecondary education will pressure accreditors toward a more student-oriented stance.

Considerable criticism has recently been aimed at accreditors because of their failure to take an explicit interest in student needs and development. Paradoxically, society's interest in accreditation has taken on increasing importance with the emergence of federal student aid programs. Since 1952 the government has used voluntary accreditation as an indicator that a postsecondary educational institution is of sufficient quality that federally supported students may attend it—a use of accreditation that has become complex and controversial. Although accreditors were initially reluctant to accept a quasi-public role, most associations have now strengthened their emphasis on the societal benefits as well as the institutional benefits of accreditation. Meanwhile, the federal government has also launched several regulatory efforts to fill perceived gaps in the guardianship of student welfare. Accrediting associations, had their focus on the benefits of accreditation for students been stronger, might have taken the initiative in several of these areas.

Today, the benefits of accreditation for students are demonstrated more pointedly than in the past, and this fact may well lead to increased support for the continued role of voluntary accreditation. However, the relationship between accreditation and students can be expected to receive even more attention in the near future. The recent criticisms that call for more direct benefits to students can be grouped into broad categories, and from these categories can be deduced productive mechanisms that accreditors might consider for the future. Thus, the evolving role of accreditation can be analyzed in relation to (1) communication with students and parents, as well as the general public, (2) involvement of students in the accreditation process, (3) protection of students as consumers, and (4) measurement of educational quality in ways that are directly relevant to students.

Communicating with Students and Parents

Providing students with a list of credible programs was a goal of some accrediting bodies as early as 1939 and is still included in the stated purposes of many specialized accrediting associations (Petersen, 1979). The assumption is often made that students make heavy use of accreditation when choosing among colleges and professional programs (Troutt, 1979, p. 199). Although this assumption appears not to have been tested systematically, discussions with prospective students disclose little evidence of its validity. Students do not seem to understand the purposes of accreditation or even to know whether the institution they plan to attend is accredited by a recognized body.

Communications from some government agencies have not helped to clarify the role of accreditation for students and the public. For example, federal officials expressed their dubious view of accreditation in a booklet designed to assist students in choosing an institution: "Generally speaking, accreditation is better than no accreditation" (U.S. Department of Health, Education and Welfare, 1977a, p. 14). A similarly nonsupportive statement is included in a guide published by the New York State Consumer Protection Board: "The agencies [accreditors] involved rarely take strong action against any school, and they devote much of their effort to protecting the schools from public scrutiny and criticism" (Council on Postsecondary Accreditation, 1980a). Some federal officials have gone so far as to state that accreditation (or at least its role in eligibility for federal funding) hinders rather than helps students. In testimony before a congressional committee just before he relinquished his post as secretary of health, education and welfare, Joseph Califano said that "federal reliance on private accreditation misleads parents and students to believe that the federal government vouches for the quality of any institution receiving federal funds" (Califano, 1979, p. 22). Califano asked Congress to sever the link between private accreditation and institutional eligibility for federal programs in the Higher Education Act (p. 21); but the recommendation, which engendered considerable discussion, was not implemented after his resignation. The time seems to have come for the postsecondary education community to undertake an educational campaign to improve public understanding of the accreditation process and its relation to government funding, particularly among college students. In fact, such a campaign is listed as a major priority by the Council on Postsecondary Accreditation (1978c, p. 7).

Some members of the accreditation community admit that the purposes and functions of their associations have not been fully communicated to the public (Young, 1979a). Apparently, public relations efforts have suffered while there has been a concentration on shaping peer review procedures, communicating with institutional constituents, and, more recently, responding to government pressures. Lack of public understanding is not surprising when one recalls that accreditation has existed for only a short time relative to the history of postsecondary education in the United States. However, the need for more systematic attention to the public image of accreditation, particularly in the eyes of students and prospective students, is increasingly apparent.

Stories abound of students who, because they have misinterpreted the meaning of accreditation or are unaware of it, unwittingly attend an unethical institution or one of poor quality. In general, although there may be little value to the student in knowing that an institution or program is accredited, knowing that it has been turned down for accreditation may be very important. However, accreditors have generally not made public the names of institutions or programs that have failed to meet accreditation standards. One reason accrediting associations have avoided publicizing adverse decisions is the voluntary nature of their membership. Associations have no authority to enforce recommendations but rather can only encourage adherence to their guidelines. A decision to remove accreditation may be costly and may involve lengthy litigation. Consequently, as a Federal Interagency Committee on Education report stated (1975, p. 38), accrediting bodies are not eager "to engage in full disclosure, to publicize those institutions which have been put on probation, or to disclose some of their findings which could be used by students and applicants." Yet, in forgoing this opportunity, a chance is lost to make accreditation more meaningful to students. The 1979 AICS draft of *Accreditation Standards* admitted that "a decision to withdraw accreditation or to censure an institution is effective only when it can be communicated publicly" (Association of Independent Colleges and Schools, 1979, p. 45). However, the 1980 revised document appears to have omitted this statement. A U.S. General Accounting Office report (1979, p. 13) recommended that the secretary of HEW "initiate efforts to increase the public's awareness of the accreditation process and what can and should be expected from it."

Even if accrediting associations fail to publicize institutions or programs from which accreditation is withdrawn, as required by COPA, they could communicate more fully with students about important issues to consider when choosing among accredited institutions and programs. Furthermore, accreditation could contribute more to the implementation of national priorities for improved student access and choice among institutions and programs. For example, since 1974 the Fund for the Improvement of Postsecondary Education has sponsored several projects designed to disclose more detailed information to help students choose among options for postsecondary education. The National Task Force on Better Information for Student Choice identified the types of information that seem important to students, including financial aid, types of careers, and the quality of instruction and instructors (El-Khawas, 1978). A second major effort, the Center for Helping Organizations Improve Choice in Education (CHOICE), worked with several colleges to collect such information and make it available to students. The colleges voluntarily provided data drawn from alumni follow-up studies and developed detailed profiles on student aid opportunities. Interest among nonparticipating colleges has been high regarding the techniques used and the positive effects on student/college relations. Some of the "Better Information" activities have now been assumed by the National Association of College Admissions Counselors. All the information could be gathered during a self-study before an accreditation review, and the new techniques could just as well have been fostered by accreditors.

Some institutions that participated in the Better Information Task Force suggested, as have the Carnegie Council on Policy Studies in Higher Education (1979, p. 63) and some accreditors (Council on Postsecondary Accreditation, 1980b), that accreditation reports be shared with students as well as with faculty members and a conscious effort be made to involve the entire education community in implementing recommendations for improvement. Distressingly, colleges probably still commonly release some of the positive aspects of the report to students and the public while dealing quietly with identified weaknesses, although accrediting bodies try to control blatant efforts at misrepresentation. As has been argued elsewhere (Stark, 1978), such selective publication of data directly contradicts the principles of academic research that colleges teach and thus strains the colleges' credibility with students. All accrediting bodies might well ask their members to encourage full discussions of evaluations on the campus.

Another example of a situation in which the accreditors could take the lead in improving communication involves specialized accreditation. Students must attend an accredited program to ensure admission to certain upper-level college or graduate programs or to take certain licensing examinations. Students may proceed through a course of study only to learn later that the program lacked specialized accreditation and that they may not be able to enter an accredited advanced school or obtain a license to practice. Other questions surrounding the use of specialized accreditation as a gatekeeper to various professions also deserve consideration. Specialized accrediting bodies promote standards intended to assure society that only qualified graduates are admitted to professional practice; but professional opportunities for graduates of nonaccredited institutions or those who have acquired knowledge outside formal educational settings may be foreclosed by such arrangements. Increasingly, such restrictions by specialized accrediting bodies are viewed by the public and some segments of the education community as self-serving. If there are valid reasons for curriculum restrictions in specialized fields, accrediting bodies would benefit from disclosing the reasons so that they can convince the public that quality, not self-interest, is their primary concern.

The time is propitious for all segments of postsecondary education to establish communication with students and other publics to improve credibility (Stark and Griffith, 1979). Because of declining enrollments, some colleges are seeking students more aggressively than in the past; the news media have not neglected opportunities to publicize hard-sell tactics in college admissions. Throughout the postsecondary education community, too, college officials are discussing "marketing" approaches for postsecondary education. Most institutional officers carefully distinguish marketing from indiscriminate selling of institutional services and specify that marketing implies a meaningful attempt to match the needs of prospective students with the services provided by the institution (Stark, 1979; Litten,

1980). Because of their information about colleges' objectives and characteristics, accreditors have an opportunity to assist colleges in appropriately marketing their services to learners. However, accrediting associations also need to market their own activities by communicating precisely what their services guarantee and do not guarantee to students and society. Petersen (1979, p. 152) has recommended that communication could be improved if accreditors could at least agree to standardize the nomenclature describing their processes and judgments.

Involving Students in the Accreditation Process

Students probably benefit most from the accreditation function when the institutions they attend take the process seriously and use the self-study and peer review processes to examine programs and procedures thoroughly. When an institution regularly assesses whether it is meeting its stated objectives and uses available information to improve the quality of education, the effect on students is indirect; students may be quite unaware that the accreditation process exists. Nevertheless, since today's postsecondary students are adults who legitimately should have a part in decisions about education, they should be on self-study teams and involved in accreditation visits. Such participation not only provides a student perspective to the evaluation but may enhance the educational experience of the students who participate. Generally, however, only a few students can be directly involved in the peer review process. There are a variety of other ways to provide student involvement in accreditation beyond appointing a few students to a committee.

One method of achieving student involvement is to conduct regular, systematic surveys of student views on a variety of college services. Some colleges that worked with CHOICE and with the Better Information Task Force found that involving students in designing and implementing surveys provided useful information for accreditation, was helpful in informing prospective students about current student views, and provided practical research exercises for enrolled students. In turn, the process led to positive relations with students, who felt their views were valued. Because an accreditation team to a large degree validates a college's own self-study, a simple "audit" can confirm that the surveys of student views conducted by students themselves were obtained through unbiased techniques. One college in the Better Information Task Force, experimenting with such an audit conducted by peers to confirm the accuracy of materials from student surveys, reported that it could be effective (Stark and Marchese, 1978).

A continuing and legitimate objection to characterizing the student as a consumer is that the term seems to imply that all responsibility for the success of education falls on the institution. Involving students in the self-study process, whether in conducting studies or as deliberating committee members, provides an opportunity for the college to discuss and clarify the responsibilities of students for their own education. To foster reciprocal responsibility of students and institutions, accreditors might well try to assess the extent to which an institution encourages its students to take responsibility for their own education. This dimension of educational quality may have been overlooked by accreditors, who have not traditionally granted students an active role in the evaluation process.

Until recently, accreditation was carefully guarded as a peer review process. However, peer review has rapidly come under question as some federal and state officials have perceived potential conflict of interest in a situation in which institutions monitor themselves through voluntary associations (U.S. General Accounting Office, 1979, p. 43). Accrediting bodies have been pressed to "take into account the rights, responsibilities, and interests of students" as well as of the general public, professional and occupational groups, and institutions (39 Fed. Reg. 30042, 1974, cited by Finkin, 1978, p. 5). As a condition for inclusion on the list of accreditors maintained by the commissioner (now secretary) of education, accrediting bodies have also been required to include on their governing board representatives of the public who can give voice to the community of interests affected by accreditation (Finkin, 1978, p. 5). One study refers to the appearance of students on some accreditation teams in small numbers beginning in 1973-74 (Kells, 1979, p.

187). The accreditation community need not fear that public representation on governing boards and student representation on accreditation teams will destroy the value of the review of quality standards. Instead, the accreditation community needs to develop positive and innovative modes of involvement that will take advantage of the viewpoints of all its constituencies.

Protecting Students from Consumer Abuses

Since 1974, government and student groups have adopted the "student as consumer" slogan to identify and advocate reforms in postsecondary education. Federal agencies, as well as student lobbying groups and independent researchers, have insisted that accrediting associations should share the responsibility for investigating specific institutional practices in the review process. The practices to be examined are based on perceived unfairness to students eligible for federal financial assistance. They encompass problems that sometimes occur in both accredited and nonaccredited schools, such as inconsistent and unclear admissions and grading practices, misleading or false advertising, use of inadequately prepared teachers, lack of promised services (for example, job placement assistance), and failure to provide specific types of information to prospective students. At one point, criteria for federal listing indicated that accrediting bodies should foster ethical practices among institutions (such as equitable refunds and nondiscrimination in admissions and employment procedures) and should ensure accuracy of representation in college advertising (see Chapter Thirteen).

Although accreditors do hold that "promoting the interests of the educational consumer" is part of their role (Council on Postsecondary Accreditation, 1978c), they have maintained that they are not the proper groups to assume responsibility for enforcing various civil laws and that accreditation should not "serve as a consumer protection guarantee for more than it attempts to evaluate" (Young, 1979a, p. 135). Others have asked whether accrediting associations do indeed "have an obligation to do more than they are now doing to assure the public that their members follow clear and comprehensive codes of good conduct which would embrace many principles of consumer protection" (Selden and Porter, 1977, p. 19). The postsecondary education community has responded with an effort to promote self-regulation initiatives (see Chapter Three). The accrediting bodies that have a large number of proprietary schools as members (the Association of Independent Colleges and Schools, the National Association of Trade and Technical Schools, and the National Home Study Council) have emphasized good business practices and student consumer protection.

From outside the accreditation community, the criticism has been sharper. For example, the argument has been made that "it is very hard to see how a quality institution can permit the existence of conditions, policies, or practices which are potentially abusive to students, regardless of how 'quality' is defined and measured" (Jung, 1977a, p. 364). One critic has observed pessimistically that "the attempt of some [U.S. Office of Education] officials to plant consumer protection in the accreditation process is as promising as a crop of Arctic coconuts" (Orlans and others, 1974, p. 21).

The idea of consumer protection has engendered equally negative reactions among many educators, particularly when the discussion starts from the premise that colleges deliberately treat students unfairly or when simplistic solutions are offered. Several groups and individuals have argued, however, that if the consumer protection concept is incorporated into the self-study process, it can benefit institutions. Self-examination by colleges of some practices in financial aid, admissions, advertising, and business affairs can result not only in an educational experience of better quality for students but also in more positive relations between students and institutions (El-Khawas, 1976; Stark and Associates, 1977). In this sense, accrediting associations would improve their services to all constituencies if they encouraged institutional members to engage in studies of fair practice that might supplement traditional accreditation.

In view of considerable negative publicity, if accrediting associations wish to uphold their claim of substantiating educational quality, they should all examine some student concerns that have been mentioned under the consumer protection rubric.

Accreditors should pay careful attention to the lengthy lists of potential abuses cited by some federally sponsored studies (Jung, 1977a) and determine which practices are sufficiently related to educational quality to merit inclusion in a self-study or peer review. Clearly, some federal stipulations should not be included. For example, a cogent argument has been made that the recent federal emphasis on student retention and job placement statistics as measures of quality both ignores institutional diversity and is based on a misconstruction of the idea of good education (Levin, 1977; Jung, 1977a). Such simplistic measures of quality would undoubtedly be among those rejected by accreditors. Yet, responsiveness to student needs may require that data on some related issues at least be collected and studied by the accreditation community to encourage a more informed discussion of the legitimate responsibility of accrediting bodies.

Several groups have tried to persuade educators to focus self-study techniques on particular institutional practices to ascertain that they deal fairly with students. For instance, the American Institutes for Research developed an institutional self-study form to help identify potential abuses of the student as a consumer. Some accrediting associations testified at a 1978 conference that pilot tests of the instrument demonstrated its helpfulness (Jung, 1977a, p. 367). Using a different approach, the American Council on Education published *New Expectations for Fair Practice* (El-Khawas, 1976) to set forth goals for conducting institutional relations with students in both business and academic matters. Project CHOICE developed a checklist for reviewing institutional public relations materials to ensure that they are pertinent to student interests and represent the college fairly (Chapman, Griffith, and Johnson, 1979). The same group also developed manuals on collecting and developing information materials for prospective students (Stark and Terenzini, 1978; Stark, 1978; Chapman, 1980). The National Center for Higher Education Management Systems has contributed a guide on presenting information to students (Lenning and Cooper, 1976). Again, any or all of these efforts could have been initiated by accrediting associations in response to demonstrated need. Although accreditors have acknowledged and occasionally endorsed some of these efforts, less frequently have they ventured independently beyond the peer review role to assess whether such techniques should be directly incorporated into the accreditation process.

Accrediting bodies have hesitated to carry the banner for consumer protection, and they have hoped to avoid independent review systems set up by federal or state governments to ensure fair practice by institutions. Nevertheless, recent proposals for amending the eligibility process have urged heavier reliance on state and federal consumer protection efforts instead of judgments by accrediting bodies (U.S. General Accounting Office, 1979, p. 10). It is well documented, however, that several states are ill equipped to efficiently perform either an accreditation function or a consumer protection function (Jung, 1977b; Orlans, 1980). Indeed, Millard observed that voluntary nongovernmental accreditation would probably never have originated if the states had been ready to deal with the problem of educational quality (Millard, 1979).

However, not all government pressure on accrediting associations that has resulted from their involvement with the federal eligibility process affects students positively. The number of new accrediting bodies recently applying for federal listing or recognition by COPA results from the increased importance of areas of study that have heretofore been outside the mainstream of postsecondary education. But to some extent the rise of new accrediting associations is also an entrepreneurial effort to obtain federal funds for educational programs that are superficial and unworthy of federal support. Accreditors have complained that federal criteria for listing are too detailed and burdensome, but other observers would hold that they are not stringent enough in demanding definitions of educational quality or in ensuring representation of legitimate educational interests. To be of greatest assistance in protecting the student, reviewers of accrediting bodies must continue to insist that only associations that are consistent and have the potential to determine quality are recognized and listed. Failure to do so would sanction meaningless proliferation of associations and further mislead students. Most educators believe a strong effort should be made to retain and to guard the integrity of the voluntary system that, although it arose in response to an institutional need, has been evolving to benefit other segments of society as well.

Student-Oriented Measures of Educational Quality

Accrediting associations have typically taken the position that educational quality cannot be defined in terms of specific standards or requirements because of the great variability in purpose and form among institutions and programs. In examining whether institutions have sound strategies for achieving their objectives, institutional accrediting associations generally focus on institutionally declared objectives and evaluate them within the framework of general criteria on institutional purpose, organization and administration, financial and physical resources, library facilities, faculty, student services, and educational program (Andrews, 1978, p. 20). Specialized accrediting associations more often use more specific criteria that reflect consensus of the professional or disciplinary group regarding acceptable educational strategies and conditions (Petersen, 1979; Young, 1980b). Thus, although an institutional accrediting association is likely to ascertain that the institution has workable governance procedures (without specifying the particular type of organization), a specialized accrediting body like the National Council on Accreditation of Teacher Education might require, for example, that practicing teachers be involved in organizational decisions related to curriculum. At still another level, the Educational Training Board of the American Speech-Language-Hearing Association might set forth a specific number of hours of clinical training that students should participate in, or the American Physical Therapy Association might evaluate programs on the basis of the number of graduates who demonstrate certain clinical competencies on a written licensure examination. Clearly, great variability in how educational quality is defined exists among the various types of accrediting bodies as well as among institutions.

Some observers have criticized the regional accrediting associations, seeing the way they allow institutions to vary as permissive, inconsistent, and lacking in credibility. Other critics have focused on the specialized accrediting bodies because of their seeming preoccupation with specific requirements (such as student-faculty ratios and number of full-time faculty members) that might or might not reflect on quality. One critic has compared the evaluation process used by accrediting bodies to a production model in which the emphasis is on the assembly line (Troutt, 1979, pp. 201–202): "Accreditation criteria of most regional associations suggest checking the curriculum is more reliable than checking the student. . . . Instead of checking on the quality of production outcomes, that is, student achievement, criteria generally check on the quality of the assembly line, that is, curricula, faculty, resources, and so on. Criteria assume a direct relationship exists between the quality of the assembly line and the quality of the product." Many other prominent figures in postsecondary education have also urged that accrediting bodies pay more attention to educational outcomes. Bowen stresses that the inputs into the education process traditionally examined by accreditors (facilities, library resources, extracurricular opportunities) must not be confused with the outputs of the process (the personal development of students). To Bowen and an increasing number of others, a valid assessment of quality must consider a range of major goals of education, including cognitive development, emotional and moral development, esthetic sensibility, practical competence, and direct satisfaction derived from education (Bowen, 1979; Astin, 1979).

Convinced as a result of his work on student development that traditional notions about assessment of institutional quality need revision, Astin (1979) has argued that new measures of the effectiveness of education must involve student feedback if they are to be valid. He suggests that any evaluation of an institution's educational objectives should include three types of measures that particularly pertain to students: successful completion of the program of study, cognitive development of the student, and student satisfaction with both the program of study as a whole and particular aspects of the experience.

Indeed, there is reason to believe that students might not only desire but also benefit from a greater emphasis on educational outcomes by accrediting bodies. When asked to judge among factors important in considering a college, students choose items concerning the quality of instruction, student satisfaction, and probable outcomes of their education, including potential entrance to satisfying careers (Lenning and Cooper, 1976). Because of its more detailed focus on specific program outcomes, specialized accreditation possibly has more utility to students than institutional accreditation.

Some accreditors have been alert to these views, and Bowen perceives that with increasing social demands for consumer protection and accountability "accreditation . . . may be entering a new era" (1979, p. 19). As an indication of new directions, a conference of education leaders sponsored by COPA emphasized educational outcomes. In addition to such joint discussion, accrediting associations have individually made some strides toward different methods of evaluation, perhaps in response to a major priority on outcome measures established by the Council on Postsecondary Accreditation (1978c). For example, the American Assembly of Collegiate Schools of Business (1980) initiated a major project on validating outcome measures within individual fields of study. Presumably, future evaluations of educational quality will more frequently use regular student feedback to gauge effectiveness in accomplishing stated purposes. Present forms of accreditation might eventually evolve into a coordinated system for verifying that the college or university has met stated educational outcomes (see Chapter Seventeen).

Perhaps the most significant statement that accreditors have made about the use of student outcomes is included in the report of a national project intended to develop evaluation criteria for accrediting nontraditional education. The report proposed that "institutional accreditation should operate within a single mode that will accommodate all of postsecondary education, recognizing both process and performance components in the evaluation of institutions" (Andrews, 1978, p. 19). Though asserting that accreditors have been effective and fair in evaluating the many types of nontraditional education, the report called for an emphasis not only on process but also on student performance in evaluation. In truth, such a stand was virtually dictated by the emergence of nontraditional education modes that attempt to substitute student accomplishment and performance for traditional measures of educational progress. The report, which has received considerable attention among accreditors, also recommended a review of institutional purposes to verify that emphasis is on educational achievement.

In the years ahead, accrediting bodies will be prompted by three developments to focus more fully on student achievement—new modes of education, new procedures used by colleges and education agencies to evaluate prior learning, and increasing attention on outcomes (for example, Pace, 1979). Many credible organizations now use tests to determine the skills possessed by graduates of educational programs. For example, the Center for Occupational and Professional Assessment of the Educational Testing Service (ETS) assesses skills for licensing and certification purposes in thirty fields from auto mechanics to gynecology (Educational Testing Service, 1980). The National Center for Higher Education Management Systems has been involved in a substantial project to assist colleges in measuring outcomes (Micek, 1979). The Higher Education Research Institute at UCLA has devised outcome studies of graduates that are being used by several institutions. Community colleges are tailoring cognitive mapping techniques and then regularly monitoring student progress.

Although such techniques were originally more common in occupational fields of study than in traditional academic disciplines, in which most assessment is done by the classroom professor, the movement toward student outcome measures has gained momentum, even in traditional academic disciplines. For example, a study by ETS for the Council of Graduate Schools identifies methods of assessing the quality of doctoral education and asserts that better measures of quality can be found without extensive financial and time commitments (Clark and Hartnett, 1978, p. 20). In this particular scheme, two clusters of interrelated indicators are proposed. The first cluster resembles traditional accreditation measures in that it includes department size, faculty publications, and physical and financial resources; the second includes measures of student satisfaction, ratings of teaching, ratings of faculty members' interpersonal relations skills, and alumni ratings of dissertation experiences (Clark and Hartnett, 1978, p. 4). Such an evaluation procedure, which draws on both traditional assessment indicators and new ones, would provide a more complete analysis of program quality that would be helpful to students in comparing programs in a particular field of study (Clark and Hartnett, 1978, p. 18). Because several groups and projects have espoused various types of outcome studies as useful to students in choosing colleges, students will probably begin to ask for such information. Accrediting associations could assist students by contributing to the development of valid assessment measures and adopting such instruments as part of their work.

Adapting to Future Needs

In view of the history of the development of accreditation and the pressures that now impinge on accrediting bodies, the accreditation process seems to be nearing the end of an evolutionary period with respect to its three potential beneficiaries —institutions, society, and students. Accreditation began as a tool developed and supported by institutions, and then by professional associations, to serve their purposes. Those original objectives, however, have changed in some instances. For example, an early purpose of accreditation—to certify to member institutions that students were adequately prepared for admission—has largely been preempted by the growth of comprehensive public high schools and the increased use of college admission tests. Although the reputation of the preparing institution is still important, most colleges and graduate schools are willing to weight standardized test scores at least as heavily as specific institutional preparation. The wide use of examinations that assess self-acquired knowledge equivalent to that learned in introductory college courses has added impetus to this trend.

Over time, forces outside the postsecondary education

community, including government agencies and groups operating in the public interest, have promoted a concern among accrediting bodies with demonstrating that postsecondary education is responsive to societal needs. Today, in fact, accountability to society may outweigh uses within and among institutions as the primary purpose of accreditation. The question "Accountability for what?" continues to be debated, however. The accreditation community has argued that accreditation should be used for education-related purposes, not as a policing mechanism in other areas. In addition, self-regulation, self-evaluation, and self-improvement can be seen as essential elements in an effective system of accountability (see Chapter Three). There is also the related question "Why seek accreditation?" Status that colleges once derived from peer approval may now be sought because accreditation is viewed as the primary route to certain federal and state funds. Thus, society has emerged as a primary beneficiary of the accreditation process because accreditors help judge the kinds of educational endeavors suitable for the public. Students continue to benefit from accreditation to the extent that the process operates to ensure that they are receiving worthwhile educational opportunities. Their participation in the process, however, is quite limited and their awareness of its significance minimal.

During this process of evolution, accrediting associations have appeared to play the role of follower rather than leader, particularly in devising new methods of assessing educational quality. Member institutions have moved ahead into new areas of outcome validation with the help of other agencies. Only when new assessment procedures are well established in the education community are accrediting bodies likely to adopt them. For example, the nontraditional education movement instituted by colleges has pushed accrediting bodies toward evaluating performance as well as the processes of education. One analyst (Hall, 1979) suggests that accrediting associations have adapted to the emphasis of nontraditional education on serving diverse students. Yet, the adaptation seems to be continuing at an accelerated rate as accreditation moves from its relatively strong societal interest to an emphasis on student outcomes. In the words of one accrediting-body executive, "A new emphasis on outcomes would not only respond to societal needs but is a logical culmination of our more flexible approach to quality assessment" (Sweet, 1979, p. 5).

The peer review system is the basis of the accreditation process. It has many advantages, not the least of which is the spread from one campus to another of good ideas beneficial to institutions in general and to students in particular. Nonetheless, as financial pressures on postsecondary education become more severe and as institutions carefully assess the costs associated with preparing elaborate self-study reports for peer review, changes in the accreditation process may be prompted by cost considerations. Maintaining the benefits of the peer review as well as accommodating increasing oversight by state coordinating boards and potential federal regulation will be a challenge, because the costs of all these processes are passed on to the already financially beleaguered student.

Accrediting associations will need to recognize that the student may now well emerge as the primary beneficiary of accreditation, particularly as institutions become anxious to provide assurance that they are performing a service valuable to students. An era in which students may choose among many colleges with empty places is quite different from an era in which only a relatively few students were chosen. Communicating with the public more adequately, involving students in accreditation processes, performing selected consumer protection services, and using new methods of outcome assessment that are meaningful to students are all approaches that can help maintain the credibility of voluntary nongovernmental accreditation and enhance the role it will play in the future.

13

Charles M. Chambers

꙾꙾꙾꙾꙾꙾꙾꙾꙾꙾꙾꙾꙾꙾꙾꙾꙾꙾꙾꙾꙾꙾꙾꙾꙾꙾

Federal Government and Accreditation

> *The great question is to discover, not what the governments prescribe, but what they ought to prescribe; for no prescription is valid against the conscience of mankind.*   Lord Acton (1877)

Accreditation developed in this country over the last seventy years as an integral and essential aspect of postsecondary education. Any examination of its relationship to the federal government must therefore be made in light of the government's own interest in education.

The U.S. Constitution does not provide for a direct role by the federal government in education. From the country's founding days, this responsibility has been assumed by the states, which have established their own institutions, as well as by private corporations chartered within their boundaries. Under the Constitution's "general welfare" clause, however, the federal government has created a vast array of special-purpose funding programs through which appropriations flow, directly or indirectly, to colleges and universities. In the interest of good

233

stewardship and, even more, in the hope of fostering greater national achievement, the Congress has been concerned that only reputable institutions with acceptable educational quality should participate in these programs. The very act of granting funds to some institutions while withholding them from others in and of itself has created a federal index of perceived quality—an index that has posed a dilemma for the federal government. Regardless of what criteria the government developed or how objectively they were applied, there would be a strong concern within the postsecondary education community and elsewhere that the federal government would thus be accrediting institutions and that this action might become the first step toward the creation of a centralized ministry of education in Washington.

Within the Office (later the Department) of Education, an effort was made to resolve this dilemma by adopting a two-stage process for funding programs in postsecondary education. (Other federal agencies varied their approaches.) The first stage is known as institutional eligibility, and at present an institution must document its status as a legal entity offering postsecondary education of some recognized quality and meeting certain federal requirements. In granting institutional eligibility, the federal government does not directly inspect each and every institution. Rather, it requires that the institution be chartered or licensed by the state in which it is operating (or in a few instances by the federal government itself), that it be accredited by a nationally recognized accrediting body (or fulfill one of several alternatives to accreditation), and that it assure the federal government that it conforms to statutory requirements in such areas as employment practices. The pool of eligible institutions has grown quite large, exceeding 8,000, including teaching hospitals, clinics, and foreign institutions enrolling American students. At the second stage, the various federal programs select from this large pool those institutions that most closely meet the programs' funding goals. For example, there may be only a few dozen institutions with the facilities to conduct genetic research or perhaps only a few hundred that are both located in certain urban areas and particularly able to serve a certain group of economically disadvantaged students. Almost all eligible institutions qualify, however, for the large student aid programs.

This two-stage process seemed an ideal way for the federal government to stay out of the role of evaluating individual institutions and yet assure itself about the soundness and quality of the institutions by relying primarily on the states and the accrediting organizations. Unfortunately, the process did not turn out to be quite that straightforward or perfunctory. The states vary widely in their requirements for authorizing institutions to operate; at least two states (Utah and Missouri) have no licensing laws. These differences are historical and political in nature and generally reflect the degree of urbanization and industrialization in a given state. Because the states are independent instruments of government, the Department of Education elected to accept at face value whatever authorization any state has granted to any institution. Thus, the federal government makes no effort to regulate this important part of the institutional eligibility stage. The federal government has encouraged states with minimal or no chartering statutes to improve their oversight of institutions within their boundaries and has supported the development of model state licensing legislation. It has been careful, however, not to go beyond these bounds. In dealing with nongovernmental accrediting bodies, the other major component in the institutional eligibility stage, the government did not have to contend with any constitutional restraints. Therefore, it has played a much more aggressive role in using, reviewing, and regulating these private associations.

A historical review of the relationship between the federal government and accrediting bodies is useful because it shows how the present relationship developed and reveals the major trends and subtle nuances of the relationship. Five basic periods can be identified: the early years, the period immediately after World War II, the national-defense years, the social-equity years, and the federal-regulation years. Note that each period is defined by a shift in the federal government's interest in education and, hence, in its relationship with accreditation.

The Early Years

From the adoption of the Constitution in 1776 to the creation of the land-grant program under the Morrill Act in 1862, there was little federal involvement in education, and no accrediting organizations existed. Yet, that period was crucial for postsecondary education in this country, because during this time deep roots were pushed down to undergird principles such as institutional autonomy, academic freedom, and the complementary roles of state and private institutions. Toward the end of this period, private associations of institutions and professional and disciplinary societies were formed—all interested to one degree or another in the quality, soundness, and well-being of various educational activities.

With the adoption of the Morrill Act, the federal government established the Bureau of Education to collect and publish data on schools and colleges in the United States. At once, the bureau faced the difficult problem of deciding which institutions should be designated colleges and which should be considered precollegiate. At about the same time, the state-by-state appearance of public secondary school systems led to the common adoption of the high school diploma as a certificate of completion. In addition, the new regional accrediting associations began developing working definitions of the term *college* as well as establishing what preparation students seeking college admission should have.

During the early part of the twentieth century, many baccalaureate graduates traveled to European universities for advanced study. The German universities in particular were reluctant to admit graduates of just any "college" and asked the Bureau of Education to rank American undergraduate institutions as first-, second-, and third-level. The bureau developed what it considered to be a set of objective criteria based on the success of a college in placing its students in the graduate programs of institutions belonging to the Association of American Universities (AAU). The higher education community was quick to sense the inappropriateness of the federal government's putting such "good/better/best" labels on institutions, and the resulting uproar reached Congress, where the publication of such a list was decried as "an outrage and an infamy to designate institutions whose sons had reflected honor on the nation" as being second- or third-rate (Capen, 1917, p. 35). Sensing strong opposition to such a list and not finding any overriding federal interest (as surely the German universities could survive without such a list), President Taft acted to prohibit its publication. When his successor, Woodrow Wilson, again declined to publish the list in 1914, the Bureau of Education abandoned the project, and the AAU, as a private organization, published its own list for the German universities. Yet, even it found such rancor within the education community that it eventually dropped the ratings and developed a single list of what it considered the most prestigious institutions.

Over the next few decades, the regional accrediting associations refined their standards for membership and developed procedures for assessing educational quality on the basis of an institution's own self-study and an evaluation by a group of visiting peers. Similar efforts made among professional societies led to the establishment of the many corresponding specialized accrediting bodies.

In summary, this period may be characterized as a time when both the federal government and the postsecondary education community learned more about their roles and relationships and when the federal government pursued a modest degree of experimenting with how much it could say about educational institutions, most notably in its growing bookshelf of directories, compendiums, and other lists of information.

The Post–World War II Years

Since World War II, the federal government's interest and involvement in accreditation has reached astonishing proportions. Because the government and the postsecondary education community had already discovered something about each other, this period has been marked by many policy changes both in statutes and in the day-to-day working practices of federal agencies and institutions. The general theme has been to use federal appropriations to encourage wider access and opportunity for postsecondary students as a way to achieve national social goals. Through the late 1950s, the two GI bills looked to the postsecondary education community as the primary means of helping the returning veteran get established or reestablished in a productive career. During the next decade, the country reacted to the Sputnik challenge and again called on colleges and universities to build broader strength in science and defense capabilities. The last decade has witnessed a mammoth effort to provide postsecondary educational opportunities to economically disadvantaged students regardless of their preparation for collegiate study.

Clearly, such dramatic policy shifts every ten years or so have tested, if not shaken, the traditional wisdom about what postsecondary education is and is not intended to do. On a historical scale, these recent decades can be described as nothing less than revolutionary, and in this environment the federal government has developed its serious interest in accreditation.

Without doubt, the major phenomenon that has influenced the relationship between the federal government and postsecondary education over the past quarter century has been the series of post-World War II veterans' education assistance programs. Accordingly, the most fundamental linkages between the federal government and accreditation were established through this legislation in the early 1950s. A brief review of the circumstances surrounding the Servicemen's Readjustment Acts, as they were technically known, is necessary to understand how the federal role in accreditation emerged so dramatically. (For a complete review of the education issues pertaining to the Servicemen's Readjustment Acts, see Orlans and others, 1979.) The first GI Bill, enacted in 1944 with World War II still underway, provided a wide range of liberal benefits to returning veterans. It was designed to ameliorate the harsh economic prospects confronting soldiers returning to a country undergoing the difficult contraction from a wartime to a peacetime economy. The hardships faced by the veteran after World War I were still fresh in the minds of most legislators, and price seemed no object. A major part of the bill provided education benefits that could be used for almost any type of education from elementary school through graduate school, including vocational, and even avocational, courses of study. Institutions were reimbursed directly by the government for the number of veterans enrolled. There was virtually no process for supervising which institutions veterans could attend. The Veterans Administration (VA) was given carte blanche to approve institutions or simply use the list prepared by each state of the institutions legally operating in its jurisdiction. There was no involvement of the Bureau of Education or any use of its comprehensive directory, *Accredited Higher Institutions.*

The education part of the package was exceptionally well received. Some twenty times the anticipated number of veterans actually pursued education, a majority of them seeking vocational training below the college level. Unfortunately, there was a severe shortage of reputable and established technical schools, and during a five-year period the number of such schools tripled. Year by year, Congress attempted to fine-tune the quality controls in the education part of the GI Bill as the reports of scandal grew. National commissions studied the problem and pointed out that many of the questionable schools lacked both accreditation and effective state regulation through licensing and that the VA itself lacked expertise about education.

The mounting concern for an extensive reorganization of the veterans' education benefits culminated in the passage of the 1952 Korean GI Bill. No longer would institutions be reimbursed by the VA; rather, payment would be made directly to the veteran in the hope that he or she would demand a dollar's worth of education for each dollar spent. Conditions were added concerning the type of institution in which the veteran could enroll and the program of study that could be pursued. The American Council on Education, among others, argued that the newly established Office of Education should administer the education benefits. There was some strong sentiment from non-education groups not to fragment the whole benefits package. In fact, the American Legion favored a veto power by the VA administrator over all participating institutions. Congress was eager to have better quality control but was equally eager to avoid having a federal agency, such as the VA, meddle in the affairs of education—especially in an area as sensitive as judging educational quality.

In the final legislation, Congress turned to the states and asked each of them to conduct, on behalf of the VA, an approval process for postsecondary educational institutions operating in the state. As a concession, but hardly a compromise, the Office of Education was directed to publish a list of nationally recognized accrediting bodies that could be considered reliable in judging the educational quality of their member institutions. This task was not considered particularly onerous because *Accredited Higher Institutions* had for years contained a listing of corresponding accrediting bodies. The meagerness of this role for OE was further dramatized by the fact that state approval agencies were not required to rely on an institution's accreditation but had full discretion to carry out inspections of any educational institution, from vocational preparation to graduate research, if deemed necessary.

Section 1775 of the bill (P.L. 82-550) contained the specific language. This language reappeared in new legislation as "boiler plate" over the next thirty years: "For the purpose of this title the commissioner shall publish a list of nationally recognized accrediting agencies and associations which he determines to be reliable authorities as to the quality of training offered by an educational institution, and the state approving agency may, upon concurrence, utilize the accreditation of such accrediting associations or agencies for approval of the courses specifically accredited and approved by such accrediting association or agency."

Despite some nettlesome problems with certain aspects of the language, such as what makes an accrediting body "nationally recognized" and when a course is "specifically accredited," the general thrust of this section is still recognized, even by its critics, as an adroit maneuver to placate the education community and at the same time to spare the government the onerous and politically untenable task of passing on the quality of individual institutions and programs in postsecondary education, especially when accreditation suggests that a reasonably good track record exists.

The Office of Education now faced the problem of deciding which accrediting bodies to place on the list. Just as, a century earlier, it had had to decide which institutions to list in its directory, OE now had to have some definition to determine which accrediting bodies were "nationally recognized" and how they could be considered "reliable." Not wishing to antagonize the education community, Commissioner Earl McGrath approached the recently established National Commission on Accrediting (NCA). NCA was supported by the presidents of the major higher education institutions and had developed a set of criteria to help it judge which specialized accrediting bodies were actually needed in higher education. The ultimate goal was to have only a small core of specialized accrediting bodies deemed essential to public health and safety, with the regional accrediting commissions assuming the primary responsibility for accrediting the entire institution. Commissioner McGrath proposed that the federal government simply adopt the NCA criteria and its list of recognized accrediting bodies.

NCA was flattered to have its criteria accepted but blushed at the suggestion of providing a precise list. NCA, of course, knew of the existence of every major accrediting body; yet, the timing was most inopportune. Its own operating goal, toward which it was only slowly beginning to move, was to limit the number of recognized bodies to an irreducible minimum. It had not yet begun a rigorous screening process, although it clearly had in mind some accrediting bodies that it considered superfluous. NCA found that it would be in an awkward position if it were to provide a full list to the commissioner and later refused to admit any of those organizations into its own membership. However, it was a fledgling organization, and if it provided only an abbreviated list, it would surely encounter strong backlash from the accrediting bodies that it omitted. In a letter dated July 24, 1952, to Commissioner McGrath, NCA director Fred Pinkham communicated his organization's decision that no list would be forthcoming and that the commissioner should feel free to prepare his own list, but only with the clear understanding that the sole purpose of such a list was to carry out the approval provisions of the GI Bill and that this list would in no way constitute an endorsement by the government of the practices of the accrediting bodies on it. NCA continued to develop its own recognition process, based on its criteria, that would be voluntary for accrediting bodies seeking affiliation with NCA.

In a classic example of administrative efficiency, the commissioner published the list of accrediting bodies contained in the Office of Education's directory, *Accredited Higher Institutions,* together with a slightly edited version of the NCA criteria. To this day, that list appears in the 1952 edition of the *Federal Register* in law school libraries throughout the country as the federal government's first official pronouncement about who was who in accreditation. Of course, the NCA letter, with its caveat, was not published, and as might be expected, the list included numerous specialized accrediting bodies that many institutions hoped NCA would be particularly successful in curtailing.

By publishing this first list, the federal government profoundly altered the nature of accreditation and, more important, its relationship to the postsecondary education community. First, the federal government had never previously purported to make an explicit statement about who was an accrediting body and what such a body did. Although a roster of accrediting bodies had been included in the earlier directory, *Accredited Higher Institutions,* its purpose there was only bibliographical. Second, accrediting bodies were now, by virtue of the statutory provision, judged to be both "recognized" and "reliable." These are the two operative words in the statutory language regarding the commissioner's authority to publish a list of accrediting bodies. To this day, they have proved to be a gold mine of flexible interpretation. Such grandly subjective terms are always problematic in legislative drafting. Indeed, during the ensuing thirty years, the regulations to interpret these two words have grown from one-half page to more than four pages in the federal code.

The emergence of this federal list, coupled with polite obstructionism from the more established specialized accrediting bodies and a mounting ambivalence on major campuses about whether they would actually deal only with NCA's groups, effectively destroyed NCA's role as accreditation's policeman in the nongovernmental education community. For the handful of prominent specialized accrediting bodies that were well integrated into an institution's academic affairs, the appearance of the federal list probably made little difference. However, for the dozen and a half or so less well-established accrediting bodies that were actually the target of NCA's attrition plans, the list was crucial. By the mid 1950s, NCA recognized that if it was to be a leader, then it must march in front of the crowd; it therefore summarily recognized essentially all specialized accrediting bodies on the government list.

Another interesting consequence of the federal government's new role in accreditation soon began to emerge in the proprietary school sector. A significant number of veterans chose to use their benefits to enroll in commercial, business, correspondence, and technical schools. Further, the proprietary sector was where most of the reported instances of poor quality had been reported, thus leading to the new state approval system. Although these schools had begun experimenting with processes of external review and evaluation through their national associations, those associations were not accepted by NCA as accrediting bodies, nor had their institutions ever been listed in the OE directory. Because the commissioner of education was now required to publish a list to assist the VA and the states in the administration of the veterans' benefits and because the lion's share of the benefits was going to proprietary schools, the commissioner could not fail to include their accrediting bodies and still discharge his statutory responsibilities.

In particular, if the commissioner failed to list an accrediting body, he would then be placed in the position of having to defend why a nationally recognized accrediting body was not considered reliable. The Office of Education, recognizing the untoward politics involved, rejected—on the basis of administrative discretion—the applications of the newly formed proprietary accrediting bodies. Washington counsel for the groups doggedly challenged this determination, and by the late 1950s the accrediting bodies for both proprietary business schools and correspondence schools appeared on the list with stature equal to that of the regional accrediting commissions and the professional accrediting bodies. The proprietary technical schools soon realized that national endorsement of their work could be achieved through federal means and in the midsixties organized their own association expressly to achieve a place on the commissioner's list.

A final complication that can be traced to the first federal list pertains to the two basic types of accreditation—institutional and specialized accreditation. Like the regional associations, the proprietary accrediting groups were institutional in nature, evaluating the entire scope of their members' educational activities. Further, the GI Bill instructed the commissioner to include on his list accrediting bodies that were deemed reliable as regards the quality of education offered "by an educational institution." Other language spoke of "approved courses," as though an institution might offer some acceptable courses, while other courses at the same institution might be unacceptable. Because there is no such thing as course-by-course accreditation, the practice has been that all courses offered by an accredited institution could be deemed eligible by the state approving agency, if desired. The clear institutional thrust of the provision for publishing the list was apparently overlooked. The earlier VA system had focused on approved institutions, and a course given by an institution with accreditation could be accepted as approved. The Office of Education could have included on the first list only the regional accrediting groups, explaining that the VA scheme did not envision subinstitutional accreditation despite the unfortunate language about "approved courses." But the seeds of confusion had been sown decades earlier when institutions having only one small part accredited by a specialized accrediting body had been included in *Accredited Higher Institutions*. Without a second thought, many specialized accrediting bodies that played no role in the VA approval system were placed on the first list. Not until the late 1970s were the misleading consequences of this fundamental oversight recognized and confronted.

The National Defense Years

The next major increase in federal funding going to colleges and universities was prompted by the appearance of a small, metallic Soviet voyager orbiting high above the earth. In response to Sputnik, Congress passed the 1958 National Defense Education Act (NDEA). Although this act is perhaps best remembered in education for its loyalty-oath requirement, it also inaugurated a new link between accreditation and federal eligibility that has continued, virtually unchanged, to this date. Unlike the veterans' legislation, this act gave the Office of Education direct responsibility for administering the benefits—that is, for actually dispersing fellowship money and related funds to students and participating colleges and universities. Thus, within the guidelines of the statute, OE would determine who would receive funds and who would not. This was a complete turnabout from the GI Bill situation, in which OE played only an advisory role to the VA and its state approval agencies.

Congress handled the problem of deciding which institutions could participate in the program by an efficient administrative arrangement. Quite simply, the operative language in the act states that funds can be used only at "institutions of higher education." This language would appear to be carte blanche for the Office of Education, because those four words, with suitable bending, could probably be applied to any postsecondary educational institution. However, the general-provisions part of the act contained definitions of various terms used in the act, including *institution of higher education*. Specifically, for purposes of the act, such an institution was one that was, first, public or nonprofit; second, authorized by the state in which it was located; and third, accredited by a nationally recognized accrediting body determined by the commissioner to be a reliable authority on the quality of education it offered. An institution also had to meet some technical requirements regarding the range of its offerings, but regardless, those that satisfied this definition were therefore said to be eligible to participate in NDEA programs.

An important distinction needs to be made. To be eligible, an institution had to be accredited, but its eligibility alone did not entitle it to receive federal funds. In essence, eligibility qualified an institution to apply for funding, but before a specific grant would be made, the Office of Education would have to review a formal proposal and determine that the purposes of the act could indeed be expected to be achieved at the applicant institution. Thus, program funding within OE became a two-tiered process with the link to accreditation relevant only at the first, or eligibility, stage.

Another important point is that the design of the statute clearly addressed institutional accreditation. Indeed, the institution is the legal entity that enters into contractual relationships with the federal government for the purpose of carrying out the goals of the funding legislation, and the institution itself is what becomes eligible, by virtue of its comprehensive accreditation. As in the GI Bill a decade earlier, the commissioner was again authorized to publish a list of accrediting bodies to be used in the eligibility process.

Because of the similarity of the NDEA language to that in the GI Bill, the commissioner simply elected to use the same list prepared for the VA. This administrative expediency perpetuated the inconsistency of the specialized accrediting bodies on the list. In particular, despite the institutional framework of eligibility, the list continued to include virtually all existing specialized accrediting bodies. In fact, at that time, virtually all eligibility determinations needed to administer the act could be made with a list of the regional accrediting commissions. Further, if asked, most specialized accrediting bodies would readily admit that they do not conduct a comprehensive assessment of an institution that could be used by the federal government to establish its overall eligibility and that they require or expect an institution to have comprehensive accreditation before it seeks their more limited certification.

Because the accreditation-eligibility language in the National Defense Education Act so closely parallels the GI Bill provision, one could easily assume that the policy was not looked at very closely—that, rather, the language was merely pasted in. There seem to have been mixed emotions in the accreditation community about this growing federal role, and perhaps serious reservations among some staff directors. However, the record does seem clear that the governing bodies of regional accrediting commissions—that is, the institutions—endorsed if not encouraged this new link between their accreditation and federal eligibility. Congress still had reservations about proprietary schools, and they were excluded, by definition, from being eligible for NDEA support.

The eligibility provisions perpetuated the language requiring the commissioner to "publish" a list of accrediting bodies. Although the clear intent of the legislation was to establish a procedure for qualifying institutions to participate in the programs, the word *publish* connotes a broader information-dissemination obligation akin to the preparation of a reference guide. In the 1952 GI Bill, the use of the word *publish* seems to acknowledge the organizational separateness of the Office of Education from the Veterans Administration. The commissioner could simply put his list on the VA bulletin board, and the VA administrator could subsequently consult it at his convenience in approving an institution. There does not seem to have been any public information function being served by the list, and language instructing the commissioner to "prepare" or "maintain" a list or to "designate" the corresponding accrediting bodies would have been much more appropriate.

With the new federal eligibility system came a new problem that was to prove distressing, especially to institutional accrediting bodies. To be granted eligibility, an institution had to be accredited by an accrediting body on the commissioner's list. Yet, accreditation was fundamentally a voluntary process. It was certainly considered worthwhile to have; however, if an independent institution, in its own wisdom, declined to seek accreditation, that was its prerogative. Indeed, there were many church-related institutions that eschewed all affiliations with secular organizations, such as professional societies and regional accrediting bodies. If they were not accredited, how could they be made eligible?

The commissioner found a solution in the old directory of accredited higher education institutions. There have always been reputable institutions that did not have accreditation, and the old Bureau of Education listed them in a separate part of the directory if their credits were accepted in transfer by three accredited institutions and they could produce letters to that effect. This expeditious procedure was known as the three-letter

rule, and for directory purposes there seemed little harm in listing such institutions in a separate section. Indeed, the amount
of information made available to the public about institutions
considered reputable, by some criterion or other, was increased.
The commissioner suggested, and Congress agreed, that a similar exception should be used to establish eligibility under the
National Defense Education Act. Again, the argument was made
that eligibility did not entitle an institution to receive funds but
only to apply for them and that any nonaccredited institution
could participate only after it met the second-tier requirements.
Thus, the exception was merely a convenient alternative to ensure that reasonably qualified institutions could be reviewed for
program grants. Put in perspective, the full impact of the federal government's involvement in accreditation becomes apparent. In essence, to participate in the NDEA funds, an institution
must have educational quality meriting accreditation, but in the
absence of such accreditation, letters from three accredited institutions showing the regular acceptance of credit transferred
from the institution will suffice. In other words, in the federal
scheme of things, obtaining letters from three accredited institutions was just as good as going through the rigors of an accreditation self-study and site visit.

By the early 1960s, the awkwardness of this expediency
was beginning to be appreciated. Subsequent legislation was
amended to allow nonaccredited institutions to qualify for eligibility if they could show "satisfactory assurance" that they
would receive accreditation within a reasonable time. If all else
failed, the commissioner was empowered to make institutions
eligible directly if, in consultation with a competent advisory
committee, he found the institution qualified. For the relationship between the federal government and accreditation, this eligibility system had all the makings of a classic Catch-22. It
mandated that accreditation be one condition an institution
must meet to become eligible. Yet, accreditation is a voluntary
process, and so some provision had to be made for institutions
that, for whatever reasons, had declined accreditation. At the
same time, accreditation is a nongovernmental activity designed
to evaluate educational quality. Consequently, whatever alterna-

tive routes to eligibility the federal government established would always appear to be a substitute for, or an equivalent of, such quality—as judged by the federal government.

Generally, the education community was not happy with the three-letter rule, and the commissioner was understandably reluctant to make independent federal determinations about individual institutions, even with an advisory committee. In the best spirit of compromise, middle ground was found in the satisfactory-assurance alternative. The genius in international agreements is said to be the use of language so intentionally vague that each party can interpret the language as it sees fit in convincing its side that the terms and conditions are to its advantage. Such an example occurred in the eligibility system, as follows. The regional accrediting bodies had established a preliminary status, generally called candidate status, for newly developing institutions. To ensure that an institution understood that candidacy was a preliminary stage, the accrediting bodies explicitly cautioned that being a candidate gave no assurance whatsoever of eventual accreditation. The Office of Education, however, took the opposite view—namely, that if an institution was able to become a candidate to pursue accreditation, then it would most likely achieve fully accredited status within a reasonable period of time. Therefore, its candidacy status could be considered satisfactory assurance of eventual accreditation, and the institution would be made eligible. In an almost Kafkaesque distortion of the principles involved, eligibility was eventually granted to one institution that was found to be making satisfactory progress toward achieving *candidacy* within a reasonable time.

The Social-Equity Years

By the mid 1960s, several new pieces of federal education legislation had been enacted. In general, each looked to the colleges and universities to provide education services that the government believed would help achieve diverse social goals it had set. Interestingly, although institutions and their accrediting bodies were coming under more and more federal scrutiny, little support was actually being given directly to them. Rather, Congress had determined that to achieve certain improvements in society's well-being, what was needed was particular types of education, research, and service that universities were uniquely qualified to provide. In essence, colleges and universities were invited to compete as independent contractors for federal funds to perform social tasks set out in the diverse programs enacted by Congress.

The commissioner of education was soon faced with growing complexity in the accreditation-eligibility system and felt an inherent reluctance to make too many direct eligibility determinations for institutions with irregular or even no accreditation. In 1968 the commissioner organized a small ad hoc advisory committee on accreditation chaired by Frank Dickey, then NCA's executive director. This advisory group had barely drawn its first breath when the entire federal role in education was extensively altered by the passage of President Johnson's extraordinarily comprehensive Great Society initiative. The central education component was the Higher Education Act, which was supplemented by other programs, such as the Vocational Student Loan Insurance Act. The impact of this legislation was soon to change many working assumptions about the role and purpose of accreditation and how accreditation should relate to the federal government.

The Great Society programs were based on the premises of opportunity for all and independence of choice. Not only would needy students be assisted in attending the colleges and universities of their choice, but they could also pursue vocational and technical studies in both community colleges and proprietary training centers. Ultimately, because of the range of benefits, more American and foreign institutions would enroll students in these programs than had served veterans twenty years earlier. Yet, unlike the GI Bill, which utilized a multimillion-dollar state approval system, virtually all this legislation adopted the OE eligibility system, with its more gentle link to accreditation developed in the college-level NDEA programs. Even in the proprietary sector, students could use guaranteed loans if the school was accredited by an accrediting body deemed reliable by the commissioner.

Although there was still a two-tiered process, many of the benefits were viewed as entitlements to students, and the second-tier review of the institution was quite perfunctory. Consequently, gaining first-tier eligibility was almost tantamount to gaining federal funds (or, more correctly, gaining students with federal financial aid). Yet, accreditation as it existed in the mid 1960s was just not well enough developed in breadth of coverage and depth of rigor to be thrust into such a pivotal role in federal funding. Congress, in essence, converted the accrediting bodies into quasi-governmental bodies by virtue of the large support it authorized. Although this eligibility process may be considered a great display of confidence in the accrediting bodies, the more likely explanation is that Congress did not want to get the federal government embroiled in the thankless task of deciding which institutions would and, more important, which would not be eligible for the expanded funding. Accreditation was not that well understood, but the postsecondary education community seemed to have much faith in it.

To their credit, the regional accrediting bodies proved equal to the challenge and broadened their memberships to include the rapidly growing community college and vocational school sectors. In a significant service to both the postsecondary education community and the federal government, the regional accrediting commissions demonstrated that the general process of self-study and peer review, designed as a way to judge that an institution had set appropriate educational objectives for itself and was reasonably achieving them, could serve as a unifying concept for quality assurance among many disparate types of institutions. As a result, the accreditation principles developed for colleges and universities received firm social validation, and they served education well a decade later when many nontraditional education programs began to emerge. Although there will always be critics of the rigor and resolve shown by the regional accrediting bodies in policing their own membership, regional accreditation was able to avoid the real danger of state education boards assuming the primary quality assurance role for vocational and technical education. Had this expanded role for the regional accrediting bodies not been achieved, the vital concept of general education—however that may be defined—would have ceased to be a significant component of postsecondary education.

As might be expected, not every state agreed to rely on the accrediting bodies. Some had established their own networks of centrally administered vocational schools and, led by Minnesota, declined to authorize their schools to pay separate fees to the regional accrediting bodies. In addition to the added costs, those states were perhaps equally worried about opening their governance practices for trade and technical education to review by outside groups of educators dominated by academicians. Subsequently, an amendment to the student aid provisions was introduced by Senator Walter Mondale and adopted by Congress. Using language similar to the accreditation-eligibility provision, the amendment stated that if the commissioner found that a state agency was a reliable judge of the quality of its public vocational schools, then those schools would be exempted from the accreditation requirement in eligibility. The Mondale amendment is more of an aberration than a fundamental undercutting of the accreditation-eligibility link. Although state vocational schools did technically operate at the postsecondary level, often they were centrally administered under a state superintendent in a fashion similar to the public school system. In general, true matriculation is not involved, and the role of state vocational schools is to provide continued or even accelerated technical training begun earlier by the student at a high school. Unlike the community college and the junior college, which foster intellectual development in their students through a more broad-based college-level curriculum and degree programs, these state technical schools are organized more like grades thirteen and fourteen of a high school distributive education program. Academic degrees are rarely involved, and transfer of credit is not expected. Some such schools would probably not meet the academic governance and faculty participation requirements of a college-level accrediting body. Finally, there is evidence that although such schools may obtain federal eligibility through their state boards, many still seek the collegial benefits of affiliating with their regional accrediting associations.

No review of the involvement of the federal government

and accreditation during the 1960s would be complete without a brief examination of the problems that arose in nursing education. The Nurse Training Act, enacted in 1964, provided direct financial assistance for a particular type of health-personnel development. Analogous training programs usually involved the review of competitive proposals by panels of peer experts. Here, Congress chose the accreditation-eligibility approach with the added requirement that each funded nursing program be specially accredited by an accrediting body that the commissioner deemed reliable as regards the quality of nurse training offered. If no such accreditation were available, then the commissioner could directly "accredit" the schools—that is, make them directly eligible. As the recognized specialized accrediting body, the National League for Nursing (NLN) appeared to be the appropriate organization, because the regional accrediting commissions did not make separate findings about nursing programs during their comprehensive review of an institution. Yet, a large fraction of the nurse training programs were located in community colleges or in hospitals and other clinical settings. Virtually none of these had NLN accreditation, and the community college sector strongly objected to specialized accreditation of individual program areas. The American Association of Junior Colleges (as it was then called) endorsed using either regional accreditation or state approval for eligibility for nurse training funds. Further, the commissioner was extremely uncomfortable with his direct accreditation role, but the sheer force of numbers left him no choice but to make eligible many schools that NLN had not accredited. In 1968 Congress gave all parties what they wanted. It decreed that either specialized nursing accreditation, regional accreditation, or approval of nursing programs by a state agency deemed reliable by the commissioner would establish eligibility. Congress apparently learned an important lesson from this episode and was cautious about making specialized accreditation a requirement for eligibility in the future. In fact, in the few cases in which it did, such as medical and dental capitation grants, virtually all the schools were accredited by well-established, nationally recognized accrediting bodies and had been for quite some time.

Understandably, by the late 1960s the Office of Education was experiencing some discomfort about its highly visible role in national accreditation policy issues. The time had come to move the commissioner's ad hoc committee into the spotlight, and in 1968 it was reestablished as the first official Advisory Committee on Accreditation and Institutional Eligibility. To be sure that this advisory committee received the level of administrative support commensurate with its responsibilities, a seventeen-person Accreditation and Institutional Eligibility Staff (AIES) was established in OE.

There had been growing interest from new accrediting bodies and their Washington-based legal counsel to get on the government's list. The establishment of the advisory committee and official support staff was considered a particularly opportune situation. In fact, the absence of any backsliding provision to permit the commisioner to remove an accrediting organization from the list guaranteed that, once on it, an organization could expect to remain on it indefinitely.

The Federal-Regulation Years

The unbridled expansion of the 1960s seemed to have obscured the original federal use of accreditation as one factor in establishing the eligibility of institutions to apply for certain federal funding. Indeed, as the decade drew to a close, a remarkable new role for the Office of Education in accreditation was espoused by AIES. In this view, the function of the advisory committee and the staff was not only assisting the commissioner in his work with accrediting bodies but also "safeguarding the *right* of the legitimate accrediting groups to be recognized" (emphasis added) on the commissioner's list (Proffitt, 1968). There are very few times in the evolution of government processes when a critical turning point comes so sharply into focus. Suddenly accrediting bodies had "rights" that the federal government would now be safeguarding. While citizens look to the federal government for protection of their national security, there appears to be nothing in federal law or practice that would create defensible rights on the part of accrediting bodies.

They neither receive nor are dependent on any federal funding and therefore cannot have some vested interest in remaining on the federal list that needs to be safeguarded. Furthermore, because accrediting bodies are expected to be "nationally recognized" before being listed by the commissioner, presumably little prestige is added by appearing on the list. Whether an accrediting body is on or off the commissioner's list, it derives its reputation and prestige from its demonstrated service and commitment to its constituents.

Up to this time, the federal government had been a rather docile recipient of the reliable information provided by the accrediting bodies about the quality of their member institutions and programs. Historically, this information was used only for federal directories, but during the 1950s and 1960s it had come to be relied on more heavily in determining institutional eligibility for federal funding. In a fundamental turnabout, the Office of Education now saw itself as a guardian and protector of the rights of recognized accrediting bodies. With the Office of Education now devoting time and energy to protecting the right of an accrediting body to be on the list, in a short time being on the list was viewed as a valuable commodity to be procured and preserved by accrediting bodies.

As always, with rights come responsibilities. Because the Office of Education was now doing something for accrediting bodies, rather than the other way around, the logical consequences seemed to be that (1) the accrediting bodies had to demonstrate that they were worthy of such favor and (2) the Office of Education, as the source of the favor, could adjust the rules as best fit its interests. In the lawyer's vernacular, the burden of persuasion was shifted from the Office of Education to the accrediting bodies. No longer would OE have to seek out the accrediting bodies that presumably were doing reliable work for use in eligibility determinations. Rather, accrediting bodies would now be expected to petition OE and demonstrate that they deserved a place on the list.

The established accrediting bodies, particularly the regional accrediting commissions, objected to making formal application to the commissioner. They stated that they were not applying to be on the federal list but were merely submitting information about their accreditation activities so that OE could determine whether they were reliable enough to be used to establish the eligibility of their member institutions. Other newly created accrediting bodies, however, were delighted by the opportunity to convince the government that they deserved a place on the list. Being listed now offered the most expedient and inexpensive route to achieving a national reputation without having to spend years or even decades building support and respect within the postsecondary education community.

In addition to turning the tables on the accrediting bodies, OE undertook a major revision of criteria by which accrediting bodies had been judged qualified to be listed. Although the technical details are beyond the scope of this chapter, there are important policy matters related to the way the criteria were developed and how they were applied by the AIES staff. First, recall that the original criteria adopted in 1952 were essentially developed by the National Commission on Accrediting. Over the next dozen and a half years, NCA worked closely with the national accrediting bodies to further refine and extend these criteria to reflect not only the minimum acceptable qualifications of an accrediting body but also the expected good practices a reputable one would follow in its work with institutions and programs.

Next, in 1969 OE published its first revision of the criteria in the *Federal Register*. Major new sections adapted from the NCA good-practice statement were added. These included the accrediting body ensuring due process for institutions, regularly reviewing its standards and criteria for accreditation, demonstrating fiscal soundness, and defining its various accrediting statuses, including any candidacy status it offered. There was never any doubt that all these items were desirable practices for a reputable accrediting body. In fact, there was tacit approval from NCA that no accrediting body should be given prominence on a federal list unless it reflected the best policies and practices in accreditation. Unfortunately, this approach only served to reinforce the primacy of the federal list itself.

Further, the adoption of such detailed specifications by

the federal government essentially established a blueprint for accrediting bodies. The commissioner of education, even with his advisory committee, was not in a position to make those difficult, subjective judgments about whether an accrediting body had achieved a position of genuine importance and influence within the postsecondary education community. In many government processes that seek to be selective through written regulations, form takes precedence over substance. Compliance with the letter rather than the spirit of a regulation can easily become the pattern. Those who stand to benefit from being selected by the federal government are generally inclined to construe or interpret the regulations quite narrowly and most favorably toward their own situation. Indeed, they frequently retain Washington counsel to be sure they can demonstrate that they meet the requirements with as little change and adjustment as possible in their own practices. Even a bureaucracy interested in achieving more than a minimal level of compliance would be thwarted by lawyers who insist on reading the necessarily vague words in such regulations in a manner least demanding of their client.

The record of the past decade since the adoption of the expanded federal regulations shows a disturbing trend. A recognition process endorsed and supported by the education community is available through COPA, but it requires that new accrediting bodies first develop their policies and procedures to serve the needs of their constituent students, programs, and institutions and then demonstrate that they have achieved recognized stature in postsecondary education. In a variation of Gresham's law, new such bodies are tending to organize themselves in exactly the format necessary to match the federal regulations in the belief that once they are placed on the commissioner's list, their eminence, if not their preeminence, will be established. The feeling is that the postsecondary education community and other constituencies will then have little choice but to accept them. This practice also results in new accrediting bodies trying to fit into a standard mold. Although the mold may be a good one, and indeed the best known at the time, the result is that those new accrediting bodies whose only goal is to

acquire OE listing do not attempt to be innovative in their process for fear of being found incompatible with the listing regulations. This fear can obviously have a chilling effect on experimentation and growth in accreditation.

Another major undesirable consequence of this expanded
federal role is that accrediting bodies that have no true depth or
maturity in their subject area will obtain some prominence by
means of the federal government. New accrediting bodies can
develop impressive handbooks and guidelines by adapting materials from other organizations while failing to develop that
broad background of professional and academic competence
that can come only from many years of dedicated work in the
field. That is, they may choose to ignore the fact that accreditation is mostly substance and only slightly form. Agencies sponsored by aggressive professional groups spare no cost in getting
on the government's list. The suggestion is not that corruption
and bribery are involved in the review of an accrediting body
but rather that, with the help of Washington counsel, documents are prepared in the form required by the OE staff so that
a satisfactory recommendation for listing will be forthcoming.
Regardless of the social need for a new accrediting body or its
commitment to the educational and public service mission of
accreditation, its bylaws, handbooks, standards, and review procedures can be made to contain all the right words, arranged in
the right order, presented in the right fashion. This approach is
clearly only a pantomime of academic principles—a matter of
putting up the right façade without ever going through the tedious and laborious apprenticeship that truly marks the recognized accrediting bodies. In an effort to keep its process from
being used as a shortcut to respectability by spurious accrediting bodies, OE amended its regulations to require that an applicant have at least two years of experience as an accrediting body.
At times this experience can consist of as little as accrediting
the half dozen or so institutions or programs represented by the
members of the organization's own accrediting commission.

There is one policy consequence of particular significance. Through the expanded regulations, the federal government no longer limited itself to the statutory requirement that

it judge only the reliability of already nationally recognized accrediting bodies for use in determining eligibility. The federal government had now become an arbiter of what constitutes good practice in accreditation even though such words appear nowhere in the statutes or in their most generous interpretation. When this shift occurred, not only did the federal government preempt NCA's role in monitoring the practices of accrediting bodies, but it also put itself in a position to redefine, on its own terms, the nature of accreditation and how accreditation relates to its many publics.

Sensing increasing national concern about civil rights, public accountability, and integrity in the management of the growing Title IV student aid programs, the Office of Education published a new set of regulations in 1974. In addition to expecting listed accrediting bodies both to be reliable, as mandated by statute, and to follow the good practices set out in the 1969 revisions, the regulations now required an accrediting body to do the following (*Federal Register,* 1974):

1. Demonstrate its capability and willingness to foster ethical practice, such as nondiscrimination and equitable tuition refunds.
2. Encourage experimental and innovative programs.
3. Consider the concerns of its constituents, such as students, the general public, and the professional or occupational fields it represents.
4. Include representatives of the public in its decision-making processes.

These new regulations made the commissioner the conscience of education and the public about which accrediting bodies were good and how they could be better.

To be sure, the years from the late sixties to the midseventies were ones of great social turmoil. Spectacular abuses in federal student aid programs were prominently reported by leading newspapers, and the affirmative action and student consumer movements were growing ever more active. Accreditation found itself at the confluence of many of these crosscurrents.

That the government would be genuinely concerned with such matters and try to act through the accrediting bodies is commendable. Unfortunately, as clearly explained by professor of law Matthew Finkin (1978), there is no statutory authority for such an expansive and flexible role by the commissioner in defining the role and responsibilities of an accrediting body. The statutes were clearly limited to the purpose of establishing institutional eligibility for federal funding programs.

The well-established accrediting bodies generally viewed these developments with alarm. The regional accrediting commissions adopted a statement that matters of social policy considered important by the government must be handled by the government and that although accrediting bodies can testify to institutional quality, they cannot and should not try to enforce or police federal social policy. Yet, the commissioner's list had grown from twenty or so accrediting bodies in 1952 to beyond fifty. Many new accrediting bodies also expressed concern in public about excessive bureaucratic regulation, but their actions betrayed a strong private allegiance to the Office of Education. Indeed, many made significant changes in their accreditation activities to comply with the federal regulations. Further, accrediting bodies that had found a cool reception at NCA particularly appreciated the willingness of the commissioner to review their applications and place them on the list and asked no questions about what role they were to play or not play in eligibility for federal funds.

In rebuttal, federal officials argued that many established accrediting bodies had grown somewhat provincial in fulfilling their social responsibilities. This charge cannot be denied, but many of the social policy areas added to the federal regulation were indeed being thoroughly debated by NCA and its successor, COPA. This debate involved a thorough review and refinement by the affected communities of interest and has led to a clearer delineation of how accrediting bodies are accountable and what they can expect of their member institutions. That many of these clarifications of good practice in accreditation are sound, appropriate, and desirable fails to address the question of what authority the federal government has to require them, in that they overlap only slightly with the role set out for the commissioner in the legislation. At best, the role of the commissioner here has been to precipitate a serious look at the ethical issues and social responsibilities by the accreditation community itself.

Federal officials have also argued that by giving prominence to the role of the accrediting bodies in determining eligibility, they have reduced the likelihood that federal and state agencies will become more aggressive in regulating institutions directly. Yet, there is a darker side to this endorsement of accreditation. If the Office of Education succeeds in having more and more reliance placed on accrediting bodies as implementers of federal social policy, then OE will need more direct control over them. The characteristics of educational quality in postsecondary educational institutions would then come indirectly under federal review. As sources of funding and authority, both the federal and state governments have proper, complementary roles in overseeing educational institutions.

This phenomenon of expanded regulation is not unknown throughout government. At all levels, sincere and perceptive administrators confront shifting social trends every day, and they can easily become frustrated by the glacial pace of legislative reform. Though sworn to enforce the Constitution and laws of the United States, many officials become impatient and begin to include their own personal policy positions in regulations, interpretive guidelines, and public speeches. Fairly narrow statutory language is given a broad, abstract interpretation that does not necessarily follow from the legislative intent. Yet, as Mr. Justice Frankfurter noted: "Laws are not abstract propositions. They are expressions of policy arising out of specific situations and addressed to the attainment of particular ends" (1947, p. 533). There has never been any doubt that the intended end to be served by the federal list of accrediting bodies was the establishment of eligibility for institutions to participate in the corresponding funding programs. If there are abuses in the administration and reporting of federal funds by institutions, Congress may legislate corrective measures and give the commissioner additional broadened authority to regulate the recipients directly. Through the work of NCA, FRACHE, and concerned executives of well-established accrediting bodies, the Office of Education was forced to acknowledge its lack of authority for much of the social activism added to its regulations for accrediting bodies.

In 1976 Congress began to take an intensive look at the abuses in the financial aid area with the intent of enacting remedial legislation. The Office of Education proposed that accrediting bodies could be relied on to police institutions more closely if the commissioner were allowed to determine that the listed accrediting bodies were reliable authorities not only on the quality of education but also on the "probity" of each accredited institution receiving federal funds. *Probity* was defined in the proposal to encompass all the social action areas introduced into the 1974 regulations as well as virtually anything else that any government official might at any time in the future feel had become an important part of an institution's integrity and responsibility, such as investment of funds in South African corporations, use of nonunion agricultural products in food-service units, conflict of interest in board appointments, salary differences between male and female employees, and contractual relations with other educational organizations.

This proposal for a fundamental policy change in federal accreditation legislation represented the first critical test of the newly formed Council on Postsecondary Accreditation. COPA was successful in galvanizing support not only among the leadership of the accreditation community but also from the postsecondary education community in general. As a result, the probity proposal was not supported by the secretary of health, education and welfare, nor by either political party, nor by either house of Congress. Instead, Congress gave the commissioner new statutory power to "limit, suspend, or terminate" an institution's participation in the student financial aid program if it were judged deficient in its "administrative and financial capabilities" or in the "equity" of its tuition refund policy; the commissioner could take this action directly without involving the accrediting bodies (P.L. 94–482, Sec. 131(b) and 133(a), 1976). The rejection of the probity proposal essentially reaffirmed the 1952 statute and established significant legislative history about Congress' intent: that reliable institutional accreditation was to be used as one factor in establishing the eligibility of colleges and universities to apply to participate in certain federal funding programs.

A more general argument has been made that the commissioner does have a direct interest in assisting accrediting bodies to improve their practices. Indeed, the argument is that as accrediting bodies become better, their accreditation decisions become more sound and valuable and the commissioner can then feel more secure in relying on their determinations as one factor in eligibility determinations. Yet, in the final analysis, the federal government probably cannot have much effect on the strength of an accrediting body. Even though the effect of federal regulation may be to stifle innovation and experimentation and bring about greater uniformity in accreditation, the nature of the federal process is such that the regulations will be met more in form and less in substance. Another indication of this inability of the federal regulatory process to go beyond form can be found in the efforts of the Federal Trade Commission (FTC) in accreditation.

As the role of accreditation increased over the last decade both in eligibility for federal funds and in entrance to various professions, the Federal Trade Commission became concerned that the specialized criteria of some accrediting agencies could be creating restraints of trade. Even if this were not the planned or intended consequence, the antitrust laws still can be applied, and, in light of the Supreme Court's refusal to review a decision finding bar association regulations about what constitutes the practice of law to be in violation of the Sherman Antitrust Act [*Surety Title Insurance Company, Inc.* v. *Virginia State Bar* 431 F. Supp. 298 (E.D. Va. 1977), *cert denied,* 436 U.S. 941 (1978)], the FTC began to examine the work of professional accrediting bodies more closely. The major initiative involved the Liaison Committee on Medical Education (LCME), as an arm of the American Medical Association.

LCME was listed by the commissioner as a reliable accrediting agency, and medical schools had to have their accred-

itation to receive the significant levels of student financial assistance known as capitation grants. During LCME's periodic
review by the commissioner's advisory committee in 1978, FTC
presented third party comment. Such comment was permitted
by the Office of Education's regulations, and the FTC staff argued that LCME was not autonomous in serving the best interests of quality medical education but suffered a serious conflict
of interest in having major control by the practitioners' (physicians') trade association. Such control, according to the FTC,
would encourage accrediting practices intended to limit the
number of persons who could enter medical school and thus
who could eventually become physicians. Because there are so
many hurdles to be cleared even after earning an M.D. degree
before one can practice medicine, all related to safeguarding
the health and well-being of the public, the committee found
difficulty with the FTC claim. After learning that the Public
Health Service was phasing out the capitation grants because of
an oversupply of physicians, it renewed LCME's term on the
list. In an ironic twist, LCME officials realized that without the
capitation grants, there was no need for them to be on the federal list. The misdirected zeal of the FTC had given them great
pause and serious discussions about relinquishing their place on
the commissioner's list ensued.

An interesting contrast to the FTC initiatives in professional credentialing involves the activities of the National Board
of Respiratory Therapy, a certifying body, and the American
Association for Respiratory Therapy, an accrediting body that
served no role in eligibility. It appeared that both groups had
been quite successful in regulating every phase of entry into careers by respiratory therapists. In particular, there were claims
that only graduates of their accredited schools could apply for
certification, that hospitals could hire only certified therapists,
and that those who worked in nonapproved hospitals could lose
their credentials. Such a monopolistic approach would totally
ignore the possibility that one could become a thoroughly qualified therapist in other ways, such as through military service or
study in a foreign country. The FTC took no action; rather,
a group of aggrieved therapists, under the class name *Viezaga,*

brought a private Sherman Act suit against the credentialing bodies and others. In a decision dated January 27, 1977, Judge John F. Grady, sitting in the Eastern Division, Northern District of the U.S. District Court for Illinois, certified that such activities were proper grounds for a class-action, antitrust suit (Docket Number 75-C3430). This decision was followed by mutual settlement of the claims in private by the parties themselves.

A more prominent case of FTC involvement in issues of educational quality is found in its Trade Regulation Rule (TRR) on "Proprietary Vocational and Home Study Schools" issued in 1978. Ostensibly the rule was intended to establish an automatic, uniform tuition-refund formula for students who withdraw during a course, together with rigid and misleading disclosure of withdrawal and placement statistics, so as to protect students from abuses that FTC claimed were rampant. The rule was challenged by a number of affected schools and their national accrediting agencies as being unjustified by the facts and as being an arbitrary and capricious intrusion into educational self-regulation. The case was *Katharine Gibbs School* v. *Federal Trade Commission* 612 F.2d 658 (2d Cir. 1979), *rehearing denied,* 628 F.2d 755 (2d Cir. 1980). In its amicus brief, COPA pointed out that rather than being an effort to improve accrediting practices, the TRR was in fact a frontal assault on the basic concepts of accreditation. The rule's requirements were, in all respects, government-established criteria of educational performance that would fundamentally alter the traditional relationships among student, teacher, and institution. The U.S. Court of Appeals found the rule unjustified and it was eventually put back on the shelf.

During this period, OE found itself with more and more applications from accrediting bodies and therefore needed to expand its support staff. AIES was reorganized as the Division of Eligibility and Agency Evaluation (DEAE). DEAE continued to push for new, revised regulations that included the probity factor just denied by Congress. The commissioner's list was well on its way to including 100 accrediting bodies when, in 1978, then-Commissioner Ernest L. Boyer learned of growing concern in the postsecondary education community about the accreditation regulations. He then held a series of meetings with postsecondary education representatives in Washington and directed his staff to prepare revisions to the regulations that were in marked contrast to the earlier DEAE proposals.

The commissioner followed a policy of strict construction of the statutes and developed draft regulations that were specifically intended to meet the limited eligibility purposes of listing accrediting bodies. This draft removed two and a half decades of accumulated embellishment and bore striking similarity to the original 1952 regulations. Although this move was entirely in keeping with the "back to basics" and deregulation mood in Washington, it also meant that many of the accrediting bodies that served no purpose in determining eligibility would be removed from the list. In a bizarre interpretation, an assistant staff counsel familiar with eligibility matters argued that the commissioner could fulfill his statutory responsibility if an accrediting body showed "a probable nexus" to eligibility either now or at some time in the future, and thus no accrediting body need be removed from the list. With the help of Washington counsel, a number of accrediting bodies slated to be removed from the list launched a spirited assault on the commissioner, questioning his motives, challenging his competence, charging star-chamber tactics, and recalling both the Holocaust and the Spanish Inquisition. The virulence and fervor of this assault on the commissioner convinced many staff members in OE, HEW, and the White House that there must indeed be some questionable patronage between OE and the accrediting bodies that caused them to be so anxious about protecting their standing and prominence on the federal list.

In its proposal for the 1980 reauthorization of the Higher Education Act, the administration suggested that the link between accreditation and eligibility be severed entirely. Because the two-tiered system did screen institutions at the second tier, or program stage, any institution that was legally authorized by a state should be considered eligible. Although this proposal might have resulted in a healthy disengagement of the parties and a separate reassessment of what each actually wants and needs from the other, it was not to be. The general mystique of accreditation, which was apparent in the 1952 deliberations on the veterans' benefits, coupled with a vigorous lobbying campaign by the regional accrediting bodies, influenced many senators and representatives, and the accreditation-eligibility system remained unchanged.

When Congress finally reauthorized the act, however, it did accomplish one significant improvement regarding the role of the Advisory Committee, which had been a continuing, but less provocative, source of concern in the whole accreditation-eligibility debate. The Advisory Committee served to advise the commissioner about eligibility and listing determinations, and indeed, the commissioner almost inevitably adopted the committee's recommendation. Yet, the committee's charter had grown equally expansive over the years, basically permitting it to oversee all aspects of postsecondary education and accreditation that ever had been, were now, or might ever be of interest to the federal government. Committee appointments had been carefully screened by the DEAE staff, and the committee looked exclusively to the staff for advice and recommendations on extremely long and involved agendas. By the late 1970s, the committee appeared to many observers to be unable to provide an independent voice to the commissioner. The committee had never been authorized by statute, despite earlier attempts, but rather was appointed by the commissioner as a discretionary committee with a two-year, renewable charter.

In consultation with the postsecondary education community, Congress established an eligibility advisory committee in Section 1205 of the reauthorized Higher Education Act. The committee charter was for the first time explicitly limited to matters of institutional eligibility. The committee is now advisory to the secretary of education and held its first meeting in March 1982. Among other things, it has shown a growing interest in coordinating a review of accrediting bodies with COPA's recognition process. Just as the federal government now relies on the certification given an institution by voluntary accrediting bodies in establishing its eligibility, it will probably come to rely on the certification given an accrediting body through COPA's voluntary recognition process.

NCA's decision in the early fifties turned out to be a fateful one. Of course, NCA had no way of predicting the long-range consequences of turning down the commissioner's request to use a list of nationally recognized accrediting bodies produced by NCA and instead telling the government to prepare its own list. The decision no doubt seemed to be the best one at the time, but in hindsight, NCA was at a fork in the road. It chose a path that eventually led to a deeply convoluted relationship between accreditation and the federal government, with the government calling the tune—and changing the tune whenever it wished, whether "safeguarding" the "right" of accrediting bodies to be on the list or seeking to link accreditation with a governmental view of institutional probity that might shift with every political turn or tide. Today, the relationship between accreditation and the government has stabilized considerably but still remains somewhat unsettled, as shown by the administration's proposal in 1980 to sever the link between accreditation and institutional eligibility (even though the proposal did not succeed in Congress).

As long as accreditation is linked to determining institutional eligibility for federal funding programs, there will be an interest within both the government and accrediting bodies to have the relationship serve each other's special interests. Accrediting bodies can probably never return to an era when their sole mission was to assess educational quality. Like it or not, they have become a central source of information about postsecondary education that the federal government relies on.

Accrediting bodies have a unique opportunity to assist institutions to better understand their own roles and responsibilities and to adopt and adhere to codes of good practice. Although accreditation must continually strive to warrant the respect and deference it is shown, it must also never forget that its ultimate concern is the educational quality of institutions and programs. Accrediting bodies must be sure of their purpose and identity. They can then take an active role in their relationship with the government—mindful that, after all, the government relies on accreditation, not the other way around. In this way, the essential philosophy of fostering educational quality through institutional self-regulation and self-accounting—the philosophy on which accreditation is built—can take root in a manner that serves the needs not only of the federal government but also of state and local governments, students, employers, and the public.

14

Louis W. Bender

ϡϢϡϢϡϢϡϢϡϢϡϢϡϢϡϢϡϢϡϢϡϢϡϢϡϢϡϢϡϢ

States and Accreditation

> *The powers not delegated to the United States by the Constitution, nor prohibited by it to the States, are reserved to the States respectively, or to the people.* **U.S. Bill of Rights**

The role of state government in relation to postsecondary education is changing. Although the U.S. Constitution ascribed general powers to the states—with the resulting authority to police and control—the states tended to avoid assuming a policing role with colleges and universities. (New York is an exception.) Instead, states allowed substantial institutional sovereignty during the country's early history. During the first half of the twentieth century, state policies were based on an expectation that colleges and universities would regulate themselves, through their institutional governing boards and voluntary nongovernmental accreditation.

Beginning after World War II and accelerating in the 1960s, however, there was a growing feeling within state government that postsecondary education, particularly public colleges and universities, required closer scrutiny, statewide coordination, and even regulation. Green (1981) has observed that the state role in postsecondary education has changed considerably during the past fifteen years—from passive provider to concerned underwriter. History may someday record that, during the last quarter of the twentieth century, state government evolved into the role of controller of the postsecondary education enterprise.

The recent changes are undoubtedly affecting the interrelationships of postsecondary educational institutions, accrediting bodies, professional organizations, the federal government, and state governments. In particular, as the role of state government in relation to postsecondary education has evolved, the relationship of state government to accreditation has also been altered.

Historical Relationship

Higher education in America preceded our form of government by more than 100 years. The colleges of the colonial period were church-sponsored, committing themselves both to the tenets of the denomination and to the education of an elite. Although several of these colleges did receive some state support and in several instances had state officials on their boards, the sovereignty of the college was, by and large, inherently respected (see Cowley, 1980, for a description of the significant exceptions). Colleges were established by means of articles of incorporation typically administered by the office of the secretary of state or the office of the attorney general of a state. There was no state-level education agency charged with the regulation of higher education. Because most colleges were church-sponsored, the ethic of separation of church and state carried over to higher education. The general assumption was that the institution and its governing board had the responsibility as well as the prerogative to oversee programs and performance. Furthermore, the Dartmouth College case in 1819 firmly established the inviolability of the corporate charter (Brubacher and Rudy, 1976, pp. 32-35).

The development of state universities, beginning in the 1800s, was spawned by (1) federal land grants to new states for universities or "seminaries of learning," (2) universities established by four Southern states after the revolution, and (3) the Land-Grant College Acts of 1862 and 1890. Some state universities were established by state constitution provisions, but most were created by statutes. State government, however, played only a perfunctory role in higher education during this early period. Because few states had an agency for higher education, institutions had contact with the state typically through the governor's office or the state budget office only. Accreditation, as such, did not yet exist, and the few recorded incidents of political intrusion into institutional affairs involved ambitious governors who attempted to use the state university for political gain.

Although normal schools began to appear in the first half of the nineteenth century, the need for public school teachers mushroomed in the twentieth century, and state after state established a system of normal schools or purchased privately sponsored normal schools. These teacher training schools were state-owned, were administered by state departments of public instruction, and operated as agencies of the state. Budgets were prepared in the same manner as for other state agencies, and administrative procedures were governmental rather than academic. These early normal schools were not viewed as peer institutions by the higher education community.

The public junior college, the forerunner of the contemporary community college, also developed during the early twentieth century and was originally not viewed as part of higher education. These institutions resulted from ambitions of school districts to extend their sphere of influence and the desire of some university presidents, such as William Rainey Harper of the University of Chicago, to spin off the first two years of general education so that the more specialized upper division of the university might be strengthened. Because most of the early public junior colleges were sponsored by local school districts, they were administered by the state in the same manner as were elementary and secondary schools.

At one end of the higher education spectrum, then, private colleges and state universities were perceived as the true institutions of higher education and were thus—at least nominally—outside the jurisdiction of state government, while at the other end of the spectrum normal schools and public junior colleges were operated as either state agencies or constituent school districts. Here the seed was planted for a change in the posture of state government, which became more directly involved in higher education when normal schools became four-year teacher's colleges and when junior colleges were eventually accepted as part of higher education.

This expansion and diversification of higher education, combined with the development of the public high school, also created problems. What was a high school and what was a college, and how should the two institutions relate to each other? There were no common standards to guide or control the various institutions. Although the practices of the state university could be used as a norm for secondary schools in preparing their students for further education, private institutions calling themselves colleges or universities varied considerably in their standards of admission, grading, promotion, and graduation. Because the federal government lacked the authority and state governments for the most part failed to take the initiative, voluntary nongovernmental accreditation gradually developed to meet these needs (see Chapter Two).

During the first half of the twentieth century, state legislatures were generally in awe of representatives of public colleges and universities. Most members of the legislature had rural backgrounds and limited formal education and therefore were timid and unprepared to challenge persons from academe. The relationship of public institutions to the governor, however, was often more direct and dynamic. Typically, a governor had power over trustee appointments and therefore wielded great influence. Furthermore, governors were frequently empowered to modify or reduce the executive budget of the state and thus could reward or punish through the power of the purse. The need for external leverage to protect the state university from political interference began to emerge, and accreditation gradually took on that role.

Every regional accrediting association could doubtless

document challenges by state authorities. For example, in 1930 Governor Theodore Bilbo of Mississippi tried to replace 179 politically unacceptable employees in state institutions, and the Commission on Colleges of what is now the Southern Association of Colleges and Schools (SACS) suspended the membership of the Mississippi institutions. As a result, graduates of those institutions became unacceptable for certification, and there was an immediate drop in student enrollments. The issue became a major part of the 1931 gubernatorial election, with Bilbo being defeated and the new governor pledging to correct the situation (Allen, 1978). Another SACS challenge occurred in 1941 when Governor Eugene Talmadge pressured the board of regents of the university system of Georgia to dismiss the dean of a college of education over a racial integration issue. Again, SACS refused to accept the intrusion into the operations of a member institution and voted to suspend the entire university system from membership. Once more, the issue was settled with the defeat of the governor in the 1942 election, and the incoming governor pledged to correct the misuse of political authority (Allen, 1978). In 1945 the board of regents of the University of Texas was charged with usurping powers properly belonging to the president and the faculty. Within a year, the Executive Council of the SACS Commission reported corrective action and "notable improvement," whereupon accreditation was restored (Allen, 1978).

As another example, in 1969 a bill was introduced in the Pennsylvania legislature that would have denied any of Pennsylvania's state-owned teacher's colleges membership in what was then the Middle States Association of Colleges and Secondary Schools. The action was in retaliation to a warning from the Middle States Association that partisan politics should cease in the appointment of trustees of state colleges. The bill was defeated when legislative testimony explained the consequences of the action because of statutes already enacted; for example, graduates from unaccredited colleges would be denied admission to the professional schools of Pennsylvania State University and would not be certified to teach in Pennsylvania schools. The proposed bill was defeated, and a new law was enacted restructuring the governance of the state-owned colleges to reduce political interference in the trusteeship of the institutions (the State College Act, 1970).

By the end of World War II, many state laws and regulations had incorporated references to accreditation, particularly specialized accreditation, and reciprocity agreements that used accreditation as the means of recognition were agreed to by many states. These developments strengthened the role of accreditation and also encouraged regional rather than state-by-state thinking. During the postwar period of rapid growth in postsecondary education, states viewed educational quality as manifesting itself primarily through criteria established by institutions—students with high test scores and faculty members with doctorates, research grants, and publications (Green, 1981). In 1959, a national commission headed by Milton Eisenhower produced guidelines for relations between state government and colleges and universities (Moos and Rourke, 1959).

The third quarter of the twentieth century witnessed a growing impact of national policies on postsecondary education. National social goals involving postsecondary education (such as the assimilation of war veterans back into civilian life, the response to the challenge of Sputnik, and aiding the underprivileged) were implemented by new federal programs—in some instances by direct funding to postsecondary educational institutions and in others by appropriations to the states as a link between the federal government and institutions. As a result, states gradually developed financial dependency on these federal funds, at least to some degree, and accreditation became a significant element in determining institutional eligibility for certain federal programs (see Chapter Thirteen).

The Education Amendments of 1972 imposed important additional changes. In that landmark legislation, Congress substituted the term *postsecondary education* for *higher education* and defined it as including not only degree-granting colleges and universities but also vocational, technical, specialized, proprietary, and nontraditional educational institutions, as well as the educational activities of other social enterprises such as hospitals and clinics. Furthermore, the legislation shifted the major recipients of federal aid from institutions to students. The primary rationale for this change was to increase access to postsecondary education for students from underrepresented groups. However, at least two other considerations were also involved: (1) a hope that, given the "free market" principle, consumer choice would help preserve private institutions and discourage low-quality institutions and programs and (2) a desire to provide federal funding to postsecondary education without bringing about federal control. In the same law, Congress provided for the so-called 1202 state planning commissions in an effort to influence state governments to play a stronger role in the planning and coordination of postsecondary education. Thus, the Education Amendments of 1972 had a major impact on the shift in posture of state governments toward stronger oversight and regulation of postsecondary education.

Just as the regional accrediting associations originally were organized around degree-granting and nonprofit institutions, most state governments were not organized to accommodate the broader configuration of postsecondary education defined by Congress. As a result, new state agencies were created or existing agencies were assigned additional responsibilities. Both these developments resulted in more bureaucracy, more paperwork, more intrusions by the state into the lives of postsecondary institutions, and greater potential for conflict with voluntary nongovernmental accrediting bodies.

Drawbacks of State Activity

State governments have consistently exhibited some basic tendencies in assuming an increasing role vis-à-vis postsecondary education. To understand some of the issues that have developed between accreditation and state governments, an examination of these shortcomings is appropriate.

Diversity of Approaches. Although the state has primary authority over education and its regulation, state regulatory legislation and regulatory agencies have typically emerged only as specific needs have appeared. Thus, a great variety of agencies among the fifty states have some regulatory power, with considerable unevenness among them in funding, staffing, authority, and effectiveness. Millard (1979, p. 129) has observed: "Given the number and variety of states it is not surprising that the agencies are differently organized in different states or that different agencies handle degree-granting institutions and proprietary institutions in many of the states. The probability of uniformity in approach among all the fifty states is practically zero."

Involvement of Many Agencies. Since 1950 the number of state agencies concerned with postsecondary education "has almost literally exploded" (Millard, 1980, p. 3). These agencies are of several types (Millard, 1980):

1. *State approval agencies.* Under the Servicemen's Readjustment Assistance Act of 1952, Congress provided direct funds for states to establish veterans' approval agencies. These are state agencies funded by contract with the Veterans Administration to approve courses and programs for veterans, and they operate under VA rules and regulations. There are currently about eighty such agencies operating in the fifty states, the District of Columbia, and Puerto Rico. Twenty-seven states have single agencies; of these, eighteen are located in departments of education. Twenty other states have two agencies, and four states have three.

2. *State authorizing or licensing agencies.* In 1982, forty-eight of the fifty states plus the District of Columbia had such agencies for proprietary and non-degree-granting institutions. Forty-one states had agencies for degree-granting institutions.

3. *State coordinating or governing boards.* The rapid expansion of postsecondary education during the 1960s and 1970s led to the creation of state coordinating or governing boards by states that did not already have them. These boards are charged with statewide planning, role delineation, and program review for postsecondary education. In some instances, they also approve budgets and programs. Virtually all states now have such bodies, although in some states (such as North Carolina) the central office of a statewide university system plays that role.

4. *Other agencies.* In addition, other state agencies (for

example, state boards of nursing) have become involved in the licensing of practitioners and, in some instances, the review and approval of training programs required for licensing. As competition for scarce resources has increased, many states have broadened the powers of their budget offices. Capital construction projects are channeled through building authorities or commissions established during the rapid-growth years of the 1960s. A variety of consumer information and consumer protection agencies have broadened their purview to encompass students as consumers of postsecondary education.

This multiplicity of agencies often results in conflicting demands, duplication of effort, and a diminishing of institutional autonomy and coherence.

The power struggle between the legislative and executive branches or the special interests of legislative committees often fosters additional jurisdictions or creates new agencies. Proposed legislation by a committee may identify an agency for oversight and implementation other than the existing postsecondary education agency. For example, an agriculture committee might propose legislation involving educational programs or standards but designate the department of agriculture as the responsible agency. As a result, different jurisdictional responsibilities, ranging from reporting requirements to direct supervision, are often located in many state agencies. Institutions may have to report on matters of campus location and development to a regional planning commission, submit construction requests to a special building authority, and conform to various environmental and building-code requirements at local, regional, and state levels.

Another phenomenon since the 1950s has been the advent and growth of legislative staffs. State legislative committees used to depend on executive agencies for information to help in policy making or turned directly to institutions. Many state legislatures have decided that neither state agencies nor institutions were providing complete and unbiased information and so have increasingly created their own staffs and instituted their own studies and investigations.

Lack of Agreement. State agencies do not always agree

on what postsecondary institutions should be doing and how they should be doing it. For example, a specialized board may have informed an institution that it has to improve its facilities and equipment, while a budget office has told it that costs have to be cut back. Moreover, state agencies' expectations can change over time, reflecting changes in political agendas. Lack of agreement is a particular problem when dealing with such an elusive concept as quality. In fact, there has not always been agreement that quality should be a state concern. For example, a 1971 Carnegie Commission report identified eleven areas in which the individual states should exercise influence or control in postsecondary education. Managerial issues dominated the list, while institutional and program quality was not explicitly mentioned (Carnegie Commission on Higher Education, 1971).

Uniform Treatment. There is also a tendency of government, particularly the federal government, to treat all institutions as a class. States make an understandable distinction between public and private postsecondary educational institutions. As a general rule, however, to be fair, government cannot be placed in a position of appearing to favor one institution over another; hence, government agencies tend to establish minimum standards. Government agencies could never examine each institution as is done in accreditation, in which an independent judgment is rendered relative to the specific purposes of each institution. Such an approach would almost inevitably provoke criticism and challenge from one or another of the interests involved.

Minimum Standards. Another tendency of state government is to establish minimum standards for use in making enforcement decisions. States fund different types of institutions at different levels. For example, California makes distinctions among the university system, the state university system, and the community college system. To a large extent, however, funds are provided by formulas based on certain assumptions about minimum levels of support. There have been some tentative experiments with incentive funding (for example, in Tennessee), but it has not been the rule. The states' primary concerns are that all citizens receive at least a guaranteed minimum level of service and that the most efficient use possible be made of public monies. Given these concepts, as well as the financial constraints in most states, states understandably do not ordinarily commit themselves to supporting institutions at the highest possible levels.

Compliance Mentality. Growing out of the tendency of state governments to focus on minimum standards is a concomitant attitude: The postsecondary educational institution is expected to provide evidence demonstrating that it does in fact comply with minimum standards. This expectation varies somewhat from agency to agency and, of course, is felt much more by public institutions than by private institutions. Nonetheless, the compliance mentality can come into conflict with the self-study concept of accreditation. The self-study process calls on the institution to identify areas that need improvement. However, weaknesses identified through the self-study can be perceived as serious shortcomings by the state government.

Regulation by Exception. A well-known tendency of all government is to regulate by exception; that is, regulations are frequently developed and applied to all institutions to combat the excesses or shortcomings of a few. For example, if one college were to begin awarding questionable amounts of credit for experiential learning, a state might attempt to establish a law or regulation that would prohibit or limit this practice, rather than focus on the violator.

Issues for States and Accreditation

Given the legal authority and responsibility that state governments have for postsecondary education, the benign neglect that prevailed for many years, the growing pressures for a stronger state role, and the radically different perspectives of state agencies and accrediting bodies, that there have not been more problems and conflicts is surprising. As a matter of fact, state governments and voluntary nongovernmental accrediting bodies have for the most part agreeably accommodated each other and on occasion even worked cooperatively. For example, the Maryland Commission for Higher Education and the Middle

States Association developed an agreement that involves joint visits to institutions.

There are basic issues that must be addressed, however, if major conflicts are to be avoided in the future. States share these concerns with nongovernmental accrediting bodies, and these two groups should work together in addressing these issues.

Institutional Authorization. Reflecting the provisions of the U.S. Constitution, most postsecondary institutions are chartered or licensed by the state in which they are primarily located. A few institutions, such as the military academies, are authorized by the federal government. State governments both authorize institutions to operate and to grant degrees; these two separate but related authorities may be exercised by one or more agencies. Some institutions (such as those in Michigan) are authorized by the state constitution, and thus they are not legally subordinate to the executive or legislative branch of government, although they are dependent on those branches for funding. In New York, the state constitution created the University of the State of New York, comprising all chartered institutions, public and private. In 1982, nine states had no licensure for degree-granting institutions. Two states, Missouri and Utah, did not provide for any form of institutional licensing, and many other states had licensing laws weak in language or not backed up with sufficient resources to make them meaningful. For example, California's licensing law permitted an institution to operate if it could demonstrate that it had at least $50,000 in assets. Because institutional accreditation requires that an institution must be properly authorized by the state in which it is located, the weaknesses in state licensing are a major concern.

The growing number of "degree mills" and the increase in fraudulent practices led the Education Commission of the States in 1973 to propose model state legislation, developed by a national task force (Education Commission of the States, 1973). Before then, only seventeen states had state licensure laws applying to degree-granting institutions; but by 1982, forty-one states reported some sort of licensing authority or function. However, in many states (nineteen in statute; others in practice, with right of review), licensing laws specifically exempt regionally accredited institutions, as well as religious institutions. This exemption creates a Catch-22 situation (accreditation says an institution must be licensed before it can be accredited, but the state says if an institution is accredited, it does not have to be licensed). This exemption inadvertently creates the image that accreditation is quasi-governmental in nature.

Professional Licensure. States also license practitioners in a great variety of professions and specialized occupations (from doctors to television repairers). Licensure is an area of considerable debate—concerning what purpose licensing serves, whether it is efficacious, whether periodic relicensing is desirable, and what role in the licensing procedure members of the group being licensed should have (see Chapter Sixteen). One issue being debated is the proper role of accreditation in professional licensure. Many licensing laws currently require that a candidate for a license have graduated from an accredited program or institution; often, these laws even specify the professional organization (for example, the American Bar Association) from which accreditation must be received. Such language has the effect of passing on to a nongovernmental body the legal authority of the state. It also puts a potent weapon into the hands of the accrediting body in dealing with postsecondary educational institutions. A college or university would be reluctant to challenge accreditation if as a result the opportunity of graduates to qualify for licensure would be jeopardized. In this situation, accreditation cannot truly be called voluntary.

Some licensing boards and commissions have recently come under new "sunset" laws requiring the legislature to review their authorization after a specified period. Such reviews have had mixed results to date. In some states, aggressive lobbying by professional groups has turned back efforts to eliminate licensing or to place public representatives on licensing boards. In other cases, the removal of licensing has caused severe problems. For example, the Florida legislature in 1979 permitted several licensing boards to go out of existence, including the one for professional psychologists. Within a matter of days after that board was terminated, hundreds of persons had purchased licenses from county governments and had become licensed practitioners without regard to previous training or experience. Under pressure, the legislature reinstated the licensure requirement, including graduation from an accredited program.

Private-Independent Status. Spokespersons for the proprietary sector often say that for-profit institutions are taxpaying, private nonprofit institutions are tax-avoiding, and public institutions are tax-supported. However, proprietary schools benefit from tax writeoffs and government contracts. Private nonprofit institutions, of course, are subsidized by reason of their tax-free status, and because they can receive tax-free gifts, most of them also receive substantial amounts of state and federal monies, directly or indirectly. The Commonwealth of Pennsylvania recognized this situation by classifying institutions as state-owned, state-supported, and state-aided. In recognition of these conditions and the important quasi-public role that they play, private institutions prefer to be called independent. The important point is that it is no longer meaningful to talk about public institutions and private institutions as clear-cut categories; both forms of postsecondary education are heavily subsidized.

The argument is often made that the greatest strength of American postsecondary education is its diversity, that a pluralistic society needs such diversity, and that the preservation of the private or independent sector is necessary to guarantee it. Further, the case is regularly made that new approaches to learning, innovative programs, and quality education are more likely to be stimulated in private institutions, with their versatility and flexibility, than in public institutions, which are usually hampered by funding restrictions and detailed review and approval procedures. To provide themselves with continued access to public funds but to protect themselves from onerous state controls, private institutions have championed the role of accreditation as a guarantor of institutional quality and as a buffer against state agency intrusions. They have argued that institutional accreditation should satisfy state requirements for licensing. The public and private sectors must come to agreement on the appropriate and complementary roles of state authorization and nongovernmental accreditation so that the postsecondary education community can send one set of signals to state governments.

The Triad Concept. Kaplin (1975) has fully described the respective roles of the federal government, state governments, and accrediting bodies (the "triad") in the governance of postsecondary education. In addition, many of the problems inherent in those relationships are explored elsewhere in this book (see Chapter Thirteen). One issue has particular relevance to the role of the states: The U.S. Department of Education, in its institutional eligibility process, requires both state authorization and accreditation (or a presumed equivalent). However, recognizing the insufficiencies and weaknesses of state authorization, the department has attempted to place a greater reliance on accreditation, implying that nongovernmental accrediting bodies should carry out a monitoring or policing function—a role that accreditation disavows. Many states similarly look on accreditation as being responsible for ensuring the operational integrity and accountability of postsecondary institutions. These expectations have been reinforced by the consumer protection movement and the growing concern that federal or state funds not be misused. The debates over this issue tend to overlook the fact that many institutions are neither licensed nor accredited, many more institutions are licensed but not accredited, and thousands of enterprises are not postsecondary educational institutions in the usual sense (organizations such as teaching hospitals and clinics) but are eligible for federal student aid funds.

Under the concept of the triad, the federal government, state governments, and nongovernmental accrediting bodies would carry out different but complementary roles to eliminate fraudulent institutions, identify weak institutions, assist institutions that wish to improve, assist in the allocation of government funds, and provide the public with useful information and advice. However, there has been more rhetoric (and finger pointing) than action. To make the triad a reality, the federal government would have to work to achieve greater uniformity in state authorization and regulation of postsecondary education through the incentive of direct financial support and the pressure of action based on the equal-protection provisions of the Constitution.

Nontraditional Education. There is very little in the way of traditional postsecondary education any more—if by that term what is meant is the institution that serves only full-time, resident students under twenty-five years of age through on-campus educational programs that consist of lectures, laboratories, and activity classes and lead to academic degrees. Almost all colleges and universities now enroll part-time students and students over twenty-five, offer instruction off campus as well as on campus and at a wide variety of times, and make use of new technology (from satellites to computers). Many also give credit for experiential learning, offer opportunities for independent study, grant external degrees, and teach noncredit as well as credit courses. Some institutions (for example, the University of Maryland and Brigham Young University) offer instruction around the world. Oklahoma State University is organizing a teleconference network that will link up fifty or more universities across the country (see Chapter Seventeen).

State agencies have been struggling to keep up with the rapid spread of new institutions, programs, and delivery systems. Their major concerns have been (1) to ensure that established institutions are not engaging in new activities that are inappropriate, unfairly competitive, or of questionable quality, (2) to deal with institutions from out of state that are establishing programs in the state and, conversely, with institutions within the state that are establishing programs in other states, (3) to cope with new kinds of institutions (such as the Community College of the Air Force or the now-defunct University of Mid-America) that do not have the usual structure or functions of an institution of postsecondary education, and (4) to develop ways to respond to the unsettling challenges of telecommunications.

Most state agencies have not been very successful in dealing with these phenomena, because they are working with an outmoded definition of *postsecondary education* and because they are using inadequate tools—licensing and regulation. For example, some states have received pressure from institutions

285

within the state to keep out-of-state institutions from operating in competition with them. These states have responded by invoking new interpretations of existing licensing laws or by enacting special licensing laws that would apply to "carpetbagger" institutions. Students of the law, however, believe that the commerce clause of the U.S. Constitution would prohibit a state from imposing requirements on out-of-state institutions that were not also imposed on institutions within the state.

Program Review. State agencies have become increasingly involved in the review of programs offered by postsecondary institutions for two reasons. First, the review of programs is, in certain fields, part of the licensing of practitioners. Second, changes in enrollment patterns and reductions in funding have recently forced cutbacks, and states have engaged in program reviews to determine how cuts should be made. Because such program reviews contribute to a greater centralization of state authority and decision making, most institutions have viewed them as a major threat to institutional autonomy and academic freedom. However, Green (1981, p. 77) notes: "The state concern and responsibility for quality in higher education is subject to two constitutionally based constraints: state responsibility for the economic regulation of the higher education marketplace and state responsibility for the provision of educational access and opportunity." Proponents of self-determination by postsecondary institutions point out that, ironically, specialized accreditation may be of critical value in militating against undue centralization of state power while providing more acceptable avenues for program review.

Student Consumer Protection. The recent growing interest in consumer protection has broadened the scope of state government concerns to include misrepresentation, breach of contract, tuition refund policies, due process, grading practices, and articulation problems (see Chapter Twelve). State agencies and accrediting bodies share most of these concerns. However, the fundamental consumer protection responsibilities of the state are in guaranteeing not only the stability of the institution but also the appropriateness and availability of programs. Effective chartering and licensing processes can address these issues.

"Sunshine" Laws. A number of states have enacted "sun-

shine" laws intended to open up the decision-making processes of public bodies to scrutiny by the citizenry. Board meetings must be open to the public, and any business discussion can occur only after appropriate public announcement. A few states have interpreted such laws narrowly, permitting certain critical matters (such as contract discussion and personnel considerations) to be restricted to executive sessions or protected under the classification of working papers. Other states have interpreted such laws broadly and, among other things, have challenged the confidentiality inherent in both the institutional self-study and the voluntary nature of the accreditation process. For example, a newspaper reporter in Virginia insisted on seeing the self-study report of a local college. Only after a lengthy explanation of the purpose and nature of this document did the reporter agree not to use the institution's self-identified weaknesses as the basis for an article. Some state agencies have attempted to use self-study reports as a basis for determining which programs to eliminate. This issue of confidentiality versus public scrutiny has yet to be effectively resolved.

Coordinating Boards. Statewide coordinating or governing boards grew rapidly during the 1960s. Some states (for example, Wisconsin) created statewide institutions by bringing all colleges and universities under a single authority. Whether these centralized organizations will expand their roles and authority, remain as they now are, or diminish in importance is not yet clear. On the one hand, dwindling resources and pressures for accountability and consumer protection suggest an increased presence. On the other hand, the disappearance of federal support will force states to decide whether these organizations are cost-effective. States that are strapped for funds may be understandably reluctant to provide more money so that a postsecondary education commission can visit and evaluate each college and university when the institutions and their accrediting bodies already conduct such procedures. Many state officials, however, question the value of accreditation, particularly institutional accreditation, and are also beginning to raise questions about the hidden costs of accreditation in time spent by faculty and staff members.

In some states (Birch, 1979, identified seventeen), legislation empowers coordinating or governing boards or other agencies to "accredit" institutions. The activities called for are not accreditation in the same sense that the concept is used by the accreditation community. In any event, most states have accepted institutional accreditation in lieu of conducting their own evaluations. However, some state licensing reviews (for example, in the District of Columbia) come close to duplicating the accreditation process.

State governments historically took the position of honoring the desire of postsecondary educational institutions to engage in self-determination and self-regulation. That position has gradually given way under a variety of forces, and states have recently engaged in more direct oversight of postsecondary education—thus challenging not only the role of the institutional board of trustees as the presumed vehicle for representing the public interest but also the role of accreditation as the nongovernmental mechanism for self-evaluation and self-improvement.

These changes in state policies and practices are a reflection of public sentiment. Many persons, including governors and state legislators, have come to believe that some postsecondary institutions are not very good and too many others are not as good as they should be or are wasteful and duplicative. They have encouraged state governments to try to address these concerns because they do not understand the role of accreditation or are not convinced of its effectiveness. Institutions and their accrediting associations have not done enough to make clear the importance and reliability of self-regulation and voluntary accreditation. Until institutions, individually and collectively, assume a greater responsibility for self-regulation, they can only expect to face increasing state regulation.

15

Charles M. Chambers

ﾞﾞﾞﾞﾞﾞﾞﾞﾞﾞﾞﾞﾞﾞﾞﾞﾞﾞﾞﾞﾞﾞﾞ

Council on Postsecondary Accreditation

> *There is a need to create ideals even when you can't see any route by which to achieve them, because if there are no ideals, then there can be no hope, and then one would be completely in the dark.* Andrei Sakharov (1974, p. 173)

Accreditation has been part of American postsecondary education for many years, but only during the past thirty years or so has any concerted effort been made to focus on the planning, policy making, and governance of accreditation at the national level. Following earlier partial efforts, the Council on Postsecondary Accreditation (COPA) was founded in 1975. Even today, however, after COPA has undergone two major reorganizations, the primary participants in COPA have yet to completely accept its legitimacy and agree on its role and authority. Understanding why "an idea whose time has come"

Much of the material in this chapter is drawn from several unpublished background papers prepared by the author for the self-study conducted by the Council on Postsecondary Accreditation (1981d).

289

finds that it has not yet fully arrived requires a knowledge of COPA's historical development and the major issues it faces today.

Early National Efforts

By the mid 1920s the American Council on Education (ACE) and other groups of college presidents were beginning to notice with concern the growing number of specialized accrediting bodies. To many, accreditation standards seemed to be becoming more rigid and financial expectations more grandiose. A series of conferences, coordinating committees, and position papers served to remind educators regularly that these problems were not going away and, indeed, that the situation appeared to be worsening.

No formal organization was charged, however, with setting an agenda and moving forward with plans to coordinate and oversee accreditation at the national level. ACE saw itself as the natural spokesperson for all matters in higher education, including accreditation. It preferred, however, to work through resolutions and position papers that presumably would be followed by other higher education groups and institutions rather than to become actively engaged in the day-to-day activities of coordinating, simplifying, standardizing, and supervising accreditation.

The great education expansion that followed the Second World War was accompanied by a parallel growth in the number of specialized accrediting bodies. At least some education leaders felt that the ACE approach was not working well enough and, in 1949, moved to establish the first national coordinating body, the National Commission on Accrediting (NCA). The fear was that the success of any professional area that gained advantage through the establishment of its own accrediting body would fuel the enthusiasm of other disciplines for establishing similar bodies. The ultimate result might be that every program on a college or university campus would be accredited by its own accrediting group, with no discernible increase in quality and with tremendous resources devoted to keeping the machinery going.

The implicit assumption had been that accreditation was the only, or at least the best, method of developing and preserving educational quality and integrity. NCA leaders, however, felt that institutions—through their autonomous boards, faculty governance, and dedication to fulfilling their missions—created the foundation for quality education in this country. Accrediting bodies, along with professional societies, state boards, and other external groups, were regarded as traffic signs scattered along the highway every now and then to help an institution stay on the right road, not as the sole means for making "good" education.

Although NCA was at first received coolly by ACE as well as the specialized accrediting bodies, it was supported by the major associations of public and private colleges and universities through direct annual assessments to the institutions. Clearly, NCA could accomplish nothing without the support of the institutions' presidents. Ideally, no college or university would submit to accreditation unless the accrediting body had been approved by NCA. In reality, NCA had no direct relationship with the many nonmember institutions, and for the thousand or so it did nominally represent, its policies were only advisory. With a small staff and budget, NCA could not police accrediting bodies. Nevertheless, presidents clearly hoped NCA would solve their problems at the national level and relieve them of confronting awkward situations on their own campuses.

The initial agenda called for NCA to eliminate unnecessary accrediting bodies, reduce duplication among the remainder, simplify their procedures, and reestablish educational leadership in institutions. That there were a few well-established accrediting bodies that could not be dropped because their work was closely tied to professional licensure was at once clear, but they could be accepted on the grounds that they were helping to protect the public safety and well-being. The ultimate goal set by NCA was to have the regional associations provide the primary external assessment of colleges and universities. For specialized areas deemed necessary, the corresponding accrediting bodies would advise the regional associations. NCA would also identify where accreditation was not needed and would encourage the respective professional associations to support quality in education through such devices as publications, conferences, workshops, and awards programs—but not accreditation.

The proposal to have the regional associations assume all accreditation responsibility was bolder than might be imagined today. Of the six regional associations, only four were accrediting at the postsecondary level when NCA was formed. Their work was given little more deference than that of several other national bodies that were publishing lists of institutions deemed to be of recognized quality by some definition or other, including the Association of American Universities, the American Association of University Women, the Carnegie Foundation for the Advancement of Teaching, the National Association of State Universities, and the U.S. Bureau of Education.

In the same year, 1949, the regional commissions established the National Committee of Regional Accrediting Agencies (NCRAA) to facilitate cooperation throughout the regions and, the hope was, to minimize some of the "evils" associated with the growth of new accrediting bodies. NCRAA eventually became the Federation of Regional Accrediting Commissions of Higher Education (FRACHE). In addition, within a decade, the two remaining regional associations, the Western Association and the New England Association, began a formal accreditation process. With the nation thus totally blanketed, the other organizations that had been publishing lists of qualified institutions gradually acceded to the regional process.

Apparently the regional associations enjoyed their newfound prominence and independence while tending to effectively hamstring FRACHE, which could set standardized national policies in accreditation only with the concurrence of five of the six member regions. Its major contribution, therefore, was to serve as a forum for testing ideas and reinforcing the best new approaches as the regional commissions faced an ever-changing education landscape, which began to include community and junior colleges, nontraditional education, and proprietary schools.

By the mid 1950s, NCA began to sense its dilemma. The regional associations had obtained stature as the preeminent ac-

crediting bodies, and there was little hope that they would encompass the specialized areas as planned by NCA. Nor did they
show any interest in becoming part of NCA. Further, with most
of the specialized accrediting bodies on the government list,
NCA stood to lose much credibility by dealing only with the
smaller set it deemed essential to the protection of public safety and well-being. Faced with growing apathy on college campuses, NCA decided it could do more by working with the accrediting bodies than by marching out of step with them. The
new strategy was twofold. First, even if the current level of
specialized accreditation was inevitable, accrediting bodies
should be expected to do their work responsibly. Second, proliferation should be controlled, and no new accrediting bodies
should be recognized unless they thoroughly demonstrated the
need for them and their competence, reliability, and experience.

During the fifties, a third organization became active in
national accreditation policy: the Office of Education (OE) in
the Federal Security Agency (replaced later by the Department
of Health, Education and Welfare). With the coming of the student aid programs, OE began to expand its role in reviewing accrediting bodies as part of determining institutional eligibility
(see Chapter Thirteen). Concern within the accreditation community about how far the federal government was going—un-
checked—was an important element in the eventual decision to
form a single national organization. The regionals were now
undergoing periodic review in Washington, together with other
accrediting bodies on the federal list. In fact, they were quick to
point out that they had not applied for, nor were they seeking,
federal recognition, but rather were complying with OE's request for information so as to be of service to their member institutions in becoming eligible for the handful of federal programs linked to accreditation. In such a setting, NCA was never
successful in convincing the regional associations that they
should be reviewed under the criteria set out by NCA.

Another direct beneficiary of the expanding federal assistance programs was the proprietary school sector. Their national associations served as accrediting bodies for many proprietary schools but were not eligible for recognition by NCA or

membership in FRACHE. The primary importance of accreditation to these schools, however, was not acceptance as institutions of higher learning or coordination of their activities with traditional colleges but rather the attainment of eligibility for federal funds. The affiliation of their accrediting bodies with OE met all their important needs, and besides, there was not the added expense of belonging to another national organization such as NCA.

Although NCA and FRACHE shared reciprocal members on their boards, the regional associations were concerned about maintaining their prominence and not appearing to be subordinate to a sister organization. FRACHE tended to view NCA as a representative of, if not advocate for, specialized accreditation. It also saw NCA's role in recognizing accrediting bodies as being effectively short-circuited by the growing federal initiative. NCA leaders, however, felt that the regional associations were slow and ponderous and had missed a golden opportunity a decade earlier to encompass all accreditation on the campuses. In alliance with other national associations, NCA was ever alert to the shifting sands and was quick to sense a mounting disenchantment with the slow responsiveness of the regional associations. Yet, both were supported directly by institutions and presumably represented their interests in accreditation.

Nevertheless, a major study (Puffer, 1970) vigorously argued the wisdom of a strong national organization for all institutional accreditation. Among other concerns, Puffer believed that the slowness of the regional association's response to the growing community and junior college movement might cause support for regional accreditation to crumble and might provoke even greater federal and state involvement. He also felt that such a strong central body could fulfill NCA's original mission—making institutional accreditation sufficient for all programs except for the most complex ones that require state licensure to protect the public.

In 1971, on the heels of the Puffer report, plans to merge NCA and FRACHE were announced. Each organization then began to consolidate its support so that it would enter the union from a position of strength. Both NCA and FRACHE increased their budgets. NCA extended recognition to the National Home Study Council, an institutional type of accrediting body, and added three representatives of specialized accrediting bodies to its board. The regional associations, having just been told (in the Marjorie Webster case) that they need not accredit proprietary schools, decided to accept proprietary accrediting bodies into FRACHE.

Making FRACHE so comprehensive was a good argument that a merger was unnecessary. It was beginning to look as though the prospects for a merger would end in a draw. With plans stalled and the likelihood of failure the longer the lack of progress continued, the national associations made clear their displeasure with the in-house maneuvering and threatened to withdraw their support and encourage their institutions to do likewise. This sobering development, coupled with the accelerating federal activity and the announced intention of the NCA director to retire, was sufficient to break the logjam, and the parties moved swiftly to form a new organization—the Council on Postsecondary Accreditation.

Development of COPA

Although the Council on Postsecondary Accreditation is a relatively young organization, it went through three stages of development in its first seven years—its original establishment in 1975, a reorganization in 1978-79, and a self-study and further reorganization in 1981-82.

Stage One: Beginnings. COPA received its charter as a nonprofit corporation from the District of Columbia on August 27, 1974. Because the national offices of FRACHE and NCA were adjacent on the seventh floor of the National Center for Higher Education at Dupont Circle, the physical merger was accomplished simply by the removal of a single interior partition. The first board meeting was held on January 15, 1975. At that meeting the board adopted the bylaws, named its president effective April 1, and completed other organizational details.

With the merger, COPA became the most comprehensive education association in the country. It is the only one with the word *postsecondary* in its title, and it represents virtually every type of postsecondary education—vocational, trade and technical, home study, community college, liberal arts, proprietary, and graduate research. Despite its important mandate and comprehensive membership, COPA had to face several onerous handicaps from its beginning—issues that occupied much of the time and attention of the new organization's leadership. First, the staff directors of the member accrediting bodies who had to be brought into cooperative working relations were given no official role in the organization. Second, postsecondary educational institutions, whose concerns COPA was supposed to address, had no direct role in its financing. Third, and most significant, the widely differing expectations of the institutional accrediting bodies, the specialized accrediting bodies, and the institutions (either directly or through their associations) had been intentionally ignored so that the consensus necessary to form COPA could be achieved. Specifically, the merger of FRACHE and NCA combined an organization of staff directors of accrediting bodies (who wanted COPA to serve as a trade association) with an organization of presidents (who wanted COPA to monitor, control, and even limit accreditation). Further, the creation of COPA gave, for the first time, a collective voice to specialized accrediting bodies and new status within the postsecondary education community to the several groups representing proprietary schools and colleges.

COPA's founders, nonetheless, achieved some significant areas of agreement. One of the first areas of agreement between FRACHE and NCA was the joint approval of the COPA bylaws in advance of the merger. The result was a genuine marriage, however contrived, in the sense that neither party felt exploited by a new set of bylaws that might not be in its best interests. The parties firmly endorsed the independence and autonomy of postsecondary education as desirable qualities on which to base strength and excellence, and they viewed accreditation as the major means for overseeing those standards of quality and integrity that were relied on by the public as well as the education community.

COPA's main functions were to recognize, coordinate,

and periodically review the work of its member accrediting bodies and to determine the appropriateness of proposed changes in accreditation activities. Next, to demonstrate its nonprofit, charitable mission, COPA restricted its activities exclusively to educational, scientific, research, mutual improvement, and professional activities. The bylaws prohibited COPA from accrediting any institutions or programs. They also required that each member recognize the accreditation of all other members—except that no relationship between members could limit an institution's independence in admitting students. For example, a professional accrediting body may require that its program be located in an institution with regional accreditation, but it cannot require that the professional program admit only students who have undergraduate degrees from regionally accredited colleges.

Stage Two: Bylaws Revisions. To achieve acceptance of the merger, COPA's founders had "papered over" many of the fundamental disagreements that separated NCA, FRACHE, the professional associations, and the proprietary sector. Therefore, shortly after COPA was founded, the board created the Task Force on Structure and Bylaws to begin immediately examining how COPA should be reorganized. In 1978 this group made its final report, which was adopted, in part, by the board.

To provide a role in COPA for the accrediting-commission directors, two constituent assemblies were created, one for institutional accrediting bodies and one for specialized accrediting bodies. The assemblies were not policy-making or legislative bodies but were intended to facilitate discussion and consensus building among the members. The assemblies elected officers, established rules of order, and set their own agendas, but they had no operating budgets. Staff support was provided by COPA, and the assemblies met twice annually—about one month before each board meeting. The chairmen regularly reported to the board, and the assemblies could place items directly on the board agenda. The assemblies did not approve policies for COPA; rather, they provided the board with their considered comments about proposed items. These comments could include formal endorsements of reports to the board for its final approval and adoption.

Even after the dissolution of FRACHE, the directors of the regional accrediting commissions continued to meet on their own as an ad hoc group. Generally, COPA staff members attended these semiannual meetings as observers. After the 1978 reorganization, this group became an official part of the institutional assembly. Its activities were coordinated through the COPA staff, and official minutes were kept. Furthermore, the regional accrediting commissions, for the first time, underwent review by the COPA board in 1980 and were thereby officially recognized by a private national organization.

During the formative period of COPA, the Council of Specialized Accrediting Agencies (CSAA) was created to give those bodies a voice in the process. CSAA was then used as a vehicle for selecting representatives to the COPA board from the community of specialized accrediting bodies. The organization met periodically, usually in conjunction with COPA meetings. With the formation of the assemblies, CSAA was kept alive to give the specialized accrediting bodies a separate voice in case it might be needed.

The bylaws revisions made clearer that COPA would recognize the accrediting bodies periodically and that this recognition would be in the form of a statement of specific scope for each member. Thus, COPA saw itself not only as certifying that an accrediting body followed accepted standards of good practice but also as limiting its recognition to a specifically defined area of accreditation. At that time, an accrediting body was not prohibited from engaging in accreditation activities in other areas, but COPA would lend no credibility to such activities.

The revisions also amplified the education interests that COPA coordinated and represented. The institutional accrediting bodies, one of the primary representatives of institutions, were seen as the major constituent and would therefore carry a larger share of COPA's funding responsibilities. Institutions were also represented by several major nonaccrediting associations. These associations would not be members of COPA, but their importance as a constituency would be reflected in their comparable representation on the board and nominal financial support. Next, many national societies directly interested in professional education programs sponsor specialized accreditation and would therefore be expected to have substantial representation in COPA and an equitable level of the funding responsibility. Finally, the public-interest nature of COPA and the accrediting bodies would be formally acknowledged through public representation on the board.

At about the same time that COPA was undergoing reorganization, two other important developments were taking place. First, ACE, in conjunction with the six other national associations participating in COPA, established the interassociation Presidents Committee on Accreditation. The committee was chaired by the ACE president and consisted of the staff directors of the seven associations and their COPA board representatives. This group met on an ad hoc basis, once or twice a year, first, to allow the board members, who are generally presidents of member institutions, to discuss issues with the staff directors and develop coordinated positions and, second, to focus on areas in accreditation of particular concern to institutions. Questions were raised about this group preempting or competing with COPA. The committee, however, designated COPA as its "chosen instrument" for national policy matters in accreditation and adopted resolutions encouraging member institutions, which represent virtually every nonprofit postsecondary college and university, to deal only with COPA-recognized accrediting bodies, a policy similar to that established for NCA thirty years earlier.

Second, in conjunction with the reauthorization of the Higher Education Act, the Office of Education (later the Department of Education) undertook a reexamination of its role in accreditation and eligibility. Both the Commissioner's Advisory Committee and the Postsecondary Education Subcommittee of the U.S. House of Representatives heard testimony from COPA and other parties regarding not only the link between accreditation and eligibility but also the proper role of the federal government in recognizing accrediting bodies. The Carter administration finally recommended that Congress sever the link between accreditation and eligibility, echoing the recommendation of an earlier Republican administration when

Frank Newman and his task force suggested in 1971 that the secretary of HEW do essentially the same thing. Congress ultimately left the current eligibility system unchanged. The old Advisory Committee was allowed to expire, and Congress authorized a new one with a much more sharply focused charter limiting it solely to advice on eligibility matters. Also during the reauthorization period, Congress amended the General Education Provisions Act to prohibit government interference in accrediting-body activities, as recommended by COPA and ACE. The new Department of Education made several major staff changes in the accreditation area, and the Reagan administration seemed intent on deregulating activities involving accreditation as much as possible. In this climate, a stronger agenda of mutual exploration and cooperation between COPA and the department has emerged (see Chapter Thirteen).

Stage Three: Self-Study. The first reorganization had barely been put in place when a comprehensive self-study of COPA was proposed. Specifically, at the organizational meeting of the new assemblies in September 1979, the institutional accrediting bodies called for an overall assessment of COPA's performance in terms of its goals, governance, financial structure, and priorities. Because 1980 marked the fifth anniversary of COPA's founding, the time was considered opportune for such a study. The specialized accrediting bodies concurred with this proposal.

In April 1980 the board authorized a self-study to be conducted by a nine-person ad hoc panel of experienced education leaders. The task force was to be independent of COPA so that it might make forthright recommendations unhindered by allegiances to one or another of COPA's constituents. To provide liaison, however, two board members were included in its membership. Pressing business caused the board to have to delay giving its final approval of the charge to the panel until April 1981.

During the summer of 1981, the panel conducted an intense review of COPA's development and activities and held public hearings at which it received written or oral comments from twenty-two organizations representing virtually all COPA's constituencies. The panel then reached consensus on a series of preliminary recommendations. Recognizing the sensitivity of its role, the panel sought to build confidence in its work, if not concurrence in its findings, by submitting its preliminary report to the COPA assemblies, which met in September. After giving full consideration to the reactions of the member accrediting bodies and making the modifications it felt were justified, the panel submitted its final report to the board at the October 1981 meeting.

In presenting the panel's recommendations to the board, chairman Howard R. Bowen stressed the fundamental principle that institutions of postsecondary education must maintain their independence from control by government agencies and domination by professional groups (Bowen, 1981). But, he stressed, with independence comes accountability, and voluntary accreditation is a unique and innovative device for encouraging and evaluating educational quality. Ultimately, therefore, accreditation must serve the educational well-being of institutions. Although there is an obvious need for close communication and understanding between institutions and accrediting bodies, the tendency for accreditation "to take on a life of its own somewhat detached from the institutions" poses a threat to institutional autonomy (Bowen, 1981). In his view, "academic autonomy requires that primary responsibility for accreditation must lie with the colleges, universities, and other academic institutions" (Bowen, 1981).

In line with this philosophy, the panel made several significant recommendations for reorganizing COPA and provided much detail about how each item could be implemented. First, the board should be reduced from forty members to fifteen, with four ex officio members. No longer would any one accrediting body have its own designated representative on the board. Second, the recognition process should be independent of the board through a new Committee on Recognition. Third, a third assembly should be established for national institutional associations. Fourth, institutions, as accreditation's chief beneficiaries, should bear a major share of COPA's cost, with the balance shared equally by COPA's member accrediting bodies. Fifth,

COPA's name should be changed to the Commission on Postsecondary Accreditation, to emphasize its central role and authority. Finally, among a series of topical priority issues, a formal review and evaluation of COPA should occur at least every five years.

At its October 1981 meeting, the board adopted all the recommendations except the name change. In the financing area, it endorsed only the principle of direct institutional support. It adopted, instead, an interim financing plan that shifted a portion of COPA's support from the institutional accrediting bodies to the specialized accrediting bodies. However, the plan still left the bulk of COPA's financing in the hands of the institutional accrediting bodies. From a recent survey of a few dozen select institutions, it seems likely that the interim financing plan will remain in force.

What Has COPA Accomplished?

Soon after COPA's formation, the board reviewed the overall purposes of the organization and set the following five major priorities:

- Dealing with the problems of proliferation and specialization.
- Evaluating educational quality, including the measurement of outcomes.
- Coping with the role of federal and state government.
- Developing a national education and information program.
- Selecting, training, and evaluating accreditation volunteers.

During its first seven years, COPA has made significant progress in addressing the first three priorities but has yet to effectively take on the last two.

Proliferation and Specialization. This problem, which was chosen by the board as COPA's number one priority, is not explicitly contained in the bylaws. It might be implicitly found in COPA's charge to promote the improvement of postsecondary education and the interests of the education consumer, if one can assume that carrying out more and more inspections of smaller and smaller pieces of an institution somehow detracts from the educational purposes that an institution is designed to accomplish. The opposite view is advocated by some of COPA's members and others—that is, only when every component of an institution has its own separate accreditation will there be any assurance of quality and integrity in postsecondary education for the student and the public. In fact, however, the prominent specialized accrediting bodies are as concerned about growing proliferation as are the regional accrediting commissions and institutions.

Since COPA was founded, more than 120 groups have expressed an interest in being recognized as accrediting bodies. All these organizations have been advised by COPA's staff that their aspirations are premature, in one way or another, and that they are so grossly out of compliance with key COPA provisions that recognition would probably not be granted. COPA has recognized several new accrediting bodies, but each was previously under final consideration by NCA at the time of the merger and successfully completed its application early in COPA's existence. The Committee on Recognition revised the criteria in 1981 and has set down, for the first time, the many educational and social considerations that must be addressed before a new applicant can demonstrate the need for additional accreditation (see Resource B).

The expectation that COPA would control proliferation is further complicated by the fact that its recognition of accrediting bodies is voluntary. No organization need apply, and many institutions, even those that endorse COPA's role, openly permit nonrecognized groups to evaluate programs on their campuses. COPA is well aware that, of the 120 groups that have sought COPA recognition, some 18 are actually visiting colleges and setting requirements to be met for their accreditation. COPA is concerned that no one has vouched for the consistency and integrity of these accreditation practices and policies, but neither COPA nor NCA before it has ever had the authority to tell an institution from whom it can or cannot seek accreditation.

As required by another of its purposes, COPA has developed formal procedures to review and recognize accrediting

bodies (see Chapter Eight). Specifically, this recognition qualifies them for membership in COPA. Although recognition is
granted for periods of up to five years, COPA has attempted to
monitor problem situations more frequently through interim reports and informal working conferences with its members. Within the first five years of its own recognition process, COPA reviewed every member at least once. As specified in the bylaws,
COPA attempts to safeguard institutional rights through appeals
and due process, but it functions neither as a policeman nor as
an ombudsman. COPA has not had the resources to continuously investigate each of its more than fifty members. Rather, its
practice has been to inform each accredited institution and
other interested parties when a particular accrediting body was
being reviewed and invite comment about that organization's
practices and performance. Finally, the board reviews the accrediting body through a system of panels and subcommittees
and grants final recognition.

Various aspects of the recognition process have not always been consistent, causing some dissatisfaction among organizations undergoing reviews. In addition, the third-party
comment approach has had mixed success. Just as buck privates
are loath to complain about their drill sergeants in public, institutional officials such as presidents, deans, and program directors are cautious about antagonizing an accrediting body unless
there are urgent and compelling reasons. In such cases, COPA
has received significant critical input that enabled the board to
supervise the accrediting body properly. If there is just general
concern and nagging dissatisfaction with an accrediting body,
COPA receives little comment. For example, when the nine regional accrediting commissions were reviewed, COPA was aware
of informal grousing that inferior schools were being accredited
and that some visiting-team members were incompetent. Yet,
not one single critical comment was received in writing from
the more than 3,000 institutions accredited by the regional
associations.

Essentially, COPA has taken the position that there are,
and should be, both institutional accrediting bodies and specialized accrediting bodies. However, it has also argued that there is

no need for the accreditation of every program in an institution and that the time demands, costs, and conflicts of multiple accreditations should be minimized (see Chapter Eighteen).

Evaluating Educational Quality. This priority is stressed in the preamble to the COPA bylaws and is the primary purpose of accreditation. As one of its first major activities, COPA performed a national study on the accreditation of nontraditional education, funded by the W. K. Kellogg Foundation. The major conclusion of the study was that accrediting bodies should focus primarily on educational outcomes, using the same approaches and expectations for all kinds of institutions and programs (see Chapter Seventeen). COPA then sponsored a national conference on this subject and produced an occasional paper (Astin, Bowen, and Chambers, 1979).

COPA also worked closely with the four uniformed services and the Department of Defense regarding the accreditation of off-campus programs on military bases. With DOD support, a major case study of fourteen military installations was made, resulting in a series of recommendations that were implemented by DOD and the regional accrediting bodies. In addition, COPA has cooperated with the Council of Graduate Schools, the American Association of Collegiate Registrars and Admissions Officers, and ACE's Office on Educational Credit and Credentials in developing policies for the proper role of accreditation in graduate education, transfer of credit, and experiential learning.

Federal and State Government. Coping with federal and state governments as their roles affect accreditation is another priority not found in the bylaws. Because increasing federal activity vis-à-vis accreditation was a key factor in stimulating COPA's formation, this omission is strange. In addition, COPA gave this issue a major amount of attention during its first five years. Perhaps the drafters of the bylaws did not want to raise red flags and therefore couched concerns about government regulation in terms of "improving and safeguarding education" (COPA Bylaws, 1975).

Views are divided within the accreditation community on whether COPA's battles with the Office of Education were necessary and successful or unnecessary and counterproductive. Most persons in the larger postsecondary education community remain relatively unaware of the conflict or are confused. However, leaders within the key national associations (for example, the American Council on Education, the Association of American Universities, and the American Association of Community and Junior Colleges) were strongly supportive of COPA's efforts to delimit and clarify the federal role as it would affect nongovernmental accreditation (see Chapter Thirteen).

State governments have become more active in the accreditation arena during the past few years. How their role might evolve remains to be seen. The fact that COPA chose as its second president a person with a strong background of experience dealing with state postsecondary education activities suggests that COPA may be preparing to handle developments in this area (see Chapter Fourteen).

Education and Information Program. COPA's bylaws speak of the organization being the national spokesperson for postsecondary education and establishing a general information program on accreditation. COPA's various publications and meetings have served to keep the accreditation community well informed. However, the larger universe of postsecondary education, except for persons actively involved as volunteers, remains largely uninformed or, worse, misinformed about accreditation. And the general public is either unaware of or indifferent to this "esoteric" function. COPA has yet to mount an effective national effort to explain the role and value of accreditation.

Volunteers in Accreditation. Once again, this priority is not mentioned in the bylaws, except that the selection, training, and evaluation of volunteers in accreditation are obvious requisites to promoting improvement of postsecondary education through accreditation and ensuring the soundness of accreditation practices. Most accrediting bodies, of course, conduct training programs, and some of them cooperate in sharing volunteers and information about their performance. COPA, however, has yet to take the lead in designing and implementing a national effort in this area.

Other Achievements. COPA has carried out the standard

range of association activities, such as adopting board policies, establishing special-purpose task forces and committees, sponsoring funded research, maintaining a national information center, distributing regular and occasional publications, administering working relations with its members, coordinating with other groups, and representing accreditation nationally. Though careful not to become overly dependent on soft funds, COPA has had a relatively robust research program. In addition to the Kellogg and DOD projects, COPA received funds from the Danforth Foundation for a project on educational outcomes and from the Carnegie Corporation for a publication on accreditation and collective bargaining. With the State Higher Education Executive Officers, COPA is cosponsoring a project, supported by the Fund for the Improvement of Postsecondary Education, to explore the problems of the regulation and accreditation of off-campus programs and distance learning through telecommunications.

COPA has a good record of cooperation and coordination with the postsecondary education community. Not only has COPA been designated as the "chosen instrument" for policy matters in accreditation by the national education associations in Washington, but because accreditation policies can be quite complex (as well as somewhat arcane), most education associations are pleased to have a single body such as COPA with whom to consult and to whom inquiries can be directed. At the same time, the whole area of developing policy and taking public positions on accreditation issues has been extraordinarily vexing for COPA. Although COPA has received a great deal of respect, the organization has had difficulty appearing to speak with one voice.

As a free-standing corporation, COPA has full authority to adopt its own policies to carry out any of its corporate purposes and functions. Unfortunately, these are binding only on COPA and not generally on its membership. In only two areas listed in its purposes may COPA adopt policies binding on the member accrediting bodies. First, it can adopt policies with which accrediting bodies must comply to be recognized for membership. These provisions generally fall into the area of good practice and due process in accreditation activities. They were inherited almost verbatim from NCA. Second, the board may develop policies for the coordination of accreditation activities implemented by its members. It has done so through the newly published interagency guidelines, which took several years to develop (see Chapter Eighteen and Resource C). Unlike FRACHE, which could adopt uniform policies with the concurrence of five of the six regional associations, COPA has no power to establish policies for accreditation even if consent among its membership is unanimous. This impotence is further dramatized by the fact that although COPA is intended to represent postsecondary accreditation at the national level, any member or group of members may publicly take different, even contradictory, positions.

Policy statements must frequently be made in rapidly shifting political situations at the national level. On occasion, there has been time only to consult the Executive Committee of the board, which can act for the board between meetings, and to get its approval for proposed positions. Yet, even when the full membership has been consulted and the board acts on a policy, a divided front can still be presented. The recent work of the Ad Hoc Committee on Policy has vastly improved the organization and management of the little comprehensive policy-making power COPA possesses. COPA has adopted a more orderly process for developing policy, and there is hope that, through such careful consensus building, the logic and persuasiveness of new policies will be so apparent that they will be broadly accepted among the membership. Then, indeed, COPA will be more able to speak with one voice. COPA's objective of being the national deliberating and policy-setting body in accreditation has in this sense been the least well-achieved priority to date.

Major Issues

COPA's short life has been a story of struggle—a struggle by various special-interest groups to determine the nature and scope of its role, their balance of representation in its governance, and, ultimately, the control of the organization through the control of its finances.

Role. Although accreditation issues will doubtless remain important, the question whether a body as broadly representative as COPA—with its espoused purpose of coordinating and improving all nongovernmental accreditation activities at the postsecondary education level—is inevitable bears some careful inspection. In looking at COPA's constituents, the following observations can be made about who has what resources and who might be willing to use them for what purposes—scenarios of what could happen if COPA were not to succeed.

First, the regional accrediting commissions would be more than able to reestablish their own national coordinating body. It could be along the lines of FRACHE, but it would more likely have more coordinating authority and would also probably include national institutional accrediting bodies. These two changes would improve it enough without the appearance that FRACHE was simply being resurrected. Rather, there would be a new national organization stressing institutional accreditation that would be proceeding in directions chartered by COPA. If the proprietary associations were not part of this body, they would doubtless spend more money for closer interagency coordination, but they probably would not reach a strong enough consensus to devote enough funds for their own national federation.

The national associations could easily agree to form a new body (a new NCA) that they and their member institutions would fund in some form, certainly to monitor accrediting bodies and perhaps to delve further into policy making. During the next decade at least, specialized accrediting bodies would probably not be able to provide enough funding to enable the Council on Specialized Accrediting Agencies (or some comparable body) to function on its own as an effective national organization. ACE could establish a commission of its own, similar to the Office on Educational Credit and Credentials, which, at a minimum, would review and recognize all accrediting bodies, institutional and specialized.

The history of the first five years of COPA does not seem

to teach that there will always be a COPA. COPA has been described as a mixture of oil and water. The implication, however, is that to keep the two from separating, the mixture must be constantly stirred or occasionally shaken. COPA has had to work in the face of a number of contradictions. It has been asked to function as both advocate and monitor of accrediting bodies, to protect institutions from exploitation while balancing the roles of comprehensive and specialized accrediting bodies, and to keep a wary eye on the federal and state governments. Although this description might sound grandiose, it is realistically the agenda of accreditation in this country. Any organization pretending to provide national leadership must address and manage each of these issues.

If COPA is to succeed, it must have the endorsement and participation of at least the regional accrediting commissions, the dozen or so major professional accrediting bodies, and most of the national associations, including ACE. Ideally, each of these major constituents would be assessed at a high enough level so that its dues, when combined with the others, would ensure a functioning national organization. Yet, dues should not be so high that if one constituent were to go its own way, it would have enough funding to establish an independent, competing organization. COPA has been fortunate in that its major funding source, the regional accrediting commissions, has much more often than not supported the organization, its goals, and its projects.

Governance. Issues related to the board and its work strongly influence any organizational plan. The most prominent feature of COPA's governance was the large size of its board. There was something unwieldy about having forty people scattered throughout the country who must meet twice a year. That problem was addressed in the latest reorganization, when the size of the board was cut back to fifteen, with four ex officio members.

The second most important governance issue concerns the nature of the board itself. Legally, the board operates under the nonprofit corporations statute of the District of Columbia and is the sole governing body for COPA. Even though virtually all board members are appointed by and represent a particular constituency, for them to vote on matters as instructed delegates would be legally improper. Rather, the board is expected to function as a single legislative body, discussing as a whole the pros and cons of each item and then acting by the majority vote of members who personally believe the action to be proper and desirable for COPA. Of course, there is much caucusing, both formal and informal, in advance of board meetings within the various special-interest constituencies. Caucusing is certainly legitimate and helps improve each board member's understanding of complex issues. Nevertheless, the expectation is that each board member will vote his or her mind after hearing the full discussion. Finally, board meetings are held in public unless closed by the chairperson on a simple plurality vote to discuss sensitive matters, such as personnel and financing.

Another important aspect of the board's work is its official recognition of member accrediting bodies. At least once every five years, accrediting bodies that voluntarily seek membership in COPA must submit written documentation that they are in compliance with some two and a half dozen criteria demonstrating the professional caliber of their accreditation services. Although this process is loosely called "accrediting the accreditors," it is not an accreditation process but rather a verification by the board that each COPA member is fulfilling an appropriate need in a fashion that protects the integrity and vitality of institutions. Organizations that fail to comply are either removed from membership or counseled through various interim reports and special reviews to improve their practices.

The recognition function has always posed a serious dilemma for COPA. On the one hand, COPA is supposed to promote and foster the role of accreditation in postsecondary education on behalf of its members. On the other hand, COPA is expected to "police" how accrediting bodies work. COPA has tried to resolve this contradiction by espousing the principle of accreditation and promoting the important benefits it provides, without appearing to give an unqualified endorsement to accreditation as practiced by each of its members. Because accreditation makes sense only when viewed in the context of an accrediting body actually doing it, this principle may be a distinction without a difference. Concurrent with the self-study reorganization, COPA put into place a greatly strengthened recognition process that shows promise of functioning quite well with the support and endorsement of the member accrediting bodies.

COPA identifies its major constituents as the institutional accrediting bodies, the specialized accrediting bodies, the national associations, the postsecondary educational institutions, and the public. This community is broad, and many of its individual members are also represented in other national organizations, which naturally have more than a passing interest in accreditation. Consequently, there are a host of formal and informal relationships with many other groups that influence, to a greater or lesser degree, what COPA is and what it can do.

Financing. Each special-interest group in COPA will continue to compare the percentage of the financing it provides to COPA with the percentage of representation it has on the board. Clearly, when a group's financial stake becomes large, that group begins wondering aloud why the organization is not more responsive to its needs. The organization becomes viewed as a trade association for that primary group. Moreover, any group that pays a greater share of the financing than its proportional representation in the governance tends to mutter about taxation without representation. Finally, groups that pay a lesser share than their relative standing in the organization tend to emphasize the nonfiscal benefits that their participation brings.

COPA is split on which approach to use in obtaining financial support. The self-study committee proposed, for both technical and policy reasons, that COPA obtain 80 percent of its funding directly from institutions and 20 percent equally from the accrediting bodies and national associations participating in COPA. The board adopted this approach in principle but delayed its implementation pending a survey of institutions to assess its feasibility. A further complication was that the national associations set the implementation of direct institutional support within a year as a condition for their willingness to form a new assembly within COPA. Nevertheless, because the survey of a sample of institutions showed little interest, the board may not be able to implement a system of institutional dues.

Although COPA's future will forever be inextricably intertwined in the agendas of dozens of competing and self-protecting constituents, COPA remains, as it was in the beginning, an ideal.

The ideal COPA would be based on the following principles:

• COPA should have as its primary purpose the fostering and improvement of nongovernmental accreditation. Other purposes should relate to this purpose or be secondary to it.

• COPA should be the national organization that brings together all the groups involved in and affected by accreditation, not just an association of accrediting associations.

• COPA should base its role on the following definition of accreditation (which was also given in Chapter One): Accreditation is a process by which an institution of postsecondary education evaluates its educational activities, in whole or in part, and seeks an independent judgment that it substantially achieves its own educational objectives and is generally equal in quality to comparable institutions or specialized units within institutions.

• COPA's primary function should be to establish standards for accrediting bodies, to review and recognize accrediting bodies that meet those standards, and to work with accrediting bodies to improve their practices in light of the standards. Other functions should relate to this function or be secondary to it.

• COPA should have as its basic philosophy that (1) the student is the central concern of the educational process and accreditation should focus primarily on student-demonstrated educational outcomes, (2) the educational institution, however it defines itself, is the legal or organizational entity sponsoring educational programs and accreditation should honor and reinforce institutional autonomy and integrity, and (3) accreditation activities involving any given institution should be conducted in a coordinated, collaborative manner, in accordance with the institution's desires.

In view of COPA's history, its experience, and the potent environment in which it must operate, the question remains, how realistic is this ideal?

Part Five

๛๛๛๛๛๛๛๛๛๛๛๛๛๛๛๛๛๛๛๛๛๛

Developing
Practices
in Accreditation

The traditional professions are facing unsettling changes and diminishing powers, and many new professions and specializations are emerging. These developments have provoked a rethinking of state licensing and regulation of the professions, with profound implications for accreditation.

Similarly, the appearance of a host of nontraditional institutions, programs, and delivery systems has posed new challenges for accreditation. Accreditation began by asking, "What is a college?" It now finds itself asking, "What is an institution of postsecondary education?" Structure, resources, and processes are being given less emphasis in accreditation in favor of increased attention to defining and evaluating educational outcomes.

Finally, institutional concerns about the gradual proliferation of accrediting bodies and their activities have led to demands for action. The answer, however, appears not to be a closed market or market allocation but rather a rational process for achieving cooperation and collaboration among accrediting bodies in ways that will serve the best interests of the institution.

315

16

Corrine W. Larson

ᙁᙁᙁᙁᙁᙁᙁᙁᙁᙁᙁᙁᙁᙁᙁᙁᙁᙁᙁᙁᙁᙁᙁᙁᙁ

Trends in the Regulation of Professions

> *Something complex and strange is happening to the old idea of professionalism and some authorities argue that it must be replaced.*
>
> Cyril O. Houle (1980, p. ix)

There are significant differences in purpose and perspective between institutional accreditation and specialized accreditation (see Chapters One, Ten, and Eleven). Institutional accreditation determines that each part of the institution is contributing to achievement of the institution's educational objectives. Specialized accreditation focuses on one area of professional preparation offered by an institution, and its underlying goal is to determine whether this program or unit is meeting standards presumed to be necessary for practitioners to enter the profession. In other words, one review is oriented toward the interests of the institution; the other, toward the interests of the profession.

The information in this chapter on credentialing was drawn from material provided by Jerry W. Miller.

317

These differences have provoked much of the confusion and controversy in discussions of accreditation. An important step in understanding the basic issues in accreditation, therefore, is to know something about the development and role of professions in society; the changes that are affecting professions and their regulation; and the issues concerning the regulation of professions that must be faced by states, education, and the professions themselves.

Growth of Professions

In an important sense, the development of professions began with the priesthood, because only these special members of the church were given access to nonconventional knowledge (Spencer, 1900). During the Middle Ages, the original seven liberal arts (grammar, rhetoric, logic, geometry, music, arithmetic, and art) formed a basic professional curriculum for practitioners within the church. Ever since, the possession of special knowledge has been seen as the essence of professionalism. The mystification of knowledge is attributed historically to the church and to church-sponsored universities. More common occupations, not requiring special knowledge but based on more readily available information and skills, were open to members of lower orders of society and were organized around guilds, which in some sense were precursors of modern labor unions.

A monopolistic hold on a body of knowledge does not in itself, however, create a profession. Professions are collections of persons similarly situated in society who come together for mutual advantage. Professions in the modern sense, distinguished by formal associations, first arose in the late Middle Ages and with the appearance of capitalism. What was there about early capitalism that gave impetus to the growth of professions? To begin with, capitalism brought trade and mobility as a replacement for the manorial way of life, and the new commercial society based its economy on commodities. Services, as distinct from products, could be treated as commodities by becoming standardized. Such standardization required cooperation, particularly agreement on technological issues and on ways to exclude those who might not meet or adopt the standards and who thus might challenge the profession.

Then, as now, exclusion from competition was best obtained through the sanction of the prevailing authority. Professions have always sought support from whatever group exercised the most power in society. First it was the church, then royalty. Thomas (1903, p. 256) wrote of professions: "They need patronage, and when either the court or the church is developed, the patronage is at hand. . . . But their development must be regarded as a phase of the division of labor, dependent on economic conditions rather than on the presence in society of any particular set of individuals or any peculiar psychic attitude of this set."

The city-state of earlier times was too restricted a form of government to provide the necessary support for a widely spread professional organization, but the coming of national and state governments established the basis for a patronage relationship between professions and the state. "The age of enlightenment in the eighteenth century and the industrial revolution of the nineteenth caused a break with the past for the professions as for many other aspects of life. Both theoretical and practical knowledge began to be built into complex systems. Simple skills taught by apprenticeship grew more refined; engineering, architecture, pharmacy, and nursing emerged as clear-cut separate occupations. The phenomenon of organized association became more highly developed than before, making possible interlocking networks of professional groups that could provide services for and exercise discipline over their members. Governments either took on the power of licensure or delegated it to other bodies" (Houle, 1980, p. 21).

Motives for establishing professions have changed relatively little over time. Professions arose because of the need to organize the market for services and because of the desire for status. Professions tied the possession of scarce knowledge and skills to economic rewards, and professional organization formalized status. (For further information, see Feldstein, 1977; Freidson, 1970; Larson, 1977.) As universities grew as primary purveyors of knowledge, professional education was naturally included in the curriculum, and special degrees were conferred. And when accreditation developed in this country, professions—along with colleges and universities—sought the added status that accreditation bestows. Professional status became linked not only with special knowledge and skills but also with credentials endorsed through specialized accreditation or state regulation.

Credentials as a Tool of Professions. The system of state licensing and professional certification or registration was developed by the professions as a way of achieving the goal of assuring the public that practitioners had met some predetermined requirements limiting the number of practitioners. Accreditation became an essential function of these systems, following the pattern established by medicine in the early 1900s (see Chapter Eleven), a pattern that has been closely followed by most professions ever since.

There are three generic forms of credentials (Miller and Mills, 1978, pp. 8-9):

1. *Licenses—documents of certification, licensure, or registration—issued by government agencies to persons who meet specified requirements.* Such documents are evidence that the state has granted a person permission to engage in a specified activity; practice by the uncredentialed is often, but not always, prohibited. Thus, credentials issued by government agencies may be mandatory for practice, or they may be voluntary or advisory in the sense that the holder, in the view of the state, has permission to use a certain title and to engage in certain activities. An example of the mandatory type of credential is a license issued by a state government to practice dentistry.

2. *Documents of certification or registration awarded by voluntary occupational or professional organizations attesting that the holder meets certain requirements or occupational standards.* The credential represents an advisory opinion by the issuing organization that the holder is qualified to engage in specified practices. It involves the authority of government only in cases in which such credentials are specified in legislation or in an administrative rule as a requirement to qualify for practice. Occupational certification may duplicate, complement, or sup-

plement credentials issued by a government agency and educational institutions or in some cases may provide a higher level of certification than those credentials. An example of this type of credential is that of Certified Association Executive (CAE).

3. *Diplomas attesting to degree or certificate status conferred by educational institutions for successful completion of an organized program of study or for equivalent educational accomplishment.* Credentials issued by an educational institution may be an award for educational accomplishment; they may also be advisory in the sense that they signify that the holder, in the view of the institution, is qualified to engage in certain occupational activities. In some senses, a degree from an accredited institution may be one requirement in qualifying for government or professional credentials. A bachelor's degree in electrical engineering is an example.

Miller and Mills go on to describe the credentialing process (p. 9): "The credentialing process is essentially the same for all three categories of certification. Credentialing involves three parties: (1) the authority issuing the credential, (2) the person to whom the credential is issued, and (3) the persons, groups, or agencies benefiting from or using the judgments of the credentialing authority. The process involves three principal steps: (1) definition of the attitudes, competences, knowledge, or skills to be certified, (2) assessment of each individual to determine whether he or she meets the requisites, and (3) issuance of a document to attest to the individual's possession of the requisites. To an increasing extent, credentialing involves a fourth step: periodic recertification that the holder continues to possess the requisites for the credential or meets new ones made necessary by advances in the field."

The ties between credentialing systems, accreditation, and professional practice are often intricate and reinforcing. In its ultimate form, the professional association conducts a successful campaign to convince the state that practitioners should be licensed in the public interest. The wording of the licensing law is proposed, or at least strongly influenced, by the professional association. The licensing board is usually dominated by members of the profession, who are often recommended by the professional association. The law not only establishes the requirements for the license and possibly its renewal but also may specify that a prerequisite to licensing is graduation from a school or program accredited by the professional association. The role of specialized accreditation, from the perspective of the profession, is secondary to the credentialing system; indeed, the role of specialized accreditation is seen as supporting the credentialing system. In voluntary certification and registration, accreditation may also be cited as a prerequisite.

How Specialized Accreditation Serves Professions. The Council on Postsecondary Accreditation sanctions thirty-seven specialized accrediting bodies covering more than fifty fields. The rationale given is that institutional accreditation alone provides inadequate safeguards, and there are compelling social or educational reasons for an additional form of accreditation. Many critics of specialized accreditation argue that the existence of specialized accreditation in a given field may also result from historical accident or the exercise of political muscle by entrenched and powerful interests in the professions or in education—muscle that colleges and universities have not been able to collectively resist effectively. But whatever the real reason, specialized accreditation is tolerated officially because of a perceived compelling educational or social need.

The most justifiable forms of specialized accreditation are found in fields preparing practitioners whose activities have a direct bearing on the health and safety of the public they serve or whose activities could cause irreparable harm to members of society. A generally accepted premise is that institutional accreditation cannot provide the extensive and intensive evaluation required for certain professional programs, perhaps the best examples being medicine and dentistry. In certain professional fields, specialized accreditation interacts with licensure and voluntary certification to provide an extra measure of protection for the public by providing assurances about the adequacy of educational preparation and therefore presumably about the competence of the practitioners. In fields in which licensure or certification is not a factor, specialized accreditation—more than institutional accreditation—implies that, across institutions, curriculum and degree requirements are similar and the competence of graduates is comparable. The evaluation process of specialized accrediting bodies is much more likely to look for specific examples of student achievement, which is thought to be predictive of acceptable practitioner performance. Much like institutional accreditation, specialized accreditation is a public expression of confidence in the expertise and integrity of an accredited program, but it has a greater concern for the ability of graduates to perform.

Specialized accreditation also has the effect of modifying the general reputation of an institution. The quality of programs within an institution is invariably uneven, and low-quality programs may benefit from the lofty reputation of an institution. Conversely, high-quality programs in an institution of lesser overall reputation may suffer without the boosting effects of specialized accreditation. Supporters of specialized accreditation have argued that it is a valuable tool either to brighten or to dim an institution's halo.

In many fields, specialized accreditation is still entirely voluntary in that many institutions choose not to submit to the process. In other fields, in which candidates must have graduated from an accredited program to sit for the professional licensure or certification examination, even some of the most prestigious institutions have little choice but to submit their programs for evaluation.

Changes Affecting Professions

The imposing role that well-established professions have built for themselves over the years, involving credentialing and accreditation, is increasingly being undermined by several recent developments.

New Occupational Groups. Technological advances and increasing specialization since World War II spawned many new occupational groups. New types of workers were required to perform new types of work. What these occupational groups have in common are ill-defined and often overlapping scopes of practice, a desire for greater autonomy in the workplace, and a tendency toward overtraining (Galambos, 1979). In the 1960s and 1970s, scores of these would-be professions, mostly in the health area, sought the protection of state licensing laws. Following the successful model pioneered by physicians, these emerging professional groups also created pressure and more than an element of confusion in service settings and in educational programs.

In this professional maelstrom, state regulatory authorities have various choices. They can seek to arbitrate the scope-of-practice claims or "turf wars" themselves, specifying in regulations who can perform which functions and on the basis of what education, training, and credentialing. They can resort to the political arena to resolve interprofessional disputes in state legislatures. Or they can leave to managers and "third-party payers"—such as insurance companies, employers, and government agencies—the power to make these judgments. If the authorities are unable to resolve the disputes using one of these methods, the issues are taken to the courts, where in general the past is only reiterated; new solutions are seldom framed through judicial review of historical decisions.

Trend Away from Solo Practice. In earlier times, professionals worked on their own. They were relatively free from supervisors and subordinates alike. Today, factors such as specialization, technology, the desire for efficiency, and economies of scale result in more group efforts and more structure. Solo practice survives but does not rule. Increasingly, doctors, lawyers, engineers, architects, nurses, and most other professionals function as members of teams or as employees in large organizations. This change makes possible even greater specialization, but it also imposes new requirements in the form of administrative and human relations skills. More important, it calls for a different understanding of the role of a professional.

Increasing Geographical Mobility. Because professionals today require great geographical mobility, their credentials must be portable. Therefore, no institution, however large, can maintain a unique credentialing system, and states operate independent systems only at the risk of both penalizing residents who may wish to move elsewhere and frustrating recruitment of out-of-state professionals. Of particular concern are (1) tendencies to give the same category of workers different names in different states, (2) fundamental differences among states in the scope of practice of a single occupational group, and (3) conflicting patterns of supervisory, training, and testing requirements. To cite just one relatively minor example to indicate the pervasiveness of the problem, even when all states adopt the same national test to credential members of a particular occupation, state boards sometimes set different passing scores on the test.

Changing Attitudes About Professions. Public attitudes about professional licensing in particular and credentialing in general are changing. Legislators have begun to realize that there may be some connection between licensing and fragmented delivery systems, high costs of professional services, and barriers to making good use of people. Consumers have discovered that licensing requirements may have little to do with competency to practice. Employers and consumers increasingly object to being told whom they can hire or use, and insurance companies are beginning to see that they need a better mechanism for ensuring appropriate payment.

Furthermore, today people are taking more responsibility for certain aspects of their lives. The myth that professional service is so complex that it cannot be understood by the layperson is falling away. The suggestion that health and well-being are primarily personal responsibilities is once again beginning to be believed.

Changing Regulations. Clearly, change in the way professions are regulated is inevitable. Consumers of professional services today are more sophisticated. They refer themselves to specialists, they learn about new scientific developments through the news media, and they are increasingly aware that they have rights in transactions with the professional network. These rights are epitomized in malpractice suits. But the rights of consumers also relate to the authority and responsibility of regulators to withdraw or limit licenses of incompetent or unethical practitioners. The modern consumer knows that he or she has the right to some control over the institutions that govern his or her life. Furthermore, third-party payers are being compelled by economic factors to become more assertive in questioning regulatory standards, costs, and the quality of professional service, and they are starting to serve as advocates for consumers and taxpayers. Because of this pressure, as well as direct consumer pressure, professions, licensing authorities, and institutions of postsecondary education are expected to show greater accountability than ever before.

The unmistakable conclusion about the regulation of professions is therefore that professions can no longer act alone to set standards. Unjustifiable standards of entry into a profession and restrictions on competition may (and probably will) be struck down by the courts acting under the authority of due process requirements or antitrust laws. Even state agencies are not immune from such public and judicial review. For example, the increasing presence of consumers on regulatory boards and the watchful eye that boards and professions keep on each other tend to ensure that more regulatory excesses are brought to public attention. The face of professional regulation is therefore changing. More often, state officials, professionals, employers, third-party payers, and consumers are all involved in forging decisions about who is qualified to perform which tasks.

In this complicated situation, the relevance of scope-of-practice restrictions in statute books has paled. They seldom reflect the realities of modern professional practice, are inherently vague in wording, are unrelated to courses of training, and differ so markedly among states and so little among professions that they institutionalize irrationality. The danger is that when these laws are opened to litigation among occupational groups, the courts are thrust into the position of making scope-of-practice determinations on the basis of unrealistic, anticompetitive laws. A more flexible and systematic way of charting scopes of practice is clearly indicated and can logically rest on determinations of proficiency—determinations that are increasingly subject to empirical demonstration.

Pressure for Credentials Based on Competence. No professional today is truly independent. Increasingly, the employer is an organization. Yet, the system of licensing the individual is based on the faulty premise that there is no interdependency among the professionals in different groups, that there are no shared functions, that each group has an exclusive scope of practice, and that services are delivered by solo practitioners. Increasingly, there will be call for information on who is competent for what and for information on what outcomes can be expected from a given service.

Decrease in the Influence of Local Standards. Several factors have lessened the influence of local standards: (1) the increased impact of national standards that accompany federal funds, such as the impact of Medicare standards on health care and the impact of federal funding requirements on education, (2) increase in the sophistication of communication technology, (3) court decisions reflecting less adherence to "local standards of care" arguments, (4) increased mobility of people, and (5) the development of regional and national systems of continuing education, which means that "unique" statewide standards will become increasingly more difficult to justify.

Increasingly Fragmented Delivery Systems. Studies have documented that licensing laws, with their competing scopes of practice, create barriers to effective use of human resources and contribute to increased fragmentation in the delivery of services (Shimberg, 1980, pp. 132-159). Neither efficiency nor coordination is facilitated by defining delivery systems through establishing requirements for practice from the perspective of a single discipline, without any consideration for how disciplines overlap or how professionals from different disciplines work together to solve problems. The fragmentation of delivery systems contributes to the high costs of service, leads to dissatisfied consumers, and gives rise to today's concern about regulations being uncoordinated, excessive, and contradictory. Furthermore, professional licensing is one of three factors at the state level that have been identified by the federal government as probable causes of inflation, an impact documented by more and more researchers (Shimberg, 1980, pp. 132-159).

Need for Greater Efficiency in State Government. State legislatures and state governments are under pressure for more efficient organization and operation. The recent emergence of "sunrise," "sunshine," and "sunset" legislation is a direct result of this pressure. Many states are carrying out a functional analysis of state government to identify common functions among agencies, and licensing boards therefore become more visible. The question is asked: If these boards have the common function of seeing to it that persons in professional groups meet certain predetermined requirements for practice, are there not some benefits to the state by centralizing certain administrative functions?

In sum, the rapid growth of professions may be a movement that has just about consumed itself. In an era when all are professionals, no profession has monopolistic control and knowledge. When professions batter against each other's limits, claims to turf must be refereed by others, or anarchy will reign. Consumerism and cost-consciousness today result in part from the tremendous growth of professions and reinforce the need for a rational system. And because today professionals are not the only ones who care about the credentialing system—which is no longer stable—the issues facing states, education, and professions themselves are now public policy questions.

Issues for States

State legislatures have begun to face the following questions: Should the state be regulating professional groups? Who should be regulated? If there should be regulation, what should it be, and who should be responsible for administering it? Legislators are discovering that there have not been adequate mechanisms for ensuring an orderly process of identifying occupations that need regulation. The traditional model of establishing peer boards and allowing them to function autonomously has resulted in a fragmentation of regulation and an inflexibility that prevents innovative uses of new or existing personnel. They are beginning to realize that each licensure law, by definition, has tended to ensure an exclusive area of practice for the licensed group, and an occupational group cannot readily alter its scope of practice or admit other practitioners into its exclusive practice area. Employers have become aware that such laws tell them whom they must hire.

State licensing boards and private certifying bodies will be asked to face the following issues:

Conflict of Interest. Opinion is mounting that there is a basic conflict of interest in a licensing board controlled by the profession but operating with the legal authority of the state. Many of the abuses (exclusionary practices, anticompetitive activities, and lack of vigor in investigating complaints and taking disciplinary actions) stem in part from the fact that boards are composed of peers from a single discipline. The notion that only members of the occupation can make judgments about the effectiveness of a profession is being challenged.

Restrictive Entry Requirements and Tests. Requirements exist that discriminate against residents of another state or another culture, that do not recognize that learning occurs in a variety of ways, or that discriminate for lack of a common standard. Using tests that do not meet rigid standards of validity, reliability, and job-relatedness was never appropriate and is now no longer legal. Given court decisions such as that in the Duke Power case and Equal Employment Opportunity Commission (EEOC) guidelines, non-job-related requirements will be more and more difficult to justify.

Anticompetitive Restrictions. Anticompetitive restrictions in the past have included prohibition against advertising or competitive bidding. The courts and the Federal Trade Commission have found that such restrictions are not in the public's interest.

Enforcement Weaknesses. Consumers have argued that licensing boards and professional disciplinary committees are insensitive to consumer complaints and that they are reluctant to investigate or take disciplinary action, and when they do, it is usually related to criminal violation, drug abuse, or questions of moral turpitude for which there is seldom agreement or solid legal interpretation. Professional credentialing practices are meant to be quality assurance mechanisms that protect the public from unqualified practitioners by weeding out incompetents and disciplining those who are guilty of professional misconduct. Professional codes of ethics and codes of behavior are beginning to be scrutinized for their relation to the public's interest.

Pressure for Increased Consumer Rights. The public seems less willing to let important decisions be made unilaterally by professionals. Consumers, patients, and clients want more choice in providers and more say in decisions. They want information on rights, choices, expectations, and costs. Increasingly they are challenging hierarchal organizations and paternalistic traditions.

Effectiveness of Licensing. The long-standing debate about the effectiveness of licensing and relicensing continues. Milton Friedman and others argue that there is no persuasive evidence that licensing does sort out the competent from the incompetent and thus serves to protect the public (Friedman, 1962; Freidson, 1970). Others accept the value of licensing but question the way in which the process operates—usually dominated or controlled by professional groups functioning under the imprimatur of the state, with little or no public oversight or control. Where there is a licensing procedure, the desirability of periodic review through some sort of relicensing procedure has been widely accepted. Many states, however, have attempted to deal with this problem by imposing some sort of continuing education requirement. For example, the licensed professional may be expected to complete a certain number of CEUs (continuing education units) over a specified period of time. This approach has been challenged because it focuses on "time served" in workshops and at conferences rather than on demonstrated proficiencies and has led to many abuses.

Issues for Education

Many colleges and universities have long accepted the role of providing preprofessional and professional education, and they are increasingly offering continuing professional education, often in collaboration with professional associations. Educators, however, face many problems—some old and some new—in relating to professions.

Purposes of Education. Educators continue to debate such questions as these: What areas of specialization are appropriate for institutions of postsecondary education? What should be the relationship between general education and specialized education, between theory and application? How much education and what kind is necessary for various occupations? The questions have not changed over the years, but the answers vary from profession to profession and are modified over time.

Relationships with Professions. Should professional education be offered in free-standing institutions (such as independent schools of music) or in units that are part of a college or university? If the latter, in what ways and to what extent should the professional unit have operational autonomy and independent identity? Economic considerations are pushing more and more institutions to adopt the position that "every tub should stand on its own bottom." Should professions influence or dictate curricula (primarily through credentialing or accreditation requirements)?

Faculty members in professional programs have dual identities: as members of the college or university faculty and as members of the profession. They often have problems reconciling these roles. Within most professional groups, there are conflicts between the "educators" and the "practitioners." The latter have customarily concentrated on the issues of credentialing and have left to the educators the operational concerns of specialized accreditation; however, the professional associations, dominated by practitioners, have in most cases retained veto power over accreditation decisions, standards, and policies.

Role of Educational Credentials. There is limited agreement, both within colleges and universities and outside them, on the meaning of a degree. Expectations concerning the competencies of graduates in the same major field of study varies considerably across institutions. Because most majors are highly work-related, institutions are under pressure to standardize this part of the degree more than any other. However, most educational credentials have limitations: "The credential is not a guarantee that every person credentialed will perform satisfactorily or that every credential holder will perform well in every situation. It merely indicates that those people who hold the credential tend to deliver adequate services with substantially more consistency than those who do not hold the credential. Given the difficulty of defining and assessing the requisites for delivery of complex highly refined services, credentialing cannot be expected to provide absolute protection to society. It has social utility because it increases the likelihood that satisfactory services will be delivered" (Miller and Mills, 1978, p. 4).

Significant among the dilemmas for educators is the extent to which they should train students for credentials and contemporary practice. Two considerations are the length that programs should be and the balance between skill training and general education. The briefest possible program may be best for filling acute personnel shortages but may do a disservice to students in fulfilling their long-range potential; nevertheless, degree requirements that are not job-related will increasingly be challenged. New training programs and curricula will probably continue to be placed under the responsibility of colleges and universities. However, because job duties are diffused among increasing numbers of occupations in an expanding technology, who should be trained to do what and what needs to be known to obtain specific expertise will no longer be at all clear (for further information, see Miller, 1976; Shimberg, 1981).

Uses of Accreditation. Should institutional accreditation give greater attention to institutional units, especially as some of them become increasingly self-sufficient? In fact, do institutional accrediting bodies need to reexamine their definition of an institution? A self-supporting law school or medical school located miles from the parent campus may be only nominally part of a university. Are the regional accrediting bodies prepared to expand their activities regarding the accreditation of free-standing specialized institutions traditionally accredited by professional associations? (For example, the Western Association of Schools and Colleges has taken its first step in this direction by accrediting the Western State University College of Law.) Can institutions most affected by specialized accreditation—universities and large community college systems—find the will to withstand, when appropriate, the use of professional licensure to impose specialized accreditation, to resist the pressures of specialized accreditation for special privileges, and to insist that specialized accrediting bodies work cooperatively and focus mainly on institutional objectives and program outcomes?

Issues for Professions

All these issues, of course, are also questions that must be addressed by professions themselves. More basic to professional groups, however, are the following three concerns.

Redefining Professions. Professions are constantly changing and evolving. Medicine has become a series of specializations, and law is rapidly following that same pattern. Simultaneously, new specializations are coming along to take over certain areas of practice from previously established professions. Each profession must continue to redefine itself or face the prospect of having its role gradually appropriated by other groups. With challenges in the courts and by the Federal Trade Commission, a profession can no longer depend on membership requirements or state sanctions to ensure a monopoly.

Evaluating Proficiencies. To most people the term *credentialed* is synonymous with being well qualified. Competence, however, is more than having knowledge about how to solve problems in an effective, efficient manner. A much less discussed area, but just as important in being able to do one's job, is the complexity of attitudes and values that cause people to entrust their destinies to a professional. Society tends to reward credentials, not competence. We must learn to assess proficiency rather than aptitude (Houle, 1980). Relying on an educational credential is no longer adequate. Education generally continues to focus on the development of cognitive skills to the relative neglect of affective and behavioral competence. Professions must identify not only occupational tasks but also the characteristics that enable workers to perform those tasks effectively (Pottinger and Goldsmith, 1979). A practice audit model to identify competencies has been developed by Pennsylvania State University, working cooperatively with selected professional groups, under a grant from the W. K. Kellogg Foundation (Continuing Professional Education Development Project, 1981). The Center for Occupational and Professional Assessment of the Educational Testing Service is also doing important work in this area.

Reconciling the Conflict Between Professional Interests and the Public Interest. The present system cannot long withstand the conflict between professions' demands for licensure and rising public awareness of the deficiencies of current regulation. There is reason for caution with respect to the continued importance of education requirements as prerequisites for particular functions. As history shows, extensive education—even overtraining—is a hallmark of professions as privileged groups in society. Education is desirable, and when it can demonstrably be related to minimal competence in particular functions, education should by all means be used as a credentialing requirement. But it is too costly to be used as a lever to protect professional monopolies.

A simple regulatory approach that the public can understand is to be desired, if it can be achieved. The regulatory system should be one that employers can implement, state authorities can enforce, and professions can support. It should also be one that educators can use in developing curricula that allow for maximum personal growth of students without channeling students into rigid, largely irrelevant course requirements. Scopes of practice should not continue to be determined by licensing laws, because they are then subject to court interpretation, and technological developments are occurring too rapidly to make such legal determinations appropriate. Ideally, scopes of practice should be based on objective determinations of competence rather than on political demarcations of competing jurisdictions. Finally, a flexible and useful regulatory system should encourage input from employers, third-party payers, and social scientists on the decisions to be made, and it should seek and make use of evidence on the impact of regulatory changes on the public.

Toward an Organized System of Regulating Professions

The existing framework for regulating professions, shared by all states, is clearly no longer suitable; in practice, it is barely defensible. Its paramount deficiencies are the following:

• Policies, criteria, or processes are lacking for determining whether a particular occupational group should be licensed. The decision to license is mainly the product of political pressure. Clout is perhaps a rational factor in deciding whether to license a group—it should not automatically be excluded from a list of appropriate considerations—but at present it is usually not balanced by a determination of what impact licensure will probably have on the cost, quality, and organization of services.

• No systematic method has been adopted for assessing the impact of a particular set of proposed licensing requirements on other licensed groups and on the delivery system as a whole. Raising questions of competition and competence might well open a Pandora's box of uncomfortable issues that most professions would prefer to keep sealed. But consumers, public-interest groups, and social scientists will not remain silent just because professions insist on couching their licensing demands and counterdemands in the rhetoric of "public interest" and "high-quality service" without specifying how inherently anti-competitive restrictions are going to achieve these desirable but vague objectives.

• Present practice does not fit the stated purpose. Although state regulation is predicated in every jurisdiction on the state's "police power" or the need to regulate health, safety, welfare, and morals, state regulation is in practice imbued with economic overtones. Some social scientists contend that entry requirements into a profession are raised during hard times and lowered during easier ones and that, in lobbying, professions place public considerations far below income concerns. These allegations may or may not be true. However, the uncontroverted fact that occupational licensure has in almost every known instance resulted from professional pressure rather than public concern supports the proposition that licensure serves professions at least as well as it serves the public. If the purpose of public protection is to be served, evidence should be submitted on the likely impact of a change in licensure on the public. Among other things, this requirement would necessitate greater leeway in innovation or demonstration projects, now virtually forbidden under licensing restrictions.

Up to now, states have served as a vehicle for the growth of professions. This function could conceivably continue—but only at the risk of frequent court battles over scope of practice, public outrage at the lack of rationality in the licensing system, continued legislative battles over licensing questions, and a near paralysis within regulatory agencies striving to serve a progressive role. Recognizing the need to stem the tide of indiscriminate licensing of newly formed occupational groups, some states have developed new criteria for licensure. Such criteria cover the capacity for harm to the public, the uniqueness of the discipline, the overlapping of its functions among related occupations, the availability of registration or some other approach less restrictive than licensure, the availability of nongovernmental regulation, and the economic impact of regulation. Acceptance of these or similar criteria for a "sunrise" process of systematically evaluating licensure requests is surely a minimal step in correcting abuses while preserving the framework of state licensure.

Similarly, as part of the "sunset" movement, most states are engaged in some sort of process for reviewing existing regulation to see whether it is useful and necessary. So far, such reviews have rarely resulted in the termination of licensing boards. But the sunset idea is in its primitive stage and offers great opportunity for the constant upgrading and updating of regulatory processes.

The trend of these developments is toward an organized system of regulation with two key characteristics. One characteristic is that regulatory requirements are no more stringent than necessary, so that compliance does not unnecessarily restrict employers, close educational or alternative pathways, or reduce licensure to merely a political game. The second characteristic is that the system is intended to serve employers and consumers as well as professions. Employers could be more strongly involved in the decision making, as well as reimbursers. Input from these groups could reduce fragmentation in the delivery system.

Although there is unmistakable progress in reducing the proliferation of professions, there is less progress in a related area: Information on comparative levels of competence is scarce. Methodological difficulties combine with professional resistance to inhibit research comparing the effectiveness of practice across related occupations. What few research results exist tend to confirm that less educated occupational groups achieve outcomes no worse than those achieved by highly educated, traditional groups. An example is new health practitioners compared with physicians. Another example is mental health therapists without doctorates compared with psychiatrists and psychologists with doctorates.

A better information system is beginning to evolve, however, at least in the area of health care. The National Commission for Health Certifying Agencies, created largely to offset confusion about occupational roles and the rapid increase in the number of credentials, is developing criteria and a methodology for ensuring a match between measured knowledge and skills and specific occupational credentials. Private health occupational certification programs that apply for membership in the commission are subject to a rigorous review to ensure that they award certificates based on valid and reliable evaluations, objectively framed. Decisions that emerge from commission determinations can benefit licensing and regulatory authorities as well as employers and third-party payers. And these determinations can be useful not only as they apply to new occupational groups but also as they are applied to already regulated professions (National Commission for Health Certifying Agencies, 1982).

Advance in technology can cause education and licensing standards to become obsolete. Traditional patterns of professional education followed by lifetime licensure must give way to new patterns. The credentialing agencies' chief responsibility is to determine the ability of the individual to practice or to use the occupational title. An equal responsibility is to remake that assessment periodically. However, the proper techniques and tools for periodically assessing competence are either unreliable or very costly. Ways will need to be found, because the system is moving toward periodic reassessment to assure continuing competence—through job-related, competence-based assessment mechanisms.

One important aspect of the future of professional practice and its regulation is continuing professional education. The policy issues in developing and implementing mandatory continuing education are many, and they include matters such as these:

- How should continuing education be defined?
- What is its purpose?
- What is its acceptable context?
- Who should be responsible?
- What unit of measurement will be used?
- Who should keep the data?
- What activities should be given credit?
- Should learning be demonstrated?
- What is an appropriate interval between credential renewal periods?

Vigorous efforts must be directed toward developing and testing methods that will foster practice-based continuing education. The individual professional will need mechanisms for determining weaknesses, and there must be opportunity for self-assessment. Interdisciplinary programs are needed more than ever, but they must be developed carefully, based on an information flow between disciplines and between states. Performance components may take some time to develop.

Implications for Accreditation

Several rather dismal scenarios for the future can be imagined. In one version, present conditions would continue but get worse; that is, more and more specialized groups would obtain state licensure and manage to control the licensing process. Through licensing, each such group would be able to get itself designated as the only acceptable accrediting body in its area of specialization. Then, given this quasi-governmental authority, that group would be in a position to impose its requirements and sanctions on postsecondary educational institutions that offer programs in that field. Colleges and universities would thereby lose even more autonomy by bits and pieces, and accreditation would become even less a voluntary enterprise. As more specialized programs within the institution were subjected to their own form of accreditation, those disciplines without accreditation (particularly subject matter areas in the arts and sciences) would either lose out in the battles for recognition and funding or would develop their own accreditation. Once institutions were blanketed by specialized accreditation, the role of institutional accreditation would come under question, and such accreditation would either disappear or change—becoming a general coordinating body or focusing on noneducational aspects (political, financial, and behavioral problems). Both specialized and institutional accreditation, in this scenario, would become tools of government and would be used to exercise greater control over the lives of institutions.

In another version, the professions would gradually fall victim to a combination of factors—loss of public confidence, court decisions nibbling away at their powers, the increasing splintering away of ever more specialized factions, and (perhaps most important) the impact of technology. Christopher Evans, in *The Micro Millennium,* predicts that "the erosion of the power of the established professions will be a striking feature of the second phase of the computer revolution" (Evans, 1979, p. 121). He points out that the vulnerability of the professions is tied up with their special strength—the fact that they act as exclusive repositories and disseminators of specialized knowledge —and that computers are already destroying these knowledge monopolies. In the ultimate, every person could therefore, in effect, become his or her own doctor or lawyer, given access to a computer.

But a more likely outcome would be the creation of a new array of lower-level specialists—such as medical diagnosticians and legal case analysts—combining some basic professional knowledge and computer skills. Established professional schools in the universities would have to (in fact, are already beginning to) rethink and revise their approaches to professional preparation, and community colleges, technical institutions, and trade schools would develop a host of new short-term programs. These new specializations would be less powerful than the traditional ones and therefore less able to impose their will on state governments or institutions. However, the resulting chaos in terms of agreement over roles and standards of practice would produce a strong public demand for controls. Past experience suggests that the newly emerging fields would strongly resist efforts to incorporate them into existing mechanisms for accreditation but rather would see accreditation as a legitimizing force and would attempt to develop their own accreditation procedures. If they were to achieve state licensing, the first scenario would play out, only with a new cast. Lacking state licensing, these new groups would be less able to impose their accreditation on institutions. However, colleges and universities would be faced with proliferating demands for accreditation and would likely react by rejecting accreditation as a failed cause.

A much more positive future can be envisioned, however, if attention is focused on the recent pioneer projects to redefine various professions (for example, in theology, business, and law). These efforts are important in three ways: (1) they are establishing ongoing mechanisms and procedures so that the redefinition of professions can continue in the future, (2) they are involving other appropriate groups—representatives from colleges and universities, state agencies, and related fields, and (3) they are focusing on proficiencies—that is, they are defining the profession in terms of abilities needed to perform. If successful, these approaches will provide professions with a meaningful definition of role, state licensing boards with a functional point of reference for judging qualifications, and postsecondary educational institutions with a focus for curriculum development. And if these approaches to redefining professions were to become the basis of regulation and accreditation of all professions, then specialized accrediting bodies would for the first time have an answer to the question "What is quality?" A quality program would be one that prepares its students so that they are fully proficient when they graduate and are able and willing to continue to learn and thus maintain their proficiencies throughout their professional careers (see Houle, 1980).

To date, three forces—the thrust of professions to define and control their own destinies, the mandate of the state to regulate in the public interest, and the desire of postsecondary educational institutions to function as meaningful social entities —have shaped the regulation of professions. The conflict inherent among these three forces has been growing, and until a purposeful linkage among them is achieved, specialized accreditation will be a political football, not a socially useful enterprise.

17

Grover J. Andrews

ჯჯჯჯჯჯჯჯჯჯჯჯჯჯჯჯჯჯჯჯჯჯ

Adapting Accreditation to New Clienteles

> *"Would you tell me, please, which way I ought to go from here?"*
> *"That depends a good deal on where you want to get to," said the Cat.*
> *"I don't much care where—" said Alice.*
> *"Then it doesn't matter which way you go," said the Cat.*
> Lewis Carroll (1865/1946, pp. 71–72)

Until the mid 1960s there were few postsecondary educational institutions desiring accreditation that did not have access to consideration by one or more of the nationally recognized accrediting bodies. Most institutions were traditional in nature and offered most, if not all, of their programs on campus, using processes and procedures well established in postsecondary education. If an institution wished to be accredited, it would apply voluntarily to the appropriate accrediting body and begin the process of self-study and peer evaluation using a set of established standards or criteria. A traditional institution could reasonably expect to become accredited if it functioned in an

342

acceptable way and had adequate learning and financial resources. The accreditation process was comprehensive in that it could accommodate most, if not all, of the institutions then seeking accreditation.

Beginning in the late 1960s, significant changes began to take place in the nature and structure of American postsecondary education. Nontraditional programs and institutions began to emerge, often with few of the characteristics normally found in or expected of traditional institutions, and nontraditional variations of programs within traditional institutions were developed. External degrees and the off-campus delivery of both new and established programs (educational outreach) became relatively common as many institutions began to serve new constituencies drawn primarily from the adult population. Other variations that subsequently became associated with the nontraditional education movement included competency-based education, mediated instruction, learning contracts, the weekend college, college-sponsored experiential learning, education "brokering," education contracts, the awarding of degrees and credits by examination, and the assessment of prior learning from life and work experience.

Four examples of institutions that have developed such innovations are these:

• *Mars Hill College.* Located in North Carolina, this small private liberal arts college redesigned its curriculum to state all its requirements in terms of competencies rather than simply in terms of required courses and credit hours. In each curricular area, at least three basic elements were developed: (1) a broad statement of competencies to be acquired by the student to successfully complete the program, (2) sets of standards and evaluation criteria that define the level of proficiency required to successfully attain each competency, and (3) sets of experiences designed to assist the student in attaining the required competencies. To complement the competency-based program, the college also provides for the assessment of well-documented learning from life and work experience, independent study, practicums, cooperative education, and credit by examination.

• *The Wright Institute.* This institution, located in Berkeley, California, uses an individualized learning contract system for its Ph.D. program. Working with a faculty committee, each student establishes specific educational goals, specifies a plan for attaining them, and indicates the procedures by which achievement will be evaluated.

• *New College of the University of Alabama.* In the New College program, individualized learning contracts are used for undergraduate students who are capable of accepting much of the responsibility for their own learning. Students are encouraged to combine nonclassroom experiences and independent study with university educational resources in structuring their contracts for achieving specific learning and career goals.

• *The Regents External Degree Program of the University of the State of New York.* This program functions as a non-instructional, examining institution that has no faculty as such, no residency requirements, and no campus or facilities. The administration employs education consultants, usually faculty members from other institutions, who develop programs and evaluate student progress. Degrees are awarded on the basis of student performance, using explicit and rigorous examinations and assessment procedures. Both associate degree and baccalaureate programs are offered.

Each of these institutions has been successful in achieving accreditation by its respective regional association or specialized accrediting body. However, new approaches to curriculum, instruction, and evaluation have raised serious questions for traditional educators and the general public about how valid nontraditional education is and whether the accrediting associations can deal effectively with this new phenomenon.

Studies on Nontraditional Education

The growth of the nontraditional movement in postsecondary education during the latter part of the 1960s and throughout the 1970s raised legitimate questions concerning the comprehensiveness of the voluntary accreditation process. Could accreditation, which was geared mainly to evaluating the education process within traditional institutions, effectively assess the quality of education in these new institutions and programs, which place less emphasis on process and more on outcomes?

Although many studies of nontraditional education were conducted during the 1970s, three national projects have been most significant in defining the concerns of nontraditional education. The first of these was the work of the Commission on Non-Traditional Study, chaired by Samuel B. Gould, which began in the late 1960s and concluded in 1973. This study identified the range and scope of the nontraditional movement; contributed to the literature on the movement; and, most important, defined the movement. The commission's definition of nontraditional education, since validated by time and experience, was as follows: "Nontraditional study is more an attitude than a system and thus can never be defined except tangentially. This attitude puts the student first and the institution second, concentrates more on the former's need than the latter's convenience, encourages diversity of individual opportunity rather than uniform prescription, and deemphasizes time, space, and even course requirements in form of competence and, where applicable, performance. It has concern for the learner of any age and circumstance, for the degree aspirant as well as the person who finds sufficient reward in enriching life through constant, periodic, or occasional study. This attitude is not new; it is simply more prevalent than it used to be. It can stimulate exciting and high-quality educational progress; it can also, unless great care is taken to protect the freedom it offers, be the unwitting means to a lessening of academic rigor and even to charlatanism" (Commission on Non-Traditional Study, 1973, p. xv). Coming early in the nontraditional education movement, this study did more to legitimate these types of educational activities than any other event. In addition to this report, two publications resulting from the study provided valuable assistance to educators in planning and implementing nontraditional educational programs: *The External Degree* (Houle, 1973) and *Planning Non-Traditional Programs* (Cross, Valley, and Associates, 1974).

The second project, conducted by the Bureau of Social Science Research for the American Council on Education and the National Institute of Education, was a study of the negotiability and acceptability of the undergraduate external degree. Completed in 1978, this study identified and reviewed every undergraduate external degree program in operation in the United States at the time.

For the purposes of its study, the bureau defined external degree programs as those that were primarily nonresidential and nonclassroom and required no more than 25 percent of a student's total work toward a degree to be campus-based, classroom instruction (Sosdian and Sharp, 1978). Of the 244 degree programs operating within the 134 institutions examined, 90 percent were either accredited or candidates for accreditation. The study also surveyed 2,647 graduates with external degrees and found that most nontraditional degree holders were successful both in achieving access to further education and in receiving work-related benefits, including formal credentials.

Graduates reported that their greatest gains from the experience were a sense of personal achievement and self-satisfaction and the opportunity to discover and enjoy knowledge. Eighty percent of the respondents reported achieving the goals of (1) learning about a subject area chosen out of personal interest, (2) improving job skills and work-related performance, (3) learning to be self-directed learners, and (4) actually obtaining the degree. Only 8 percent of the graduates believed that the external degree was less valuable to them than a degree earned through a traditional program.

The study also surveyed a sample of those who employed external degree holders participating in the project. Employers found no significant difference in preparation between their personnel who held external degrees and those who had graduated from traditional degree programs.

The third study was the Council on Postsecondary Accreditation's Project to Develop Evaluative Criteria and Procedures for the Accreditation of Nontraditional Education. Completed in 1978, the project reviewed all the accreditation procedures of the accrediting bodies recognized by COPA, made a detailed analysis of the programs and the accreditation experiences of sixty-two institutions, and conducted a national survey of 1,500 educators. The project (Andrews and others, 1978) concluded that—

- The nontraditional education movement is a positive and creative force in American postsecondary education, providing added stimulus for needed reform, and is specifically focused on the issues of equality of access, quality of results, and individual achievement (p. 9).
- Nontraditional education is basically a variation within, not a departure from, the traditional purposes, processes, and outcomes of American postsecondary education (p. 18).
- Separate standards or criteria should not be applied in the evaluation of traditional and nontraditional educational institutions. Rather, a single set of procedures and criteria that recognizes both process and performance components should be used in the evaluation of all institutions (p. 19).

Although the study documented that the basic system of institutional accreditation was oriented mainly toward institutional processes—governance, faculty, facilities, and internal systems of quality control—it also found that accreditors had been reasonably successful in adapting and applying the process-oriented model to the evaluation of nontraditional education.

In his research for COPA on the accreditation procedures used with nontraditional programs, John Harris reported: "Staffs and visiting teams did not indicate any difficulty in applying current or 'traditional' accreditation policies, standards, or procedures to the wide spectrum of institutions and programs represented in this study. There were very few cases where either a visiting team or staff representative found a fundamental inconsistency between any given standard and an institutional practice" (Andrews and others, 1978, p. 73).

The 1,500 educators who responded to the project's national survey strongly encouraged a move toward the assessment of educational outcomes in the accreditation process. In a section of the survey dealing with the future role of regional accreditation, the respondents selected as their primary concern that accrediting bodies should "focus more on educational results and less on structure and process" (Andrews and others, 1978, p. 112). In response, the COPA project recommended that all postsecondary education would benefit from broadening current accreditation procedures, which focus on educational process, to include an educational outcomes orientation.

Many observers and research findings have indicated that the most important single concept emerging from the nontraditional education movement is the emphasis on educational outcomes. However, the accreditation community is left with a serious dilemma: How can a voluntary nongovernmental accreditation system shift from an evaluation of the processes intended to achieve the institution's purpose and mission (administration, organization, financial resources, academic programs, student services, and physical resources) to an evaluation that includes measuring the institution's success in achieving its intended educational outcomes? How can educational institutions be persuaded to adapt an educational outcomes mode and therefore accept and implement an outcomes-oriented accreditation process?

The COPA study provides useful conceptual information for answering these questions. American postsecondary education, it points out, should be viewed as a continuum with the strictly traditional institutions and programs on one end and the highly nontraditional institutions and programs on the other. Institutions that are predominantly traditional emphasize structure and process, with minimal attention to educational outcomes, while those that are predominantly nontraditional emphasize educational outcomes, with minimal attention to structure and process (Andrews and others, 1978, p. 43). Accrediting bodies and postsecondary educational institutions may find the COPA taxonomy useful in identifying the traditional or nontraditional orientation of institutional program elements. If the accrediting body has developed a process/performance model of evaluation, then the degree to which an institution emphasizes traditional or nontraditional education can be accommodated in the accreditation process.

The study concluded that the institution should have the prerogative of determining the degree to which it will adopt traditional or nontraditional educational practices. Furthermore, as long as the institution can demonstrate the rigor of its educational program and the educational achievements of its students by recognized and acceptable means, any institution should have the right to seek and obtain the recognition offered by accreditation.

An accreditation procedure that emphasizes learning outcomes can be equitably and comprehensively applied to all postsecondary educational institutions or programs regardless of their orientation. Recommendation Eleven of the COPA study provides the conceptual framework for developing a comprehensive process for the accreditation of postsecondary education (Andrews and others, 1978, p. 124):

> The accrediting association responsible for the evaluation of an institution or program [should] require that the institution or program place major emphasis on learning to demonstrate that it:
>
> 1) Has clear educational goals and objectives that are sufficiently explicit to be assessable and that presuppose in their realization the learning necessary for successful performance in the fields for which students are being educated;
> 2) Maintains a system of educational delivery that embraces and affords the opportunity for learning;
> 3) Applies performance criteria that, if met, would reasonably assure graduates of competence in the area for which they are being prepared; and
> 4) Employs effective instruments to assess student attainments which would be acceptable if independently examined by recognized scholars.

Thus, the proposed national policy on nontraditional education recommended by the COPA project addresses the relationship of accreditation, nontraditional education, and educational outcomes—seeking an overall improvement in the effectiveness of American postsecondary education (see policy statement in Resource D). If the recommendations of the COPA project are fully implemented, the voluntary accreditation process will be sufficiently comprehensive to accommodate all forms, structures, and delivery systems in postsecondary education today.

Responses to the COPA Project

Although COPA itself has not moved aggressively to implement the recommendations that resulted from the project, several accrediting bodies, particularly the regional accrediting commissions, have been responsive to the project's general findings.

The Commission on Higher Education of the Middle States Association of Colleges and Schools was the first to respond to the COPA study by making a complete review of the state of the art of outcomes assessment and reviewing its own procedures to assess their effectiveness in dealing with all types of postsecondary educational institutions. The executive director of the Middle States Commission, Robert Kirkwood, in correspondence with the author, made this observation: "The experience we have had in working with Empire State College, with the Regents' External Degree program, and with Thomas Edison College of New Jersey has simply reinforced our belief [that] nontraditional institutions must be dealt with in the same way that traditional institutions are. We have, of course, placed increasing emphasis on outcomes studies as a part of our evaluation process, and that was one of the recommendations of the study. The less distinction we make between our approaches to traditional and nontraditional institutions the better, and I am firmly convinced that the emphasis on outcomes is the wave of the future for all accrediting activities." In June 1981 the Middle States Commission completed and ratified a major revision of its basic accreditation document, *Characteristics of Excellence in Higher Education,* and revised its *Handbook for Institutional Self-Study* to make it more consistent with the revision.

The Commission on Colleges of the Southern Association of Colleges and Schools (SACS) responded to the COPA project with an ambitious three-year study to review and evaluate its entire accreditation process and standards. Under the direction of a nine-member steering committee and using six study committees, the project sought to develop an accreditation process that would deal in a comprehensive and uniform manner with collegiate institutions. The executive director of the SACS commission, Gordon W. Sweet, has indicated in conversation that he fully expects the final product to be a new set of procedures and criteria for accreditation that emphasizes the assessment of educational outcomes and institutional effectiveness. His comments appear to be strongly supported by the work to date of the SACS project. One of the six study committees was charged with examining the state of the art of outcomes assessment in postsecondary education. In its final report the committee states: "The subcommittee believes that while indicators of quality are needed that apply to the components of inputs and processes, there is also the need to have quality indicators for program and service outcomes. Based on the review of the state of the art, this subcommittee concludes that while the feasibility for using an input-process-outcome model of accreditation is somewhat based on theory and speculation, the commission should move to develop this model to assess institutional effectiveness" (Commission on Colleges, 1981b, p. 9).

The Southern Association verified these findings and those of the COPA project by conducting an extensive survey of its constituent colleges. There were 1,704 respondents. The responses to one question about the accreditation process are significant, considering that most of the respondents were traditional educators working in traditional institutions (Commission on Colleges, 1981a, p. 42):

Question

The method of education is partly represented by the relationship between means and outcomes. The accrediting process can emphasize primarily the *means* of education (faculty, library, facilities, and so on) or the *outcomes* of education (what the student learns and can do as a result of education). Traditionally, accrediting agencies have emphasized means more than outcomes. In the future, would you like to see the accrediting process emphasize:

Responses	*Percentage*
1. Means totally	2.35
2. Means much more than outcomes	18.37
3. Means somewhat more than outcomes	24.12
4. Means and outcomes equally	33.98
5. Outcomes somewhat more than means	11.09
6. Outcomes much more than means	6.57
7. Outcomes totally	.12

The Accrediting Commission for Senior Colleges and Universities of the Western Association of Schools and Colleges has modified its *Handbook of Accreditation* on the basis of the COPA study and has a committee at work reviewing its basic standards. The executive director of the Western Association Senior Commission, Kay Andersen, sought and received a two-year grant from the W. K. Kellogg Foundation and the Hewlett Foundation for training accreditation teams following the findings of the COPA project.

The executive director of the Commission on Colleges of the Northwest Association of Schools and Colleges, James Bemis, reported that the COPA project had had a significant impact on the accreditation activities of his commission. The results he identified include a better understanding of the activities of nontraditional educational institutions by accreditation teams, revisions in accreditation procedures and standards, and an increasing proportion of Northwest Association colleges modifying their purpose and function to provide more flexible models of education. Bemis also stated that "now and in the future, we need to have a much better understanding of our end products as a basis for fostering excellence and institutional improvement."

The Commission on Institutions of Higher Education of the New England Association of Schools and Colleges has included a chapter on accreditation and nontraditional study in its new manual of accreditation. This chapter states that "the accrediting process generally should move toward assessment of the results of education rather than its process, and developments in nontraditional studies and degrees provide opportunities to do so" (New England Association of Schools and Colleges, 1980, p. 90).

The director of the Commission on Institutions of Higher Education of the North Central Association of Colleges and Schools, Thurston E. Manning, reported that a special committee has been established to consider issues of accrediting nontraditional institutions and programs.

Significant developments are also taking place in the recognition of nontraditional education by accrediting bodies for selected professions. With most professional groups moving rapidly toward more rigorous continuing professional education, the basic educational requirements for entry into the professions are also being reviewed; a shift toward a more explicit educational outcomes approach is occurring. For example, the Association of Theological Schools is engaged in a project to define proficiencies required for the ministry. The Accreditation Board for Engineering and Technology has just completed a set of standards for continuing education for engineers and is beginning a three-year period of field testing before implementing them nationwide. Pennsylvania State University is conducting a major project funded by the W. K. Kellogg Foundation to define proficiencies needed for selected professions. When completed, this project will provide valuable information for use by the various professions, continuing education providers, and specialized accrediting bodies.

In addition to these activities, significant educational outcomes research projects have been carried out by Jonathan Warren for the Educational Testing Service, Peter Ewell for the Student Outcomes Project of the National Center for Higher Education Management Systems, Aubrey Forrest for the College Outcomes Project of the American College Testing Program, and Wayne Brown for the Performance Funding Project established by the Tennessee Higher Education Commission. Although much useful information on procedures for assessing outcomes of postsecondary education may be found in the results of these research projects, little research has been conducted on what happens when the educational outcomes concept is applied to the evaluation and accreditation of postsecondary educational institutions. The current project of the Commission on Colleges of SACS is the first comprehensive effort to identify, define, and apply the outcomes concept to the accreditation process.

Educational Outcomes—Pros and Cons

Despite the increasing attention given to the subject of educational outcomes by COPA and the regional accrediting bodies, colleges and universities have been slow to respond to this new emphasis. (Vocational-technical schools and training programs sponsored by business and industry, the military services, and other groups do, however, specify expected educational results.) Only a dozen or so degree-granting institutions have attempted the admittedly difficult and time-consuming process of defining educational outcomes and developing means for their evaluation. Most colleges and universities have not ventured beyond the generalized statements of mission that appear in their catalogues, and the degrees they award do not carry with them many assurances of the common competencies of the recipients (Miller and Mills, 1978).

Persons advocating a greater emphasis on educational outcomes have been puzzled by the seeming reluctance of most institutions to move in this direction. They argue that not only would such an approach prove helpful in accreditation, but it would also accommodate several other important developments. Defining educational outcomes would—

- Respond to external demands for more effective accountability in education.
- Apply the concept of management by objectives to the teaching/learning process—a concept that is increasingly being used in other aspects of administration.
- Serve as a unifying element in the general kind of institutional assessment (market analysis) that colleges and universities should undertake regularly if they are to function successfully in a future that brings with it changing enrollment patterns, pervasive economic problems, increasing competition from noncollege enterprises, and the use of new technology such as telecommunications and computers (see Niebuhr, 1980).

Why, then, are most colleges and universities apparently

reluctant to set about the process of stating their educational intentions in specific ways and then determining their success in achieving them? The answers are several:

- Institutions in the past, especially during the period of rapid growth in the 1950s, 1960s, and 1970s, did not have to concern themselves with results. Enrollments were growing rapidly, and public support for postsecondary education was high and unquestioning.
- Designing and implementing an effective program focused on educational outcomes requires a great deal of time and effort, especially in broad-based areas such as arts and sciences.
- Perhaps most important, faculty members have resisted defining educational outcomes because it diverts their time and energy, uses up institutional resources that might otherwise go to faculty support, and poses the implicit threat of providing a basis for faculty evaluations.

Other objections are also voiced by faculty members—for example:

- The most important educational outcomes cannot be put into terms that lend themselves to evaluation.
- Many educational outcomes evolve later in life, long after graduation.
- The teaching/learning process is a unique interaction between professor, student, and environment; educational outcomes are therefore unpredictable.

These and other questions are dealt with at length in the growing literature on this topic. Not only researchers but also administrators and faculty members in an increasing number of institutions are finding ways to address these concerns, and despite faculty qualms, more and more institutions are likely to develop explicit educational outcomes that lend themselves to evaluation —by means of student reports, faculty evaluation, external assessments, and longitudinal studies of alumni, as well as other means (see Astin, Bowen, and Chambers, 1979). Some pioneering institutions have demonstrated that it can be done, and administrators within the institutions—admissions, public relations, publications, institutional research, development, and alumni officers, as well as presidents and other general administrators—increasingly see the crucial value of stated educational outcomes.

New ways of providing quality programs have emerged as postsecondary educational institutions have recognized and responded to the educational needs of many segments of society. Although these innovations have been catalysts for change in the accreditation process, the new focus on outcomes does not eliminate traditional concerns about how an environment for education is created. The major focus of the accreditation process, therefore, should be on the overall effectiveness of the education offered by an institution. An accrediting organization should not set any specific level of performance criteria as such.

Instead, the goal of an outcomes-oriented accreditation process should be that an institution will develop, implement, and evaluate its effectiveness on a regular basis. In so doing, an institution should be expected to—

1. Translate its mission and needs-assessment data into specific goals, objectives, and measurable educational outcomes.
2. Provide for a systematic procedure for measuring the effectiveness of its methods for achieving its goals and desired outcomes.
3. Provide for a systematic and regular means of collecting, organizing, and analyzing outcome data.
4. Have effective procedures for using the data collected for decision making, policy setting, planning, and resource allocation for institutional improvement.
5. Be able to demonstrate to others its effectiveness in achieving its educational outcomes.

The role of the accrediting association, then, should be to verify that the institution has articulated appropriate educational outcomes and has implemented appropriate procedures in a regular and consistent manner to maintain and improve its educational effectiveness.

Each of the studies cited in this chapter has helped to identify and document how increasingly diverse American postsecondary education became during the 1960s and 1970s. These studies also tend to confirm the views of those who claim that the new institutions and programs, with their focus on results rather than process, are providing an effective and efficient form of education that can lead to constructive change within all of postsecondary education. This change will be greatly facilitated if COPA will complete the task it began with its project on nontraditional education—by implementing the recommendations and establishing the national policies that were proposed. Such a move would serve society by ensuring that the educational needs of the population will be met with quality programs.

18

Sara Ayers Bagby

꒞꒞꒞꒞꒞꒞꒞꒞꒞꒞꒞꒞꒞꒞꒞꒞꒞꒞꒞꒞꒞꒞꒞

Interagency Cooperation in Accreditation

> *Somehow and somewhere there germinated in [man's] mind the idea that association, cooperation, would serve his ends better than unbridled egoism in the struggle for existence.*
> William Archer, quoted in Cardiff (1945/1972, p. 13)

A prophetic warning scrawled on the chalkboard greeted the members of the COPA Task Force on Interagency Cooperation at a meeting in November 1978:

> Cooperate
> Or
> Perish
> Accordingly

This play on the acronym for the Council on Postsecondary Accreditation dramatized the importance of the work before the group and warned of the possible consequences if the accreditation community failed to heed the edict.

The problem before the task force involved the interrelationships between an increasingly complex system of post-secondary education and the distinct, independent accrediting organizations dealing unilaterally with institutions and their various components. Typically, a college or university with several accreditations was faced with separate, unrelated contacts with accrediting bodies, all of which might have different accreditation cycles, evaluation criteria, data requests, and terminology. Institutional officers had become concerned about what appeared to be uncoordinated, conflicting requests from growing numbers of organizations. Accreditation personnel, for their part, were encountering what appeared to be reluctance among many institutions to participate, through accreditation, in quality assessment and improvement of educational programs.

During the late 1970s, both accrediting bodies and institutions became more aware that cooperative, coordinated accreditation efforts among accrediting bodies and within institutions could be developed. Research revealed both the extent of multiple accreditations and positive attitudes toward cooperation. Moreover, the climate in which educational systems operate was changing swiftly; colleges and universities moved into the 1980s with spiraling costs, reduced or level budgets, fewer faculty members and staff members, and concerns about shifts in population and government control. The theme of the decade became coordination, consolidation, and cost-effectiveness. Thus, reassessing the potential benefits of cooperative efforts appeared both appropriate and necessary. The COPA task force, representing accrediting bodies and institutions of postsecondary education, was the beginning of what has become a major effort to address the need for cooperation and coordination—a problem that had its roots in the very nature of voluntary nongovernmental accreditation and the manner in which it had evolved.

Development of Accreditation

Accrediting bodies have tended to view themselves (and their responsibilities) as independent rather than as part of a general movement or a community of interest. A growth period of approximately seventy years, the diversity of organizations, and the lack of a national coordinating body during the early years contributed to this isolation. Institutional accrediting bodies originally did not consider their interrelationships with specialized accrediting bodies. The specialized groups, when approached by regional associations, tended to resist incorporation into the institutional review. Some specialized accrediting bodies feared being "swallowed up" if the regional association coordinated or controlled the evaluation process within an institution. Each type of group seemed to have a pervasive concern about encroachment by the other.

Some evidence does exist to substantiate a lack of interaction among accrediting bodies, both historically and today. Although comparable data are not available for all regions, data on institutions accredited by the Middle States Association of Colleges and Schools' Commission on Higher Education indicated that although 60.6 percent of institutions were accredited by two to five accrediting bodies (Kells and Parrish, 1979, p. 15), only one visiting team in five had representatives from another accrediting body present during the on-site evaluation (Kells, 1979, p. 182). Although coordinated visits are only one of many possible methods of coordination among accrediting bodies, other cooperative efforts were unlikely to have been carried out, nor are there data to indicate that they were, in either the Middle States region or other regions of the country.

In addition, the development of groups operating autonomously may have been encouraged inadvertently by criteria established by organizations or agencies that recognize or list accrediting bodies. Some criteria emphasize operational independence as a basic principle for accrediting bodies. Operational independence has generally been accepted as meaning a lack of interference or undue pressure from the group or groups that sponsor the accrediting body. However, accrediting bodies, in an effort to comply with guidelines on operational independence, may have also considered autonomy in relation to other organizations. The triangular relationship among accrediting commissions, sponsoring bodies, and recognizing organizations is complicated. Furthermore, concurrence is lacking on what interrelationships of roles are appropriate, which adds to the confusion about operational independence.

Meanwhile, the knowledge explosion and technological advances have fostered conflicts over what roles professions should play, especially in establishing standards and assessing quality for increasingly specialized fields of study. Institutions have developed more and more out-of-state programs, and as a result, the issue of territoriality has had to be faced and resolved by regional accrediting bodies. All accrediting bodies are confronted with problems that are inherent in evaluating free-standing educational enterprises that are expanding their programs to include multipurpose instruction and expanding their areas of service from one to several states. Some of the once clear-cut boundaries established by common agreement or based on scope of recognition are no longer applicable. The present structure of postsecondary education includes universities and colleges, large university systems, branch campuses within and outside the United States, and broad or highly specialized program areas, all of which may overlap. With increasingly complex fields of study and educational enterprises, operational independence among accrediting bodies may no longer be possible.

During this evolution of education and the accreditation process, institutions as a general rule dealt individually with each accrediting body and rarely took the initiative in establishing institutional interagency relationships. When institutions did act collectively in the mid 1940s to establish the National Commission on Accrediting (NCA), the accrediting bodies were omitted from the decision-making process. NCA attempted to control the proliferation of specialized accreditation activities through a recognition process; yet, it ignored the lack of coordination among accrediting bodies. Meanwhile, the National Committee on Regional Accrediting Associations (later the Federation of Regional Accrediting Commissions of Higher Education) represented the nine postsecondary education commissions of the six regional associations. National institutional bodies, which accredited free-standing single-purpose institutions, belonged to neither organization. Thus, there was no coordinating organization for accreditation as a whole and no sense of community among accrediting bodies.

With the founding of the Council on Postsecondary Accreditation in 1975, all members of the accreditation community had a potential forum. Even so, only after the COPA by-laws were revised in late 1978 did accrediting bodies have a direct mechanism for meeting with one another, as well as representation on COPA's board and Committee on Recognition.

That accreditation has been able to develop with a single-ness of stated purpose—to encourage and assist institutions in evaluating and improving educational quality—is surprising. Wide-scale cooperation has understandably not prevailed in accreditation, given its history, the independent relationships between institutions and professional associations, and (until recently) the lack of interaction among types of accrediting bodies. Nevertheless, each accreditor recognized by COPA performs its functions in accordance with published procedures and criteria and within a framework of good practice as determined through the COPA recognition process. Accreditors are expected to approach each institution as a purposeful social entity whose interrelated parts reflect and contribute to the whole. This basic agreement (in principle if not always in practice) on purpose, process, and institutional prerogatives implies that accreditation —by its nature, if not by its history—can be viewed as a cooperative, even collaborative, process.

Proliferation or Lack of Coordination?

During the 1970s, there was a growing awareness of the importance of interagency cooperation. As the number of accrediting bodies grew, so did concern about external groups that might influence the organization, operation, and focus of both the institution and programs within the institution. Today, many college and university administrators are increasingly aware of and interested in accreditation as it affects their institutions. Some consider accreditation an intrusion into institutional affairs. Others recognize that America's highly technological, rapidly changing society has produced more fields of specialization in the workplace and that postsecondary educational institutions—especially universities, multipurpose colleges, and large community colleges—are offering more specialized programs and courses. They acknowledge that no governing board, administration, or general faculty today can, by itself or in concert, understand the complexities, the changing roles, and the potential of these many specializations: It needs the assistance of outside specialists. Neither view addresses, as well as each might, the costs of accreditation in time and money, the institutional anxieties over the accreditation process, or the conflicts that can occur because of various accrediting bodies' stipulations.

Selden's expectation that "in facing the future we may confidently expect that the number of professions and semi-professions will continue to increase and that each will be based on programs of education provided by colleges and universities" (1960, p. 66) has become reality. In addition, Selden and Porter (1977, pp. 4-15) document a rapid increase in the importance of accreditation as a result of the expansion of its uses. The initial purposes of accreditation, according to Selden and Porter (1977, p. 3), were (1) to establish minimum educational standards, (2) to insist on the maintenance of minimum educational standards to protect the public, institutions, and graduates, (3) to stimulate continued self-improvement by institutions and programs, and (4) to protect institutions from improper external or internal pressures. From these purposes, the uses of accreditation have expanded for institutions, professions, and society. Areas such as acceptability of transfer of credit, justification for certain federal and private funds, student recruitment, criteria for certification and licensure, and consumer protection for students illustrate the current broad application of accreditation.

The increased importance and expanded uses of accreditation may have contributed to the proliferation of accrediting bodies. Each use has value in and of itself and may in some cases be related only indirectly to the initial purpose for which accreditation was created. Selden and Porter remind their readers that accrediting bodies are well suited to carry out functions related to identifying, improving, and preserving educational quality. They warn, however, that "accrediting bodies need to be reasonably independent, and this independence must include the right *not* to undertake tasks, however worthy, for which they are ill suited or which they cannot adequately support" (1977, p. 19).

Thus, there is interaction among the emergence of professional programs and organizations in response to technological and societal change, the way this culture values and encourages diversity and growth, the demand by the public and students for accountability and evidence of excellence, and the varied uses of accreditation status. All contribute to the current somewhat tenuous relationship between institutions and the accreditation community. The initial effort to attack the proliferation of accreditation activities was by restricting the development of new accrediting bodies through the creation of the National Commission on Accrediting in the 1940s. Only in the 1970s was attention given to coordination, collaboration, or cooperation among accrediting bodies as a mechanism to decrease institutional concerns and enhance the effectiveness of accreditation.

Which, then, is the issue: proliferation of accrediting bodies or lack of coordination among agencies—or both?

- Given the past experience of NCA, the Office of Education, and COPA, can the number of accrediting bodies be controlled?
- If control is possible, is it desirable?
- What are the legal and educational implications of attempts to restrict the development of accrediting bodies?
- Given the past experience of interaction among accrediting bodies, can interagency cooperation decrease the adverse effects of multiple accreditations?
- If cooperative endeavors are possible, are they desirable?
- What are the implications for institutions and programs of increased coordination of accreditation?

The State of the Art

Much-needed data on accrediting bodies—their structure, functions, standards, and procedures—are now available. A major national study of regional commissions by Phillips (1979) and one of COPA-recognized groups by Petersen (1979) provide the information required to assess the similarities and differences among accrediting bodies and to identify areas for cooperation more readily. (See Chapters One, Ten, and Eleven for a review of accrediting-body characteristics.) Equally important research projects include studies of multiple accreditation, opinions within institutions about accreditation and interagency cooperation, and the extent of current cooperative relationships. These studies were a response to the increased focus on interagency cooperation.

Growing Emphasis on Cooperation. Although there is no identifiable progression of events leading to the heightened awareness of interagency cooperation, significant activities in the 1970s suggested that some professionals in the postsecondary education and accreditation communities were considering the potential of cooperative efforts.

- The Council on Postsecondary Accreditation was conceived and founded as the "balance wheel" for the various groups involved in or affected by accreditation. One major function of this national coordinating organization is to develop policies and procedures to encourage coordination of accreditation activities.

- Conferees at the first COPA invitational conference, in February 1975, discussed comparable annual reports, interpretation of accreditation status, and good practices. They reached general agreement on the purposes of accreditation. Many recommendations framed at this first conference involving all accrediting groups focused on COPA's role in coordinating the preparation of guidelines to foster consistency among the accrediting bodies' use of terminology, self-study mechanisms, and reporting formats. The conference stimulated further work on identifying similarities and differences among accrediting groups and on improving the effectiveness of communication about the accreditation process to the public.

- In 1976 the chairman of the COPA board established the Task Force on Interagency Cooperation to develop guidelines for the coordination of accrediting bodies with institutions or programs needing or desiring two or more accreditations. The task force developed the guidelines as well as a proposed glossary of terms, a proposal for a funded project, a research study on existing interagency cooperation, a national conference on the subject, and a national assessment of institutional attitudes toward coordination efforts.

- In 1978 the COPA board adopted a statement on proliferation in accreditation. The statement identified increasing numbers of accrediting organizations, overlap and duplication, and lack of effective coordination as some of the defects in the accreditation system. Although strengthening the recognition process was once again cited as a partial solution, the task force suggested extensive consultations with prospective accrediting bodies as a way to try to avoid duplication, as well as efforts specifically aimed at facilitating the consolidation and coordination of accreditation activities.

• In 1979 the National Conference on Interagency Cooperation was held. It used group-process consensus-building techniques to address the issues of common terminology, the role of institutional leadership, coordinated self-studies, a common data base, site-visit procedures, selection and training of visiting-team members, consultations between accrediting groups, and the advantages and disadvantages of interagency cooperation for institutions and accrediting groups. The conference produced numerous recommendations, precipitated further task force and committee work on the many facets of interagency cooperation, and encouraged individual accrediting organizations to further explore coordination.

• The COPA board approved interim guidelines on interagency cooperation in 1978, established a second task force the following year, and accepted the work of this group and the interim guidelines as fully approved guidelines in 1980 (see Resource C). However, the 1978 guidelines were not printed and distributed until the spring of 1981.

• Meanwhile, other groups focusing on cooperation among organizations illustrated the trend toward collaboration. An American Council on Education subcommittee, composed of representatives of large institution-based associations, called for interassociation coordination, including a moratorium on the formation of new associations until procedures for effective coordination and collaboration could be developed. The American Society of Association Executives predicted consolidation of associations as a means of reducing power struggles between competing associations in the same profession. The consolidation or absorption of professional societies would have a direct impact on the sponsorship of existing accrediting bodies.

Extent of Multiple Accreditations. How extensive is the problem of several organizations accrediting a given institution and its component parts? So that an objective response could be made to complaints "about the burdens and purported wastefulness of multiple accreditation relationships," Kells and Parrish (1979, p. 1) "systematically gathered and analyzed information about the nature and extent of such relationships." Data indicated that—

- Institutions not *regionally* accredited—which account for 20 to 40 percent of the institutions, by region, listed in *Accredited Institutions of Postsecondary Education* (American Council on Education, 1980b)—have few accreditation relationships; 92 percent are accredited by one accrediting body, 7 percent by two, and fewer than 1 percent by three.
- Of regionally accredited institutions, 40 percent are accredited by the regional accrediting body only, two-thirds have two or fewer accreditation relationships, and 90 percent have five or fewer. Thus, only 10 percent—or about 300 institutions, essentially large universities—have more than five accreditation relationships.
- The maximum range of multiple relationships is from nineteen to twenty-five accreditations, and this volume occurs very rarely—in fewer than 1 percent of the institutions in any region and fewer than 0.2 percent nationwide.
- In rank order, the ten most active specialized accrediting bodies, accounting for 75 percent of all specialized accreditation in regionally accredited institutions, cover the fields of chemistry, nursing, teacher education, allied health, music, engineering, dentistry, social work, business, and law.
- There is a strong relationship between number of organizations accrediting an institution and its size and highest degree granted.

Sixty percent of regionally accredited institutions had more than one accreditation. Although the study determined that many institutions had more than one accreditation, it did not attempt to assess attitudes toward multiple accreditations.

Opinions About Accreditation and Interagency Coopera-
tion. In an attempt to assess institutional needs and attitudes,
COPA sponsored a study of views about accreditation and interagency cooperation (Pigge, 1979). The purpose of the study was
to determine the extent to which institutions currently involved
in multiple accreditation relationships viewed participation in
cooperative accreditation arrangements. A random sample of
one-third of the institutions with multiple accreditations was
used. The research design precluded the assessment of interest
in coordinated accreditation activities in institutions presently
having only one accreditation. Data indicated that—

- The overwhelming majority of both institutional and program administrators wanted to participate in future cooperative endeavors, regardless of their past level of experience in
  such activities.
- Respondents gave positive evaluations of past cooperative activities, citing benefits such as the coordinated self-study, reduction in fees and costs, and an increase in the helpfulness
  of the entire process.
- Regarding the value of accreditation in general, respondents
  believed that accreditation improves the overall quality of
  the institution and its programs (94 percent), that the benefits outweigh costs (73 percent), and that there is a need
  for both institutional and specialized accreditation (82 percent).
- Respondents, however, confirmed concerns about duplication, lack of coordination in standards, terminology, self-
  studies, data requested, site visits, and decision-making processes. A majority of respondents indicated concern about
  one or more burdens such as fees, report preparation, site-
  visit expense, and contradictory demands by accrediting
  bodies.
- Factors identified as related to the success of cooperative
  endeavors include clear understandings among the accrediting bodies and with the institutions; written agrements; the
  coordinating of responsibility; the nature of self-study understood by all; visiting teams of appropriate size and represen-

tative of all accrediting bodies; team leaders who believe in
the value of cooperative endeavors; and written reports that
reflect the purposes, standards, and scope of activities of all
the accrediting bodies involved.

Current Cooperative Relationships. Although cooperative
interagency activities have not pervaded the accreditation community, there is evidence that many accrediting bodies recognize the need for them. Joint endeavors vary in the extent of
coordination and length of experience and involve organizations differing widely in type, sponsorship, and scope of accreditation activities. Some examples of interagency cooperation are
these:

- Postsecondary education accrediting commissions of both regional and specialized accrediting bodies have shared information and worked on common problems.
- Regional commissions have for many years coordinated site
  visits with one or more specialized organizations when requested by the institution being reviewed. Many accrediting
  groups, as a standard procedure, inform institutions seeking
  accreditation that either coordinated or concurrent visits are
  possible.
- The American Association of Bible Colleges (AABC) and the
  Association of Theological Schools (ATS) each have formal
  agreements with regional accrediting commissions for collaborative accreditation of free-standing institutions seeking
  both regional and AABC or ATS accreditation.
- National specialized institutional accrediting bodies have developed joint procedures for accrediting institutions with
  programs that come under the purview of two or more of
  the organizations.
- The American Dietetic Association, the American Home
  Economics Association, and the Foundation for Interior Design Education Research have developed an information exchange system, coordinated site visits, modified terminology
  for consistency, developed joint data-gathering forms, and
  identified information for a single core document that can

be used, with appropriate attachments, by any of the three groups.

- Some professional organizations have jointly sponsored an accreditation mechanism through either a coordinating body for associations within a field (such as the American Medical Association's Council on Allied Health Education and Accreditation), a single accrediting body (for example, the National Council for Accreditation of Teacher Education), or a coordinating board for professions (as in the case of the Accreditation Board for Engineering and Technology).

These examples illustrate cooperative arrangements among regional accrediting commissions, among specialized accrediting bodies, among national institutional accrediting bodies, and between combinations of these types. The examples support the premise that cooperation can occur in many areas and can take a variety of forms. The critical questions for many accrediting bodies are: Do institutional administrators want coordination of the accreditation activities within their institutions? What are the cost/benefit ratios of cooperative efforts?

Basis for Cooperation. Pigge's data on attitudes toward cooperative endeavors and factors related to the success of such efforts closely corresponded with the principles on which the COPA Task Force on Interagency Cooperation based the *Guidelines on Interagency Cooperation in Accreditation*. The task force identified the facilitation of cooperation among accrediting bodies as a major objective of COPA and stated the following principles as the basis for cooperation:

- Consistent with the concept of voluntary accreditation, each institution of postsecondary education should decide for itself whether to seek accreditation by any accrediting group or combination of groups.
- Institutions desiring coordinated accreditation activities, particularly among organizations that accredit programs located within the same academic administrative unit (for example, a school of professional studies), should be offered every possible assistance and cooperation.

• Coordination begins with designating responsibility within the institution for liaison with the various accrediting bodies.
• To be successful, coordination requires advance planning by both the institution and the accrediting bodies involved.
• Representatives of each accrediting body will be responsible to their own organization for investigating and reporting activities carried out as part of the accreditation cycle.

A wide range of opportunities for cooperative endeavors exists, and no single model for cooperation is appropriate for all institutions and organizations. Levels of integration of accreditation activities can differ widely within one institution, between the institution and the accrediting bodies, and among organizations.

Guidelines. The Task Force on Interagency Cooperation, in an attempt to illustrate possible coordination between an institution and the groups that accredit it and its programs, developed guidelines on the wide range of opportunities for cooperative endeavors. These guidelines were produced after much discussion and concern about whether they were practical and workable. Both accrediting organizations and institutions expressed concern that they might be forced into a relationship that was more cumbersome, costly, and time-consuming than their current relationship. With a few exceptions, accrediting bodies operate with a small staff and many volunteer participants. Because a key to successful cooperation is extensive planning, some feared that superimposing the needed coordination would unduly burden an already overloaded staff. Others saw coordination as a means of reinforcing and complementing the functions of an individual organization and therefore easing the problem of limited staff and financial resources.

A major concern was expressed about the independence of accrediting bodies and institutions—the autonomy to decide whether to use coordination mechanisms. The subsequent repercussions of their choice was another concern. Many operational facets were debated, such as designation of a coordinating organization, equal time allocation during visits, potentially conflicting commission actions, and resolution of variations among accrediting bodies regarding policies such as pre–site-visit consultation. Nonetheless, the guidelines were adopted as options from which accrediting bodies could develop a suitable coordinated accreditation process.

In summary, the guidelines address—

- The responsibility of an institution to assume the leadership role in suggesting the most advantageous modes of cooperation among the accrediting bodies involved.
- The need for and form of written agreements among cooperating groups.
- Designation of accreditation responsibilities, with recommendations for various configurations with both institution and program accreditors as the coordinating organization.
- The application of accreditation standards and the responsibilities of team members to be knowledgeable about similarities and differences among the sets of standards being used.
- Procedures for contacting institutional officials regarding the self-study, the visit, and other expectations.
- The variety of self-study options, such as a common self-study, a core self-study with appropriate supplemental materials, separate but coordinated self-studies for the various accrediting bodies, and nontraditional self-studies.
- Suggestions about the formation of common pools of site visitors, the possible sharing of training conferences, and site-visit procedures.
- Filing of site-visit reports and accrediting-commission actions.
- Use of cooperative endeavors to reduce direct and indirect costs for the total accreditation process.

For a complete text of the *Guidelines on Interagency Cooperation in Accreditation,* see Resource C.

For both accrediting organizations and institutions, the major components of the guidelines involve the initial agreement and planning process, coordination of standards and requirements, and operational procedures. Basic to any interaction between an institution and accrediting bodies, however, is the necessary level of internal coordination of each. An institution may have a designated person for coordinating all types of review—state, research grant, certification, internal assessment, and accreditation. An institution might have a highly coordinated internal process and still deal separately with each review process and body. Accrediting groups could have a high level of agreement on accreditation terminology, cycle, process, and standards; a sophisticated information-exchange system; and joint training sessions for staff, site visitors, and council members—with little or no coordination among accrediting bodies as each deals with an institution. Pigge's data seem to call for a relatively high level of coordination both internally and among accrediting bodies.

Once an institution has requested consideration by more than one accrediting body, some areas of potential cooperation include development of a common or core self-evaluation report, multiple agency responsibilities for site visitors, joint site visit and report, and coordinated accreditation action. Whatever the type or level of cooperation, three key factors determine its success—the commitment of the persons involved to the method selected, extensive planning, and effective communication throughout the process.

The extent to which the guidelines have already influenced practice is unknown, especially because there was a three-year time span between their development and their publication and distribution to institutions and accrediting bodies. However, the guidelines provide choices from which a suitable coordinated accreditation process could be developed. Their purpose is to enable an institution "to integrate the various external accreditation reviews into [the institution's] own internal planning and evaluation activities as it sees fit" (Young and Chambers, 1980, p. 101).

Limitations of Cooperation. Although coordination among accrediting groups is generally accepted as a desirable goal, interagency cooperation has limitations. Particular types of coordination may be rejected by the institution, the accrediting body, or both. Young suggested that "the ideal situation for accreditation as it relates to the institution can best be described by the

word *coherent*. . . . The problem, of course, is that bringing coherence to a process involving more than fifty accrediting bodies
and an additional number of sponsoring and collaborating organizations is not an easy matter" (1980a, p. 2).

A limited survey of accrediting personnel by the author
revealed both philosophical and logistical concerns. Respondents
seem to agree that cooperative efforts are difficult but possible.
Some accrediting bodies have indicated to institutions a willingness to work with other accrediting organizations (especially on
joint site visits) but have had no (or few) opportunities to date.
Representatives of other, more experienced groups cite problems, such as the following:

• Confusion may exist on campus about the scope of authority accorded the various accrediting bodies, with the coordinating organization automatically perceived as in control of
all areas to be evaluated rather than each accrediting group
operating within its own scope of recognition. The coordinating
organization may or may not have the resources to coordinate
the process effectively.

• There may be significant differences in accreditation
procedures. Examples are the extent and type of interaction before the site visit, the selection and announcement of site
visitors, the visit schedule, and the format and schedule for reporting findings to the institution. These differences can create
confusion for the institution and unfair criticism of the accrediting body that is "different."

• The additional costs of coordination are real and have
not been accurately assessed.

• The logistical problems created by multiple accreditation teams on a campus concurrently, if not properly handled,
may result in less effective time use, distractions from the purpose of the visit, and overlapping or confusion in data gathering.
The necessarily increased focus on the mechanics and procedure
of coordination may be a detriment to a serious assessment;
procedure could become more important than substance.

• The overriding concern is whether each cooperating organization is able to obtain adequate and accurate information

needed by its independent accrediting commission to make decisions.

Accrediting-organization personnel state the need for more information on options, pros and cons, and ways to produce cost-effective interagency cooperation. Basic issues are the diversity and complexity of accrediting bodies (and institutions), the lack of "natural alliances" among many accrediting bodies, the need for extensive planning and knowledge of goals and procedures by all personnel involved, and the autonomy of accrediting groups to establish procedures (including review schedules) and standards to best perform the task for which they were established. The number one problem listed by a discussion group at the 1979 COPA Conference on Interagency Cooperation was the lack of definitive data on the impact of cooperation on the quality of the accreditation process. This group also, however, listed the potential advantages of cooperative efforts:

- Cooperation between accrediting groups is perceived as advantageous to institutions.
- Cooperation may dispel some of the myths about accreditation and particular accrediting organizations.
- Some positive spin-offs are possible for both institutions and accrediting bodies.
- Cooperation may prevent some duplication of effort by institutions and accrediting bodies and may reduce proliferation of accrediting bodies.
- More cooperation between accrediting groups may assist in resolving problems of "turf" or assist institutions in resolving such problems.
- Working together could lead to common data bases and practices and may serve to keep accrediting bodies' houses in order.

Whatever the limitations, problems, or promise of interagency cooperation, if cooperative efforts are to expand beyond the current level, institutions must take the lead, and accrediting organizations must be willing to experiment.

The Future

Aristotle described change as the transition of potentiality to actuality. At least three scenarios can be considered for the future of interagency cooperation: maintaining the status quo, strengthening the autonomy and independence of accrediting bodies, or increasing the coordination of accreditation activities. The possibility and feasibility of each scenario involve not only forces within postsecondary education and its system of self-regulation but also forces outside it.

External factors likely to have the greatest impact on the operation of educational institutions are economic and political forces, national and international. Inflation and the erratic nature of the economy produce an anxious, uneasy climate for politicians and institutional personnel alike. The continued stress on accountability and "quality control" produces a "do more for less" environment. Both state and federal governments attempt to "regulate" educational endeavors, although there is an increasing emphasis on reducing governmental control through self-regulation. The economic squeeze is tightened by the state tax income base and the failure to obtain voter approval for bond monies for education. New laws on consumer protection and court rulings in areas once decided only in the education arena increase the complexity of institutions' and accrediting organizations' procedures. Public involvement in the governance of institutions, and more recently within the structure of accrediting bodies, brings a different, and often more objective, point of view; matters such as educational objectives and outcomes, cost-effectiveness, and meaningful credentials for graduates often concern public representatives. In addition, societal and technological change will be reflected in professional requirements and, therefore, in programs and courses in postsecondary education. Never before has population distribution had more implications for education, employment patterns, social and economic systems, and life-styles.

Futurists have predicted societal value shifts that may have implications for postsecondary education and its assessment: the shift from a linear approach to systems approaches in problem solving, from a concern with means to a concern for the ends or results of educational processes, and from thinking that organizational independence is crucial toward a greater acceptance of the desirability, if not necessity, of cooperation and collaboration. In a nation of political and economic upheaval, with changing values and opinions, in an age of rapid technological advancement, and in a world of conflict and shortage that increasingly emphasizes interdependence and interrelationships, the status quo is not viable for any aspect of life—including postsecondary education.

Factors that push toward strengthened coordination in accreditation, therefore, include the realities of social, economic, and political change. Coordination has been enhanced by continued movement toward agreement on policies and procedures by accrediting groups, by increased sharing of resources and information among such organizations, and by the strengthening of a coordinating organization for all accrediting activities. Cooperative efforts are further encouraged by societal pressure on institutions to demonstrate outcomes and cost-effectiveness, the movement of institutions toward issuing periodic "audit statements" of core data for accreditation purposes, and the emphasis on institutional self-regulation with accreditation as a key component.

Among the forces that foster the desire for autonomy for accrediting bodies are increased state and federal government quasi-accreditation activity, infighting among related professional groups, institutions' using the accreditation process for political purposes rather than as a positive tool for improvement, and reducing accreditation studies by conducting evaluations "for cause only."

COPA policy will greatly influence future activities in interagency cooperation. In a personal communication (July 1, 1981), Richard Millard, president of COPA, reviewed the events leading to the development of the guidelines and emphasized the importance of cooperative endeavors: "All of these are closely interrelated and underline the fact that interagency cooperation and its encouragement must be a continuing central concern for COPA in the years to come. It lies close to the heart of COPA's reason for being; and if COPA is not successful in this, many of its other activities, as important as they are or may be, tend to become peripheral."

The future of interagency cooperation involves institutions, accrediting groups, and the professional organizations representing both. Interagency cooperation poses problems and holds promise. The challenge is to frame the future through conscious assessment and planning, rather than to be propelled into a future determined by external forces.

Kenneth E. Young

٭٭٭٭٭٭٭٭٭٭٭٭٭٭٭٭٭٭٭٭٭٭٭٭

Epilogue:
The Future
of Accreditation

The future of accreditation should flow from basic philosophical principles rather than political expediency.　　　　　Howard R. Bowen (1981)

Political expediency has too frequently impeded or diverted the development of accreditation. Federal agencies, state governments, professional associations, institutions of postsecondary education, and accrediting bodies themselves have all on occasion misused or misrepresented accreditation for questionable purposes.

For example, accrediting bodies have attempted to get themselves written into federal statutes, and many have succeeded in placing themselves in state licensing laws. Institutions have sometimes falsely claimed, often without being corrected by the accrediting body involved, that the failure of a state to provide funds for a new building or other needs would jeopardize accreditation. State agencies have demanded that accrediting bodies rate institutions or programs so that decisions could be made to reduce or cut off funding for those rated lowest.

379

And federal officials have tried to force accrediting bodies to judge institutional "probity," which apparently would have meant whatever the government wanted it to mean. These examples, and many others, have always been exceptions rather than the rule; but they have occurred often enough to cause confusion and to slow progress.

What is truly remarkable, given all these alarums and discursions, is that, during a relatively short historical period, accreditation has evolved into an important (some would say essential) aspect of American postsecondary education. Furthermore, it has developed a reasonably clear philosophy that is generally well accepted within the accreditation community and is embodied in the following principles:

- Accreditation is a form of self-regulation and is central to other self-regulatory activities in postsecondary education, the "self" being the institution of postsecondary education.
- Accreditation began as a voluntary enterprise and remains largely voluntary.
- Accreditation is therefore essentially nongovernmental; although government can make use of the results of accreditation, it should do so in ways that will not destroy its nongovernmental character.
- Accreditation at the same time has become a quasi-public enterprise; it serves certain public ends and must be responsive to appropriate public concerns.
- Accreditation is basically an evaluative process; it has moved gradually from evaluating presumed conditions of good education to being increasingly concerned with the results of education and from emphasizing external review to being much more dependent on self-evaluation.

Accreditation, however, continues to wrestle with a number of problems. It will not survive just because it is a good idea. Its future success will depend on the thoughtful, considered efforts of individuals, institutions, and organizations. An examination of the future of accreditation should take into account the problems carried over from the past that still must be faced.

Recommendations for how those problems can be addressed by institutions, accrediting bodies, the Council on Postsecondary Accreditation (COPA), and government are therefore set forth. In addition, educators and leaders in accreditation should be aware of coming changes in education and society and how they will affect the long-term future of accreditation.

Continuing Problems in Accreditation

Selden (1960) listed seven issues that seemed the most important at that time:

1. What accreditation criteria can be developed that place less emphasis on minimum standards and more on continued institutional reevaluation, experimentation, and improvement?
2. How can accreditation be made more stimulating for institutions of quality?
3. How can the inevitable increase in the accreditation of graduate schools be designed without impairing independent research and individual scholarship?
4. How can the need for quality assurance in specialized institutions and professional programs be met without increasing the number of professional accrediting bodies?
5. How can accreditation be simplified without limiting its effectiveness?
6. How can accreditation adequately satisfy the needs of various groups and the public for more information about the degree of quality of individual institutions?
7. How can government's growing interest in postsecondary education be met without increasing its involvement in accreditation?

The progress made during the last twenty years in responding to most of these concerns is reassuring. Accreditation has moved away from a preoccupation with minimum standards to a greater emphasis on continued reevaluation. Experimentation is encouraged, and fostering the improvement of education is seen as the primary purpose of accreditation. These changes have made accreditation potentially more worthwhile for the Harvards of the nation, although not all institutions of high quality and great prestige have made effective use of it. The "inevitable increase" in the accreditation of graduate schools has not been realized, except in some professional fields; the traditional disciplines have shown remarkable resistance to proposals that they adopt accreditation. Furthermore, although the battle to reduce the number of specialized accrediting bodies has not been won, the growth of new groups has been limited. Accreditation has become both more simplified and more complex; that is, the essential elements of the accreditation process have received increasingly widespread acceptance and consensus, while their application has become increasingly diversified.

Some issues, of course, persist. The accreditation community continues to struggle with the issue of confidentiality versus the public's right to be better informed. Accreditation will always live with the problem of being a nongovernmental process that is inevitably used for certain governmental purposes. And accreditation is still dogged by several persistent issues, in particular.

Control. The basic issue identified by Selden more than twenty years ago—the struggle over standards—remains a thorny problem. The issue of control has two major dimensions: government versus the private sector and, within the private sector, institutions of postsecondary education versus external groups (particularly professional associations). The bias of this book is clear: that accreditation fundamentally is and should remain a nongovernmental activity and that institutions should play the leading role in the process. Although that point of view is widely shared, the issue has not been resolved.

Voluntarism. The most important area in which the battle over control continues to be fought has to do with the voluntary nature of the process. Significant aspects of the voluntary character of accreditation have been lost as the federal government has managed in some instances to convert accreditation to its purposes and as state agencies, acting at the behest of certain professional groups, have written accreditation into licensing statutes. If accreditation is to become truly voluntary again, institutions, working collectively, are the only ones that can resolve this problem.

Sense of Community. Although progress has been made since the advent of COPA, the staff members of accrediting bodies do not yet view themselves primarily as fellow professionals. They come into accreditation from a wide variety of backgrounds and for many reasons. In some positions, turnover is rather rapid; in others (particularly the top roles), incumbents often stay too long. There are no educational programs to prepare a person to work in this field, and in-service training is virtually nonexistent. Accreditation will never be able to resolve its own problems until its corps of professionals acquires a sense of colleagueship and a program of formal professional development.

Cooperation. For far too long, the postsecondary education community, including such groups as the National Commission on Accrediting and COPA, have been preoccupied with a concern about the proliferation of accrediting bodies to the neglect of the issue of cooperation between these groups. Acknowledging the need for cooperation, one university president quipped that two accrediting organizations are one too many if they cannot or will not work together. COPA has made interagency cooperation a major priority, and there are signs of progress. However, much more needs to be accomplished.

Greater cooperation is also needed between accrediting bodies and other education associations, especially the president-based organizations such as the American Council on Education, the Association of American Universities, and the American Association of Community and Junior Colleges. Institutions look to these organizations for leadership and guidance and will see accreditation issues as being important only to the extent that they receive attention from these associations.

In addition, cooperation is required within the various associations that sponsor accrediting bodies. The regional associations must address the long-neglected issue of articulation between secondary and postsecondary education commissions, and the professional organizations must coordinate multiple accreditation activities (for example, medicine and allied health programs, law and legal-assistant programs, the various levels of nursing, and regular and continuing professional education).

Focus on Outcomes. Many of these issues may lend themselves to being resolved as efforts to define educational objectives are expanded. If professions increasingly define their fields of practice in terms of proficiencies, then professional training programs, state licensing requirements, and accreditation standards can all use common terminology and relate to one another in a meaningful way. If institutions of postsecondary education continue to move toward defining their degrees in terms of proficiencies and listing educational outcomes for each program, then institutional accrediting bodies and institutions will have a common focus.

An Effective National Mechanism. That accreditation functioned for so many years (more than sixty) without a unifying national presence is amazing. Not until COPA came on the scene in 1975 were virtually all the nationally recognized accrediting bodies brought together in a single organization. And even then, during its early years COPA spent most of its energy in, first, organizing and then reorganizing itself and, second, waging a costly battle with the Office of Education over prerogatives and relationships. COPA has reorganized yet again, but now—for the first time—institutions are formally represented, through their own assembly within COPA. This reorganization has not only provided institutions a role inside COPA, but it has also clearly stamped COPA as the organization responsible for serving all interests in accreditation, not just functioning as a trade association for accrediting bodies. Whether COPA can survive the pushes and pulls of the many special-interest groups among its constituencies and build the necessary support from institutions remains to be seen.

Public Understanding. Accreditation continues to have difficulty impressing the nature and purpose of the accreditation process on the public in simple, understandable terms. Despite the qualities of independence and voluntary action that have marked this country throughout its history, many Americans came to this nation from other societies and brought with them a strong sense of government control, epitomized by the concept of the Inspector General—a concept reinforced by the word *accreditation*. Thus, the accreditation process is seen by many as education's version of the "white glove" inspection; to become accredited is to pass inspection and receive a seal of approval. Using other inappropriate models, people often compare accreditation to the collective bargaining of a labor union, to the adversarial mode of a legal proceeding, to quality control as practiced in manufacturing, to social mechanisms such as arbitration and conciliation, and to the political tools of negotiation and compromise.

Accrediting bodies therefore have difficulty persuading their publics to view them as facilitators; to view the accreditation process as a matter of goals clarification, self-evaluation, and peer review; and to view achieving accreditation as becoming a member of an organization, evidence of acceptance by peers. One of the difficulties, of course, is that this description is not completely accurate. Some accrediting bodies are dominated by individual membership associations, and institutional membership is only nominal or virtually nonexistent; some accreditation practices still smack more of the external inspector than the friendly facilitator; and some accreditation standards do seek to impose fairly rigid requirements on reluctant institutions. Fortunately, these situations are decreasing year by year, but their existence does confuse the casual observer.

To help explain the role of accreditation, leaders in accreditation can and do point to examples of peer review and self-evaluation elsewhere in society:

- The scientific method rests on making hypotheses, testing them over time, and subjecting them to rigorous peer review and criticism.
- Certain sports, such as diving, gymnastics, and ice skating, involve the setting of individual goals and performance formats, and the performance is evaluated by a body of peers using group-determined criteria.
- Personnel evaluation, when conducted for purposes of individual improvement rather than leading to judgments about

promotion and salary, begins by asking employees to define
their personal and vocational goals and to evaluate themselves. This evaluation is then subjected to review and discussion, leading to the design of a plan for self-development.

• Grants by foundations and government agencies commonly
call for funded projects to state expected outcomes and
build in an evaluation process, involving both internal and
external review, to determine whether the objectives have
been realized.

• The court system rests on a form of peer review—the jury.

Recommendations for Institutions

How the accreditation process is used and adapted to
meet the challenges of the years ahead will be the pivotal factor
in whether accreditation will not just survive but flourish. The
following recommendations are made in the hope of helping
postsecondary educational institutions, accrediting bodies, the
Council on Postsecondary Accreditation, and government take
steps toward ensuring that the accreditation process will prevail
in a form best suited to meet the changing needs of the future
and continue to serve both the postsecondary education community and the public well.

Institutional leaders—members of governing boards, chancellors, presidents, provosts, and other key decision makers in
colleges and universities—must recognize that accreditation is a
major, continuing concern. They must see accreditation as an
activity that the institution can and should control rather than
an activity that controls the institution. They must view accreditation as central to an institution's ongoing efforts to define itself, set future directions, establish priorities, evaluate its successes and failures, and improve its performance over time.
They must believe that accreditation is too important to be dis-
regarded or delegated to others.

1. *The governing board should regularly give attention to
accreditation issues.* The general subject of accreditation should
be on the governing board's agenda at least once each year. Accreditation issues that merit board attention include these:

What have we done this year to clarify or change our objectives? What have we found out about ourselves? What accrediting bodies are we working with and why? What are the costs and benefits? How can we make more effective use of our membership in these organizations? Should we drop or add memberships? Some boards do not even receive copies or summaries of accreditation reports; progress reports should be made to the board on all accreditation actions (Association of Governing Boards of Universities and Colleges, 1983).

2. *The president must assume responsibility for accreditation.* The chief executive officer of the institution should regard accreditation as a significant, ongoing responsibility. That person should develop an institutional policy on accreditation, and decisions about entering into or renewing memberships with accrediting bodies should be made by the president, only after careful thought. The institution's posture on accreditation should be made clear to the entire staff and faculty and should be periodically discussed. Accreditation should be seen as a means for bringing a common focus to institutional efforts such as long-range planning, institutional research, development, recruiting and admissions, and public relations. The president should plan to periodically devote time to serving on accreditation teams or commissions and should encourage other key officials and leading faculty members to do the same.

3. *An accreditation liaison officer should be appointed.* One person, reporting to the president, should be designated to be responsible for all accreditation matters and to serve as institutional liaison with all accrediting bodies dealing with the institution. This person should maintain up-to-date records on accreditation memberships and statuses, costs, and faculty and staff participation. This person should also work with units within the institution in identifying opportunities for cooperation and collaboration among accrediting bodies serving the institution.

4. *Institutions should insist that accrediting bodies make their demands clear and related to quality-based standards.* Institutions should require that clear distinctions be made, by accrediting bodies and within the institution itself, between con-

cerns that will affect the accredited status of the institution and concerns that will not. Most accreditation reports include a variety of recommendations that are intended to be helpful to the institution but which are not of such consequence that accreditation would be jeopardized if they were not followed. Institutions should also take the position that the accrediting body is obligated to show that there is a research-based relationship between a requirement for accreditation and educational quality.

5. *Each institution should take a stand on COPA.* Every institution, as an important part of its policies on accreditation, should determine its position with regard to the Council on Postsecondary Accreditation. Does the institution believe that there should be a national organization overseeing accrediting bodies? Is COPA the appropriate organization? Is it doing what it should be doing? And if the answers to these questions are positive, should the institution then deal only with COPA-recognized accrediting bodies? The institution should also make use of COPA as the instrument for dealing with problems in accreditation.

6. *Institutions should work collectively to eliminate the quasi-governmental status of accrediting bodies.* If accreditation is to become truly voluntary again, then institutions must work to eliminate the quasi-governmental status given certain accrediting bodies by various state licensing laws and federal statutes. This objective can be attained only by collective action, with institutions working through their appropriate national associations.

7. *When the accreditation process does not measure up, institutions should work collaboratively to change it.* When college and university administrators or faculty members talk to their colleagues from other institutions about accreditation (which is all too rare), they usually discover that they have had similar experiences, good and bad. However, having identified a common problem, institutional leaders seldom take the next step and work together in an effort to resolve the problem. Just two or three presidents can have significant impact on an accrediting body. A larger group can turn an organization completely around.

8. *Institutions should, as a last resort, withdraw their support from an accrediting body when the accreditation process does not function well and cannot be changed from within.* Overall, accreditation has received, and continues to receive, strong support from the institutions that are both its subjects and its financial backers. However, a few institutions have ceased their support of one or another accrediting body. What generally happens is that when a college or university's officials do not believe that their institution or program has changed or advanced as a result of participation in the accreditation process, they drop their support—not only by refusing to pay accreditation fees and membership dues but, more important, by seriously exploring whether faculty members and staff members should participate as volunteers at institutional expense. Withdrawal of support is, of course, the most significant way that institutional leaders can signal that the accreditation process is not as useful as it could be for their institutions.

Recommendations for Accrediting Bodies

The recommendations for accrediting bodies are divided into three categories: recommendations aimed at accrediting bodies in general, those aimed at institutional accrediting bodies only, and those aimed at specialized accrediting bodies only.

General

1. *Accrediting bodies should define proficiencies needed for their staff members and design staff development programs.* Because accreditation is not a large enough enterprise to have developed a sense of profession, there are no professional programs designed to prepare practitioners. Staff members move into this work from a variety of backgrounds and with little or no previous preparation. The most common pattern is for a faculty member or junior administrator in an institution of postsecondary education to become active as a volunteer in accreditation and, having impressed others, to be invited to take on a professional position with an accrediting body. Accrediting

bodies have no formal training programs for their staffs. The accreditation community, perhaps through the leadership of COPA, should set about defining the proficiencies needed for the various levels of work in this field and then identifying subject matter (evaluation concepts, psychometric techniques, organizational analysis, self-assessment processes, and group dynamics) and designing learning experiences (individualized study materials, workshops, and internships) to prepare and upgrade staff members. Accrediting bodies should also introduce annual evaluations. Ironically, the persons most identified with reviewing and judging others in most instances have no formal program of self-review.

2. *The accreditation community should cooperatively develop a volunteer training program.* In its early years, COPA listed the development of a cooperative program within the accreditation community for the selection, training, evaluating, and sharing of volunteers as a major priority. However, as of 1982, nothing major had been done to implement such a program, which is badly needed. Volunteers usually become involved in accreditation because they are recommended by someone. Occasionally, a person acts on his or her own, but accrediting bodies tend to be somewhat wary of the self-nominated individual, wondering about motives or qualifications. Persons become leaders in accreditation through years of service—as members of visiting teams, as chairpersons of teams, as members of special committees, and finally as officers of a commission and then perhaps the association. This "moving through the chairs" usually requires from five to ten years of service, and the experience is a highly effective professional development program for those who stay the course. However, it discourages faculty members and staff members with other important responsibilities, and because the corps of experienced people can be used only sparingly, it leaves accrediting bodies highly dependent on relatively inexperienced volunteers. Therefore, it is crucially important that COPA and the accreditation community move vigorously ahead with a volunteer training program.

3. *Every accrediting body should offer assistance to its member institutions regarding the development and conduct of*

an effective self-study process. Training programs should be offered to help prepare selected representatives from institutions. In addition, staff members from accrediting bodies should spend more of their time working with institutions to help them design and conduct the self-study.

4. *A professional (an accrediting-body staff member) should accompany the accreditation team at least for those visits that might prove troublesome.* Even with the best of volunteers, an accrediting body cannot depend on the occasional worker to provide two important elements—continuity and consistency. Therefore, every accrediting body should ideally be sufficiently well staffed to send a professional along with the team for the first day of the visit, to set the ground rules and iron out any problems. Surprisingly, this is not the practice with many accrediting bodies. Even the North Central Association of Colleges and Schools' Commission on Institutions of Higher Education, the oldest and largest of the regional accrediting bodies, does not follow this practice. This expectation should become a requirement for recognition by COPA.

5. *Accrediting bodies should require institutions and programs to focus on educational outcomes.* Despite the early leadership shown by COPA pointing toward an increasing focus on educational outcomes, follow-up by the accreditation community has been limited and slow. COPA should adopt a more explicit requirement on this subject. Institutional accrediting bodies should move as quickly as possible toward a requirement that each accredited institution define its expected educational outcomes and evaluate their achievement as part of the self-study. Specialized accrediting bodies, if they have not yet done so, should initiate projects leading to the development of proficiencies for their professions.

6. *Accrediting bodies must move aggressively into cooperative and collaborative arrangements.* COPA has adopted interagency cooperation as a high priority. The COPA board has approved guidelines for interagency cooperation that were developed by a task force and tested by the accreditation community, and COPA will be demanding evidence of cooperative activities as part of its review process. Each accrediting body should

now review its own practices—terminology, data requests, self-study requirements, site-visit procedures, and decision-making processes—to determine that there are no roadblocks to cooperative efforts.

Institutional Accrediting Bodies

1. *The regional associations must work on developing common standards.* The concept of regionality has no legal force. Because regional accrediting bodies are nongovernmental, they cannot require that an institution seek accreditation from one association rather than another. This condition could become a problem if institutions were to come to believe that one regional accrediting body were "better" or "easier" than another. The regional associations can avoid problems only if they rededicate themselves to their earlier-proclaimed goal of developing "national standards regionally administered." This goal will require purposeful, cooperative action toward developing common standards, procedures, terminology, training programs, and evaluations.

2. *The problems of separate accrediting bodies for elementary, secondary, and postsecondary education must be addressed.* The structure, procedures, and financial arrangements of the elementary and secondary education commissions of the regional associations raise substantial questions about whether they are in fact nongovernmental, voluntary, and regional. These commissions have in most instances developed close ties with state education agencies and operate through state committees with direct or indirect state financial support. The regional commission actually functions as a standard-setting, coordinating, data-gathering, and reporting body. Another problem is that relationships between the various commissions within a given association have never been close and have occasionally erupted into conflict. Regional associations must address these problems—either writing off elementary and secondary accreditation activities as more appropriate to state agencies and groups or revising their present policies and structures to integrate these accreditation activities in a meaningful way. Self-study is as appropriate for accrediting bodies as for institutions.

3. *Regional accrediting bodies must come to terms with the changing meaning of membership.* They must be clear about what it now means, and they should work diligently to translate that meaning into appropriate action. In reviewing the meaning of membership, they should be careful to avoid easy, superficial answers. Colleges and universities are no longer exclusively, or in many cases even primarily, degree-granting institutions. A university may have more in common with a think tank or a high-technology company than with a nearby college. A community college may find more to talk about with a trade or technical school than with a liberal arts institution. The important underlying concern, however, is that accreditation cannot afford to lose the sense of peer review that has undergirded the process from the beginning.

4. *In national institutional accrediting bodies, the accreditation function must be sufficiently set off from other functions to guarantee its credibility and effectiveness.* National institutional accrediting bodies do not suffer from the problems of a diversified membership. They are organizations serving clearly defined types of institutions (although some of them are cautiously beginning to broaden their roles). Whereas the regional accrediting bodies provide a particular service—accreditation—to a wide array of institutions, the national groups offer a range of services, including accreditation, to a small, select number of institutions. The problem with this arrangement is that accreditation may be seen, and therefore used by some groups, as just another membership service, working hand in glove with lobbying and other activities intended to advance the interests of the membership.

Specialized Accrediting Bodies

1. *Professional associations should turn over responsibility for accreditation to associations composed of institutions.* Specialized accreditation took a different track from institutional accreditation rather early on when individual membership associations took it over, leaving associations of educational units (the medical schools and law schools) to function as junior partners or second-tier follow-ons or, more often, out of the

picture altogether. The reasons for this development are quite understandable. During the years when specialized accreditation was beginning, many professional schools were quite bad. Asking these institutions to reform themselves did not make sense, but practitioners could muster the clout to effect change. Once a solid corps of acceptable institutions had developed, however, the professional associations would have been wise to turn over primary responsibility for accreditation to the institutions. They still would be wise to do so (although such a course of action is doubtful). In accreditation matters, the American Medical Association should defer to the Association of American Medical Colleges, the American Bar Association should defer to the Association of American Law Schools, and so on. In particular, the National Education Association, a major labor union, should remove itself from a direct role in accreditation—leaving that responsibility to the American Association of Colleges for Teacher Education. Where there is no national organization of specialized programs in a field, one should be organized—separate and apart from the individual membership association. If an effective group cannot be established and maintained, this should raise questions about the ability of this profession to sponsor an accreditation function. The individual membership group should be provided with meaningful representation on an accrediting commission and its review teams and special committees, but it should not control the accreditation process. Its energies, rather, should be turned to the important tasks of defining (and periodically redefining) the profession and establishing the competencies for professional practice.

2. *Professional associations should support efforts to remove references to particular accrediting bodies in state licensing requirements and statutes.* Because individual membership groups have dominated specialized accreditation, and because their primary interest was in ensuring the competence (or in limiting the numbers) of practitioners, the link that developed between specialized accreditation and state licensure was only to be expected. This alliance, however, has weakened the important concept of voluntarism in accreditation and yet has not served to assure the public of the competence of practitioners.

Recently, the interassociation Presidents Committee on Accreditation, under the leadership of the American Council on Education, identified as one of its priorities the task of getting state licensing boards to drop their references to specified accrediting bodies. This exceedingly important objective should be supported by all institutions and their associations, as well as professional associations—which should recognize that the true test of accreditation should be its value to the institution it professes to serve.

3. *New fields of specialization should consider alternatives to establishing separate accrediting bodies.* Many newer and smaller fields of specialization have instituted, or are considering establishing, accrediting bodies—in misguided efforts to gain acceptance or increase their authority. Given the prevailing economic restraints and the more detailed requirements of COPA recognition, some of these groups will probably drop the idea of accreditation. In any event, many of them would be well advised to think through more carefully what ends they wish to achieve. In most instances, their purposes would be better served by devoting their resources to developing guidelines and offering at-cost consultation services. Others might better follow the model of the American Chemical Society, which sponsors a program approval service. Still others should join allied groups in sponsoring a collaborative accreditation service. COPA should be actively advocating these alternatives.

Recommendations for COPA

COPA began as an organization born of a shotgun marriage and crippled by political compromises. That it has not only survived but also managed to clarify and strengthen its role is surprising and reassuring. However, it will continue to be less than it should be unless some additional steps are taken. To gain a sense of how far COPA has yet to go, compare it—as an example but not a model—to the role played in intercollegiate athletics by the National Collegiate Athletic Association.

1. *COPA must become financially independent of the accrediting bodies.* COPA will never be able to fully play the role

it was designed for until it ceases to be dependent on the accrediting bodies (and, for all practical purposes, their executive directors) for its financial support. Under present funding arrangements, a combination of two or three of the largest accrediting bodies could threaten to quit the organization and thus place COPA in financial jeopardy. COPA should move to a system whereby institutional accrediting bodies would serve as a collecting mechanism for dues paid by accredited institutions. The dues could be quite nominal (no more than $100) for most institutions, with those having several accreditation relationships paying substantially more.

2. *COPA should pursue another of its original priorities— the conduct of a national information and education program about accreditation.* The general public is woefully ignorant about accreditation, and most faculty members and staff members in institutions of postsecondary education have limited and inaccurate perceptions. Such a project would require outside funding, but its obvious value should make it a matter of interest to a national foundation.

3. *COPA should develop policy documents that set forth its positions on basic issues.* A recent example is its 1982 publication *Policy Statement on the Role and Value of Accreditation* (see Resource D). Among the topics that should be addressed are accreditation and the federal government, accreditation and state government, accreditation and the professions, and when does accreditation meet a social need? Once positions on these issues have been developed and approved, COPA should be more aggressive in tackling questionable practices by recognized accrediting bodies. The organization should not necessarily wait until the regular five-year review but should take up issues as they become evident. In doing so, COPA should make effective use of concerned college and university presidents, as was done recently in meetings with certain accrediting bodies whose practices have caused adverse reactions.

Recommendations for Government

To say that accreditation should be nongovernmental is not to say that government should never use accreditation. The

overriding concern is that government use accreditation properly—that is, with full knowledge of its value and limitations and
with care not to impose unrealistic demands on it. The government should find useful the information that an institution has
voluntarily and successfully gone through an accreditation process. But the government must assume responsibility for verifying other conditions required by law.

1. *The federal government does not need and should not
have an advisory committee, a staff, and an elaborate review
process to make effective and appropriate use of accreditation.*
The Department of Education should concentrate on its rightful
concern—determining institutional eligibility for certain federal
funds. It should also be working toward achieving some sem-
blance of consistency among other federal agencies as they deal
with institutions of postsecondary education. To the extent
that accreditation is used as a consideration in determining eligibility, it should be used for what it is—a confirmation that an
institution has declared its objectives, conducted a guided self-
study, undergone an external review, and qualified for membership in a nationally recognized accrediting body. Recognition
by COPA or by a substantial number of states should constitute national recognition.

2. *States that have no chartering and licensing laws for
institutions of postsecondary education, or inadequate ones,
should strengthen their statutes to bring them up to the standards recommended by the Education Commission of the
States in its 1973 model state legislation.* If a state fails to
strengthen these laws within a reasonable amount of time, the
federal government should declare that institutions from those
states will have to undergo a federal review to ensure their eligibility.

3. *State agencies should establish cooperative agreements
with institutional accrediting bodies.* Some state agencies have
already entered into working agreements with institutional accrediting bodies—agreements that permit representatives of appropriate state agencies to have access to self-study reports and
to accompany site-visit teams. Such cooperative arrangements
should be encouraged, although care must be taken to ensure
that the state does not control or redirect the accreditation pro-

cess. Moreover, the issue of confidentiality must be handled with sensitivity.

The Long-Term Future

Now—just as accreditation appears to be coming into its own, with a basic philosophy, an emerging sense of community, and an apparatus for bringing credibility and coherence to the field—changing conditions pose new problems. Postsecondary education is undergoing massive changes, and the nation is moving into a postindustrial society.

Changes in Postsecondary Education. Peter Drucker (1981, p. 26) wrote: "The biggest 'infrastructure' challenge in this country in the next decade is not the billions needed for railroads, highways, and energy. It is the American school system, from kindergarten through the Ph.D. program and the postgraduate education of adults. And it requires something far scarcer than money—thinking and risk-taking." Herman Niebuhr, Jr., has written extensively about this challenge. In his 1980 and 1982 articles, he identifies four major components of what he calls "the crisis in higher education": (1) the demographic component—the drop in eighteen-year olds from now until the end of the century, (2) the resource component—the impact of inflation, declining state and federal support, and projected losses in tuition revenues, (3) the competition component—the large and growing sponsorship of postsecondary education by other social institutions and the challenge of high technology (cable television, satellites, and low-cost computers), which promise a veritable revolution in learning systems, and (4) the legitimacy component—the declining reputation of colleges and universities since the late 1960s.

Drucker, Niebuhr, Harold Hodgkinson, Morris Keeton, Patricia Cross, and others argue that many institutions of post-secondary education must change or die. The changes they foresee will make these institutions into very different kinds of enterprises—working in close collaboration with business and industry, labor unions, professional associations, libraries, museums, and other noncollege entities; employing part-time fac-

ulty members to teach mostly part-time adult students; and de-
livering courses in a variety of formats and settings. All these
activities, of course, can presently be found in various institutions around the country, but such approaches will have to become the predominant mode. If that prediction seems surprising, note that Harvard University currently enrolls 16,000
degree candidates in all its regular programs but each year serves
an additional 45,000 part-time adult students, most of whom
are enrolled in noncredit continuing professional education activities (National University Continuing Education Association,
1982, p. 1).

Accrediting bodies, which are so dependent on the role of
the governing board to protect the public interest and the role
of the faculty to assure quality standards, have been greatly
strained by the nontraditional institutions and programs that
have already appeared. They may be overwhelmed by the "revolution" now under way. If they are to avoid that possibility, accrediting bodies must find answers to a new set of questions
(which sound much like recycled old questions).

1. *What is an institution of postsecondary education, for
purposes of accreditation?* In an unpublished paper, John Harris
and James Huffman argue that certain "forms" are essential to
an educational institution and that these forms should not be
neglected as accreditation is justifiably turning more attention
to "results" (Harris and Huffman, 1981). They state that if institutions of postsecondary education are to remain relatively
autonomous and self-regulating, they must have the following
characteristics:

- The institution should be incorporated as an entity that is
  separate from the agency that sponsors it.
- The governing board should insulate the institution from its
  direct sponsor.
- In turn, there ought to be a marked and functional difference between the responsibilities of the governing board and
  the responsibilities of the executives of the institution.
- The whole governing structure should be such that dispari-
  ties between mission and function are quickly identified and

corrected, pursuit of truth is protected, and appeals and grievances can be properly aired.

- Finally, the form of organization should provide appropriate channels for all constituencies with vital and enduring interests in the institution to contribute to shaping its direction and policies (pp. 8–9).

2. *What is the meaning of a college degree?* At one time, a college degree signified that students of fairly similar abilities, interests, and backgrounds had gone through comparable educational experiences, but that has not been so for many years. A growing concern over this condition led to the establishment of the National Task Force on Educational Credit and Credentials and publication of the task force's report and recommendations (Miller and Mills, 1978). Colleges and universities have been slow to implement the recommendations, and new efforts have been initiated. The Association of American Colleges is sponsoring a project to redefine the meaning and purpose of the baccalaureate degree, and the Association of American Medical Colleges is similarly reviewing the medical degree. The American Association of Community and Junior Colleges will be conducting a study of the associate degree, and the Council of Graduate Schools has been working on definitions for graduate degrees. These projects are attempting to redefine the fundamental skills, essential knowledge, and personal qualities that should be attested to by the awarding of a degree.

3. *What are the differences between credit and noncredit courses?* David Stewart prepared two papers on this subject for the American Council on Education's Commission on Educational Credit and Credentials (Stewart, 1982a, 1982b). For better or worse, academic credit is a basic element in a college degree, and in most public institutions, state funding is provided on a formula basis related to full-time-equivalent enrollments in credit courses. An increasing number of institutions are granting credit for courses offered jointly by the college or university and some noncollege sponsor, perhaps with the postsecondary institution playing only a nominal role. And institutions with declining enrollments can be strongly tempted to convert noncredit courses into credit courses.

4. *Can accreditation function effectively without the strong sense of membership that has until now been an essential element?* What membership will really mean in the future is not clear. The regional accrediting bodies have already become so diversified that critics have questioned their viability or have proposed the creation of more meaningful subdivisions. The regional organizations are already admitting to membership non-degree institutions (except for the Middle States Association); vocational-technical, specialized professional, and proprietary schools; institutions without boards of trustees, full-time faculty members, or campuses; and institutions sponsored by corporations and government. What will all these institutions have in common? Can regional accrediting bodies continue to broaden their membership to include an increasing number, perhaps a majority, of noncollege enterprises? And can regional commissions turn away otherwise accreditable institutions when their "traditional" members are increasingly collaborating with such entities and adopting their nontraditional approaches?

Or will the increasingly amorphous nature of the regional associations lead to the development of new institutional accrediting bodies along the lines of the Association of Independent Colleges and Schools and the National Association of Trade and Technical Schools—that is, national organizations of special types of institutions? Organizations such as the American Association of Community and Junior Colleges and the American Association of State Colleges and Universities have, on occasion, considered the possibility of sponsoring their own accrediting commissions (although their support of the regional accrediting bodies has prevailed). But organizations such as the National Association of Manufacturers or the National Association of Broadcasters might decide to sponsor their own accrediting bodies.

5. *As more new kinds of institutions come into postsecondary education, will they in fact value and seek accreditation?* In the past, new types of institutions—community colleges, technical schools, nontraditional institutions—have eagerly sought accreditation as a badge of respectability. But they were the "outs" joining the "ins," the minority becoming part of the majority. Colleges and universities no longer dominate postsec-

ondary education—in number of institutions, number of students served, or number of dollars spent or earned. As many of the traditional institutions become more like the nontraditional —with teleconferencing by satellite, interactive computers, training contracts with business and industry, collaboration with professional associations, and a growing preoccupation with part-time adult students—they too may question the value of an accreditation system designed for a different type of institution. If the ties to federal funding and state licensure are loosened, the commitment of some institutions to accreditation may also be sorely tested. The director of evaluation for the Commission on Vocational, Technical, and Career Institutions of the New England Association of Schools and Colleges publicly stated at a 1979 COPA meeting that if eligibility for federal funds were not tied to accreditation, his commission would go out of business.

The Coming Postindustrial Society. The United States (and much of the rest of the world) is moving into a new and quite different stage of development, described by Daniel Bell (1973) as the "postindustrial society." America is becoming a society of changing values (Yankelovich, 1981), a high-technology society (Evans, 1979), and a learning society (Husén, 1974). If the futurists are right, Americans will soon be living in a radically different world, with the following implications.

1. *The public schools may continue to disintegrate.* Factors contributing to this trend include the increasing movement of students into private schools, conflicts between unionized teachers and disaffected taxpayers (particularly the growing number of childless adults), the declining quality of students majoring in education, a decrease in the number of teachers entering the field and an increase in the number leaving the field because of low salaries and poor working conditions, the impact of the computer and television on learning modes, the continuing problems of the cities and the suburbs, and pervasive economic difficulties. Accreditation of elementary and secondary schools would inevitably be affected by these changes, and therefore so would accreditation of postsecondary educational institutions, which must relate to the schools students attend before entering college.

2. *The lines between secondary and postsecondary education (already blurred) may become meaningless as high technology opens up new worlds of learning to everyone.* For example, not only are first-graders learning how to operate computers and use them as learning tools, but they are also doing their own programming (Papert, 1980). The regional associations may have to redefine roles and relationships among their various commissions, and all accrediting bodies may face new problems in defining the meaning of *postsecondary education.* Further, new areas of research are increasingly blurring the lines between traditional disciplines. The most important and exciting new learning is occurring in hybrid areas such as genetic engineering and biochemistry. These developments will probably lead, eventually, to a reorganization of knowledge and therefore of academic departments—with a consequent impact on specialized accreditation.

3. *The increasing role of television and computers appears to be producing already disturbing declines in reading and writing skills.* Some writers assert that an educational system founded on the written word will be forced to reexamine its basic assumptions. If communication skills are to be important in this new society, then ways must be found to offset these trends. Once again, accrediting bodies will be caught in the shifting tide of changing definitions.

4. *The work force is already experiencing major changes.* There is now a smaller pool of workers made up of younger, better-educated employees who see a job as an entitlement and demand self-fulfillment from their work but who are less motivated by the traditional incentives of pay increases and promotions. These changes are occurring while the nation is going through the agonies of economic adjustment and is contending with the growing competition of other nations. At the same time, there is an increasing number of older retired persons and a growing, seemingly permanent underclass of the unskilled unemployed. Society will look to education—colleges and universities in particular—to respond to these problems, or other social institutions will develop their own educational programs in response. Either way, accrediting bodies will face the challenge of sorting out appropriate from inappropriate educational programs as well as the effective from the ineffective.

5. *The United States may increasingly become a nation of "electronic cottages" providing the opportunity for many to learn and work at home rather than having to go to a campus or an office.* If so, will millions of students still travel to a college or university each year and pay thousands of dollars for the privilege of living in dormitories and sitting in lecture classes? For many students, the psychological and social values represented in the ritual of "going away to college" will probably prove sufficiently strong to offset the financial and other advantages of learning at home. As the costs of postsecondary education continue to climb, however, patterns of schooling may change significantly. The External Degree Program of the New York Regents or the computerized credit-banking system of the Community College of the Air Force may become much more prevalent arrangements, thus posing new challenges for accreditation.

6. *As computers make specialized knowledge and techniques more commonly available, professions may decline in power.* A computer can research legal precedents more thoroughly and quickly than a lawyer and can make more accurate diagnoses of illnesses than most doctors. Will this power shift affect the ability of professions to establish standards of professional preparation and licensure? As the traditional professions experience continuing redefinition and fragmentation, will they be able and willing to control accreditation in their changing fields?

7. *In a dynamic, technological society, credentials—as evidence of competence—may become ever more important, but demands will probably increase for assurances that credentials have real social utility.* Society has recently decided that professions should move from lifetime credentialing to periodic recredentialing. The courts have already established that when credentials can be used for advantage or disadvantage, they must be proved pertinent, valid, and reliable. These trends will probably continue in the future. What will be—should be—the role of accreditation as part of these developments?

8. *"Learning processes are lagging appallingly behind and are leaving both individuals and societies unprepared to meet the challenges posed by global issues"* (Botkin, Elmandjra, and

Malitza, 1979, p. 9). Individuals and societies have traditionally adopted a pattern of continuous "maintenance learning"—the acquisition of fixed outlooks, methods, and rules for dealing with known and recurring situations—interrupted by short periods of innovation stimulated by the shock of external events. But for long-term survival, particularly in times of turbulence, change, or discontinuity, society requires "innovative learning" —learning that can bring change, renewal, restructuring, and problem reformulation. Such learning requires anticipation and participation. If one accepts this analysis and prescription (which received remarkably little attention from the postsecondary education community), what should be the role of accreditation in encouraging and assisting postsecondary education to move from "maintenance learning" to "innovative learning"?

Faced with the almost overwhelming nature of these predicted changes in virtually every aspect of life, one could easily fall into a state of anomie. Or one could become pessimistic about the capacities of a social process as fragile as accreditation to cope with so many changed conditions. A look backward can be reassuring, however. In its brief seventy years or so, the accreditation process has not only survived dramatic social changes but also benefited from them, adapting and strengthening. *Process* is the key word. Marshall McLuhan (1965) staggered the communications industry by arguing that "the medium is the message." Students of accreditation have slowly come to understand that the process is preeminent; the players can change, conditions can change, but the process will prevail.

Accreditation was not created in one day or in seven. It evolved and is still evolving, and the record suggests it will continue in the same general direction in which it has traveled in the past. Recent developments suggest that institutions of postsecondary education will play a more active role in accreditation. Certainly, with increasingly tight budgets, institutions are going to be more aggressive in demanding that the cost/benefit relationships of accreditation be convincingly demonstrated. At the same time, two of the basic requirements of accreditation—

Resource A

๒๒๒๒๒๒๒๒๒๒๒๒๒๒๒๒๒๒๒๒๒๒๒

Accrediting Groups Recognized by COPA

The Council on Postsecondary Accreditation (COPA) periodically evaluates the accreditation activities of institutional and professional associations. After determining that those activities meet or exceed COPA provisions, COPA publicly recognizes accrediting groups through an official listing in *Accredited Institutions of Postsecondary Accreditation* (*AIPE*), jointly published by the American Council on Education and COPA. The following list of accrediting bodies recognized by COPA is taken from the forthcoming 1982–83 edition of *AIPE* and reprinted by permission of COPA. The listing is current as of July 1, 1982. Groups that are regional in nature are identified with their geographical areas; all others are national in their activities.

407

Institutional Accreditation

American Association of Bible Colleges
John Mostert, Executive Director
Box 1523
130-F North College Street
Fayetteville, Arkansas 72701
Tel. (501) 521-8164

Association of Independent Colleges and Schools
James M. Phillips, Executive Director
Accrediting Commission, AICS
1730 M Street, N.W.
Washington, D.C. 20036
Tel. (202) 659-2460

*Middle States Association of Colleges and Schools
(Delaware, District of Columbia, Maryland, New Jersey, New York, Pennsylvania, Puerto Rico, Virgin Islands)*
Robert Kirkwood, Executive Director
Commission on Higher Education
3624 Market Street
Philadelphia, Pennsylvania 19104
Tel. (215) 662-5606

National Association of Trade and Technical Schools
William A. Goddard, Executive Director
2021 K Street, N.W., Room 305
Washington, D.C. 20006
Tel. (202) 296-8892

National Home Study Council
William A. Fowler, Executive Secretary
Accrediting Commission, NHSC
1601 Eighteenth Street, N.W.
Washington, D.C. 20009
Tel. (202) 234-5100

*New England Association of Schools and Colleges
(Connecticut, Maine, Massachusetts, New Hampshire, Rhode Island, Vermont)*
131 Middlesex Turnpike
Burlington, Massachusetts 01803
Tel. (617) 272-6450

Charles M. Cook, Director of Evaluation
Commission on Institutions of Higher Education

Daniel S. Maloney, Director of Evaluation
Commission on Vocational, Technical, Career Institutions

*North Central Association of Colleges and Schools
(Arizona, Arkansas, Colorado, Illinois, Indiana, Iowa, Kansas, Michigan, Minnesota, Missouri, Nebraska, New Mexico, North Dakota, Ohio, Oklahoma, South Dakota, West Virginia, Wisconsin, Wyoming)*
Thurston E. Manning, Director
Commission on Institutions of Higher Education
159 N. Dearborn Street
Chicago, Illinois 60601
Tel. (312) 263-0456

*Northwest Association of Schools and Colleges
(Alaska, Idaho, Montana, Nevada, Oregon, Utah, Washington)*
James F. Bemis, Executive Director
Commission on Colleges
3700-B University Way, N.E.
Seattle, Washington 98105
Tel. (206) 543-0195

*Southern Association
of Colleges and Schools
(Alabama, Florida, Georgia,
Kentucky, Louisiana, Mississippi,
North Carolina, South Carolina,
Tennessee, Texas, Virginia)*
  795 Peachtree Street, N.E.
Atlanta, Georgia 30365

Gordon W. Sweet, Executive
Director
Commission on Colleges
Tel. (404) 897-6126

Kenneth W. Tidwell, Acting
Executive Director
Commission on Occupational
Education Institutions
Tel. (404) 897-6164

*Western Association
of Schools and Colleges
(American Samoa, California,
Guam, Hawaii, Trust Territory of
the Pacific)*
  Kay J. Andersen, Executive
Director
Accrediting Commission for
Senior Colleges and Universities
c/o Mills College, Box 9990
Oakland, California 94613
Tel. (415) 632-5000

Robert E. Swenson, Executive
Director
Accrediting Commission for
Community and Junior Colleges
P.O. Box 70
Aptos, California 95003
Tel. (408) 688-7575

Specialized Accrediting

ALLIED HEALTH (Through the
American Medical Association)
  COPA recognizes the Committee
on Allied Health Education and Accreditation (CAHEA) as an umbrella
agency for twenty-six review committees representing forty-seven collaborating professional organizations in the accreditation of programs in the following areas of allied
health. All questions concerning accreditation of these programs should
be directed to CAHEA at the address given. The programs are Assistant to the Primary Care Physi-
cian, Cytotechnologist, Diagnostic
Medical Sonographer, EEG Technician, EEG Technologist, EMT-Para-
medic, Histologic Technician, Medical Assistant, Medical Assistant in
Pediatrics, Medical Laboratory
Technician (associate degree and
certificate programs), Medical Record Administrator, Medical Record
Technician, Medical Technologist,
Nuclear Medicine Technologist, Occupational Therapist, Ophthalmic
Medical Assistant, Perfusionist,
Physical Therapist, Radiation Ther-
apy Technologist, Radiography,
Respiratory Therapist, Respiratory
Therapy Technician, Specialist in
Blood Bank Technology, Surgeon's
Assistant, Surgical Technologist.

*American Medical Association
Committee on Allied Health
Education and Accreditation*
  John G. Fauser, Director
Department of Allied Health
Education and Accreditation,
AMA
535 North Dearborn Street
Chicago, Illinois 60610
Tel. (312) 751-6272

ARCHITECTURE
First professional degree programs

*National Architectural Accrediting
Board*
  John Wilson Jeronimo,
Executive Director
1735 New York Avenue, N.W.
Washington, D.C. 20006
Tel (202) 783-2007

ART
Institutions offering professional
preparation

*National Association of Schools
of Art and Design*
  Samuel Hope, Executive
Director
Commission on Accreditation
11250 Roger Bacon Drive,
Suite 5
Reston, Virginia 22090
Tel. (703) 437-0700

BUSINESS
Bachelor's and master's degree
programs

*American Assembly of Collegiate
Schools of Business*
William K. Laidlaw, Jr.,
Executive Vice-President
11500 Olive Street Road,
Suite 142
St. Louis, Missouri 63141
Tel. (314) 872-8481

CHEMISTRY[1]

CHIROPRACTIC EDUCATION
Institutions offering professional
degrees

*The Council on Chiropractic
Education*
Ralph G. Miller, Executive
Secretary
3209 Ingersoll Avenue
Des Moines, Iowa 50312
Tel. (515) 255-2184

CLINICAL PASTORAL
EDUCATION[2]
Professional training centers

*Association for Clinical Pastoral
Education, Inc.*
Charles E. Hall, Jr., Executive
Director
Interchurch Center, Suite 450
475 Riverside Drive
New York, New York 10027
Tel. (212) 870-2558

CONSTRUCTION EDUCATION
Baccalaureate programs

*American Council for Construction
Education*
I. Eugene Thorson, Executive
Vice-President
P.O. Box 1266
103 South Fourth Street,
Suite 6
Manhattan, Kansas 66502
Tel. (913) 776-1544 or
(913) 532-5964

DENTISTRY AND DENTAL
AUXILIARY PROGRAMS
First professional programs in
dental education; degree and
certificate programs in dental
auxiliary education

American Dental Association
Robert J. Pollock, Jr., Secretary
Commission on Dental
Accreditation
211 East Chicago Avenue
Chicago, Illinois 60611
Tel. (312) 440-2721

DIETETICS
Coordinated baccalaureate
programs

The American Dietetic Association
Philip Lesser, Administrator
Department of Education
430 North Michigan Avenue
Chicago, Illinois 60611
Tel. (312) 280-5040

---

[1]The American Chemical Society is not recognized by the Council on Post-secondary Accreditation. A list of schools approved by the society may be obtained from the Committee on Professional Training, American Chemical Society, 1155 Sixteenth Street, N.W., Washington, D.C. 20036.
[2]Clinical Pastoral Education is offered and accredited in health care facilities. Many theological seminaries recognize the accreditation of these programs and allow students credit toward theological degrees. A list of these institutions may be obtained from the ACPE headquarters.

ENGINEERING
Professional engineering programs
at the basic (baccalaureate) and
advanced (master's) levels;
baccalaureate programs in
engineering technology; and
two-year (associate degree)
programs in engineering technology

Accreditation Board for
Engineering and Technology
David R. Reyes-Guerra,
Executive Director
345 East 47th Street
New York, New York 10017
Tel. (212) 705-7685

FORESTRY
Professional schools

Society of American Foresters
Ronald R. Christensen, Director
of Professional Programs
5400 Grosvenor Lane
Washington, D.C. 20014
Tel. (301) 897-8720

HEALTH SERVICES
ADMINISTRATION
Graduate programs

Accrediting Commission on
Education for Health Services
Administration
Gary L. Filerman, Executive
Secretary
One Dupont Circle, N.W.,
Suite 420
Washington, D.C. 20036
Tel. (202) 659-3939

HOME ECONOMICS
Undergraduate programs

American Home Economics
Association
Katherine B. Hall, Director
Office of Professional Education
2010 Massachusetts Avenue, N.W.
Washington, D.C. 20036
Tel. (202) 862-8355

INDUSTRIAL TECHNOLOGY[3]

INTERIOR DESIGN
Programs at the two-year,
three-year, baccalaureate, and
master's levels

Foundation for Interior Design
Education Research
Edna Kane, Director of
Administration
242 W. 27th Street,
Suite 6B
New York, New York 10001
Tel. (212) 929-8366

JOURNALISM
Program (sequences) leading to
undergraduate and graduate
(master's) degrees in journalism

American Council on Education in
Journalism and Mass
Communication
Baskett Mosse, Executive
Secretary
Accrediting Committee
563 Essex Court
Deerfield, Illinois 60015
Tel. (312) 948-5840

LANDSCAPE ARCHITECTURE
Professional programs

American Society of Landscape
Architects
Samuel E. Miller, Director of
Education and Research
Landscape Architectural
Accreditation Board
1733 Connecticut Avenue, N.W.
Washington, D.C. 20009
Tel. (202) 466-7730

---

[3]The National Association of Industrial Technology is not recognized by the
Council on Postsecondary Accreditation. A list of programs accredited by the association may be obtained from Jeffrey T. Luftig, Director/Secretary, National Association of Industrial Technology, c/o College of Technology, Sill Hall, Eastern Michigan
University, Ypsilanti, Michigan 48197.

LAW
Professional schools

American Bar Association
   James P. White, Consultant on
   Legal Education
   Indianapolis Law School
   Indiana University–Purdue
   University at Indianapolis
   7351 W. New York Street
   Indianapolis, Indiana 46202
   Tel. (317) 264-8071

and

Association of American Law
Schools
   John A. Bauman, Executive
   Director
   One Dupont Circle, N.W.,
   Suite 370
   Washington, D.C. 20036
   Tel. (202) 296-8851

LIBRARIANSHIP
First professional degree programs

American Library Association
   Elinor Yungmeyer,
   Accreditation Officer
   Committee on Accreditation
   50 East Huron Street
   Chicago, Illinois 60611
   Tel. (312) 944-6780

MEDICAL ASSISTANT AND
MEDICAL LABORATORY
TECHNICIAN
Diploma, certificate, and associate
degree programs

Accrediting Bureau of Health
Education Schools
   Hugh A. Woosley,
   Administrator
   Oak Manor Offices
   29089 U.S. 20 West
   Elkhart, Indiana 46514
   Tel. (219) 293-0124

MEDICINE
Programs leading to first
professional degree and programs in
the basic medical sciences

Liaison Committee on Medical
Education
   (in odd-numbered years
   beginning each July first
   contact)
   Edward S. Petersen, Secretary
   Council on Medical Education,
   AMA
   535 North Dearborn Street
   Chicago, Illinois 60610
   Tel. (312) 751-6310

or

   (in even-numbered years
   beginning each July first
   contact)
   J. R. Schofield, Secretary
   Association of American Medical
   Colleges
   One Dupont Circle, N.W.,
   Suite 200
   Washington, D.C. 20036
   Tel. (202) 828-0670

MUSIC
Baccalaureate and graduate degree
programs; also non-degree-granting
institutions

National Association of Schools of
Music
   Samuel Hope, Executive
   Director
   11250 Roger Bacon Drive,
   Suite 5
   Reston, Virginia 22090
   Tel. (703) 437-0700

NURSING
Associate, baccalaureate, and higher-degree programs; also diploma and practical nurse programs

COPA recognizes 293 diploma programs accredited by the NLN at hospital schools of nursing; in addition, 109 practical nursing programs are accredited by the NLN, approximately 45 percent in academic settings; 271 diploma programs conducted by hospitals or independent schools of nursing are also accredited by the NLN. For information on the above programs not listed here, contact Mary F. Liston, Deputy Director for Program Affairs, NLN.

National League for Nursing
Margaret E. Walsh, Executive Director and Secretary
10 Columbus Circle
New York, New York 10019
Tel. (212) 582-1022

Practical nursing programs only

National Association for Practical Nurse Education and Service
Janice C. Williams, Executive Director
254 West 31st Street
New York, New York 10001
Tel. (212) 736-4540

OPTOMETRY
Professional programs in optometry and optometric technology

American Optometric Association
Sally A. Bowers, Executive Secretary
Council on Optometric Education
243 N. Lindbergh Boulevard
St. Louis, Missouri 63141
Tel. (314) 991-4100

OSTEOPATHIC MEDICINE
First professional degree programs

American Osteopathic Association
Douglas Ward, Director
Bureau of Professional Education
212 E. Ohio Street
Chicago, Illinois 60611
Tel. (312) 280-5800

PHARMACY
First professional degree programs

American Council on Pharmaceutical Education
Daniel A. Nona, Executive Director
One East Wacker Drive
Chicago, Illinois 60601
Tel. (312) 467-6222

PHYSICAL THERAPY
First professional degree programs

American Physical Therapy Association
Patricia Yarbrough, Director
Department of Educational Affairs
1156 Fifteenth Street, N.W.
Washington, D.C. 20005
Tel. (202) 466-2070

PODIATRY
Professional schools

American Podiatry Association
Warren G. Ball, Director
Council on Podiatry Education
20 Chevy Chase Circle, N.W.
Washington, D.C. 20015
Tel. (202) 537-4970

PSYCHOLOGY
Doctoral programs leading to professional practice of psychology

American Psychological Association
Meredith P. Crawford, Administration Officer for Accreditation
1200 Seventeenth Street, N.W.
Washington, D.C. 20036
Tel. (202) 833-7600

PUBLIC HEALTH
Graduate schools of public health and master's degree programs in community health education

Council on Education for Public Health
Patricia Evans, Executive Director
1015 Fifteenth Street, N.W., Suite 403
Washington, D.C. 20005
Tel. (202) 789-1050

REHABILITATION
COUNSELING
Master's degree programs

Council on Rehabilitation
Education
   Ivan M. Lappin, Executive
   Director
   162 North State Street,
   Room 601 C
   Chicago, Illinois 60601
   Tel. (312) 346-6027

SOCIAL WORK
Baccalaureate and master's degree
programs

Council on Social Work Education
   Sidney Berengarten, Director
   Division of Education Standards
   and Accreditation
   111 Eighth Avenue, Suite 501
   New York, New York 10011
   Tel. (212) 242-3800

SPEECH PATHOLOGY AND
AUDIOLOGY
Master's degree programs

American Speech-Language-
Hearing Association
   Billie Ackerman, Assistant
   Director
   Education and Scientific
   Programs
   10801 Rockville Pike
   Rockville, Maryland 20852
   Tel. (301) 897-5700

TEACHER EDUCATION
Baccalaureate and graduate
degree programs

National Council for Accreditation
of Teacher Education
   Lyn Gubser, Director
   1919 Pennsylvania Avenue, N.W.,
   Suite 202
   Washington, D.C. 20006
   Tel. (202) 466-7496

THEOLOGY
Graduate professional schools and
programs

Association of Theological Schools
in the United States and Canada
   Leon Pacala, Executive Director
   42 East National Road
   P.O. Box 130
   Vandalia, Ohio 45377
   Tel. (513) 898-4654

VETERINARY MEDICINE
First professional degree programs

American Veterinary Medical
Association
   R. Leland West, Director
   Scientific Activities, AVMA
   930 North Meacham Road
   Schaumburg, Illinois 60196
   Tel. (312) 885-8070

Resource B

༞༞༞༞༞༞༞༞༞༞༞༞༞༞༞༞༞༞༞༞༞༞༞

Provisions and Procedures for Becoming Recognized as an Accrediting Agency

As the nongovernmental organization dedicated primarily to the improvement of postsecondary education in the United States through voluntary accreditation, the Council on Postsecondary Accreditation reviews the accrediting practices of those bodies desiring recognition by the council. Such review and recognition acknowledge accreditation's broad public responsibilities as well as the specific interests of the many groups affected by accreditation (1) by helping to ensure the integrity and consistency of accreditation policies and procedures, (2) by encouraging continual improvement of accrediting practices, (3) by providing guidance to institutions and programs about the status of agencies in the accrediting community, and (4) by providing assurance about the accreditation status of institutions and programs to students, employers, state and federal agencies, and other interested groups.

Prepared by the Council on Postsecondary Accreditation (COPA), May 15, 1982; reprinted by permission of COPA.

Provisions for Recognition

COPA's provisions for recognition should be construed as an outline, not a blueprint, since recognition must ultimately rely on the best evidence available. COPA considers these provisions on the premise that they are indicia of a quality program of accreditation. At the same time, nothing in these provisions shall require any conduct contrary to the provisions of any pertinent federal or state statute, including, in particular public meeting or record laws.

A. Concerning Its Organizational Structure and Scope, an Agency—

1. Is a nongovernmental body;
2. Demonstrates operational independence for making objective judgments relative to accreditation status, policies, procedures, and criteria;
3. Conducts specialized accreditation on a national basis or institutional accreditation on a national or regional basis;
4. Has the staff and financial resources to maintain effective evaluation and reevaluation procedures;
5. Accredits institutions or programs that are classified as primarily postsecondary, are properly chartered and licensed to operate, and offer instruction leading to degrees, diplomas, or certificates with recognized educational validity;
6. Accredits entire institutions to determine that each part contributes to the institution's educational objectives, or accredits specialized academic programs which are generally accepted as preparing for the entry level(s) into the profession or occupation; and
7. Applies for recognition of the full scope of the postsecondary accrediting activities for which it assumes responsibility.

B. Concerning Its Public Responsibility, an Agency—

1. Demonstrates the need to be met by its accreditation activity, as well as its reliability, competence, and experience by

providing evidence of acceptance of its policies, evaluative criteria, procedures, and evaluative decisions by the community of interests directly affected by the agency, namely, educators, educational institutions, other accrediting bodies, practitioners, and employers;

2. Reflects within its evaluation, policy, and decision-making processes the community of interests directly affected by the agency, including effective public representation;

3. Describes fully in official public documents its accrediting scope, evaluative criteria, and procedures;

4. Publishes at least annually a current listing of the status of all institutions or programs accredited by it and also makes public all final accrediting actions taken; and

5. Makes publicly available the academic and professional qualifications of the members of its policy and decision-making bodies and its administrative personnel.

C. Concerning Its Evaluative Practices and Procedures, an Agency—

1. Periodically reviews its evaluative criteria and procedures and modifies them when necessary only after providing advance notice and opportunity for comment by affected persons, institutions, and organizations;

2. Provides appropriate and fair procedures for processing applications for accreditation and for appeals from accreditation actions and decisions;

3. Evaluates an institution or program only at the invitation of the chief executive officer of the institution involved, except that an agency may reserve the right to initiate an evaluation of an accredited institution or program when circumstances indicate questionable compliance with agency criteria;

4. Maintains clear definitions of each accreditation status, including preaccreditation status if offered, and has clear, written procedures for granting, denying, reaffirming, modifying, suspending, revoking, or reinstating any status;

5. Requires as an integral part of its accrediting process a

self-analysis of the program or institution and an on-site review by a visiting team;

6. Provides appropriate consultative guidance about the accrediting process to the institutions or programs;

7. Designs data-gathering instruments which stimulate self-evaluation and improvement, which require only those data directly related to the evaluation and accreditation process, and which make maximum use of information already available in the institution;

8. Appoints to visiting teams, in consultation with institutional or program officials, persons who are competent by virtue of experience, training, and orientation and takes reasonable precautions to ensure that those selected will develop and articulate objective opinions and decisions free of self-interest and professional bias;

9. Demonstrates that its process of accreditation, including length of terms, reporting requirements, sizes of teams, and fees or dues, is reasonably related to the purposes of accreditation;

10. Provides opportunities during the on-site visit for discussion between team members and faculty, staff, administrators, students, and other interested parties;

11. Considers accreditation actions only after the chief executive officer of the institution and director of the program have been given opportunity and time to comment on the report of the visiting team;

12. Permits the withdrawal of a request for any status of accreditation at any time prior to the decision on that request;

13. Notifies institutions and programs promptly in writing of accrediting decisions, giving reasons for the actions;

14. Provides an evaluation report to the institution which the institution is free to distribute; and

15. Maintains the confidentiality, insofar as possible, of those aspects of the accreditation process which if disclosed would jeopardize the purposes of accreditation and weaken the process.

*D. Concerning Educational Philosophy and Related
Procedures, an Agency—*

1. Recognizes the right of institutions or programs to be evaluated in the light of their own stated purposes so long as these are consistent with purposes generally recognized by the postsecondary education community and are appropriate to the recognized scope of the accrediting agency;
2. Develops and interprets its evaluative criteria to allow and encourage institutional freedom and autonomy;
3. Develops and applies criteria clearly relevant to evaluating the educational quality of institutions or programs;
4. Examines and evaluates institutions or programs in relation to the operational goals of the total institution and to educational outcomes; and
5. Allows for educational experimentation and innovation.

*E. Concerning Other Matters of Procedure,
Cooperation, and Coordination, an Agency—*

1. Demonstrates willingness to work with other accrediting bodies in cooperative accrediting processes;
2. Advises COPA of any procedural or organizational changes within the accrediting body or its parent body which might affect its accrediting activities or its recognition status; and
3. Files regularly with COPA those documents and other materials pertaining to its activities and complies with requests by COPA for other data or information.

Preapplication Procedures for Agencies Seeking
Initial Recognition or Change of Scope

Any agency desiring to apply to COPA for initial recognition as an accrediting body and any currently recognized agency proposing to apply for a substantial change in accrediting scope must complete the preapplication process prior to making formal application for COPA recognition. To be eligible to enter this process, the agency must be nongovernmental and must propose to accredit institutions or programs that are classified primarily as postsecondary as defined in the COPA "Provisions for Recognition." The COPA board of directors has established a fee of $2,000 for agencies seeking initial recognition and $500 for recognized agencies desiring a change in scope.

An agency's participation in the preapplication process will be monitored by the COPA Committee on Recognition. The process involves consultation and communication with the agency by the COPA staff and the Committee on Recognition. The specific aspects and length of the process will vary depending on such factors as whether initial agency recognition or a change of accrediting scope is involved or whether the agency already has been carrying out the accrediting function for which recognition is sought.

The preapplication process is divided into two phases. Phase I is focused on the demonstration of need for the proposed accreditation. Phase II involves demonstration of the capacity of the applicant agency to meet that need.

An agency must first submit materials responding to items 1-6, Phase I, for consideration by the Committee on Recognition. If encouraged to continue, the agency will then submit materials responding to items 7-9, Phase I. Materials in support of Phase II will be submitted only after satisfactory completion of Phase I.

Phase I: Demonstration of Need

The basic purpose of the COPA recognition process is to ensure that accreditation serves the interests of students, the professions, the postsecondary education community, and the general public in the most efficient and effective manner possible. These interests are best served if accrediting functions are established or expanded in areas only when a need for accreditation in relation to the interests of these constituencies can be demonstrated conclusively. Although the assessment of need is complex, it must be carried out in regard to the following basic principles: (1) accrediting structures and processes should not fragment the educational process but should contribute to the concept of education as an integration of disciplines into a meaningful whole; and (2) duplication of accrediting in the same general area is to be avoided since it invites inconsistent and contradictory standards and accrediting actions and thus leads to confusion on the part of students, institutions, and the public.

The specific elements involved in demonstrating a need for accreditation will vary depending on the circumstances of the particular situation. However, the following generally will be required:

1. Specification of the precise scope of the proposed accreditation in relation to geographic areas, degree levels, and/or the specific disciplinary programs to be accredited;
2. Specification by numbers and locations of educational institutions and/or programs to be served;
3. Description of all accreditation, program approval, or other programs of the agency that review professional standards and of the relationship of the proposed accrediting function to other programs of the agency;
4. For specialized accreditation, specification of the nature of of the profession, including entry-level requirements, certification/licensing requirements, and relationships with other disciplines and professions;
5. Identification of all other groups offering accreditation in the same or related areas;
6. Demonstration that accreditation is needed to protect the interests of students, to benefit the public, and to improve the quality of education;
7. Demonstration that the need is clearly recognized and that the proposed accreditation is strongly supported by the following constituencies as appropriate in the given instance:
    a. chief executive officers of the postsecondary institutions affected by the accreditation;
    b. deans, directors, and faculty of specific educational programs subject to the accreditation;
    c. affected student groups;

     d.   professionals and professional organizations in the field to be accredited;

     e.   employers of graduates of the educational programs;

     f.   groups representing related disciplines and professions;

     g.   agencies carrying out accreditation in the same or closely related areas;

     h.   agencies with responsibilities for professional certification or licensure, state educational planning and coordination, or similar functions; and

     i.   interested publics as reflected in responses to a call for comment.

8.   Assessment of the benefits in relation to the costs of accreditation; and

9.   Exploration of the feasibility of meeting the need for accreditation through existing accrediting structures or in collaboration with other accrediting agencies.

Phase II: Demonstration of Capacity

The second phase of the preapplicant process focuses on the capacity of the agency to carry out the proposed accreditation. This involves:

1.   Development of accrediting standards and procedures;

2.   Field tests of procedures and materials, including

     a.   supervised trial evaluations for accreditation; and

     b.   assessment of responses by institutions/programs;

3.   Evaluation of proficiency in conducting accreditation processes; and

4.   Demonstration of the stability of the agency and the adequacy of its personnel and financial resources.

Application Procedures for Agencies Seeking Initial or Continued Recognition or Recognition of a Change of Scope

Applications for initial recognition by COPA and for recognition of a substantial change of scope may not be acted upon until the applicant agency has been reviewed through the

COPA preapplication process. The Committee on Recognition will plan review schedules for each year, and recognized agencies shall be notified by COPA staff of pending reviews for renewal of recognition. This notice will be given at least twelve (12) months prior to the panel review and eighteen (18) months before the scheduled final COPA board action.

The following steps shall constitute the application process:

1. Letter of Intent

After notification by COPA, the agency shall send COPA a letter of intent to proceed with an application for recognition. This letter shall be filed with the COPA office within sixty days of COPA's original notice.

2. Nomination of Agency Visitors

For agencies seeking initial recognition, the Committee on Recognition may nominate a visitor(s) to observe an on-site visit(s) and a meeting of the agency's accrediting commission. At least two nominations shall be provided for each position.

Neither members or adjunct members of the Committee on Recognition nor COPA staff may serve as visiting-team members.

For agencies seeking continued recognition, such visits may or may not be necessary. Provisions are made for visits to these agencies should the review, outlined in item 17 below, produce justification for such a visit.

All visits to agencies shall be conducted in accordance with procedures outlined in "Guidelines for Visits to Agencies Engaged in the COPA Recognition Process."

3. Agency Response to Visiting-Team Nominations

After receiving visiting-team nominations, the agency shall have thirty days in which to notify COPA if any nominees are unacceptable to the agency. Such persons shall be eliminated from further consideration for the visiting team. Failure to respond by the deadline date shall validate the slate nominated.

4. Nomination of Reviewers and Readers

The members of the Committee on Recognition shall normally serve as the reviewers for all applicant agencies. If it becomes necessary to add adjunct members for any review session, such members will be added in accordance with procedures established by the committee.

The applicant agency will be provided with the roster of committee members proposed as reviewers. The Committee on Recognition shall also nominate an outside reader-consultant.

The reviewers and the reader-consultant shall be responsible for considering written materials generated by the recognition process.

5. Agency Response to Reviewer and Reader Nominations

After receiving reviewer and reader nominations, the agency shall have thirty days in which to notify COPA if any nominees are unacceptable to the agency. Such persons shall be eliminated from further consideration for these positions. Failure to respond by the deadline date shall validate the slate nominated.

6. Agency Materials Submitted

At least six months before the scheduled review, the agency shall submit an application for recognition. An application shall consist of a narrative account of the agency's compliance with each provision for recognition as well as essential supporting documents.

The agency shall submit fifteen copies of the application. The format for all materials submitted is 8½″ × 11″ paper with each set of materials punched to fit a standard three-ring notebook. Nonstandard-size materials which cannot be punched, such as bound handbooks and procedural statements, should be enclosed in prepunched, labeled, unsealed envelopes.

7. Appointment of Visiting Team, Reviewers, and Reader

Following the receipt of an agency's application, the COPA staff, in consultation with the chairman of the Committee on Recognition, shall notify the visitor(s), reviewers, and reader of their selection and shall notify the agency.

The process of nominating and selecting the visitor(s), reviewers, and reader shall be in accordance with the written policies of COPA. Nominees shall also be informed of these policies prior to their acceptance.

8. Visits to Agencies

Visits to agencies shall be conducted two to six months prior to the scheduled review.

9. Public Notice

The COPA staff shall publish notice of the agency's scheduled review in *Accreditation* and in the *Chronicle of Higher Education*. Notices of spring reviews will appear in the previous fall newsletter, fall reviews in the previous spring issue; notices in the *Chronicle of Higher Education* shall appear no later than four months prior to the scheduled review.

Notices shall follow a standard format consisting of the agency name, scope, date of review, and final date of receipt of third-party comment. COPA shall not publish any other information concerning the review nor any article which might be construed as prejudicial to the review process.

10. Petition for Third-Party Comment at Review

Not later than two months before the scheduled review, any third party wishing to offer oral testimony at the agency's review must submit a statement indicating those parties which it represents and outlining in detail the substance of its proposed testimony. Such comments must address the agency's compliance with specific COPA provisions.

11. Written Third-Party Comment Submitted

Not later than two months before the scheduled review, third parties wishing to offer written comment must submit such a statement. This statement must identify the parties represented by such comment and must address the agency's compliance with specific COPA provisions.

12. Visiting-Team Reports Submitted

Not later than two months before the scheduled review, the visiting team shall submit its report following an outline published in COPA's "Guidelines for Visits to Agencies Engaged in the COPA Recognition Process."

13. Reader Report Submitted

Not later than two months before the scheduled review, the outside reader-consultant shall submit a report on the agency's application.

14. Access to Applications and Third-Party Comment

An agency's application and materials submitted by third parties shall be available in the COPA office for public review. COPA shall not distribute or release these materials.

15. Materials Sent to Reviewers

The following materials shall be forwarded to the reviewers not later than one month before the scheduled review:

a. Narrative section of agency's application and essential supporting documentation
b. Third-party written comment or outline of oral testimony
c. Reader report
d. Visiting-team report
e. COPA "Provisions and Procedures for Recognition"
f. Instructions for reviewers.

16. Materials Sent to Agencies

At the same time materials are sent to reviewers, the agency shall be provided copies of any third-party comment, visiting-team and reader reports, and a detailed schedule of the review session.

17. Consideration by the Committee on Recognition

Immediately prior to the April or October meeting of the COPA board, the Committee on Recognition shall meet to consider the agency's application. The review shall follow this order:

a. Oral presentation by agency representative(s) to reviewers;
b. Comment on agency application by outside reader-consultant;
c. Comment from chairperson of visiting team, if any;
d. Question-and-answer period between reviewers and agency representative(s) concerning the materials and testimony submitted;
e. Oral third-party testimony, if any;
f. Agency response to written or oral third-party comment;
g. Summary review between agency representatives and reviewers.

The review shall consider only those materials, testimony, and comment relevant to COPA Provisions for Recognition and presented in accordance with these procedures.

18. Recommendations of the Committee on Recognition

The Committee on Recognition shall then convene in executive session to discuss its findings and prepare a written report containing recommendations for the board.
The Committee on Recognition may either:

a. request, in the case of previously recognized agencies, an agency visit to determine compliance with COPA provisions;

Such a request shall defer the committee's recommendation for six months, and such visits and review shall follow procedures outlined in items 2, 3, 8, 12, 16, and 17 of this document. During the period of deferral, no "public comment" shall be made concerning the circumstances leading to the agency visit.

OR

b.   prepare recommendations for board action on applications for recognition.

Possible recommendations of the committee are:

(1)   Recognition for five years;
(2)   Recognition for five years with a request for interim report(s) to the Committee on Recognition indicating progress in the correction of deficiencies;
(3)   Recognition for three years with provisions stipulated;
(4)   Action deferred for one year pending one or more of the following:
(a)   Receipt of additional information by the Committee on Recognition to determine agency compliance with COPA provisions;
(b)   Response to the concerns of the Committee on Recognition about failure to meet COPA provisions;
(c)   Response indicating the correction of deficiencies outlined by the Committee on Recognition;
(5)   Denial of the application for recognition.

After committee review of the final written recommendation, this recommendation is forwarded to the applicant agency at least four months before final board action.

*19. Agency Consideration of Committee
on Recognition Report*

The applicant agency is provided opportunity to comment on the recommendation formulated by the Committee on Recognition. This comment should deal with erroneous conclusions based upon errors of fact or interpretation and/or new developments which address concerns raised by the Committee on Recognition. The agency may not request a delay for a decision by the COPA board based upon the report of the Committee on Recognition.

20. Agency Comment to the COPA Office

The agency shall forward its comment on the report of the Committee on Recognition to the COPA office three months in advance of final board action.

21. Consideration of Agency Comments by Committee on Recognition

Immediately prior to the meeting at which the board will take final action on an agency's application, the Committee on Recognition shall meet to consider agency responses to its initial report and shall prepare the final report to the board.

22. Board Action

At its next meeting, the COPA board shall hear and take action on the recommendations of the Committee on Recognition.

23. Notification of Action to Agency

Promptly following the board action, COPA staff shall provide the agency with a complete text of the action taken as well as specific details of additional agency responsibilities.

24. Agency Response to Deferral and Requests for Reports

If an agency's application is deferred or the Committee on Recognition requests interim reports, the agency shall respond to the committee as directed, and the committee shall consider the application or interim report at its next regular meeting following the scheduled receipt of materials.

25. Procedures Regarding Petition for Review of Adverse Decisions

When a serious disagreement arises concerning an action of the Committee on Recognition or the COPA board which cannot be resolved through normal COPA recognition procedures, the agency shall follow COPA's published "Procedures Regarding Petition for Review of Adverse Decisions."

26. Publication of Recognition Action

Actions on recognition shall be published in a standard format without editorial comment.

Costs of Recognition

The applicant agency shall bear related costs of the foregoing procedures including expenses for the reader and the visitor(s) if they are required to visit an agency, program, or institution during the review. Related costs shall not include the normal meeting of the Committee on Recognition.

Procedures Regarding Complaints

The Council on Postsecondary Accreditation is concerned about the improvement and sustained quality of postsecondary education, but it is not a clearinghouse or mediator for consumer complaints against institutions or programs of study, nor do such complaints fall within COPA's mandate. COPA, however, will receive and attempt to mediate certain appropriate complaints against its recognized accrediting bodies submitted by institutions or programs.

An appropriate complaint for this purpose is defined as one involving issues between an institution or program and a COPA member concerning alleged violations of a member's criteria or procedures but does not include a dispute about a finding of fact by the member agency unless the complainant makes a prima facie showing that the finding is clearly erroneous in view of the reliable, probative, and substantial evidence on the whole record before the member agency.

Without Documentation

A complaint against a member agency must be accompanied by documentation showing that all remedies for resolution through the accrediting body's own processes have been exhausted. Failure to be specific when filing a complaint with COPA against a recognized agency will result in the following:

1. Receipt of the complaint will be acknowledged;
2. Copies of all material received will be sent to the agency against which the complaint is being made;
3. No further action will be taken by COPA.

With Documentation

Receipt of an appropriate complaint with documentation that the complainant has exhausted all administrative remedies for complaints resolution provided by the agency will result in a specified series of actions.

1. A letter of inquiry will be sent by the president of COPA to the chief executive of the agency against which the complaint is lodged asking for verification that the complainant has utilized all the processes afforded by the agency. A copy of this letter shall go to the complainant.
2. If the agency acknowledges that the complainant has exhausted all remedies through that agency, the agency will be asked to supply COPA with a summary of actions which led to the original complaint.
3. Upon receipt of a member's response to COPA's inquiry, the president shall encourage the parties to resolve their differences. If the differences are not so resolved in a reason-

able time and they appear to be substantial, the president of COPA shall appoint three members of the COPA board to investigate the complaint. Such investigation might include, but does not have to include, a visit(s) to the site(s) of the alleged violation or to the headquarters of the agency against which the complaint was lodged and such hearings as may be deemed necessary.

4. This three-person investigation panel shall have access to any and all information pertinent to its investigations, including transcripts or minutes of official proceedings by the member agency.

5. A report of the investigation and the findings shall be forwarded to the Executive Committee along with any recommendations. The Executive Committee shall then report to the board its recommendations regarding the complaint.

6. The board shall be the body of final authority.

Intra-Agency Complaints

Should there be complaint(s) by one recognized agency against another recognized agency, the resolution procedure shall be conducted informally. Agency representatives will be convened by COPA to discuss the matter of contention and to work out a mutually acceptable solution to the problem.

Costs of Complaint Pleadings

The board shall provide a procedure for the equitable distribution of costs in the processing, investigation, and resolution of all complaints.

Procedures Regarding Petition for Review of Adverse Decisions

An adverse decision regarding recognition by COPA shall be defined as denial of initial or renewed recognition, revocation of recognition, or denial of a request for change of scope.

In the event of an adverse decision by the board, the accrediting agency may petition for review of the decision on the grounds that the board has ruled erroneously by disregarding its own provisions for recognition, failing to follow its stated procedures, or failing to consider all the evidence and documentation presented in favor of the application.

Should there be petition for review, certain procedures will apply:

1. Not later than thirty days from the date of an adverse decision, the agency shall notify the president of COPA in writing of its intention to petition for review of the decision, and not later than sixty days from the same date it shall submit documentation supporting such petition.
2. The chairman of the council, with approval of the Executive Committee, shall then appoint a hearing panel comprising five persons, none of whom shall be members of the board.
3. The hearings shall be held at a mutually convenient time and place and shall be conducted in accord with due process.
4. The hearing panel may either affirm the board's decision or recommend to the board that it reconsider the decision, giving reasons in either case.
5. The status of any member shall remain unchanged during the review, and there shall be no public notice of the adverse decision until the review is completed and the board has finally determined the matter.
6. The petitioning agency shall bear the cost of any transcript which it requests.
7. The board shall provide a procedure for the equitable distribution of all other costs incurred by a petition for review.

Resource C

꘎꘎꘎꘎꘎꘎꘎꘎꘎꘎꘎꘎꘎꘎꘎꘎꘎꘎꘎꘎꘎꘎꘎꘎

Guidelines on Interagency Cooperation in Accreditation

Basic Principles

Cooperation among accrediting agencies may occur in many areas and may take a variety of forms. The programmatic accrediting agencies provide the institutional accrediting agencies with standards of excellence in the specialized fields and assistance in evaluating them. The institutional accrediting agencies in turn provide the programmatic accrediting agencies with assistance in an appraisal of the institution, especially institutional control and management. Institutional accrediting agencies, programmatic accrediting agencies, and institutions should work closely together in the total accrediting process.

It is the intent of this task force to identify a range of opportunities for cooperative endeavors, rather than to propose a single structure for cooperation. There is agreement that coop-

Prepared by the Task Force on Interagency Cooperation and approved by the COPA board October 7, 1980; reprinted by permission of COPA.

eration is a desirable goal and that sincere, continuing effort toward cooperation is essential if accreditation's position as a positive force is to be enhanced in advancing quality education.

Toward this end, the following principles are set forth:

1. Facilitating cooperation between and among institutional and programmatic accrediting agencies should be an objective of COPA, the accrediting agencies, and the institutions served by them.
2. Consistent with the concept of voluntary accreditation, each institution of postsecondary education should decide for itself whether to seek accreditation by any appropriate agency or combination of agencies.
3. Institutions desiring coordinated accrediting activities, particularly among agencies accrediting programs located within the same academic administrative unit (for example, a school of professional studies), should be offered every possible assistance and cooperation.
4. Coordination begins with the designation of responsibility within the institution for liaison with the various accrediting agencies.
5. To be successful, coordination requires advance planning by both the institution and the accrediting agency or agencies involved.
6. Representatives of each accrediting agency will be responsible to their parent agency for investigation and reporting activities carried out as part of the accrediting cycle.

Definitions and Cooperative Arrangements

For the purpose of distinguishing among institutional and programmatic agencies, the following operational definitions are presented:

1. *An institutional (general) accrediting agency* accredits an institution as a whole and therefore includes all areas, activities, and programs of the institution. Normally, institutional accreditation testifies to (a) the appropriateness of

the objectives of the institution; (b) the adequacy of its organization, program, and resources, both material and human, when viewed against its objectives and generally accepted accrediting standards; and (c) evidence of the accomplishment of institutional objectives in reasonable measure. Moreover, the criteria of eligibility provide that degree programs, however specialized, must rest upon a base of liberal or general studies required by all or most students. However, accreditation of the institution as a whole is not, and should not be interpreted as being, equivalent to specialized accreditation of a part or program of the institution and should not be represented as such.

2. *Programmatic (specialized) accrediting agencies* accredit program(s) within the total institution (or in the case of single-purpose institutions, may accredit the institution as a whole). The focus of specialized accreditation is on the effectiveness with which the program meets its objectives and those of the institution, and the accrediting standards for quality education. Normally, specialized accreditation reviews the relationship of the program to the larger unit, the adequacy of the organization and resources for program maintenance and development, and evidence of accomplishment of programmatic objectives. However, specialized accreditation does not purport to make judgments on the institution as a whole (except in some cases of single-purpose institutions).

The Study of Interagency Cooperation, undertaken by the task force, documented cooperative arrangements which have developed among accrediting agencies. The following relationships were identified:

1. Institutional and institutional accrediting agencies, including:
   • Regional and regional
   • Regional and national
   • National and national
   • Regional or national and programmatic (functioning as an institutional)

2. Institutional and programmatic
3. Programmatic and programmatic

Each accrediting agency functioned in accordance with its own purpose and recognized scope of activity. The unique contribution of both institutional and programmatic accrediting to the total evaluative process was recognized, as were the possible benefits accruing to the institution, the program, and the agencies from the coordinated effort.

Guidelines for Cooperation

1. *Institutional role:*
   The institution should assume a leadership role in suggesting how cooperating accrediting agencies can best work together to provide optimum service to the institution.
2. *Need for written agreements:*
   Written agreements should be established among accrediting agencies that propose to cooperate. In initial form these may be relatively simple and deal primarily with matters of principle, becoming more specific as the cooperating agencies resolve procedural differences through experience. Sharing of the written agreement with all participants in the accrediting process will reduce potential misunderstandings and conflicts.
3. *Designation of accrediting responsibility:*
   a. Between two or more institutional accrediting agencies
   - An institution with operations that cross regional boundaries must be prepared to deal with all of the regional accrediting agencies involved; however, the regional accrediting agency for the parent campus normally will serve as the coordinating agency.
   - A specialized institution for which there is a national specialized institutional accrediting agency (such as American Association of Bible Colleges, Association of Independent Colleges and Schools, National Association of Trade and Technical Schools, National Home Study Council) is encouraged to deal with the appropriate specialized agency. If the institution desires to

seek only regional accreditation, the institution should
so inform the specialized agency.

- A specialized institution seeking accreditation from
two or more national, specialized accrediting agencies
must determine what constitutes its predominant emphasis (specialization), and that determination will
identify the appropriate coordinating agency.
- A specialized institution for which there is a programmatic accrediting agency that accredits free-standing specialized institutions (such as American Bar Association, Association of Theological Schools, National
Association of Schools of Music, and so on) is encouraged to deal with the appropriate programmatic agency.
If the institution desires to seek accreditation from an
institutional accrediting agency as well, the programmatic agency would serve as the coordinating agency.
If the institution desires to seek only institutional accreditation, the institution should so inform the programmatic agency.

b. Between institutional and programmatic accrediting
agencies

- When a multipurpose institution seeks a coordinated accreditation process involving both an institutional accrediting agency and one or more programmatic
accrediting agencies, the institutional accrediting agency will serve as the coordinating agency. In instances
where there are one or more clusters of related programmatic agencies, there should be a coordinating
agency for each cluster which in turn would work with
the institutional accrediting agency.
- When external coordination is not possible, an institution should seek accreditation for an academic administrative unit or subunit within the institution after
it has achieved appropriate accreditation of the more
inclusive entity (total institution, college school, division, department, program—in that order).

c. Between programmatic accrediting agencies

- When an institution seeks accreditation involving

two or more programmatic accrediting agencies (located within the same or in different academic administrative units), the chief administrative officer of the institution, with mutual agreement and consent of the involved accrediting agencies, shall designate the coordinating agency, with responsibility normally going to the agency representing the program with the largest enrollment. This agency will coordinate the accrediting activities (joint and/or autonomous) consistent with the established guidelines.

4. *Accreditation standards:*
The accreditation standards of the participating accrediting agencies (institutional and programmatic) shall apply during the review. Team members should be aware of the range of standards being utilized. Procedures followed during the visit and the subsequent reporting phase must reflect the standards as required by each agency. In instances where standards may overlap or vary, the visit and the report must incorporate data relevant to the specific agencies.

5. *Contacts with institutions:*
Accrediting agencies which utilize staff previsits should arrange a joint institutional visit to negotiate details of the cooperative accrediting process. Where all parties are not involved in a previsit, participating agencies will contact the institution individually regarding the self-study, the visit, and other expectations. However, these contacts must be carefully coordinated to eliminate conflicting instructions regarding the joint accrediting process. Participating institutions should be flexible in establishing visitation dates.

6. *Self-study alternatives:*
When the institution, or an administrative unit within an institution, is seeking accreditation from more than one agency, the self-study may take a variety of forms, including the following: (a) common self-study, (b) core self-study, with varying supplemental analyses, (c) separate self-studies, with certain common elements, (d) a nontraditional alternative.

Institutions may wish to prepare single reporting documents designed to meet all requirements of each agency. The nature and format of the self-study document should be negotiated at the time a joint accrediting cycle is initiated. Where the team will function as a unit (such as an institutional agency and programmatic agency visiting a single-purpose institution), a common self-study is indicated. In multipurpose institutions, joint visits may be concurrent rather than coordinated. In the consultative stages establishing the accrediting process, a procedure for responding adequately to the data needs of all the accrediting agencies should be negotiated.

7. *Visiting team and on-site visit:*
    Written agreements should include the team's composition; the complementary skills required and the responsibility for their selection; designation of the chairman (who will normally be from the coordinating agency); procedures to be followed during the visit; the format of the written report; the process of its development; the nature of recommendations; and their reporting to the institution.

    Cooperating agencies are encouraged to share data about potential site visitors, forming common pools of names where possible or exchanging information in specific situations. All site visitors may be selected from the common pool by the coordinating agency, or the cooperating agencies may determine criteria (size of team, areas of competency desired, background experience related to institution to be visited, and so on) and specify the number of team members to be selected by each cooperating agency. Where there are only two cooperating agencies, cochairmen may be designated by each agency. The chairman (cochairmen) is responsible for making logistical arrangements.

    A specialized accrediting agency can add a valuable dimension by working cooperatively with an appropriate institutional accrediting agency in the selection of a generalist to serve on the team. Where an institutional accrediting agency needs certain expertise on a team, the appropriate specialized accrediting agency can provide assistance. In developing cooperative team arrangements, however, the integrity of the review process must be preserved. Generalists cannot effectively replace specialists, or vice versa, and a large team representing several accrediting agencies may not be as effective as coordinated multiple teams.

8. *Commission action:*
Accrediting decisions on reports are made in accordance with the policies established by the participating agencies. Where a common team report is filed, each accrediting commission should receive a copy. Where no common report is feasible, each accrediting commission takes action on the report prepared by its team representatives. Each commission should take such action as its standards require and as supported by the report data. Accrediting actions by any commission (institutional or programmatic) should be shared with participating accrediting agencies.

9. *Fees and costs:*
Because the costs of an accrediting cycle could be reduced through coordination among accrediting agencies, fees and costs should be determined between and among accrediting agencies prior to the accrediting process. The institution is responsible for paying the usual or reduced fees to each agency to cover any cost of general agency services related to the accrediting cycle. Direct costs of a site visit can be reduced through such cooperative arrangements as a joint team, and therefore the fee to the institution can be proportionately reduced. In instances where a cooperating agency does not assess a fee to the institution, its proportionate costs will have to be determined and that agency would honor its share. Each agency should handle its own billing.

It should be noted that one of the most significant reductions in the cost burden to the institution can result from a combined self-study, reporting system, and so on.

Resource D

ⰉⰉⰉⰉⰉⰉⰉⰉⰉⰉⰉⰉⰉⰉⰉⰉⰉⰉⰉⰉⰉⰉⰉⰉⰉⰉ

Policy Statement on the Role and Value of Accreditation

Accreditation is an activity long accepted in the United States but generally unknown in most other countries because other countries rely on governmental supervision and control of educational institutions. The record of accomplishment and outstanding success in the education of Americans can be traced in large part to the reluctance of the United States to impose governmental restrictions on institutions of postsecondary education and to the success of the voluntary American system of accreditation in promoting quality without inhibiting innovation. The high proportion of Americans benefiting from higher education, the reputation of universities in the United States for both fundamental and applied research, and the widespread availability of professional services in the United States all testify to postsecondary education of high quality and to the success of the accreditation system which the institutions and professions of the United States have devised to promote that quality.

Adopted by the COPA board April 15, 1982; reprinted by permission of COPA.

I

Accreditation is a status granted to an educational institution or a program that has been found to meet or exceed stated criteria of educational quality. In the United States accreditation is voluntarily sought by institutions and programs and is conferred by nongovernmental bodies.

Accreditation has two fundamental purposes: to assure the quality of the institution or program and to assist in the improvement of the institution or program. Accreditation, which applies to institutions or programs, is to be distinguished from certification and licensure, which apply to individuals.

The bodies conducting institutional accreditation are national or regional in scope and comprise the institutions that have achieved and maintain accreditation. A specialized body conducting accreditation of a program preparing students for a profession or occupation is often closely associated with professional associations in the field.

Both institutional and specialized bodies conduct the accreditation process using a common pattern. The pattern requires integral self-study of the institution or program, followed by an on-site visit by an evaluation team and a subsequent review and decision by a central governing group. Within this general pattern the various accrediting bodies have developed a variety of individual procedures adapted to their own circumstances. Increasingly, attention has been given to educational outcomes as a basis for evaluation.

Members of the Council on Postsecondary Accreditation have been found by COPA to meet specific criteria of procedure and organization regarded as necessary for the effective conduct of the accrediting process. A COPA-recognized accrediting body can be regarded as qualified to conduct evaluations of institutions and/or programs seeking accreditation, and accreditation by such bodies is generally recognized and accepted in higher education.

Institutional or specialized accreditation cannot guarantee the quality of individual graduates or of individual courses within an institution or program but can give reasonable assurance of the context and quality of the education offered.

II

An institutional accrediting body considers the characteristics of whole institutions. For this reason an institutional accrediting body gives attention not only to the educational offerings of the institutions it accredits but also to other such institutional characteristics as the student personnel services, financial conditions, and administrative strength.

The criteria of an institutional accrediting body are broad, as is demanded by the attention to an entire institution and by the presence in the United States of postsecondary institutions of widely different purposes and scopes. Such criteria also provide encouragement to institutions to try innovative curricula and procedures and to adopt them when they prove successful. The accreditation of an institution by an institutional accrediting body certifies to the general criteria that the institution:

a.   Has appropriate purposes;
b.   Has the resources needed to accomplish its purposes;
c.   Can demonstrate that it is accomplishing its purposes;
d.   Gives reason to believe that it will continue to accomplish its purposes.

Institutional improvement is encouraged by an institutional accrediting body through the requirement that the accredited institution conduct periodic self-evaluations seeking to identify what the institution does well, determining the areas in which improvement is needed, and developing plans to address needed improvements. While the certification of accreditation indicates an acceptable level of institutional quality, any institution, however excellent, is capable of improvement, which must come from its own clear identification and understanding of its strengths and weaknesses.

Institutional improvement is also encouraged by the institutional accrediting body through the advice and counsel provided by the visiting team, which comprises experienced educators drawn primarily from accredited institutions, and by the publications of the accrediting body.

III

A specialized accrediting body focuses its attention on a particular program within an institution of higher education. The close relationship of the specialized accrediting body with the professional association for the field helps ensure that the requirements for accreditation are related to the current requirements for professional practice.

In a number of fields (for example, medicine, law, dentistry) graduation from an accredited program in the field is a requirement for receiving a license to practice in the field. Thus, specialized accreditation is recognized as providing a basic assurance of the scope and quality of professional or occupational preparation. This focus of specialized accreditation leads to accreditation requirements that are generally sharply directed to the nature of the program, including specific requirements for resources needed to provide a program satisfactory for professional preparation. Because of this limitation of focus to a single program, many specialized accrediting bodies require that the institution offering the program be institutionally accredited before consideration can be given to program accreditation.

Specialized accreditation encourages program improvement by application of specific accreditation requirements to measure characteristics of a program and by making judgments about the overall quality of the program. For a nonaccredited program, the accreditation requirements serve as specific goals to be achieved. In addition to accrediting standards, assistance for program improvement is provided through the counsel of the accreditation visiting-team members, which include practitioners of the profession and experienced and successful faculty members and administrators in other institutions.

IV

Institutional and specialized accreditation are complementary. The focus of an institutional accrediting body on an institution as a total operating unit provides assurance that the general characteristics of the institution have been examined and found to be satisfactory. The focus of a specialized accrediting body on a specific program provides assurance that the details of that particular program meet the external accreditation standards. Institutional accreditation, concerned with evaluating the institution as a whole, does not seek to deal with any particular program in great detail, although programs are reviewed as a part of the consideration of the entire institution. Specialized accreditation, speaking to a specific program, does not seek to deal significantly with the general conditions of the institution, although certain general conditions are considered in the context in which the accredited program is offered. Occasionally there are institutions offering but a single program ("freestanding" schools), which may seek institutional and/or specialized accreditation. In such cases, the certification of the accreditation is that appropriate to either institutional or specialized accreditation and does not imply both certifications, although a specialized body accrediting such an institution is expected to look at the whole institution, just as the institutional body is expected to consider the single educational program.

V

In fulfilling its two purposes, quality assurance and institutional and program improvement, accreditation provides service of value to several constituencies.

To the public, the values of accreditation include:

a. An assurance of external evaluation of the institution or program and a finding that there is conformity to general expectations in higher education or the professional field;
b. An identification of institutions and programs which have voluntarily undertaken explicit activities directed at improving the quality of the institution and its professional programs and are carrying them out successfully;
c. An improvement in the professional services available to the public, as accredited programs modify their requirements to reflect changes in knowledge and practice generally accepted in the field;

d. A decreased need for intervention by public agencies in the operations of educational institutions, since their institutions through accreditation are providing privately for the maintenance and enhancement of educational quality.

To students, accreditation provides:

a. An assurance that the educational activities of an accredited institution or program have been found to be satisfactory and therefore meet the needs of students;
b. Assistance in the transfer of credits between institutions or in the admission of students to advanced degrees through the general acceptance of credits among accredited institutions when the performance of the student has been satisfactory and the credits to be transferred are appropriate to the receiving institution;
c. A prerequisite in many cases for entering a profession.

Institutions of higher education benefit from accreditation through:

a. The stimulus provided for self-evaluation and self-directed institutional and program improvement;
b. The strengthening of institutional and program self-evaluation by the review and counsel provided through the accrediting body;
c. The application of criteria of accrediting bodies, generally accepted throughout higher education, which help guard against external encroachments harmful to institutional or program quality by providing benchmarks independent of forces that might impinge on individual institutions;
d. The enhancing of the reputation of an accredited institution or program because of public regard for accreditation;
e. The use of accreditation as one means by which an institution can gain eligibility for the participation of itself and its students in certain programs of governmental aid to postsecondary education; accreditation is also usually relied upon

by private foundations as a highly desirable indicator of institutional and program quality.

Accreditation serves the professions by:

a. Providing a means for the participation of practitioners in setting the requirements for preparation to enter the professions;
b. Contributing to the unity of the professions by bringing together practitioners, teachers, and students in an activity directed at improving professional preparation and professional practice.

Resource E

ﻙﻙﻙﻙﻙﻙﻙﻙﻙﻙﻙﻙﻙﻙﻙﻙﻙﻙﻙﻙﻙﻙﻙﻙﻙﻙﻙﻙﻙ

Glossary

General

Accreditation—Concept. Postsecondary accreditation is the concept—broadly developed in the United States—whereby groups of educational institutions, professional practitioners, or educators form voluntary, nongovernmental associations (1) to encourage and assist individual institutions or programs in the evaluation and improvement of their educational endeavors and (2) to identify publicly those institutions or specialized units which meet or exceed commonly accepted standards of educational quality.

Accreditation—Process. Postsecondary accreditation is a process by which an institution or a specialized unit of postsecondary

This glossary was developed by a COPA task force and reviewed by COPA's Committee on Recognition. It was reported to the COPA board at its meeting on April 12-16, 1982, as a document that "may be used by those who wish but it will not be published [by COPA]."

449

education periodically evaluates its educational activities and
seeks an independent judgment by peers that it achieves substantially its own educational objectives and meets the established standards of the body by which it seeks accreditation.
Generally, the accreditation process involves (1) a clear statement of the institution's or unit's educational objectives; (2) a
self-study by the institution or unit which examines its activities
in relation to those objectives; (3) an on-site evaluation by a selected group of peers which reports to the accrediting body; and
(4) a decision by this independent body that the institution or
unit does or does not meet its standards for accreditation.

Accreditation Liaison Officer. An accreditation liaison officer is
the person in an institution of postsecondary education designated to work with one or more accrediting bodies on matters
relating to the accreditation of the institution and/or its specialized units.

Accrediting Body. An accrediting body is a voluntary, nongovernmental association that administers accrediting procedures
for entire institutions or for specialized units. A *recognized* accrediting body is one formally acknowledged by the Council on
Postsecondary Accreditation (COPA) as having met COPA's
provisions and procedures for recognition. A *listed* accrediting
body is one determined by the secretary of education to be a reliable authority on educational quality as part of the Department of Education's process for determining an institution's eligibility for certain federal funds.

Educational Quality. Because of the great diversity in purpose
and form represented by American higher education, educational quality cannot be defined adequately in terms of specific
standards or requirements applied uniformly to all institutions
and specialized units. For purposes of accreditation, however,
an institution or specialized unit with accreditable educational
quality is one that has appropriate objectives, a sound strategy
for achieving those objectives as judged by the standards of the
body providing accreditation, an ability to assemble and apply

resources adequate to that strategy, and an ability to measure the attainment of its objectives.

Institution of Postsecondary Education. An institution of postsecondary education, for purposes of accreditation, is an enterprise whose main objective is the offering of educational programs and/or the evaluation of educational attainments primarily for persons who have completed secondary school. Such an institution will (1) be chartered or licensed (where available) for such purposes; (2) have stated educational objectives appropriate to the postsecondary level which lend themselves to evaluation; (3) be under the legal control of a lay board (or its equivalent); and (4) have a faculty which plays a meaningful role in determining educational standards.

Institutional Integrity. A postsecondary educational institution exhibits a high degree of integrity when it conducts all its activities fairly and justly, providing adequate notice of its policies and procedures and conscientiously adhering to accepted good practices. While accreditation focuses its attention upon those matters most closely related to an institution's educational offerings, it recognizes that educational quality is fostered and protected in an institutional setting with well-established policies and procedures in all important areas of operation, and it expects an accreditable institution to be forthright in stating and reliable in adhering to these policies and procedures.

Public Interest. The interest of the public at large in any activity arises from the effects of that activity on the general welfare. In particular, there is a public interest in the proper operation of institutions of postsecondary education, because their activities result in the education and training of persons to take responsible positions in society. Similarly, since accreditation provides for an institution or its units a judgment about its educational quality in which the public places confidence, there is a public interest in the activities of accrediting bodies. In recognition of this public interest in accreditation, accrediting bodies are expected to issue useful, accurate public reports on their activities, to appoint one or more public representatives to their commissions, and to follow due process in their decision making.

Public Representative. To help ensure appropriate representation of the public interest, public representatives are usually drawn from persons who do not have other interests in accreditation. Thus the public representatives on accrediting bodies are not employed by postsecondary educational institutions or by an accrediting body or by an agency of government which deals primarily with postsecondary education. On occasion persons who hold nonremunerative appointments with postsecondary institutions, such as members of governing boards, may serve as public representatives on accrediting bodies.

Self-Regulation. Self-regulation is based on the recognition that most human activities are ruled satisfactorily through the awareness of their effect on or acceptance by others. Accreditation—as a voluntary and nongovernmental activity, as a process organized around self-study and peer review, and as an advocate for institutional autonomy—plays a major role in preserving the self-regulatory quality of American postsecondary education. Other dimensions of self-regulation in postsecondary education include the maintaining of guidelines for, and institutional commitment to, good practice, as well as the willingness of accrediting bodies to monitor by exception between accreditation reviews (that is, to investigate only matters which appear to be contrary to presumed acceptable practices).

Accrediting Process

Application. An application is the formal request submitted to an accrediting body by an institution of postsecondary education when it or one of its specialized units wishes to be considered for accreditation or for candidacy for accreditation.

Criteria. Generally speaking, criteria—along with *standards, requirements,* or *essentials*—are statements reflecting an accrediting association's expectations of an accreditable institution or specialized unit. While different distinctions among these terms are made by the various accrediting bodies, within a single body the criteria (and/or standards, requirements, or essentials) provide a common frame of reference within which institutions or specialized units are evaluated and accredited. The auxiliary verbs used in the wording of criteria are *shall* and *must*.

Educational Objectives. Educational objectives are statements developed by postsecondary educational institutions which describe the goals of the teaching/learning process within an institution or unit and in the context of which an accrediting body makes its evaluation. Such objectives, in order to be useful for the purposes of accreditation, must lend themselves to evaluation.

Guidelines. Guidelines are explanatory statements which amplify the criteria (standards, requirements, essentials) for accreditation. They usually provide examples of the way criteria may be interpreted to allow for flexibility while remaining within the framework of the criteria. The auxiliary verbs used in the wording of guidelines are *should* and *may*.

Self-Study. The self-study is a comprehensive analysis of the educational resources and effectiveness of an institution or specialized unit in relation to its educational objectives. The immediate product of this process is the self-study report or educational statement. Just as the self-study is the foundation of the accrediting process, the self-study report is the essential document in the process.

On-Site Evaluation. The on-site evaluation consists of the visit to an institution or educational unit by a team of peers appointed by the accrediting body specifically for their competencies relevant to the institution or unit being evaluated. The on-site visit follows the completion of the self-study and the submission of the self-study report to the accrediting body. This visit enables the evaluation team to determine the accuracy and completeness of the self-study and to evaluate the applicant's effectiveness within the context of its stated educational objectives and in light of the accrediting body's criteria.

Types of Accreditation

Institutional Accreditation. Institutional accreditation is a status accorded an institution of postsecondary education which embraces the whole institution as it defines itself and therefore includes all areas, activities, and programs. Normally, institutional accreditation testifies to (a) the appropriateness of the objectives of the institution; (b) the adequacy of its organization, program, and resources, both material and human, when viewed against its objectives and generally accepted accrediting standards; and (c) evidence of the accomplishment of institutional objectives in reasonable measure. Moreover, the criteria of eligibility provide that degree programs, however specialized, must rest upon a base of liberal or general studies required of all or most students. However, accreditation of the institution as a whole is not, and should not be interpreted as being, equivalent to specialized accreditation of a part or program of the institution and should not be represented as such. The nine commissions of postsecondary accreditation in the six regional accrediting associations accredit a variety of institutions within their geographic regions. Also, several national accrediting bodies provide institutional accreditation for special-purpose institutions throughout the United States. And, finally, specialized accrediting bodies, when they accredit single-purpose institutions, provide institutional as well as programmatic accreditation.

Specialized Accreditation. Specialized accreditation is a status accorded a special unit within an institution of postsecondary accreditation, which may be a college, school, division, department, program, or curriculum. In the case of a single-purpose institution, specialized accreditation also constitutes institutional accreditation. The focus of specialized accreditation is the effectiveness with which the program meets its objectives, those of the institution, and the accrediting standards for quality education. Normally, specialized accreditation reviews the relationship of the program to the larger unit, the adequacy of the organization and resources for program maintenance and development, and evidence of accomplishment of programmatic objectives. However, specialized accreditation does not purport to make judgments on the institution as a whole, except in the cases of single-purpose institutions.

Accreditation Classifications

Accreditation. Accreditation is a status granted an institution or specialized unit which has undergone the accrediting process and has been judged to meet or exceed the commonly accepted standards of educational quality informing the accrediting body's criteria.

Candidate for Accreditation. Candidacy for accreditation is a status that may be granted by an accrediting body indicating that an institution or unit has expressed its desire to become accredited and that the accrediting body judges the institution or unit to have the potential for achieving accreditation within a reasonable period, normally a maximum of six years. Candidacy, however, does not assure accreditation. (This status may also be referred to as preaccreditation status.)

Conditional Accreditation. Conditional accreditation is a status indicating that an institution or a unit has certain deficiencies which must be corrected within a specified period of time in order for the institution or unit to remain accredited. (While some accrediting bodies may make certain distinctions among these terms, conditional accreditation may also be referred to as *probationary* or *provisional accreditation*.)

Membership. Membership is the status held by an accredited institution or unit with some accrediting bodies. In some cases accreditation automatically results in membership; in others, accreditation does not imply membership in the body; in others still, membership is an additional status available to an accredited institution or unit as an option.

Accreditation Actions

Adverse Action. An adverse action is the placing of an institution or specialized unit on probation, the censuring of such an institution or unit for failing to refrain from or to initiate some activity, or the withholding or withdrawal by an accrediting body of accreditation or candidacy for accreditation status. Time limitations or other conditions imposed as part of accreditation decisions normally do not constitute adverse actions.

Appeal. An appeal procedure is the opportunity afforded an institution or specialized unit to request a formal review of an adverse action. An appeal is based normally on a challenge of factual information in the evaluation report, on disagreement with the interpretation of facts, or on an alleged violation by the accrediting body of its published procedures. Dissatisfaction with the reasons behind an accreditation decision is not, in itself, considered an acceptable basis for appeal. An appeal body should be different from that group involved in the original decision.

Complaint. A complaint is a written, signed allegation that an institution or specialized unit has engaged in actions which do not conform to its stated policies and procedures or that could seriously retard or disrupt its educational effectiveness. When a well-founded, written complaint is received, the accrediting body asks the institution or unit to respond, and if circumstances appear to warrant further action, the accrediting body may conduct a confidential investigation, with the knowledge of and in consultation with concerned parties. The results of the investigation will be reported to the accrediting body for its consideration and possible action.

A complaint is also a written allegation by an institution or unit that a COPA-recognized accrediting body has violated its own criteria or procedures. When it is established that an institution or unit has used all appeals processes afforded it by the accrediting body, the COPA president shall first encourage the parties to resolve their differences informally and, when necessary, will appoint a three-person investigation panel which shall pass its recommendations to the COPA board through the COPA Executive Committee.

"Show Cause." A "show cause" notice is one which announces a contemplated adverse action by an accrediting body and invites the institution or specialized unit to provide persuasive evidence and argument that the projected action should not be taken. Such notices normally provide several months for the preparation of such evidence and argument.

Substantive Change. A substantive change within an accredited institution or a specialized unit is one which significantly alters its objectives, scope, or control (such as the establishment of a relatively permanent instructional operation at a new geographic location). An accredited institution or unit planning a substantive change is responsible for providing in advance the planning documents for such a change to the concerned accrediting body or bodies, and, in some instances, accreditation approval must be received in advance.

Accreditation-Related Activities

Approval. Approval is an act of an officially authorized state governmental agency certifying that a unit or program within an institution of postsecondary education complies with established minimum legal requirements.

Certification. Certification is a process by which a nongovernmental organization grants recognition to a person who has met certain predetermined qualifications specified by that organization and who voluntarily seeks such recognition.

Eligibility. Eligibility is a status granted by an agency of federal or state government indicating that an institution of postsecondary education qualifies as a recipient of a specified funding program.

Licensure. Licensure is a process by which an agency of government grants permission (1) to persons meeting predetermined qualifications to engage in a given occupation and/or to use a particular title and (2) to institutions to perform specified functions.

Listing. Listing is the activity required by legislation of the secretary of the U.S. Department of Education, who maintains a list of nationally recognized accrediting bodies determined to be reliable authorities on educational quality. Accreditation by a listed accrediting body is one consideration in determining the eligibility of an institution to receive certain federal funds.

Program Registry. Program registry is a procedure by which a nongovernmental association, through a reporting relationship, (1) determines that one or more programs within an institution meet specified requirements and (2) maintains and publishes lists of these programs. Also called *program approval* upon occasion, program registry does not normally involve self-study or on-site visits.

Recognition. Recognition is the process followed by the Council on Postsecondary Accreditation whereby accrediting bodies apply and are reviewed at least every five years in accordance with established provisions and procedures. The purpose of this recognition is to provide institutions of postsecondary education and other users of accreditation with guidance concerning accrediting bodies.

Satisfactory Assurance. Satisfactory assurance is a determination by the secretary of education, as called for by law, that, considering the resources available to an institution, the period of time (if any) during which it has operated, the effort it is making to meet accreditation standards, and the purpose for which this determination is being made, an institution will meet the accreditation standards of a listed accrediting body within a reasonable time. An institution meeting this test and other requirements can become eligible to apply for certain federal funds.

Bibliography

Abbott, F. G. *Government Policy and Higher Education: A Study of the Regents of the University of the State of New York, 1784–1949.* New York: Cornell University Press, 1958.

Acton, Lord (J. E. E. Dahlberg). "History of Freedom in Antiquity." Lecture delivered at the Bridgenorth Institute, May 28, 1877. In *The History of Freedom and Other Essays* (London: Macmillan, 1907). Quoted in G. Himmelfarb (Ed.), *Essays on Freedom and Power* (Glencoe, Ill.: Free Press, 1948).

Agnew, D. C. *Seventy-Five Years of Educational Leadership.* Atlanta: Southern Association of Colleges and Schools, 1970.

Aikin, W. M. *The Story of the Eight-Year Study.* New York: Harper & Row, 1942.

Allen, F. L. *The Big Change: America Transforms Itself, 1900–1950.* New York: Harper & Row, 1952.

Allen, G. J. "A History of the Commission on Colleges of the Southern Association of Colleges and Schools, 1949–1975." Unpublished doctoral dissertation, Georgia State University, 1978.

Alverno College Faculty. *Assessment at Alverno College.* Milwaukee: Alverno Productions, 1979.

American Assembly of Collegiate Schools of Business. "Accreditation Research Project: Report of Phase I." *AACSB Bulletin,* 1980, *15*(2), 1–46.

American Council on Education, National Commission on Higher Education Issues. *To Strengthen Quality in Higher Education.* Washington, D.C.: American Council on Education, 1982.

American Council on Education, Task Force on Educational Credit and Credentials. *Recommendations on Credentialing Education Accomplishment.* Washington, D.C.: American Council on Education, 1978.

American Council on Education. *Policy Guidelines for Refund of Student Charges.* Self-Regulation Initiatives: Guidelines for Colleges and Universities, No. 1 (August 1979). Washington, D.C.: American Council on Education, 1979a.

American Council on Education. *Joint Statement on Principles of Good Practice in College Admissions and Recruitment.* Self-Regulation Initiatives: Guidelines for Colleges and Universities, No. 2 (October 1979). Washington, D.C.: American Council on Education, 1979b.

American Council on Education. *Collegiate Athletics Policy Statements.* Self-Regulation Initiatives: Guidelines for Colleges and Universities, No. 3 (November 1979). Washington, D.C.: American Council on Education, 1979c.

American Council on Education. *Joint Statement on Transfer and Award of Academic Credit.* Self-Regulation Initiatives: Guidelines for Colleges and Universities, No. 4 (January 1980). Washington, D.C.: American Council on Education, 1980a.

American Council on Education. *Accredited Institutions of Postsecondary Education: 1980–81.* Washington, D.C.: American Council on Education (for the Council on Postsecondary Accreditation), 1980b.

American Council on Education. *Joint Statement on Standards of Satisfactory Academic Progress to Maintain Financial Aid Eligibility.* Self-Regulation Initiatives: Guidelines for Colleges and Universities, No. 5 (December 1981). Washington, D.C.: American Council on Education, 1981a.

American Council on Education. *Academic Integrity and Athletic Eligibility.* Self-Regulation Initiatives: Guidelines for

Colleges and Universities, No. 6 (December 1981). Washington, D.C.: American Council on Education, 1981b.

American Council on Education. *Confidentiality of College and University Faculty Personnel Files: Its Appropriate Role in Institutional Affairs.* Self-Regulation Initiatives: Guidelines for Colleges and Universities, No. 7 (December 1981). Washington, D.C.: American Council on Education, 1981c.

American Medical Association. "Report of the Council on Medical Education to House of Delegates of American Medical Association." *Journal of the American Medical Association,* July 22, 1905, *45,* 269.

American Medical Association. Minutes of the Meeting of the Council on Medical Education of the American Medical Association in New York in December 1908.

American Medical Association. *A History of the Council on Medical Education and Hospitals of the American Medical Association, 1904-1959.* Chicago: American Medical Association, 1960.

American Physical Therapy Association. *Accreditation Handbook.* Washington, D.C.: American Physical Therapy Association, 1982.

Anderson, J. T. "A Study of Accreditation Standards and Predictors of Student Achievement." Unpublished doctoral dissertation, University of South Carolina, 1973.

Andrews, G. J. *Assessing Nontraditional Education: A Summary of the Project REPORT.* Washington, D.C.: Council on Postsecondary Accreditation, 1978.

Andrews, G. J., and others. *Assessing Nontraditional Education.* (4 vols.) Washington, D.C.: Council on Postsecondary Accreditation, 1978.

Arnstein, G. E. "Accreditation, State Licensing, and Approvals: Why the System Isn't Working." *Phi Delta Kappan,* 1975, *56,* 396-398.

Arnstein, G. E. "Two Cheers for Accreditation." *AGB Report,* July/August 1979, *21,* 35-41.

Ashworth, K. H. "Gresham's Law in the Marketplace of Ideas: Are Bad Degrees Driving Out the Good?" *Chronicle of Higher Education,* October 6, 1980, p. 64.

Association of Colleges and Schools of the Southern States. *Pro-*

ceedings of the Thirty-First Annual Meeting. Birmingham, Ala.: Birmingham Publishing Company, 1926.

Association of Governing Boards of Universities and Colleges. *The Board's Role in Accreditation.* Washington, D.C.: Association of Governing Boards in Universities and Colleges, 1983.

Association of Independent Colleges and Schools Accrediting Commission. *Accreditation Standards: Policies, Procedures, and Criteria—Committee Draft.* Washington, D.C.: Association of Independent Colleges and Schools, 1979.

Association of Independent Colleges and Schools Accrediting Commission. *Accreditation Standards: Policies, Procedures, and Criteria.* Washington, D.C.: Association of Independent Colleges and Schools, 1980.

Astin, A. W. "Student-Oriented Management: A Proposal for Change." In A. W. Astin, H. R. Bowen, and C. M. Chambers, *Evaluating Educational Quality: A Conference Summary.* Washington, D.C.: Council on Postsecondary Accreditation, 1979.

Astin, A. W., Bowen, H. R., and Chambers, C. M. *Evaluating Educational Quality: A Conference Summary.* Washington, D.C.: Council on Postsecondary Accreditation, 1979.

Atkin, J. M. "Institutional Self-Evaluation Versus National Professional Accreditation or Back to the Normal School?" *Educational Researcher,* November 1978, pp. 3–7.

Balitzer, A. *A Nation of Associations: The Origin, Development, and Theory of the Political Action Committee.* Washington, D.C.: American Society of Association Executives and the American Medical Action Committee, 1981.

Baysore, G. C. "The Selection, Training, and Evaluation of Examiners in Selected Accrediting Associations." Unpublished doctoral dissertation, University of Denver, 1971.

Bell, D. *The Coming of the Post-Industrial Society: A Venture in Social Forecasting.* New York: Basic Books, 1973.

Birch, G. E. "State Higher Education Responsibility for the Evaluation and Accreditation of Public Four-Year Institutions of Higher Education." Unpublished doctoral dissertation, Center for the Study of Higher Education, University of Arizona, 1979.

Bloom, B., and others. *Taxonomy of Educational Objectives, Handbook I: The Cognitive Domain.* New York: McKay, 1956.

Botkin, J. W., Elmandjra, M., and Malitza, M. *No Limits to Learning: Bridging the Human Gap.* A report to the Club of Rome. New York: Pergamon Press, 1979.

Bowen, H. R. "Goals, Outcomes, and Academic Evaluation." In A. W. Astin, H. R. Bowen, and C. M. Chambers, *Evaluating Educational Quality: A Conference Summary.* Washington, D.C.: Council on Postsecondary Accreditation, 1979.

Bowen, H. R. Remarks on behalf of the Self-Study Advisory Panel made before the Board of the Council on Postsecondary Accreditation, Washington, D.C., October 13, 1981.

Brickman, W. W., and Lehrer, S. *A Century of Higher Education: Classical Citadel to Collegiate Colossus.* New York: Society for the Advancement of Education, 1962.

Brubacher, J. S., and Rudy, W. *Higher Education in Transition: A History of American Colleges and Universities, 1636–1976.* (3rd ed.) New York: Harper & Row, 1976.

Burns, N. "Accreditation by the North Central Association of Colleges and Secondary Schools." In R. J. Deferrari (Ed.), *Self-Evaluation and Accreditation in Higher Education.* Washington, D.C.: Catholic University of America Press, 1959.

Butts, R. F. *The College Charts Its Course: Historical Conceptions and Current Proposals.* New York: McGraw-Hill, 1939.

Califano, J. A., Jr. Testimony Before the Subcommittee on Postsecondary Education, July 19, 1979. Washington, D.C.: U.S. Department of Health, Education and Welfare, 1979.

Campbell, J. P. "On the Nature of Organizational Effectiveness." In P. S. Goodman, J. M. Jennings, and Associates, *New Perspectives on Organizational Effectiveness.* San Francisco: Jossey-Bass, 1977.

Capen, S. P. "College Lists and Surveys Published by the Bureau of Education." *School and Society,* July 14, 1917, pp. 35–41.

Capen, S. P. "Seven Devils in Exchange for One." In *Coordination of Accrediting Activities.* American Council on Education Studies, Series 1, Volume 3, Number 9. Washington, D.C.: American Council on Education, 1939.

Cardiff, I. L. *What Great Men Think of Religion.* New York: Arno Press, 1972. (Originally published, 1945.)

Cardozo, M. H. *The Association Process, 1963-1973.* Washington, D.C.: Association of American Law Schools, 1975.

Carmichael, O. M., Jr. *New York Establishes a State University.* Nashville: Vanderbilt University Press, 1955.

Carnegie Commission on Higher Education. *The Capitol and the Campus: State Responsibility for Postsecondary Education.* New York: McGraw-Hill, 1971.

Carnegie Council on Policy Studies in Higher Education. *Fair Practices in Higher Education: Rights and Responsibilities of Students and Their Colleges in a Period of Intensified Competition for Enrollments.* San Francisco: Jossey-Bass, 1979.

Carnegie Foundation for the Advancement of Teaching. *The Control of the Campus: A Report on the Governance of Higher Education.* A Carnegie Foundation Essay. Washington, D.C.: Carnegie Foundation for the Advancement of Teaching, 1982.

Carroll, L. *Alice's Adventures in Wonderland.* New York: Random House, 1946. (Originally published, 1865.)

Casey, R. J., and Harris, J. W. *Accountability in Higher Education.* Washington, D.C.: Council on Postsecondary Accreditation, 1979.

Chapman, D. W. (Ed.). *Improving College Information for Prospective Students.* Washington, D.C.: Council for Advancement and Support of Education, 1980.

Chapman, D. W., Griffith, J. V., and Johnson, R. H. *A Checklist for Evaluating College Recruitment Literature.* Ann Arbor: Project CHOICE, University of Michigan, 1979.

Chickering, A. W., McDowell, J., and Compagna, D. "Institutional Differences and Student Development." *Journal of Educational Psychology,* 1969, *60,* 315-326.

Clark, M. J., and Hartnett, R. T. *The Assessment of Quality in Graduate Education: Summary of a Multidimensional Approach.* Washington, D.C.: Council of Graduate Schools, 1978.

Commission on Colleges. "Progress Report of the Project for the Review of the Process and Standards of Accreditation."

Atlanta, Ga.: Southern Association of Colleges and Schools, 1981a.

Commission on Colleges. Report of the Subcommittee to Survey the State of the Art of Outcomes Assessment in Higher Education. Atlanta, Ga.: Southern Association of Colleges and Schools, 1981b.

Commission on Non-Traditional Study (S. B. Gould, Chairman). *Diversity by Design.* San Francisco: Jossey-Bass, 1973.

Commission on Private Philanthropy and Public Needs (J. H. Filer, Chairman). *Giving in America: Toward a Stronger Voluntary Sector.* Washington, D.C.: Commission on Private Philanthropy and Public Needs, 1975.

Committee on Accreditation and Agency Evaluation. *Proceedings, June 20, 1979.* Washington, D.C.: Office of Education, U.S. Department of Health, Education and Welfare, 1979.

Conference Minutes. Conference of associations of delegates assembled at Williamstown, August 3 and 4, 1906.

Conference Minutes. National Conference Committee of the Associations of Colleges and Preparatory Schools assembled at Williamstown, June 28 and 29, 1907.

Continuing Professional Education Development Project (University of Pennsylvania). *Continuing Professional Education Development Project News,* April 1981.

Council on Postsecondary Accreditation. *Accreditation.* Newsletter.

Council on Postsecondary Accreditation. *Bylaws.* January 15, 1975.

Council on Postsecondary Accreditation. *Presidents' Bulletin.* Newsletter.

Council on Postsecondary Accreditation. *Provisions and Procedures for Becoming Recognized as an Accrediting Agency for Postsecondary Educational Institutions or Programs.* Washington, D.C.: Council on Postsecondary Accreditation, 1975. (Revised 1981; see Resource B.)

Council on Postsecondary Accreditation. *Summary of Data Reported by the Thirty-Eight Specialized Accrediting Agencies.* Washington, D.C.: Council on Postsecondary Accreditation, 1978a.

Council on Postsecondary Accreditation. *Statement on Prolifer-ation in Accreditation.* Washington, D.C.: Council on Postsec-ondary Accreditation, 1978b.

Council on Postsecondary Accreditation. *The Balance Wheel for Accreditation.* Revised annually. Washington, D.C.: Council on Postsecondary Accreditation, 1978c.

Council on Postsecondary Accreditation. *Presidents' Bulletin,* February 1, 1980a.

Council on Postsecondary Accreditation. "AAHE Panels Debate Evaluation Issues, Costs: Spokesmen Support Public Accredi-tation Reports." *Accreditation,* Spring 1980b, p. 3.

Council on Postsecondary Accreditation. "HEA Proposal Pro-vides New Incentive for States Initiatives in Accreditation." *Accreditation,* Winter 1980c, p. 1.

Council on Postsecondary Accreditation. *The Balance Wheel for Accreditation.* Revised annually. Washington, D.C.: Council on Postsecondary Accreditation, 1981a.

Council on Postsecondary Accreditation. *A Guide to Interagency Cooperation.* Washington, D.C.: Council on Postsecondary Accreditation, 1981b.

Council on Postsecondary Accreditation, Assembly of Special-ized Accrediting Bodies. *Quality Assurance in Professional Education: A Policy Statement on the Role and Value of Specialized Accreditation.* Washington, D.C.: Council on Postsecondary Accreditation, 1981c.

Council on Postsecondary Accreditation. *Final Report: Find-ings and Recommendations.* Self-Study. Washington, D.C.: Council on Postsecondary Accreditation, 1981d.

Cowley, W. H. *Presidents, Professors, and Trustees: The Evolu-tion of American Academic Government.* (D. T. Williams, Jr., Ed.). San Francisco: Jossey-Bass, 1980.

Cross, K. P., Valley, J. R., and Associates. *Planning Non-Tradi-tional Programs: An Analysis of the Issues for Postsecondary Education.* San Francisco: Jossey-Bass, 1974.

Dayton, C. W., and Jung, S. M. *Accreditation Agency Field Test of Institutional Self Study Form: Improving the Consumer Protection Function in Postsecondary Education.* Palo Alto, Calif.: American Institutes for Research, 1978.

Deferrari, R. J. (Ed.). *Self-Evaluation and Accreditation in*

Higher Education. Washington, D.C.: Catholic University of America Press, 1959.

de Tocqueville, A. *Democracy in America.* (H. Reeve, Trans; 2 vols.) New York: Knopf, 1946. (Originally published, 1840.)

Dickey, F. G. "The Social Value of Professional Accreditation." *Journal of the American Medical Association,* 1970, *213,* 591-594.

Dickey, F. G., and Miller, J. *A Current Perspective on Accreditation.* Washington, D.C.: American Association for Higher Education (ERIC Clearinghouse on Higher Education Series), 1972a.

Dickey, F. G., and Miller, J. "Federal Involvement in Non-Governmental Accreditation." *Educational Record,* 1972b, *53,* 138-142.

Dickey, F. G., and Miller, J. "State Chartering Approval and Licensure." In J. L. Wattenbarger and L. W. Bender (Eds.), *New Directions for Higher Education: Improving Statewide Planning,* No. 8. San Francisco: Jossey-Bass, 1974.

Donaldson, R. S. *Fortifying Higher Education: A Study of College Self-Studies.* New York: Fund for the Advancement of Education, 1959.

Drucker, P. "The Coming Changes in Our School Systems." *Wall Street Journal,* March 3, 1981, p. 26.

Education Commission of the States. *Model State Legislation for Approval of Postsecondary Educational Institutions and Authorization to Grant Degrees.* Report of the Task Force on Model State Legislation for Approval of Postsecondary Educational Institutions and Authorization to Grant Degrees. Report No. 39. Denver: Education Commission of the States, 1973.

Educational Testing Service. *ETS Developments,* 1980, *22,* 2.

El-Khawas, E. *New Expectations for Fair Practice.* Washington, D.C.: American Council on Education, 1976.

El-Khawas, E. "Accreditation's Responsibility to Education Consumers." *Accreditation,* August 1977, pp. 4-5.

El-Khawas, E. *Better Information for Student Choice: Report of a National Task Force.* Washington, D.C.: American Association for Higher Education, 1978.

Epictetus. "The Golden Sayings of Epictetus." (H. Crossley,

Trans.) In C. W. Eliot (Ed.), *The Harvard Classics.* Vol. 2. New York: Collier, 1909.

Evans, C. *The Micro Millennium.* New York: Washington Square Press, 1979.

Federal Interagency Committee on Education, Subcommittee on Educational Consumer Protection. *Toward a Federal Strategy for Protection of the Consumer of Education.* Washington, D.C.: U.S. Department of Health, Education and Welfare, 1975.

Federal Register, 34, 30042 (1974).

Federation of Regional Accrediting Commissions of Higher Education. *Code of Good Practice in Accrediting.* Chicago: Federation of Regional Accrediting Commissions of Higher Education, 1966.

Feldstein, P. J. *Health Associations and the Demand for Legislation: The Political Economy of Health.* Cambridge, Mass.: Ballinger, 1977.

Ferster, H. V. "Criteria for Excellence: A Content Analysis of Evaluation Reports by a Regional Accrediting Association." Unpublished doctoral dissertation, State University of New York at Buffalo, 1971.

Finkin, M. W. *Federal Reliance on Educational Accreditation: The Scope of Administrative Discretion.* Washington, D.C.: Council on Postsecondary Accreditation, 1978.

Fisk, R. S., and Duryea, E. D. *Academic Collective Bargaining and Regional Accreditation.* Washington, D.C.: Council on Postsecondary Accreditation, 1977.

Flexner, A. *Medical Education in the United States and Canada: A Report to the Carnegie Foundation for the Advancement of Teaching.* Bulletin No. 4. Boston: Updyke, 1910.

Fowler, W. A. "The Triad is Not Alive or Well!" Paper presented at the Keystone Staff Development Workshop for State Licensing/Approval Officials, Keystone, Colo., July 1976.

Frankfurter, F. "Some Reflections on the Reading of Statutes." *Columbia Law Review,* 1947, *47,* 527–546.

Freidson, E. *Professional Dominance: The Social Structure of Medical Care.* Chicago: Aldine, 1970.

Fremont-Smith, M. R. *Philanthropy and the Business Corpora-tion.* New York: Russell Sage Foundation, 1972.

Friedman, M. *Capitalism and Freedom.* Chicago: University of Chicago Press, 1962.

Fuess, C. *The College Board: Its First Fifty Years.* New York: Columbia University Press, 1950.

Fuess, C. M. *A Nutshell History of the New England Associa-tion of Colleges and Secondary Schools.* Burlington, Mass.: New England Association of Schools and Colleges, 1960.

Galambos, E. C. *Implications of Lengthened Health Education: Nursing and the Allied Health Fields.* Atlanta: Southern Re-gional Education Board, 1979.

Gardner, J. *To Preserve an Independent Sector: Report of the Organizing Committee as Revised and Approved.* Washington, D.C.: Coalition of National Voluntary Organizations/Nation-al Council on Philanthropy, 1979.

Garfield, J. A. Address to Williams College Alumni, New York, December 28, 1871. In J. A. Bartlett, *Familiar Quotations.* (14th ed.; E. M. Beck, Ed.) Boston: Little, Brown, 1882.

Geiger, L. G. *Voluntary Accreditation: A History of the North Central Association, 1945-1970.* Chicago: North Central As-sociation of Colleges and Secondary Schools, 1970.

Gellhorn, W. "The Abuse of Occupational Licensing." *Univer-sity of Chicago Law Review,* Fall 1976, *44,* 6-27.

Georges, E. "The Economics of Accreditation." Unpublished doctoral dissertation, Colorado State University, 1977.

Graham, B. "The Non-Profit Economy." *Washington Post,* March 11, 1979.

Green, K. C. "Program Review and the State Responsibility for Higher Education." *Journal of Higher Education,* 1981, *52* (1), 67-80.

Grimm, K. L. "The Relationship of Accreditation to Voluntary Certification and State Licensure." In *Part II: Staff Working Papers, Accreditation of Health Educational Programs.* Wash-ington, D.C.: National Commission on Accrediting, 1972.

Gross, S. J. "The Myth of Professional Licensing." *American Psychologist,* 1978, *33,* 1009-1016.

Group Attitudes Corporation. *American Attitudes Toward*

Higher Education. Washington, D.C.: Group Attitudes Corporation, 1982.

Hall, J. W. "Regional Accreditation and Nontraditional Colleges: A President's Point of View." *Journal of Higher Education,* 1979, *50*(2), 171–177.

Harcleroad, F. F. *Educational Auditing and Accountability.* Washington, D.C.: Council on Postsecondary Accreditation, 1976.

Harcleroad, F. F. *Accreditation: History, Process, and Problems.* Higher Education Research Report No. 6. Washington, D.C.: American Association for Higher Education, 1980a.

Harcleroad, F. F. *Voluntary Organizations in America and the Development of Educational Accreditation.* Washington, D.C.: Council on Postsecondary Accreditation, 1980b.

Harcleroad, F. F., and Dickey, F. G. *Educational Auditing and Voluntary Institutional Accrediting.* Washington, D.C.: American Association for Higher Education, 1975.

Harmon, J. D. (Ed.). *Volunteerism in the Eighties.* Washington, D.C.: University Press of America, Inc., 1982.

Harper, W. S. "A History of Criticisms of 'Extra-Legal' Accrediting of Higher Education in the United States from 1890 to 1970." Unpublished doctoral dissertation, University of Missouri–Columbia, 1972.

Harris, J., and Huffman, J. "Defining an 'Academic Institution' for the Purpose of Accreditation." Unpublished paper, Middle Tennessee State University, 1981.

Heilbron, L. H. *Confidentiality and Accreditation.* Washington, D.C.: Council on Postsecondary Accreditation, 1976.

Hofstadter, R. *The Age of Reform.* New York: Vintage Books, 1955.

Hofstadter, R., and Metzger, W. P. *The Development of Academic Freedom in the United States.* New York: Columbia University Press, 1955.

Hopkins, D. R. "The Development of the Six Regional Voluntary Accrediting Associations in Higher Education: An Historical Analysis." Unpublished doctoral dissertation, University of Georgia, 1974.

Houle, C. O. *The External Degree.* San Francisco: Jossey-Bass, 1973.

Houle, C. O. *Continuing Learning in the Professions.* San Francisco: Jossey-Bass, 1980.

Husén, T. *The Learning Society.* London: Methuen, 1974.

Independent Sector. *Independent Sector: 1981–82 Annual Report.* Washington, D.C.: Independent Sector, 1981.

Jacob, P. E. *Changing Values in College: An Exploratory Study of the Impact of College Teaching.* New York: Harper & Row, 1957.

Jung, S. M. "Accreditation: Improving Its Role in Student Consumer Protection in Postsecondary Education." *North Central Association Quarterly,* 1977a, *51,* 363–373.

Jung, S. M. *Executive Summary of Final Technical Report: A Study of State Oversight in Postsecondary Education.* Palo Alto, Calif.: American Institutes for Research, 1977b.

Jung, S. M. *Accreditation and Student Consumer Protection.* Washington, D.C.: Council on Postsecondary Accreditation, 1979.

Jung, S. M., and others. *A Study of State Oversight in Postsecondary Education.* Palo Alto, Calif.: American Institutes for Research, 1977.

Kaplin, W. A. *Respective Roles of Federal Government, State Governments, and Private Accrediting Agencies in the Governance of Postsecondary Education.* Washington, D.C.: Council on Postsecondary Accreditation, 1975.

Kaplin, W. A. *Towards a Development of the Triad Concept: A Synthesis of the Belmont Retreat on Institutional Licensure, Eligibility, and Accreditation.* Washington, D.C.: George Washington University, 1976.

Kaplin, W. A. *Accrediting Agencies' Legal Responsibilities: In Pursuit of the Public Interest.* Washington, D.C.: Council on Postsecondary Education, 1982.

Kaysen, C. "The Growing Power of Government." In C. C. Walton and F. DeW. Bolman (Eds.), *Disorders in Higher Education.* Englewood Cliffs, N.J.: Prentice-Hall, 1979.

Kells, H. R. "The Reform of Regional Accreditation Agencies." *Educational Record,* Winter 1976, *57,* 24–26.

Kells, H. R. "The People of Institutional Accreditation: A Study of the Characteristics of Evaluation Teams and Related Aspects of the Accrediting Process." *Journal of Higher Education*, 1979, *50*(2), 178-198.

Kells, H. R. "Proliferation and Agency Effectiveness in Accreditation: An Institutional Bill of Rights." Talk delivered at a meeting of the American Association for Higher Education, Washington, D.C., March 1980a. Also in *Current Issues in Higher Education* (American Association for Higher Education), 1980, *2*, 19-32.

Kells, H. R. "The Purposes and Legacy of Effective Self-Study Processes: Enhancing the Study-Planning Cycle." *Journal of Higher Education*, 1980b, *51*, 439-447.

Kells, H. R. *An Effort to Improve the Performance of Regional Accreditation Evaluation Teams.* Oakland, Calif.: The Western Association of Schools and Colleges, 1980c. (ED 196 381)

Kells, H. R. "Some Theoretical and Practical Suggestions for Institutional Assessment." In R. I. Miller (Ed.), *New Directions for Institutional Research: Assessing the Performance of Institutions,* No. 29. San Francisco: Jossey-Bass, 1981.

Kells, H. R. *Self-Study Processes: A Guide for Postsecondary Institutions.* (2nd ed.) Washington, D.C.: American Council on Education, 1983.

Kells, H. R., and Kirkwood, R. "Analysis of a Major Body of Institutional Research Studies Conducted in the Northeast 1972-1977: Implications for Future Research." Talk delivered at a meeting of the Northeast Association of Institutional Research, Pennsylvania State University, University Park, October 1978. (Also in the proceedings of the meeting.)

Kells, H. R., and Kirkwood, R. "Institutional Self-Evaluation Processes: A Major Retrospective Analysis." *Educational Record,* Winter 1979, *60*, 24-45.

Kells, H. R., and Parrish, R. M. *Multiple Accreditation Relationships of Postsecondary Institutions in the United States.* Technical Report No. 1. Washington, D.C.: Council on Postsecondary Accreditation, 1979.

Kells, H. R., and Robertson, M. P. "Postsecondary Accreditation: A Current Bibliography." *North Central Association Quarterly,* 1980, *54*(4), 411–426. (Copies of the bibliography are available from the Council on Postsecondary Accreditation, One Dupont Circle, N.W., Suite 760, Washington, D.C. 20036.)

Kennan, G. F. Address at Notre Dame University, May 15, 1953.

Kirkwood, R. "The Myths of Accreditation." *Educational Record,* Summer 1973, *54,* 211–215.

Kirkwood, R. "Institutional Responsibilities in Accreditation." *Educational Record,* Fall 1978, *59,* 297–304.

Koerner, J. D. "Who Benefits from Accreditation: Special Interests or the Public?" Paper presented at the Seminar on Accreditation and the Public Interest held by the National Commission on Accrediting, Washington, D.C., November 6, 1970. Mimeographed.

Koerner, J. D. "Preserving the Status Quo: Academia's Hidden Cartel." *Change,* March-April 1971, *3,* 52.

Kokalis, J., Jr. "Proprietary Schools: The Origin and Growth of National Institutional Accrediting Bodies." Unpublished doctoral dissertation, University of Pittsburgh, 1982.

Lao Tzu. *Tao Te Ching.* 426 B.C. In R. M. Persig, *Zen and the Art of Motorcycle Maintenance.* New York: William Morrow, 1974; Bantam Books, 1975.

Larson, M. S. *The Rise of Professionalism: A Sociological Analysis.* Berkeley and Los Angeles: University of California Press, 1977.

Lehman, I. J. "Changes in Critical Thinking, Attitudes, and Values from Freshman to Senior Years." *Journal of Educational Psychology,* 1963, *54,* 305–315.

Lenning, O. T., and Cooper, E. M. *Guidebook for Colleges and Universities: Presenting Information to Prospective Students.* Boulder, Colo.: National Center for Higher Education Management Systems, 1976.

Levin, N. J. "Consumer Information: Mirage and Meaning." In J. S. Stark and Associates, *The Many Faces of Educational Consumerism.* Lexington, Mass.: Heath, 1977.

Levin, N. J. "The Accreditation-Eligibility Link." *New York University Education Quarterly,* Winter 1981, *12*(2), 10–18.

Lindeman, E. C. *The Democratic Man.* (Edited by R. Gessner with a foreword by M. Otto). Boston: Beacon Press, 1956.

Litten, L. H. "Marketing Higher Education: Benefits and Risks for the American Academic System." *Journal of Higher Education,* 1980, *51,* 40–59.

McCarthy, C. F. *The Federal Income Tax.* Englewood Cliffs, N.J.: Prentice-Hall, 1978.

McConn, C. M. "Academic Standards Versus Individual Differences—the Dilemma of Democratic Education." *American School Board Journal,* 1935, *91*(6), 44.

Machiavelli, N. *The Prince.* (W. K. Marriott, Trans.) In *Great Books of the Western World,* Vol. 23. Chicago: Encyclopedia Britannica, 1952. (Originally published, 1513.)

Mackenzie, R. A. "The Management Process in 3-D." *Harvard Business Review,* November/December 1969, pp. 80–87.

McLuhan, M. *Understanding Media: The Extensions of Man.* New York: McGraw-Hill, 1965.

Manser, G., and Cass, R. H. *Voluntarism at the Crossroads.* New York: Family Service Association of America, 1976.

Marcus, L. R., Leone, A. O., and Goldberg, E. D. *The Path to Excellence: Quality Assurance in Higher Education.* ASHE-ERIC Higher Education Research Report No. 1. Washington, D.C.: Association for the Study of Higher Education, 1983.

Marts, A. C. *Philanthropy's Role in Civilization.* New York: Harper & Row, 1953.

Micek, S. S. "Identifying, Measuring, and Evaluating Educational Outcomes." *North Central Association Quarterly,* 1979, *53,* 408–419.

Millard, R. M. "Postsecondary Education and 'The Best Interests of the People of the States.' " *Journal of Higher Education,* 1979, *50*(2), 121–131.

Millard, R. M. "Evaluating Quality: Roles, Relationships, Responsibilities of States, Federal Agencies, and Accrediting Associations." Paper presented to the Fourth Annual Advanced Leadership Seminar for State Academic Officers Inservice Education Program, San Antonio, Texas, July 1980.

Miller, J. W. "Structure of Accreditation of Health Educational Programs." In *Part I: Staff Working Papers, Accreditation of Health Educational Programs.* Washington, D.C.: National Commission on Accrediting, 1972.

Miller, J. W. *Organizational Structure of Nongovernmental Postsecondary Accreditation: Relationship to Uses of Accreditation.* Washington, D.C.: National Commission on Accrediting, 1973.

Miller, J. W. "Education, Accreditation, and Licensure." Paper presented at the Professional Examination Service Conference, New York City, November 11-12, 1976.

Miller, J. W., and Boswell, L. E. "Accreditation, Assessment, and the Credentialing of Educational Accomplishment." *Journal of Higher Education,* 1979, *50,* 219-225.

Miller, J. W., and Mills, O. (Eds.). *Credentialing Educational Accomplishment.* Report and Recommendations of the Task Force on Educational Credit and Credentials. Washington, D.C.: American Council on Education, 1978.

Moos, M. C., and Rourke, F. R. *The Campus and the State.* Baltimore: Johns Hopkins Press, 1959.

National Commission for Health Certifying Agencies. *Criteria for Membership and Their Interpretive Guidelines.* Washington, D.C.: National Commission for Health Certifying Agencies, 1982.

National University Continuing Education Association. *Governmental Policies and Continuing Higher Education.* Washington, D.C.: National University Continuing Education Association, 1982.

Nevins, J. F. *A Study of the Organizational Operation of Voluntary Accrediting Agencies.* Washington, D.C.: Catholic University of America Press, 1959.

New England Association of Schools and Colleges. *Proceedings.* Burlington, Mass.: New England Association of Schools and Colleges, 1980.

Niebuhr, H., Jr. "A Renewal Strategy for Higher Education." *Continuing Higher Education,* Spring 1980, pp. 1-9.

Niebuhr, H., Jr. "An Alternative to Decline: A Once-in-a-Century Update of American Higher Education." *Change,* November/December, 1982, *14*(8), 16--21.

North Central Association Quarterly, 1978, *52* (Winter). (Contains several articles describing regional institutional accreditation.)

Office of Education. "The Office of Education's System for Determining Institutions' Eligibility for Federal Postsecondary

Education Program Funds." Testimony of Graeme Baxter before the Subcommittee on Postsecondary Education, Committee on Education and Labor, U.S. House of Representatives, May 9, 1979.

Orlans, H. *Private Accreditation and Public Eligibility.* Lexington, Mass.: Heath, 1975.

Orlans, H. "The End of a Monopoly? On Accrediting and Eligibility." *Change,* February/March 1980, pp. 32–37.

Orlans, H., and others. *Private Accreditation and Public Eligibility.* Washington, D.C.: National Academy of Public Administration Foundation, 1974.

Orlans, H., and others. *GI Course Approvals.* Washington, D.C.: National Academy of Public Administration Foundation, 1979.

Oulahan, C. "The Legal Implications of Evaluation and Accreditation." *Journal of Law and Education,* April 1978, 7, 193–238.

Oxford English Dictionary, The Compact Edition. Oxford: Oxford University Press, 1971.

Pace, C. R. *Measuring Outcomes of College: Fifty Years of Findings and Recommendations for the Future.* San Francisco: Jossey-Bass, 1979.

Pandarus. "One's Own Primer of Academic Politics." *American Scholar,* Autumn 1973, 42(4), 569–592.

Papert, S. *Mindstorms: Children, Computers, and Powerful Ideas.* New York: Basic Books, 1980.

Perlis, L. "The Volunteer." *Voluntary Action News* (AFL-CIO), October 1974, p. 5.

Persig, R. M. *Zen and the Art of Motorcycle Maintenance.* New York: William Morrow 1974; Bantam Books, 1975.

Petersen, D. G. "Accrediting Standards and Guidelines: A Profile." *Educational Record,* 1978, 59, 305–313.

Petersen, D. G. *Accrediting Standards and Guidelines: A Current Profile.* Washington, D.C.: Council on Postsecondary Accreditation, 1979.

Petersen, D. G. (Ed.). *A Guide to Recognized Accrediting Agencies, 1980-82.* Washington, D.C.: Council on Postsecondary Accreditation, 1980.

Pfnister, A. O. "Accreditation in the North Central Region." In *Accreditation in Higher Education.* Washington, D.C.: Office of Education, U.S. Department of Health, Education and Welfare, 1959.

Phillips, J. M. *Opinions of Educational Executives About Accreditation Practices and Procedures at Their Institutions.* Washington, D.C.: National Commission on Accrediting, 1974.

Phillips, J. M. "Regional Accrediting Criteria: A Study to Assess Their Relative Importance and Variability in the Evaluation of Colleges and Universities." Unpublished doctoral dissertation, Catholic University of America, 1979.

Pigge, F. L. *Opinions About Accreditation and Interagency Cooperation: The Results of a Nationwide Survey of COPA Institutions.* Washington, D.C.: Council on Postsecondary Accreditation, 1979.

Pinkham, F. O. "The National Commission on Accrediting Progress Report." In *Proceedings of the Northwest Association of Secondary and Higher Schools.* Seattle: Northwest Association of Schools and Colleges, 1952.

Pottinger, P. S., and Goldsmith, J. (Eds.). *New Directions for Experiential Learning: Defining and Measuring Competence,* No. 3. San Francisco: Jossey-Bass, 1979.

Proffitt, J. R. Memorandum from Director, Accreditation and Institutional Eligibility Staff, U.S. Office of Education, to Harold Howe III, U.S. Commissioner of Education, December 9, 1968.

Proffitt, J. R. "The Federal Connection for Accreditation." *Journal of Higher Education,* March/April 1979, *50,* 145–157.

Puffer, C. E. (Ed.). *Regional Accreditation of Institutions of Higher Education.* Washington, D.C.: Federation of Regional Accrediting Commissions of Higher Education, 1970.

Pugsley, R. S. "The Consumer Interest in Voluntary Accreditation." *North Central Association Quarterly,* 1977, *51,* 353–362.

Reid, R. H. *American Degree Mills.* Washington, D.C.: American Council on Education, 1959.

Romine, S. "Objectives, Objections, and Options: Some Perceptions of Regional Accreditation." *North Central Association Quarterly,* 1975, *49,* 265-275.

Ross, J. C. *An Assembly of Good Fellows: Voluntary Associations in History.* Westport, Conn.: Greenwood Press, 1976.

Rudolph, F. *The American College and University: A History.* New York: Knopf, 1965.

Sakharov, A. D. *Sakharov Speaks.* (Edited and with a foreword by H. E. Salisbury). New York: Knopf, 1974.

Saunders, C. B., Jr. "Association View of Federal Impact on Education." *Educational Record,* Spring 1975, *56,* 89-95.

Schuller, D., and others. "The Assessment of Readiness for the Practice of Professional Ministry: Rationale and Research Method." *Theological Education,* Fall 1973, pp. 48-65.

Schuller, D., and others. *Readiness for Ministry.* Vol. 1. Vandalia, Ohio: Association of Theological Schools in the United States and Canada, 1975.

Schuller, D., and others. *Readiness for Ministry.* Vol. 2. Vandalia, Ohio: Association of Theological Schools in the United States and Canada, 1976.

Selden, W. K. *Accreditation: A Struggle over Standards in Higher Education.* New York: Harper & Row, 1960.

Selden, W. K. "Historical Introduction to Accreditation of Health Educational Programs." In *Part I: Staff Working Papers, Accreditation of Health Educational Programs.* Washington, D.C.: National Commission on Accrediting, 1971.

Selden, W. K. *Accreditation and the Public Interest.* Washington, D.C.: Council on Postsecondary Accreditation, 1976.

Selden, W. K., and Porter, H. V. *Accreditation: Its Purposes and Uses.* Washington, D.C.: Council on Postsecondary Accreditation, 1977.

Semrow, J. J. "Towards Maximizing the Analytical Aspects of the Evaluating/Accrediting Process." *North Central Association Quarterly,* 1974, *49,* 283-290.

Shaw, W. B. (Ed.). *The University of Michigan: An Encyclopedia Survey.* Vol. 1. Ann Arbor: University of Michigan Press, 1942.

Shimberg, B. *Occupational Licensing: A Public Perspective.* Princeton, N.J.: Educational Testing Service, 1980.

Shimberg, B. *Licensure: What Vocational Educators Should Know.* Columbus, Ohio: National Center for Research in Vocational Education, 1981.

Silvers, P. "An Assessment of Evaluation Teams in Regional Accreditation of Baccalaureate-Granting Institutions." Unpublished doctoral dissertation, University of Arizona, 1982.

Smiley, D. F. "History of the Association of American Medical Colleges, 1876-1956." *Journal of Medical Education,* 1957, *32*(7), 512-525.

Smith, C., and Freedman, A. *Voluntary Associations: Perspectives on the Literature.* Cambridge, Mass.: Harvard University Press, 1972.

Sosdian, C. P. *External Degrees: Program and Student Characteristics.* Washington, D.C.: National Institute of Education, U.S. Department of Health, Education and Welfare, 1978.

Sosdian, C. P., and Sharp, L. M. *Guide to Undergraduate External Degree Programs in the United States—Spring 1977.* Washington, D.C.: National Institute of Education, U.S. Department of Health, Education and Welfare, 1977.

Sosdian, C. P., and Sharp, L. M. *The External Degree as a Credential: Graduates' Experiences in Employment and Further Study.* Washington, D.C.: National Institute of Education, U.S. Department of Health, Education and Welfare, 1978.

Spencer, H. *Principles of Sociology.* Vol. 3. New York: D. Appleton, 1900.

Stark, J. S. " 'Fair Practice': By Whose Standards?" *CHOICE Comments,* 1978, *1*(1), 2.

Stark, J. S. "Birds of a Feather: Marketing and Better Information." *CHOICE Comments,* 1979, *2*(1), 2.

Stark, J. S., and Associates. *The Many Faces of Educational Consumerism.* Lexington, Mass.: Heath, 1977.

Stark, J. S., and Griffith, J. V. "Responding to Consumerism." In L. T. Benezet and F. W. Magnusson (Eds.), *New Directions for Higher Education: Building Bridges to the Public,* No. 27. San Francisco: Jossey-Bass, 1979.

Stark, J. S., and Marchese, T. J. "Auditing College Publications for Prospective Students." *Journal of Higher Education,* January/February 1978, *49*, 82-92.

Stark, J. S., and Terenzini, P. T. *The CHOICE View.* Ann Arbor: Project CHOICE, University of Michigan, 1978.

Stewart, D. "The Politics of Credit." Paper prepared for the Commission on Educational Credit and Credentials of the American Council on Education. Washington, D.C.: American Council on Education, 1982a.

Stewart, D. "Guidelines for Planning and Programming with Academic Credit." Paper prepared for the Commission on Educational Credit and Credentials of the American Council on Education. Washington, D.C.: American Council on Education, 1982b.

Study of Accreditation of Selected Health Educational Programs. "The Relationship of Accreditation to Licensure and Certification." Commission report. Washington, D.C.: National Commission on Accrediting, 1972.

Stufflebeam, D. L., and others. *Educational Evaluation and Decision Making.* Itasca, Ill.: Peacock, 1971.

Sweet, G. W. "Accreditation: Challenge and Change." *Accreditation,* Spring 1979, *4.*

Thomas, L. Address at Douglass College, Rutgers University, April 1978.

Thomas, W. I. "The Relation of the Medicine-Man to the Origin of the Professional Occupations." *Decennial Publications, University of Chicago,* 1903, *4,* 241-256.

Thompson, R. L. "The On-Site Visit: Professional Responsibility and Ethical Conduct of Evaluators." *North Central Association Quarterly,* 1975, *49,* 376-379.

Thrash, P. A. "Accreditation: A Perspective." *Journal of Higher Education,* 1979, *50,* 115-120.

Trivett, D. A. *Accreditation and Institutional Eligibility.* Washington, D.C.: American Association for Higher Education, 1971.

Troutt, W. E. "The Quality Assurance Function of Regional Accreditation." Unpublished dissertation, George Peabody College for Teachers, Vanderbilt University, 1978.

Troutt, W. E. "Regional Accreditation Evaluative Criteria and Quality Assurance." *Journal of Higher Education,* 1979, *50,* 199-210.

U.S. Department of Health, Education, and Welfare, Office of Education. *Nationally Recognized Agencies and Associations.* Washington, D.C.: U.S. Department of Health, Education and Welfare, 1968, 1980. (Periodically revised.)

U.S. Department of Health, Education and Welfare. *Helpful Hints for Selecting a School or College: Look Out for Yourself.* Washington, D.C.: U.S. Department of Health, Education and Welfare, 1977a.

U.S. Department of Health, Education and Welfare, Office of Planning, Budgeting and Evaluation. *Improving the Consumer Protection Function in Postsecondary Education: Executive Summary, Planning/Evaluation Study.* Washington, D.C.: U.S. Department of Health, Education and Welfare, 1977b.

U.S. General Accounting Office. *What Assurance Does Office of Education's Eligibility Process Provide?* Report to the Congress of the United States by the Comptroller General, January 17, 1979. Washington, D.C.: U.S. General Accounting Office, 1979.

United Way of America. *A Brief Interpretive History of America's Voluntary Sector.* Annual Report. Alexandria, Va.: United Way of America, 1977.

University of the State of New York, Office of Self-Assessment. *A Handbook for Self-Assessment: Self-Assessment for Colleges and Universities.* Albany: University of the State of New York, 1979.

Ward, H. B. Presidential address in Cleveland, 1908. In D. F. Smiley, "History of the Association of American Medical Colleges, 1876-1956." *Journal of Medical Education,* 1957, *32*(7), 512-525.

Warner, W. K. *Accreditation Influences on Senior Institutions of Higher Education in the Western Accrediting Region: An Assessment.* Oakland, Calif.: Western College Association, 1977.

Warner, W. K. *Accreditation Influences on Postsecondary Institutions in the Northwest Accreditation Region: An Assessment.* Seattle: Commission on Colleges, Northwest Association of Schools and Colleges, 1978.

Warner, W. K., and Andersen, K. J. "The Role of Accreditation in Consumer Protection." *Educational Record,* 1982, *63*(2), 32–34.

Weisbrod, B. A. *Toward a Theory of the Voluntary Non-Profit Sector in a Three Sector Economy.* Reprint No. 152. Madison: Institute for Research on Poverty, University of Wisconsin, 1975.

Weisbrod, B. A., and Long, S. H. *The Size of the Voluntary Nonprofit Sector: Concepts and Measures.* Madison: Institute for Research on Poverty, University of Wisconsin, 1977.

West, R. W. "New England Association of Schools and Colleges, Inc." *North Central Association Quarterly,* 1978, *52*(3), 418–425.

Wiebe, R. H. *The Search for Order, 1877–1920.* New York: Hill & Wang, 1967.

Wiggins, W. S., and Shepherd, G. R. "The Role of the Council on Medical Education and Hospitals of the American Medical Association." *Journal of Medical Education,* 1959, *34,* 819–825.

Wilson, W. "School and College." In *Proceedings of the Middle States Association of Colleges and Secondary Schools.* Philadelphia: Middle States Association of Colleges and Schools, 1907.

Winninger, R. A. "An Analysis of Criteria Used in Accreditation Reports." Unpublished doctoral dissertation, University of California, Los Angeles, 1970.

Wriston, H. M. "The Futility of Accrediting." *Journal of Higher Education,* 1960, *31,* 327–329.

Yankelovich, D. *New Rules: Searching for Self-Fulfillment in a World Turned Upside Down.* New York: Random House, 1981.

Young, K. E. "Evaluating Institutional Effectiveness." *Educational Record,* 1976, *57,* 45–52.

Young, K. E. "COPA: A New Force on the National Scene." *North Central Association Quarterly,* 1978, *52,* 359–362.

Young, K. E. "New Pressures on Accreditation." *Journal of Higher Education,* 1979a, *50*(2), 132–144.

Young, K. E. "Accreditation and the Office of Education." *Educational Record,* 1979b, *60,* 212–219.

Young, K. E. "Accreditation Must Be Viewed as a Coherent Process." *Accreditation,* Spring 1980a, p. 2.

Young, K. E. "Comparing Institutional and Specialized Accreditation." *Accreditation,* Winter 1980b, p. 2.

Young, K. E., and Andrews, G. J. "Potential for Leadership by Accrediting Agencies." In S. V. Martorana and E. Kuhns (Eds.), *New Directions for Experiential Learning: Transferring Experiential Credit,* No. 4. San Francisco: Jossey-Bass, 1979.

Young, K. E., and Chambers, C. M. "Accrediting Agency Approaches to Academic Program Evaluation." In E. C. Craven (Ed.), *New Directions for Institutional Research: Alternative Models of Academic Program Evaluation,* No. 27. San Francisco: Jossey-Bass, 1980.

Zook, G. F., and Haggerty, M. E. *The Evaluation of Higher Institutions.* Vol. 1: *Principles of Accrediting Higher Institutions.* Chicago: University of Chicago Press, 1936.

Index